TRAVELERS ON THE WESTERN FRONTIER

TRAVELERS
ON THE
WESTERN

FRONTIER

Edited by

John Francis McDermott

University of Illinois Press
URBANA CHICAGO LONDON

Manufactured in the United States of America
Library of Congress Catalog Card No. 77–100375
252 00088 9

To

DELYTE W. MORRIS

Creator of Two Universities

in admiration

Foreword

MORE AND MORE through the nineteenth century the western frontier was crowded with visitors. The itch for travel so natural to us all brought men and women from every part of the United States and every country of Europe. The desire to see strange places and strange people, the desire to see for oneself what one had been reading about, the desire to be one up on one's neighbors and friends led then as now to seeking a firsthand view of that alluring new world beyond the frontier. Soldiers and government explorers and businessmen had the call of profession and occupation. Botanists and other natural historians took on themselves the scientific duty of examining nondescript lands and life. Ethnologists perforce must study the Indian in his habitat. Men of God found it a professional duty to sacrifice the comforts of home to carry the Word to the Heathen. Sportsmen wanted fresh and dramatic hunting grounds. Whatever their reasons, painters, preachers, priests, gold-seekers, gentlemen-sportsmen, Army officers, map-makers, traders, curious foreigners, and common tourists who did not bother to think up any reason at all for their excursions flocked across the Mississippi to look for themselves at the Plains and the Rockies and all the fascinating objects and activities to be seen there.

Who traveled without a notebook? Home went the wanderers to compose an official report or to develop from their notes an account of their travels with which to enchant the public. Some, more modest, dropped their diaries into a family desk drawer, to remain untouched until a persistent scholar on the hunt many years later would trace them to their hiding places. Admiring or pious descendants sometimes copied—bless them!—the letters written home by a young adventurer. Happy are we for the multitude of letters, diaries, reports, reminiscences, and books of travel which have preserved for us the many facets of life and landscape of this trans-Mississippi frontier from its French-Spanish days through the decades of the nineteenth century.

For how otherwise can we re-create this western world now a

century or two centuries past, how can we come to an understanding of people and places and action? Each traveler, if you will, saw the West through his own limited experience—but he did see it. Our garnered knowledge will not be complete, our conclusions may not always be sound, but from the travelers we can eventually discover what the western world was like.

In the Conference on Travelers on the Western Frontier we considered some of the materials available to those who wish to see the frontier as it really was. Like other recent meetings under the auspices of Southern Illinois University, this one at Edwardsville was not called together to make a complete survey of the theme of the occasion; it was not a symposium intended to define or pronounce judgment on the entire body of the literature of travel west of the Mississippi or to speak pontifically the last word on the subject. Once again it was a gathering of a small group of scholars with a particular interest in common, each of whom contributed a paper on some aspect of the literature of western travel that interested him. Other phases and facets, other points of view could have been pursued, presented, represented. Other excellent scholars might well have been on the program with us. Such a collection of papers cannot ever pretend to completeness, no such volume can ever be final. We were content, therefore, to present papers which we thought worth our effort and which we hoped others would find worth reading.

Above all, we hope that they will stimulate others to join in the investigation of the vast riches of travel literature that await the historical scholar. That it already has had some such effect is evident in Professor Flanagan's plan to make a collection of Mississippi River travel pieces from the New York *Spirit of the Times* (to be published by Southern Illinois University Press in its "Travels on the Western Waters" series) and in Professor Joost's intention to publish in full "John Brown's" letters reporting Doniphan's expedition to Santa Fe in the Mexican War.

Our volume opens with scenes from the diaries of Missouri River travelers—an obvious beginning, for the river was the earliest road into the western country. To this has been added a checklist of ninety-five firsthand reports of voyaging on the river between 1794 and 1861, clearly containing the material for a book on the subject. We close with a paper on "Roads West from St. Louis" by William B.

Baker, who has tapped hitherto unused cartographic sources on the laying out of early roads out of St. Louis which have in time become the superhighways of the West.

A prime purpose of the conference being to stimulate investigation of travel literature, four of the papers are given over to reports on resources. Archibald Hanna has indicated something of the vast riches of the Western Americana Collection in the Yale University Library, Dwight L. Smith has reported on manuscripts at the Newberry Library, and Dale L. Morgan on those in the Bancroft Library. Many another great manuscript collection might have been represented by a similar paper, but these will at least indicate what awaits the interested scholar in these treasuries. Herman R. Friis has discussed another only slightly exploited source: the documents and reports of the United States Congress.

Other essays explore certain nineteenth-century newspapers and periodicals which are mines of material that have remained almost untouched. John T. Flanagan shows that the files of the New York *Spirit of the Times,* well known enough for humorous tales of frontier life, overflow with serious accounts by travelers. This is true also of *The American Turf Register and Sporting Magazine,* as noted by John Porter Bloom. Two newspapers have been chosen for like search. Nicholas Joost has exposed the quantities of travel literature to be found in the columns of that quite unusual journal, the St. Louis *Reveille* (1844–51), and Nicholas Canaday, Jr., has made a like investigation of the New Orleans *Picayune* from its founding in 1836 until the Civil War.

The uses to which travelers' accounts can be effectively put is demonstrated in three other papers. Donald D. Miner has examined four such writers who were able to see the Indian as the human being he was rather than as the popular stereotype of noble redskin or ferocious savage. Richard E. Oglesby, seeking out the Mississippi keelboatman, found him in reality not the glamorous hero often met with in recent writing but rather a type, "half horse, half myth." John C. Ewers, tracing the experiences of the French scientist Jean Louis Berlandier as working ethnologist among the "wild Comanches" of Texas in 1828, has disclosed the vast documentation available for a single traveler.

Once again thanks are due to Southern Illinois University for being host to the Conference on Travelers on the Western Frontier at Edwardsville on February 22–23, 1968, and for making possible the publication of these papers. Vice President Charles D. Tenney was kind enough to preside at the dinner meeting which closed the conference, Professor James D. Brown, Assistant to the Vice President for Academic Affairs, chaired the opening session, my long-time friend Ralph E. Morrow, Chairman of the Department of History and Acting Dean of the School of Graduate Studies at Washington University, presided at the second session, and my present colleagues, Fred W. Voget, Professor of Anthropology, and James C. Austin, Professor of English, were chairmen of the third and fourth sessions. I am grateful to them all for their participation. My personal thanks to my friends and colleagues who shared in an interesting and pleasant occasion and whose papers are here submitted to the public; and to Mrs. Alan Seaburg, who prepared the index. Again, and always, I am truly indebted to my wife, Mary Stephanie McDermott, for help in the organization of the conference. Finally, as I have noted with similar publications, my heartfelt sympathy for the editor who sees us through the press and my happy appreciation of the handsome dress given our papers.

It is a pleasure to express here my admiration for the administrative achievement of Delyte W. Morris, President of the Southern Illinois University System, without whom there would be no university at Edwardsville.

JOHN FRANCIS MCDERMOTT
Southern Illinois University
Edwardsville, February 28, 1969

Contents

TRAVELERS ON THE WESTERN FRONTIER

Up the Wide Missouri: Travelers and Their Diaries, 1794-1861

John Francis McDermott

I

"I NEVER EXPECTED to go to the mountains in a boat carrying a *Piano*," John Mason Brown wrote with pleased surprise in his diary aboard the American Fur Company steamboat *Spreadeagle* on May 2, 1861. "But here we have Piano, Melodeon, flutes, violins and banjos and . . . persons on board who play them well." The twenty-four-year-old attorney, who had closed his desk in St. Louis to make a summer trip up the Missouri, was delighted to find among his fellow tourists a number of interesting companions. There was the English gentleman with "baggage enough for a regiment and fire arms sufficient to arm a platoon of riflemen," who was accompanied by his wife and a "young lady protegee." It was this party, Brown soon discovered, that made "excellent music in the after cabin" and determined him to work his way quickly into that "musical world." Some New Yorkers—one of whom was a young painter, William de la Montagne Cary, on his first look at the far West—were also making this "pleasure excursion to Fort Benton." Brown's assigned cabin-mate was another St. Louisan. Aboard, too, was a brother of a Louisville friend. Good prospects, indeed, for an entertaining vacation trip.[1]

Life on the *Spreadeagle* was comfortable and amusing. For the sport of it the young fellows formed a military company to drill away a few hours. On the first Sunday all on the boat were quiet, "endeavor-

[1] This diary and other works quoted or cited are identified, under year of travel, in the Checklist that follows this paper. (The Brown diary is no. 93.) Pagination will be given in footnotes only where there is no dateline in the text.

ing to preserve the solemnity of the day," a state always difficult to maintain on a steamboat. Some passengers tried their rifles at objects ashore. The captain thereupon "fined each a bottle of wine for Sabbath-breaking, and sternly collected it." Another day the passengers amused themselves by court-martialing the barkeeper. There were historic sights to watch for: the grave, high up on a bluff, of the notorious Omaha chief Blackbird, who was said to have controlled his people by a skillful use of arsenic; on another bluff the grave of Sergeant Charles Floyd of the Lewis and Clark expedition, who had died in August, 1804. Brief stops at the river towns allowed the travelers to stretch their legs ashore. At St. Joseph Brown met the son of a junior partner in Constable and Sons, the Edinburgh publishers of Walter Scott. New passengers added to the daily diversion. "A *professional* in the Negro Minstral line, who plays the violin beautifully," helped to while away time on the way to Omaha. On May 24 the English passengers called attention to the fact that it was Queen Victoria's birthday and "held some observances of their own for the day."

The river itself provided diversion as well as tedium. A mile above Sioux City, to clear a bar, a great part of the freight had to be unloaded and then brought up on a small steam ferry. But a more difficult obstruction faced the captain three days later. "We left half our cargo below," noted Brown, "crossed the Bar, discharged the remainder above, and returned empty to take on board that left below." This method, he added, "the only one, is as might be supposed very tedious and wearying to the men, as well as injurious to the Cargo." But to some the delay offered a prospect of adventure. "So much time was consumed in the various transfers that we tied up at the spot where we first unloaded, leaving some adventurous spirits, whose zeal for camp experience could not be repressed, to pass the night above the bar and across the river. The participants in the scheme were the New Yorkers who came in the next morning heartily tired of the experiment."

The very next day there was a strike by about twenty of the *engagés*, who thought their services in handling the freight were indispensable and walked off the boat. Since they had no provisions, after missing breakfast and dinner they were willing to return to work. But now the captain told them they were wanted no longer and they were left to shift for themselves in the woods. At one of the lightenings to cross a bar Brown and some others transferred to the smaller steamer

Chippewa, also a Fur Company boat. When they rejoined the main party at Fort Berthold they learned that one of the cooks on the *Spreadeagle* "had been shot through the head and killed instantly by one of the negro cabin-boys." At the Great Bend, ten of the passengers piled off with their guns, as tourists generally did, to walk across the mile-and-a-half neck of land, while the boat made the circuit of "between 38 and 45 miles."

It was the wild country that all the passengers looked forward to with great eagerness. On the second day out of St. Louis Brown had already begun "to talk mountain talk with the trappers and voyageurs aboard." One evening his cabin-mate Albert Clark showed him the "scar upon his head inflicted by a Grizzly Bear that tore away a part of his scalp in a hand to hand fight . . . in which the bear was victor, leaving Mr. C. for dead and herself escaping unhurt or but slightly wounded." Brown found himself "much amused," too, "as well as instructed by the conversation of Major Graham, a man of collossall proportions who has traveled most extensively through all the wilder portions of our Country." By the time the *Spreadeagle* had passed Omaha the young men had taken to wearing red, blue, or gray shirts; said Brown, "We have all assumed mountain costumes, save only belt and knife."

At the Yankton Agency the entire band of Yankton Sioux—at least twenty-five hundred of them—had gathered to await the arrival of the tribal annuity. "The majority of them rushed on horseback and on foot to the landing to see us," wrote our diarist, "and the effect of red, blue & green blankets, gaudy trappings and various tawdry finery was very picturesque." Near the lately abandoned Fort Clark a council with the Rees was held aboard the steamboat but this the tourists found more than a trifle tedious, for old Pierre Garreau had first to turn the Arikara talk into French and then Charles P. Chouteau the French into English.

After fifty days en route the *Spreadeagle* and the *Chippewa* reached Fort Union just above the mouth of the Yellowstone River. Brown was amused by a tame grizzly kept at the fort, "who diverted himself by boxing the pigs." With three of his fellow passengers the young man "made music" to the huge delight of the Indians and the white residents. Presently the *Spreadeagle* was loaded with twenty-four thousand buffalo robes for the return to St. Louis, and the passengers with Mr. Chouteau went aboard the *Chippewa* to continue on to Fort Benton.

But their water travel was nearly over. Two days later, when they had just passed the ruins of Forts Stewart and Kipp some eighty miles above Fort Union, while they were smoking their after-supper pipes,

> the cry of *Fire*! was raised below. The rush and excitement were terrifying but the boat being near shore a hawser was got out a head and after some delay the human freight was safely landed. I managed to save my gun, pistol, overcoat, valise and blankets, besides various property of others. 200 kegs of Powder were aboard, fire in the hold. The knowledge of this deterred us from making exertions that might have saved the greater part of the cargo. The boat floated down after the hawser burned and the powder exploded with a tremendous noise. Boat and cargo total loss.

Thus John Mason Brown reported what a passenger on a Missouri River steamboat could see and experience in 1861.

II

But let us turn back sixty-seven years to that seventh day of June, 1794, when Jean Baptiste Truteau, in a pirogue with eight oarsmen, set off from St. Louis for the country of the Mandan Indians, where he was under orders from the Director of the Compagnie de Commerce pour la Découverte des Nations du Haut du Missouri to establish a post for the control of the trade of all the Indian tribes he might discover beyond the Poncas. Happily for us who are curious to know what life on the Missouri was like in those distant days, this often unhappy leader of a poorly planned and prepared expedition did faithfully carry out his instructions to "keep a daily record of all that may be done for the Company, in which he shall give information of the daily operations: as, an exploring expedition; a treaty with one or the other nation; the arrival of foreign Indians; works of the establishment; a circumstance which is worth the trouble of being written down; finally everything that may happen to be done and ordered each day by Senor Truteau for the benefit of the Company, in chronological order. He shall send each year a copy to Senor Clamorgan, and keep the duplicate."[2]

Until he reached the mouth of the Kansas, five weeks after departure, Truteau made no notes of the route, which was well known thus far. Besides, he wrote, "I have been delayed so often by the force of the [rapidly rising] waters and the continual rains, that the details would be too lengthy." After three days of heavy rain near the first old village of the Kansas Indians, some twelve leagues from the mouth of their river, he declared, "I thought I would perish by the water that time." And he added sharply for the benefit of the company officials: "I shall say in passing that everyone who embarks on long trips, in the summer season, should take precautions with good tarpaulins to cover their equipment and not with deer or buffalo skins, which, in spite of all possible care and the time one spends in drying them, rot promptly in the heats of summer and expose the merchandise to be damaged by the ravages of the weather. This is a thing which the director of the company had not well provided for, having made me leave with bad skins, half spoiled and small, old tarpaulins."

High water and swift current, obstructions in the river, and insufficient manpower were repeatedly frustrating, but another problem was food supply. The journey seemed interminable. By September 11, when they camped for the night just below the Niobrara River, Truteau noted that he had remaining "only about a *minot* and a half of maize and fifty pounds of flour for nine men," but he still had over a hundred leagues to go before they would reach the Arikaras. On September 29 he wrote that the provisions were "absolutely" exhausted. Such supplies had been supplemented, of course, along the entire journey by game shot by one of their number who was the official hunter of the party. But the procuring of meat had to be so managed that it would not call the attention of Indians to their passage up the river. At the mouth of the James River late in August, Truteau reported he had "spent a part of a day drying over the fire the flesh of a deer" shot by their hunter, "a necessary precaution not only to avoid fasting but in order not to be obliged to fire our guns in dangerous places. For more than ten leagues below the village of the Omahas,

2 Truteau quotations in this section are from A. P. Nasatir, ed., *Before Lewis and Clark* (St. Louis, 1952), I, 250 ff.

we had carefully extinguished our fires and every morning we threw the wood of our leanto into the fire, taking care to leave as little trace as possible." Small wonder Truteau was more than five months in reaching his destination!

Equally informative in its detail of a traveler's experience was the account written by Antoine Tabeau while he was resident trader among the Arikaras for Pierre Loisel of St. Louis a decade later than Truteau. Tabeau's was not a day-by-day record but a narrative written on the spot while he was "living in a Ricara hut, surrounded by four families and by a continual crowd of admiring imbeciles," repeatedly disturbed by disputes and disagreements, so that he had "hardly been in the mood to write and above all with any pleasure."[3]

Tabeau described first of all—and vividly—the difficulties of navigation that confronted every traveler up the river. One constant danger was the crumbling of the river banks. "Notwithstanding all the prudence and the foresight possible, these accidents cannot always be prevented," he wrote.

> We ourselves owed our safety [on one occasion] to extraordinary good fortune. . . . After repeated efforts made in vain to pass an obstruction (*embarrass*), which extended very far out into the water, we were forced to give it up and, as the opposite bank was impracticable, we tried to open up a passage between the shore and the *embarrass*. In order to do this it was necessary to cut down many tree-trunks that blocked it, to pull away roots, and to enlarge the channel by digging out the earth. Having spent three hours and a half in this work, we were about to unmoor the barge, fastened at the foot of the *embarrass*, in order to guide it to the passage; it had scarcely advanced its length, when a tree, twelve feet in circumference . . . was uprooted and fell with a horrible noise within ten or twelve feet of the helm. Another similar to it followed at the same instant and their fall, submerging one end of the *embarrass*, lifted the other end and raised the trunks we had cut more than twenty feet up into the air. Had the barge remained five minutes longer, where it had been three and a half hours, I do not believe we should have seen any remains of it.

The ordinary experiences of the boatmen were extraordinary.

[3] Tabeau (no. 8), p. 52.

"We encountered," wrote Tabeau, "all the inconveniences that this river could present to *voyageurs,* whom the currents have impeded. Sometimes our *engagés,* by swimming, carried a long tow line to throw over a stump or some solid root and we ascended in this way by means of repeated towing, making sometimes only two or three miles a day. Sometimes they were in the water, tearing up roots or hewing down trees which closed our passage." At times "the only way was to seize the branches and to ascend in this manner by passing them from one hand to another, a maneuver less expeditious than fatiguing." When night overtook them in such places, "the rowers wearied with toil, having lain the best they could upon the boats, refreshed themselves only with difficulty from the labors of the day."

Always there were mosquitoes to endure. "During the whole day the boats were enveloped as in a cloud and the *engagés,* who were compelled by the extreme heat to keep the body naked, were covered with blood and swellings. Often our hunters not being able to endure them, returned at full speed to throw themselves into the boats. What is more they could not aim their weapons when covered with these insects." So bad were the mosquitoes that there was seldom a full crew well enough to work the boat.

Beyond all this there was generally a shortage of provisions. Loisel had aboard his boat some hundreds of pounds of flour, but this amount could furnish subsistence to thirty men for a few days only. Besides, added Tabeau, "boiled flour without fat is a very mean nourishment for men who work without intermission." Their hunters did frequently have the luck to meet old buffalo bulls along the bluffs, ones that had not had the strength to go away with the herd in search of the new grass. "It is to be presumed that many we killed paid but a few hours earlier their debt to nature. The savages even claim that they thus expose themselves to view on the hills in order to invite the hunter to free them from a life that they have come to find burdensome. We rendered them this service cheerfully; but their flesh, though hard and glutinous, seemed to us quite tasty."[4]

The laconic notes of John C. Luttig, heading a Missouri Fur Company expedition to the Upper Missouri in 1812, confirm everything Truteau and Tabeau had to say about the pains of travel on the

4 *Ibid.,* pp. 59–62.

river. A week after leaving St. Louis, according to Luttig's diary, "Mr. Majet, Patroon of the large Boat fell over Board on account of a log shamming against the Rudder, he saved himself by taking hold of Rudder, and got on Board." Four days later the boat was "obliged to stop on account of head wind and strong Current" and a new mast had to be arranged. On June 15, while they were camped on shore for the night as usual, at "about one oclock this Morning it began to blow furiously, [we] were obliged to put out our fires, the wind blowing from all quarters . . . [at 5 P.M. we] started about 1 Mile[,] took the Cordell[,] the Boat swung and went down the River like the Wind in full Speed, leaving all hands on shore . . . the other Boat came to[o] close swept by the Current[,] we unshipped our Rudder, run against a tree and brocke her mast, this ended this doleful Day." On June 26: "Baptiste Latoulipe of St. Louis, fell over Board and [was] never seen again, the two Boats being close together, he could not rise or was entangled by the roots of a large Tree, which he was going to strike with his Pole." On July 4, Luttig wrote, they "had prepared to salute the day of Independence" but "a Salute from Heaven prevented us, a thunder storm arose at 2 in the Morning and the Bank of the River where we camped fell in upon us momently. Mr. Manuel Lisa was nearly drowned in his Bed, and we had to run off, rowing and poling all Day."[5]

A decade later Prince Paul Wilhelm of Wuerttemberg, traveling as a passenger in a boat of the French Fur Company of St. Louis, had much the same experience. To him the noise of banks caving in resembled "the report of a cannon fired at some distance, and at night this noise together with the roar of the river and its whirlpools, the creaking and grinding of driftwood causes a frightful uproar." On one occasion "a violent gust of wind . . . caused us to lay by. The danger was great because tall timber stood close to the bank which was being drawn into the river by the washing effect of the water. A few huge old trunks fell close to the boat into the water. They would have submerged us without fail had they fallen on us." One day "a sudden gust of wind seized us from the side and threw the vessel with great force against the bank." A thick branch tore the rudder away and a young American passenger was struck overboard by an overhanging branch—he was fortunately rescued by a Negro slave who leaped into the water

[5] Luttig (no. 16), pp. 29, 32, 39, 42–43, 46.

to save him. During a severe electrical storm with no drop of rain, "lightning ignited several trees close to us, which burned with a bright flame."[6]

Every traveler had like adventures and misadventures to report. Even after the advent of steam, Maximilian, Prince of Wied-Neuwied, John James Audubon, E. de Girardin, and many others were witnesses to the pain and difficulty that driftwood, snags, sawyers, sandbars, high and low water, and swift current caused navigators and crews and passengers.

III

The boats worked so laboriously and so slowly upstream came in all sizes. Truteau referred to his large "boat," which we must presume large only in contrast with small canoes, for he had but a crew of eight men. Tabeau mentioned in his narrative thirty men engaged in the Loisel expedition he was memorializing, but there were apparently two boats in this party. Wilson Price Hunt, rushing upriver to the wintering place of his main contingent of Astorians at the Nodaway River in 1811, counted sixteen men aboard including himself, John Bradbury, and Thomas Nuttall. In the same year Henry Marie Brackenridge declared Manuel Lisa's boat, worked by a *patron* and a twenty-man crew, the finest that had yet been sent up the Missouri. General Henry Atkinson, setting out on a military expedition against the Arikaras in 1825, used eight wheel-driven (treadmill fashion) keelboats.

None of these principals bothered to say anything by way of description of their boats—one does not describe the commonplace. But a visitor to this strange new world found everything interesting; Brackenridge pictured Lisa's boat in his diary of the Spaniard's voyage up the Missouri:

> Mr. Lisa . . . took much pains in rigging his boat with a good mast, and main and topsail; these being great helps in the navigation of the river. . . . [Several of the crew] have already made a voyage to the upper Missouri, of which they are exceedingly proud, and on that ac-

6 Paul Wilhelm (no. 23), pp. 248–249, 240–241, 258, 261.

count claim a kind of precedence over the rest of the crew. We are in all, twenty-five men, well-armed, and completely prepared for defence. There is, besides, a swivel on the bow of the boat, which, in case of attack, would make a formidable appearance: we have also two brass blunderbusses in the cabin, one over my birth, and the other over that of Mr. Lisa. These precautions were absolutely necessary from the hostility of the Sioux bands. . . . The greater part of the merchandise, which consisted of strouding, blankets, lead, tobacco, knives, guns, beads, &c. was concealed in a false cabin, ingeniously contrived for the purpose; in this way presenting as little as possible to tempt the savages. But we hoped, that as this was not the season for the coming on the river of the wandering tribes, the fall being the usual time, we might pass unnoticed.[7]

Maximilian described the keelboat *Flora* in which he traveled from Fort Union to Fort McKenzie (July, 1833) as

a strong-built sloop, about sixty feet long by sixteen broad, with a deck, a mast, and sail. The goods were deposited in the middle space; at the stern there was a cabin, ten paces long and five or six broad, with two berths. . . . At the back of this cabin there was a little window, with a sliding shutter, and, on each side, a port-hole, which, in fine weather, admitted light and air. Round the vessel there was a ledge, about a foot and a half broad, on which the men walked backwards and forwards when, the water being low, they had to propel the boat by means of poles. In the fore part of the vessel was the apartment of the *engagés*, and, on the deck, an iron grate for cooking: here, too, the game which we had taken was hung up. About half of our men were destined to tow the vessel when there was no wind. . . . The number of men, destined by Mr. McKenzie for the voyage to the Blackfeet, consisted of double the usual crew of a keel-boat, and, including us travellers, amounted to fifty-two persons.[8]

Ill-fed, ill-paid, overworked, the crews of these boats were better known for their endurance than for their intelligence or ability. Little except muscle power was expected of them, as would still be true later of the rough labor on the steamboats. Discipline was sometimes difficult. At any time the men might break out of bounds. The

[7] Brackenridge (no. 14), p. 201 (April 2, 1811).
[8] Maximilian (no. 29), Thwaites ed., XXIII, 24–25.

voyage would not begin too badly. Bourgeois and captain expected a spot of trouble at St. Charles, traditionally the last place for a fling before the long voyage into the depths of the wilderness beyond. A few miles above St. Charles Lisa had to put ashore because some of the men were still remaining at the village. Wrote Brackenridge:

> It is extremely difficult to make a start on these voyages, from the reluctance of the men to terminate the frolic with their friends, which usually precedes their departure. They set in to drinking and carousing, and it is impossible to collect them on board. Sometimes they make their carousals at the expense of the Bourgeois: they are credited to the tavern keeper, who knows that their employer will be compelled to pay, to prevent the delay of the voyage. . . . It was found impossible to proceed any further this evening [April 2]; the men in high glee from the liquor they had drank before starting; they were therefore permitted to take their swig.[9]

One custom the new traveler always found pleasing was the singing of the boatmen. When Hunt's boat pulled away from St. Charles, the Canadian crewmen, Bradbury observed, were "measuring the strokes of their oars by songs, which were generally responsive between the oarsmen at the bow and those at the stern: sometimes the steersman sung, and was chorused by the men." Leaving Fort Osage, then the very last settlement of whites, was a time for reflection. "Our men were kept from thinking too deeply, by the cheering songs, which were encouraged by Mr. Lisa, and the splashing of the oars, which kept time with them."[10]

But not all crews were so amenable, nor all *patrons* or *bourgeois* so effective in managing them. Prince Paul in 1823, though only a passenger, practically had to take charge of the boat in which he was traveling.

> Soon after our departure from St. Charles the spirit of irregularity and unlawful deportment toward superiors had developed among the crew. During the previous night this had matured to serious disaffection. With much difficulty we succeeded in getting the men into action, about seven o'clock in the morning. We had scarcely advanced four miles when the quarrel broke out anew. In spite of all my admo-

[9] Brackenridge, p. 201.
[10] Bradbury (no. 15), p. 39. Brackenridge, p. 219.

nition an open and furious attack against the captain, Dutremble, followed. Since the latter did not have the necessary courage to quell the rebellion, four of the most desperate fellows took the property and guns, that had been issued them by the French Company as part payment for their services. As there was no doubt that the worst kind of quarrel and possibly bloodshed would follow, I applied all my eloquence to calm the better-minded part of the crew. When I had won them over to our cause, I, in company with the men on whom I could rely did not delay in instituting drastic measures. Thereupon the instigators of the uprising became frightened, and since we happened to be close to the land, they jumped from the boat and fled into the forest. I considered it ill-advised to have the well-armed fugitives pursued, altho I had difficulty in restraining the remaining crew. I never heard anything of the runaways, who probably turned to the English settlements. By this most disagreeable incident the captain of the boat was placed in an embarrassing situation. In all there remained only thirteen men, fit for work, on board. From the very outset there had been too few men to battle the high water, so we now had to lay by for the time being. Dutremble set out to return to St. Louis by land, to announce the deplorable incident to the merchants and to procure an addition to the crew. I considered it advisable to inform the trading company of everything in a detailed written statement, and requested them to indicate a safe means of avoiding similar vexation on the journey. I remained with the boat at a promontory on the left bank, with the understanding that we should continue with the aid of the sail, should favorable wind set in. Dutremble with the reinforcement was to follow by land. . . .

On the evening of the twenty-fourth Dutremble came and brought five men with him. Among these were three negroes and one mulatto, all slaves owned by the French Missouri Company. I received a very polite letter from the company, in which they requested me, also in the future to look after their interest on board the boat.

. . . we made halt on the evening of the fifth, after we had made only six English miles this day. Since the water of the river had gone down, it would have been an easy matter to have made a much greater day's journey, especially since several intervals of the breeze might have been utilized if the crew had not been so obstinate. After the last incident of insubordination the spirit of insolence and disobedience against the captain had increased to such an extent that the management of the boat depended more upon the will of the crew than upon that of Dutremble. The camp for every noon and night stop was determined by the crew. Moreover, they stopped at any time that it suited them, and if the officer interposed objection he was attacked and intimidated with the vilest and most abusive words. The water in the hold of the boat which had accumulated thru the seepage and the frequent showers disseminated a pestilential stench. In vain we applied all our eloquence to induce the crew to dip out the water. Caillou and old de Rouain had to perform this repulsive task themselves in the end, so that it might be possible to sleep on the boat and to protect the goods in the boat against decay. . . .

On the morning of June 7 we could not start before nine o'clock. The crew offered as an excuse the fact that during the night it had rained heavily, whereby the bank had been made too slippery to pull the boat by the tow-line. Since at the beginning of the journey the crew had performed a like duty under much more trying circumstances I could not understand the real cause for this delay. All morning as also a good part of the day and night the crew played cards. Having no money they played for whiskey which was issued to them daily in definite portions. The result was that the winners got drunk and the losers, to whom the beverage had become a necessity, gave vent to their displeasure by the most violent utterances. They then begged for an extra issue of whiskey, and since the captain on several occasions had been so weak as to give in to their pleading, I foresaw that there would be no end to this mischief, if I did not interfere with a firm hand. I promised the crew an extra amount of liquor from my own supply on condition that they should abstain from the game of cards and work diligently. Failing to do so I threatened to turn those whom I knew to be the instigators of the trouble over to the sheriff in Franklin for punishment. Since the men recognized that I was in earnest the threat worked at least as long as we were in the state of Missouri.

The Prince had yet more to contend with when he reached the frontier town of Franklin.

Hardly an hour had elapsed after our arrival when the presence of the nearby saloons was clearly seen. The entire crew was drunk and made a great noise. Under the circumstances it is incomprehensible to me how we escaped an accident on account of the gun powder which constituted the main portion of our ship's load. The indiscriminate use of pipes made an explosion seem imminent at any moment. I had decided not to go on land till the following morning, since neither the town nor the inhabitants seemed very inviting. Soon, however, I received visits of all sorts of stupidly bold and curious people who addressed me with all sorts of indiscreet questions and whose intention seemed to be to make fun of me—a stranger. When they saw that they did not gain their purpose, they committed other incivilities. They even tried to gain possession of my papers, while they described me as an adventurer and spy. My hunter, in order to rid me of these unpleasant guests, interested Caillou and a few boat hands who were not yet entirely drunk, in my behalf, requested the obtrusive company, with whom I was engaged in a lively discussion, to leave the boat. This the Franklinites did not seem inclined to do good naturedly. I had to speak again in my own behalf and was finally so lucky to persuade both parties to leave the boat and settle their affair on land. Here a terrible fight resulted. At this time a Frenchman, Mr. Benouai, from Bordeaux, a very fine man, came on board to quiet me. Benouai promised the full protection of the law if I should stop at his place. He urged me not to accept the invitation of the young men, who under the pretext of friendship would try to take me to the town in order to start a quarrel there. He also advised me not to leave the boat unarmed. I promised the obliging Frenchman a visit on the following day, and soon learned to appreciate the sincerity of his intentions. Under the pretext of reconciliation two persons came to me, and after having made some awkward excuses, requested me to accompany them to the boarding house to celebrate a feast of good fellowship. At first I excused myself in a polite manner, but when they became more and more insistent and laid hands on me, I chased them from the boat amid the uproarious laughter of their comrades. As this decisive procedure seemed genuinely American to the Franklinites, the affair dropped there.[11]

IV

Except for an occasional curious young man with time on his hands like Brackenridge, in the days before the steamboat there were few adventure-seekers voyaging up the Missouri for the sport of it. Travelers undertook such arduous, uncomfortable, and time-consuming trips only because business or profession demanded it. But for all who ventured up the river, early or late, the grand focus of interest was the Indian, his trade, and his way of life. Were one a businessman,

[11] Paul Wilhelm, pp. 241–276, 288–289.

soldier, botanist, ethnologist, artist, or plain tourist, the red man in his native country was his loadstone and his concern, and the diaries kept by these nonliterary voyagers are invaluable for their detailed information and fascinating for their firsthand impressions.

Truteau had been instructed to "discover" new Indian nations above the Poncas and to report to his employers on their customs and their trade potential. The great part of his diaries, as well as the "Description of the Upper Missouri," which he composed for Lieutenant Governor Zenon Trudeau after his return to St. Louis, is devoted to the conditions governing trade with the Indians and to a close observation of their society.

The prime difficulty for the trader on his way upriver, he stressed, was to pass safely and securely by one tribe in order to reach another with his goods. Although there might be moments of alarm, there was no great danger of losing one's scalp, for such extreme violence on the part of the Indians would almost certainly result in trade being cut off entirely the next year. But each tribe in turn would try to stop a trading party in order to force an exchange of its best goods for the pelts on hand and to prevent, if it could, direct contact with the next tribe above. This was, after all, merely good business sense on the part of the Indian, but for the trader it was a great trial.

The Omahas, at this period a powerful tribe, "never failed to try to persuade the French," Truteau declared, "that it was for the conservation of their profit and the safety of their lives that they detained them saying that this people called the Poncas [next above them and reported rich in prime pelts] were not civilized, that they think only of robbing, striking, or killing those who entered their country." It was "because of the great friendship" the Omahas had for the French "that they did not wish any evil to befall them." Brushing aside the solemn irony of the Omahas, Truteau asserted that "the real motive which urges them to act is their own interest, for in depriving this nation of a direct commerce with us they would obtain all the best pelts, beaver, and otter, for a mere bagatelle, which they sold again very dear, and they exchange the same pelts either with us or with nations situated on the Mississippi for good merchandise which they obtain very cheap."[12]

Truteau had succeeded in slipping by the Omahas and did go

[12] Nasatir, I, 266.

as far as the Arikaras, but he actually wintered about ten leagues above the Poncas. There in December he had to sustain a visit from Blackbird, then at the height of his power, who "put a climax" to his difficulties.

> This great chief of the Omahas was [*sic*] the most shrewd, the most deceitful and the greatest rascal of all the nations who inhabit the Missouri. He is feared and respected and is in great renown among all strange nations, none of whom dare to contradict him openly or to move against his wishes. They do not set out either for war or for the hunt unless he has given his consent to it. His name is recited in all assemblages and speeches are made in his absence in the most distant places to which they go. All the neighboring tribes hear his word and crown him with presents when he goes to visit them. If any of his men acquire beautiful merchandise or beautiful horses and he appears to desire them they instantly give them to him. He never goes about on foot, but always mounted on the most beautiful horse in the village. He has slaves for his work, and better to say, they are all his slaves, for should he wish to sleep he has one or two hired attendants who gently rub his legs and feet while he sleeps. If these ordinary valets are absent, he presses into that service even the greatest and bravest of the tribe.
>
> When it is time to awaken him it is necessary to do it with caution, being careful not to cry in his ears nor to stroke him with the hand, but they use a feather which they pass lightly over the face or tickle gently certain parts of his body. Finally he is a man who by his wit and cunning has no parallel among all the savage nations of this continent. He is able to do or cause to be done good or evil as it pleases him. It is not his war-like actions that have brought him so much power, for he has been inclined towards peace, but because of the fear that his men and his neighbors have of certain poisons which he uses, they say to kill off those who displease him. He takes from the French who come to trade with him their most beautiful merchandise and gives them in exchange very few hides, that those who have lost only one hundred to one hundred and fifty percent from the cost price are fortunate. He promises much and never keeps his word. He takes every year from the Poncas and from his own men a quantity of beaver and otter hides. But he saves them for the nation situated on the Mississippi which brings him every spring in exchange, scarlet cloth, china ware and unwrought silver, and some little brandy for which he has a great passion, and the greater part of his men follow

his example only paying hides of deer good or bad for guns, kettles, powder, balls, etc., which they take on credit. If they trade with beaver or otter it is at the price they set, and always to the loss of those with whom they trade. The chief pretended for some time to take an interest in the French, but at the bottom all the beautiful talk which he held, the grand promises which he made, having nothing for an end but the pillage for himself, under a false cover of friendship which he seems to display for them; and after being satisfied he leaves the trader to debate with his men to snatch his goods at the best bargains possible. In this extremity it is always necessary to have recourse to the chief of the second rank, to the braves and to the soldiers, who are so many bloodsuckers who extort from you the other third of the goods for their good services. . . .

[Blackbird] takes freely a third at least of the merchandise which comes to his village. Upon the arrival of the French at his villages he causes an exhibition of the goods to be made and then carries off and appropriates whatever is pleasing to him. The *engagés* are even forced to open their cases or haversacks which he examines. He takes from them a part of their tobacco and other little effects which they may have. The second chief[s] carry on their robbery also, and one is not able to object to them, and always with promises of good pay which ease their own mind and are a loss to the trader. As to the common people the trade is carried on with much profit, but the loss which this chief and his followers bring to the traders which takes from them the better or greater part of their effects at a low price, places them in a condition to make no gain. This Omaha post is about the most disadvantageous on the whole river at the present time as much through the great knowledge they have of trading through the English on the Mississippi, as through the evil disposition of this nation and of their chiefs in our regard. It is said that some *coureurs de bois* formerly made great profits. They had not at that time this pernicious communication with the nations dependent upon the English. . . .

So, Gentlemen, if I have dwelt a little long on this subject of this chief and his nation whose character I have studied this winter, his way of thinking and acting, it was to instruct you with the truth of what takes place among this nation, for I forsee that you have need of direct communication up as well as in descending the Missouri. Do not hope to continue secret voyages with safety. Sooner or later all your goods will be taken or stolen and perhaps your people killed.

> For it is certain that knowing now the plans of the French to trade on the Upper Missouri, and the time when they are accustomed to go up, they will watch and search in war parties, both the upper and lower country in order to surprise them. They are already very roused up against us on this subject and particularly against Jacques d'Eglise, who hastens stealthily along the road every summer they say. I have persuaded the chief that I had stopped at his village on passing in order to see him and talk with him, but having found no one I had continued the route.[13]

In the two years he spent on the Upper Missouri Truteau had time enough to become closely acquainted with the Indian. Among the most entertaining entries in his diary are those which tell us of the Indian opinion of white behavior. Noting the ease of divorce among these tribes, for example, the traveler made note that the "Indians who are told of our marriages cannot conceive how white men, who have so much intelligence and knowledge can be so blind or ignorant as not to know that marriage is a source of grief and trouble for them. They regard it as a monstrous thing to be tied to one another without hope of ever being able to break this tie . . . they stand firm and unmoved in saying that we are slaves to women."[14]

The Indian men generally were not susceptible to jealousy: "They give as their reason the fact that when a man dies he does not take his women along with him into the land of the dead; and they say that those who quarrel, fight and kill one another for the ownership of a woman are fools and mad." Frequently they offered the youngest and most beautiful of their women to the principal men of the nation. The girls and women "live in such great freedom that they seem to be a property common to all." The young Canadians and Creoles who arrived in these villages were "usually seen to be galloping at full speed like horses that have broken loose into the fields of Venus, whence they rarely emerge without having been supplied with the sickness that is inseparably attached thereto. . . ."

Women were "ranked on a low level, one that approaches slavery." Among all the tribes they had "the complete burden of family

[13] *Ibid.*, I, 282–285.

[14] This, and the remaining citations of Truteau observations, are from the translation of his "Description of the Upper Missouri" (no. 2) made for me by Alma M. Myer for a forthcoming publication.

life: it is they who construct the camps, cut and take the meat to have it dried, dress the skins of the animals that the men kill, when hunting, to make lodges, clothing, footwear for themselves, their husbands and their children, carrying loads on the march, cultivating the fields, and harvesting their products." They never took part in the assemblies or the feasts of the men.

Contrast this with custom among the whites, declared an old Pawnee Republican chief, who in his youth had visited the French settlements of the Illinois:

> There is nothing more beautiful nor admirable, my brother, than the manners, the customs and especially the industry of the white men in all they do. . . . [But] I find three great faults in their way of living and in their customs, that we, although completely savage, do not have. Their ambition to amass that white iron, called silver, their hardheartedness in the matter of food, which they sell even to the people of their own village and their own family, and their weakness towards women. I have often seen white men give feasts where many people were present. The women and girls were always the first to be seated at the table and they occupied the most comfortable places. The men stood up behind them and were eager to serve them the best pieces there were, as well as to pour them something to drink, as slaves do for their masters. And what is more, it is the men who do the work, cut and cart wood, cultivate the fields, harvest the wheat, the maize, etc. while the women, always well-dressed, stay at home, occupied only with sewing [and] gossiping.

Was it possible, continued the chief, "for the men to submit to the women and serve them so humbly; after the Master of life, is not man the king and master of all other animals? Is it not he to whom the great spirit has given the strength and courage to fight enemies and to kill the most savage beasts? Why then does he humble himself to serve a weak and lowly woman, when it is she who should serve and obey him?"

Truteau was notably impressed at the Dance of the Calumet by the "rivalry to see who will make the greatest effort to give mutual presents." The Indians say, he reported, that "this festival resembles a battle between two hostile tribes with both sides making every effort to gain the victory; each side excites itself into a passion. The old men incite them, relating in a loud voice what they themselves did in former times on like occasion; the women, the girls and the tenderest youth make the air resound with shouts of joy and praise for the most liberal. Everyone strips himself stark naked on the spot to give his clothing and finery as gifts, and each one gives as good as he gets. I have seen some of them give all their horses, their arms, and in general all they possess." These excesses continue with a "Bacchic furor rather than true liberality" until a "brave will brutally snatch the drum from the hands of the man who is beating the cadence, crying out that it is enough and that it is not reasonable to strip oneself so completely of everything; then the gifts and the dance cease . . . each keeps for his own what was given to him."

Truteau himself had an embarrassing experience at such a party given by the Arikaras to the Cheyennes one summer. Because he had brought nothing with him on this visit and therefore wanted to avoid receiving or giving presents, he kept himself at a little distance from the place of the dance. But an old Cheyenne brought him forward and made him sit among the chiefs and principal men of the two tribes. After the dance had begun, a young Cheyenne chief signed to him to rise and stripped off all the clothes he was wearing down to his breeches and shoes, and taking Truteau by the hand led him into the center of the open space. "A young woman, who was without doubt his, came forward, carrying in her arms a coat, trimmed with imitation galloon, a hat with a plume, a shirt, and a pair of big mitasses, after their fashion, made of antelope skin that was as soft as linen, the whole trimmed with porcupine, and she placed them at my feet."

The man spoke to his wife, and "she did something I never expected—she stretched out her two hands towards me and rubbed me from head to foot, and then she herself passed them over her whole body. I was so astonished at the actions of this man and this woman that I stood stock-still with my arms crossed, and let her do all she wished. He dressed me again from head to foot with the clothes I have just named, and having covered me with a robe that was also worked in porcupine, he led me back to my place amid cries of acclamation and applause of all the spectators. Some moments later I gave him as good as I got, making him a present of all my clothes."

The Frenchman knew that among those who might read or hear about this anecdote "some will doubtless be amused, and others . . .

scandalized that a man who not only professes a pure and holy religion, but who furthermore has received a complete education in the principles and maxims of virtue and propriety, so suitable to civilized societies, should permit himself to be conducted willingly into the midst of so many persons of both sexes in a state so contrary to modesty." But they must know that "this nakedness of certain parts of the body which among us is shocking to propriety because of the practice and ideas we have attached to it, is not any more noticed among the peoples who compose this assemblage than any other part of the body, because of the customs and habits, in which they are born and raised, of appearing in this state."

Furthermore, a man "who roams about in strange countries and who frequents peoples whose customs and manners differ entirely from those of his [own] country, is obliged on certain occasions, no matter how religiously or strictly he observes his own, to diverge from them in order to conform to those of the people among whom he is living, and sometimes to follow that common saying, 'One must howl with the wolves.' " He had known very well that the act of stripping and reclothing him was "an act of generosity and gallantry very usual amongst them." But the actions of the young woman and her purpose puzzled him until, on inquiring from various other persons, he learned that the "young man and young woman, having, like all their tribe, a great veneration for the white men and great confidence in their power, believed that through having touched me thus and later rubbing herself . . . the children she would bear would be exempt from sickness and would live a very long time." One learns to get along. "If those poor ignorant people have these absurd opinions, what should I do about it?"

Other customs Truteau found less pleasing, less commendable. Their manners were commonly repulsive.

> They break wind in front of everyone without caring about anyone. . . . Their familiar discourse is generally nothing but dirty words and lewdnesses, the women's as well as the men's. . . . The women strip themselves naked to sleep; they pass their water before everyone. They never wash their dishes, which are made of wood or bark, nor their spoons. . . . When the women have wiped their children with their hands they rub them on wood or dry them with some straw or leaves, and then handle the meat to cook and eat it. They seldom

> wash their faces nor their hands; they never cut their nails. They snuffle and blow like beasts when they eat, and they put their food on plates from which their dogs have just eaten, without washing them, and most often on wood or bark full of filth, and even on the ground, and thus they take their repast. . . . They never wash their clothes; to get the grease off they rub them with a sort of white earth mixed with water, or else they let them rot on their backs, especially the women, who are always full of lice, which they never kill in any other way than by squashing them between their teeth. Their camps are usually very dirty. . . .

In Tabeau's narrative, too, the most interesting observations are those reporting the manners and customs of the tribes of the Upper Missouri and the description of various ceremonies. He commented on the prevalence of suicide among the Arikara women, discussed Arikara concern over the interpretation of dreams, described the self-torture in some of their ceremonies, commented on their ideas of warfare and on the institution of military police among them, noted their marriage ceremonies and their gluttonous feasting, reported their ceremonies for assuaging grief, for piercing children's ears, for the blessing of the grain, pictured the thunderbird, described the "fair" held annually in September in which the medicine men all gathered to show off their powers, decided that the Arikara women could only have been called by some travelers the "Circassians of the Missouri" either in derision or irony.

Through his eyes we see how elaborately the young Sioux dandy dressed for sauntering about the village:

> He has shoes fully ornamented, with a skunk skin trailing at each heel and decorated with a piece of scarlet. The lower part of the leg is bound with two narrow cords, trimmed with quills of the porcupine. Leggings of very white antelope-skin, of which one has a cutout fringe, and the other, streaked with black, are joined and crossed above and are like Bavaroises. These fringes are ornamented with shells and with various spurs, the little clashes of which are sonorous enough to attract attention. A long, wide chemise of antelope-skin, all its edges fringed, perforated and festooned below with different figures, has two narrow points which trail under the arms and is closed only from the elbows to the wrists where there are wrought and pendant cuffs. All this is trimmed with little bells.

Upon the shoulder straps, diverse shells are fixed, and a band of fine leather, ornamented with porcupine quills and painted with figures of different colors, covers the throat and the stomach. Above it, is a collar of bear-claws, between which are little tassels of blue beads. Triple rolls of brass wire are in the ears, which are also trimmed with a double row of shells and feathers. Upon the head are scattered, without order, little balls of swan's down. The hair, separated into two tresses, covered with fine red leather, hangs very low in front. The face is daubed with white, blue, black, and vermilion. In the left hand is a spear, of which the long handle, gay with rags and fine leather and ornamented with porcupine, is held in the middle and kept in countenance with a pouch of the pekan. The head and tail of this animal, being the most brilliant and ornamented parts, hang side by side. A chichikoi, filled with small pebbles which make a noise, is attached to the left wrist. The other hand is reserved for gestures. Thus accoutered, the dandies promenade, two by two, with slow steps, fluttering about, chuckling, and favoring the ladies with sheep's eyes. It is clear that all the dandies are not in Paris and one can imagine the vanity of him who gives the time to make this examination, on perceiving that I am looking at him attentively.[15]

Equally detailed is Tabeau's report of the initiation of young men into the highly honored Band of Dogs:

The second order is that of the dogs. To have the honor of being received into this order, it is necessary to give proof of some warlike deed, if it be only the theft of a horse. After these honorable proofs, the candidates are admitted to a novitiate and, while it lasts, they have the entire body painted red, as also the few garments that they wear. They have at hand, as the pirains, the whistle and the chichikoi, of which they make a very different use. Having become dogs by profession, they appear to have acquired their instinct. They imitate them in everything; they steal around furtively everywhere; and enter the lodges softly, from whence they carry away what they can, sometimes the kettles with the food. They return all that is not eatable, although everything is lawful prize, as everyone, being warned, can keep himself upon his guard and pursue them with great blows of the stick, without which they would be offended. On the contrary, although they flee at the first threats, they return cautiously from the rear to the attack. As they are always many times dis-

[15] Tabeau, p. 177.

persed, a blast of the whistle, while they flee, announces something seized and, instantly, from every side comrades come and follow the thief. The most comic thing is to see all the real dogs of the village, trained to recognize the whistle, rush forth as the others, mingle indiscriminately with them, and receive their share. If anyone is disposed to treat them kindly, he allows them to enter the lodges where, without saying a word, they glide into the corners in the posture of dogs and show only the nose outside of their covering. If pieces of cooked or raw meat are thrown to them, they throw themselves pell-mell upon them and quarrel voraciously over them.

This metamorphosis generally lasts many months, after which only certain distinctive marks and ways of acting are retained that show a man to be of the order. For instance, they often mount upon the roofs, where they sing, or rather, shout for a part of the night. Their women follow them sometimes and join in at the end of each couplet, which is always the same, a hundred times repeated.[16]

Tabeau also wrote at length about the significance of the white buffalo to the Plains Indian and described the Mandan dance ceremony intended to draw the white cow near to the village:

[The old] men assemble in the evening in the medicine lodge and announce through the heralds that the cow is not very far away; but that she waits until the braves shall make sacrifices in her honor. At once the men bring in their wives to this altar of Paphos, clad only in a single garment which covers them. While the master of ceremonies arranges them at the farther end of the lodge, the nude old men touch them, bellow, roar, paw the earth, strike it with their heads and make the dust fly. At last, they imitate the bull pursuing the heifer. During this performance, a small fire is lighted in the center of the lodge in which some odoriferous herbs are burnt and, in the smoke of which, the victims themselves come to be perfumed without observing decency very much. They defile then before a number of young men seated in a row. Each husband has put into the hands of that one who has pleased him a little stick, which his wife recognizes in passing and which she seizes as if to take it away; but, the cavalier resisting, she drags him outside the lodge and, all the others doing the same, the company finds itself in a moment in couples on the prairie, where the old men, always bellowing and keeping at a distance, seem to censure their weakness and to manifest their sorrow. On re-entering the lodge, the husbands thank them very humbly, and the ceremony continues

[16] *Ibid.*, pp. 193–194.

all the night, the actors only changing partners at each scene. Among the Gros Ventres, they are paid. The cavalier, requesting a favor, the husband weeps upon his head, brings him that which he holds most precious, entreats him to do good to him and, if he can prevail upon him, he is very grateful still for this marked service. The fête lasts from ten to fifteen days; but, as the cow is really near, the herds have arrived two or three days after the first performance. This early success the Mandanes attributed to the captains' people, who were untiringly zealous in attracting the cow.[17]

Truteau and Tabeau are but the earliest travelers to report in intimate detail the tribes of the Missouri. Meriwether Lewis and William Clark, John Bradbury, the members of Stephen H. Long's western expedition, Paul Wilhelm of Wuerttemberg, Maximilian of Wied-Neuwied, George Catlin, John James Audubon, Rudolph Friederich Kurz on their occasions ashore found much to set down in their journals and letters about the Kansas, the Otos, the Omahas, the Poncas, the Sioux, and every other tribe of this great valley, the result of extensive acquaintance and thoughtful study.

V

Between the rough experience of Jean Baptiste Truteau and the pleasant summer holiday of John Mason Brown there were travelers of every sort and purpose on the wide Missouri and many a chiel among them was taking notes which have proved invaluable to us as records of facts and impressions, as personal reactions and scientific report, as vivid glimpses of life along the river road to the great Northwest. John Bradbury, commissioned by the Botanical Society of Liverpool to hunt plants in the American West, was as much interested in frontier manners, in meeting Daniel Boone and John Colter, in hearing the story of Hugh Glass's encounter with the grizzly bear, as in trees and plants. Henry Marie Brackenridge, who had begun studying Spanish in St. Louis, for practice read *Don Quixote* aloud with Manuel Lisa while the fur trader's boat raced with Wilson Price Hunt's Astorians to the Arikara country—the race itself can be followed in the diaries kept by Bradbury and Brackenridge on the rival keelboats.

[17] *Ibid.*, p. 197.

Audubon wrote with satisfaction to his family that Captain Joseph Sire of the *Omega* had laid in "500 Dozen of Eggs for the trip upward" and "15 Dozen of Claret" as well as brandy and whiskey. When the *Omega* passed the town of Glasgow without stopping, "the blackguards on shore were so greatly disappointed that they actually fired on us with rifles."[18] The journalist of General Henry Atkinson's expedition in 1825 saw at the mouth of "the Jack [James River] a skin flying on a pole as a flag with the figure of a man drawn upon it pointing down the Missouri which is supposed to indicate the descent of some trader & intended for the information of the companies men who may have been left behind on employment in other places."[19]

On New Year's Day, 1805, at the Mandan wintering camp of the Lewis and Clark expedition, wrote Sergeant John Ordway,

> we fired a Swivel & drank a Glass. about 9 o.C. 15 of the party went up to the 1st village of Mandans to dance as it had been their request. carried with us a fiddle & a Tambereen & a Sounden horn. as we arived at the entrence of the vil we fired one round then the music played. loaded again. then marched to the center of the village [and] fired again. then commenced dancing. a frenchman danced on his head and all danced around him for a Short time then went in to a lodge & danced awhile, which pleased them verry much they then brought victules from different lodges & of different kinds of diet, they brought us also a quantity of corn & Some buffalow Robes which they made us a present off. So we danced in different lodges untill late in the afternoon. then a part of the men returned to the fort the remainder stayed all night in the Village.[20]

Aboard the *Key West* in 1860 Lieutenant Carr of the U.S. Army, according to the journal of a fellow officer, August V. Kautz, quarreled with Dix, the pilot at the wheel, "because he whistled the steamer's whistle and frightened some game at which Mr. Carr wished to shoot." The pilot struck Carr, who then paraded his men and tried to arrest Dix. "In doing so, the pilot fired repeatedly at Mr. Carr, one shot taking effect in his shoulder."[21]

[18] Audubon (no. 44), p. 65; Audubon (no. 43), I, 460.
[19] Atkinson and O'Fallon (no. 25), p. 17.
[20] Ordway (no. 12), p. 175.
[21] Kautz (no. 89), p. 205.

Notes of a different sort were being taken by other observers with pen and pencil and brush, often in such profusion as to form pictorial diaries of their travels. Rudolph Friederich Kurz, young Swiss artist, took home to Bern in 1852 a portfolio of sketches unmatched for its detail of the ways of the Indian and the fur trader on the Missouri. Karl Bodmer's diary—if he ever kept one—has not been located, but his surviving pencil sketches and his magnificent collection of watercolor portraits, of riverscapes, trading forts, and Indian groups form an ethnological and historical record of great value. Father Nicolas Point's amateurish paintings of life among the tribes he knew at the Catholic mission in Idaho are rather charmingly naive, but the sketches he drew of forts on the Upper Missouri as he returned downriver in 1847 are documents as precise as they are precious for their uniqueness. George Catlin, E. de Girardin, John Mix Stanley, Will Hays, William de la Montagne Cary, Charles Wimar, and many another artist exploring the West have pictured for us this frontier as they found it.

"Different travellers have different eyes," declared Audubon in his journal.[22] Missionaries, Army officers, topographers, ethnologists, geologists, businessmen, sportsmen, artists, chance wanderers—what interested one might be of no concern to another but among them they saw everything. Trivialities, curiosities, personalities, continental exploration, the fur trade, the Indians, the pains and pleasures of travel in a rough new world—everything common or uncommon that made up life along the wide Missouri in those faraway decades between 1794 and 1861 is reported, described, drawn in the diaries, the letters, the sketches of its travelers.

A Checklist of Accounts of Travel on the Missouri River, 1794-1861

All works and travelers cited in "Up the Wide Missouri" will be found in this list, but to them have been added others to form a moderately extensive working bibliography of the Missouri River from the traveler's

22 Audubon (no. 43), II, 10.

point of view. Accounts selected have been limited to firsthand reports, written at the time of travel or very soon after.

It will be noted that a number of books invaluable for Missouri River history have not been included in the Checklist even though they contain much on-the-spot reporting of activities on the river during this period: fur-trade studies such as Richard E. Oglesby's *Manuel Lisa and the Opening of the Missouri Fur Trade* (1963) and John E. Sunder's *The Fur Trade on the Upper Missouri, 1840–1865* (1965); and histories of the river and its traffic like H. M. Chittenden's *History of Early Steamboat Navigation on the Missouri River: Life and Adventures of Joseph La Barge* (1903), Phil E. Chappell's "A History of the Missouri River with a List of Missouri River Steamboats" (*Kansas Historical Collections*, IX [1905–06], 237–316), and William E. Lass's *A History of Steamboating on the Upper Missouri River* (1962). Indispensable as these works are, they are outside the scope of this Checklist. So, too, is A. P. Nasatir's *Before Lewis and Clark: Documents Illustrating the History of the Missouri, 1785–1804* (1952), though its two volumes contain many letters and reports concerning the Missouri drawn from French and Spanish archives.

Sound argument might have been made for including important documents of another sort: the diaries kept by men stationed at some point on the river during these years, such as Francis A. Chardon's *Journal at Fort Clark, 1834–1839* (edited by Annie Héloise Abel, 1932) and James Kennerly's "Diary, 1823–1826" (edited by Edgar B. Wesley, *Missouri Historical Society Collections*, VI [October, 1928], 41–97), recorded while he was sutler at Fort Atkinson (Council Bluffs). They (and numerous others) have been omitted, however, because the point of view of the essay and of the Checklist has been that of the actual voyager on the waters of the Missouri, not of a resident on its banks. Truteau and Tabeau wrote as travelers, visitors; Chardon and Kennerly as stationary agents.

On the other hand it will be seen that a number of pictorial reporters have been included even though they have left no written word of their western wanderings. Karl Bodmer, John Mix Stanley, Charles Wimar (1859), William de la Montagne Cary, for example, recorded in their sketches river views and scenes of life and action as vivid and as valuable as any set down in penciled journals.

This Checklist, then, provides only a first accounting of travel reports of the Missouri River during a limited period of years. A definitive checklist of such literature would run without doubt to four or five times as many items. Obviously the years before 1794 and especially after 1861 would produce numerous other titles. An extended search of periodicals (both scholarly and popular), of St. Louis and St. Joseph newspapers, and of manuscript collections would uncover many reports and diaries to enlarge this roster of Missouri River travel literature.

1794–95

1. Truteau, Jean Baptiste

"Journal of Travels on the Missouri, 1794–1795."

Truteau left St. Louis 7 June 1794 as field director of the newly formed Compagnie de Commerce pour le Découverte des Nations du Haut du Missouri and returned to St. Louis two years later. His instructions directed him to keep a daily journal of occurrences, which he entitled: "Extrait des journaux de voyage de J. Bte. Trudeau sur le haut Missouris adressés à Messrs les directeurs de la Compagnie à St. Louis des Illinois depuis le 7 juin 1794 au 4 juin 1796." The first and third parts of this journal are available in translation in A. P. Nasatir, editor, *Before Lewis and Clark: Documents Illustrating the History of the Missouri, 1785–1804* (2 volumes, St. Louis Historical Documents Foundation, 1952), I, 259–311, and in *South Dakota Historical Collections*, VII (1914), 403–474. The third part, commonly called Part II, covering the period 24 May–20 July 1795, known to Thomas Jefferson and long in the Department of State Archives, was translated and published by Nettie H. Beauregard in the *Missouri Historical Society Collections*, IV (1912), 9–48. Part I (7 June 1794–26 March 1795), discovered by Roscoe R. Hill in Legajo 187, Archivo General de Indias, Papeles Procedentes de Cuba, was originally published (French text only) in the *American Historical Review*, XIX (January, 1914), 299–333. A long-missing second part, 26 March–23 May 1795, exists in manuscript. Although Truteau did not return to St. Louis until 4 June 1796, no portion of diary later than 20 July 1795 is known to exist.

The Truteau Papers, consisting of the three parts of the diary together with Truteau's "Description du haut Missouri" (no. 2), are now being prepared for publication in their entirety in English. The complicated history of the manuscripts, not pertinent here, will be discussed in the forthcoming edition.

2. Truteau, Jean Baptiste

"Description du haut Missouri" (1795).

This account (still in MS) of the Upper Missouri River and its tribes was composed by Truteau at the request of Lieutenant Governor Zenon Trudeau (3 May 1795). The eleven chapters of this 152-page manuscript are concerned with

La rivière Missouri et les nations sauvages qui habitent dans son bassin

Origine, croyance et cérémonies des sauvages dans le culte qu'ils rendent à la divinité
Moeurs des Sauvages du Haut Missouris
Habit, logement, complexion et tempérament des Sauvages du Haut Missouris
Amours et mariages des Sauvages du Haut Missouris
Manière de faire la paix, d'aller en calumet et de le danser
La danse du calumet
La danse du Soleil
La danse du Boeuf
Manières inciviles et grossières des Sauvages
Guerre des Sauvages

Three passages from a copy of the "Description" given by Nicolas Boilvin of St. Louis to Dr. Samuel L. Mitchill in the winter of 1805–06 were published by Mitchill in his *Medical Repository*, Second Hexade, III (1806), 313–315; VI (1809), 52–56, 120–124. Another extract was found in the J. N. Nicollet Papers by Dr. Annie Héloise Abel-Henderson and was published by her in the *Mississippi Valley Historical Review*, VIII (June–September, 1921), 149–179. See also the entry for Perrin du Lac (no. 7).

1795–96

3. Mackay, James

"Voyage of Monsieur Mackay General Agent for the Company of the Misuri." [Louis Houck, editor, *The Spanish Régime in Missouri* (2 volumes, Chicago, R. R. Donnelley and Sons, 1909), II, 182–192. Also in Nasatir, *Before Lewis and Clark*, I, 356–364.]

Mackay left St. Louis "at the end of August, 1795," reached the Platte River 14 October, and wintered at the Maha village, where he still was as late as 18 January 1796.

4. Mackay, James

"Extracts from Capt. McKay's Journal." [Milo M. Quaife, editor, "Extracts from Capt. McKay's Journal—and Others," *Wisconsin Historical Society Proceedings, 1915*, pp. 186–210. Also printed in *Medical Repository*, Second Hexade, IV (1807), 27–36, and in Nasatir, *Before Lewis and Clark*, II, 490–499.]

The few paragraphs of journal (Quaife, pp. 193–195) are in effect eyewitness summary rather than daily report.

1796–97

5. Evans, John

"Extracts of Mr Evans Journal." [Quaife *et al.* as in no. 4.]

On 8 June 1796 Evans was dispatched by Mackay from the Missouri Company's post at the Maha village to the Arikara, where he arrived 8 August, and the Mandan village, which he reached 23 September. Evans was still among the Mandans on 13 March 1797.

1797

6. Mackay, James

"Mackay's Table of Distances." [Edited by Annie Héloise Abel-Henderson, *Mississippi Valley Historical Review*, X (March, 1924), 428–446.]

Title of original document: "Table des distances le long du Missouri en remontant depuis l'embouchure jusqu'à celle de la Rivière Blanche, Prises par James Mackay en 1797."

1802

7. Perrin du Lac, [François-Marie]

Voyage dans les deux Louisianes, et chez les Nations sauvages du Missouri, par les États-Unis, l'Ohio et les Provinces qui le bordent, en 1801, 1802 et 1803; avec un apperçu des moeurs, des usages, du caractère et des coutumes religieuses et civiles des Peuples de ces diverses contrées. [Lyon, an XIII—1805.]

There seems to be no reason to doubt that Perrin du Lac did make the voyage up the Missouri described (pp. 197–217). According to his statement Perrin left St. Louis 18 May 1802, ascended as far as White River, and was once more in St. Louis on 20 September. As he acknowledged (p. 196), he was guided by a "former trader" who had once been employed by the Compagnie du haut du Missouri and, without naming the trader, he admitted helping himself freely to that trader's papers then in the government archives in St. Louis. "Tous ces mémoires sont resté dans les archives, dont je les ai tirés moi-même pour en extraire les parties les plus essentielles." Professor Fernand Grenier of Laval University has shown that Perrin du Lac lifted from Truteau's manuscripts—at times word for word—the matter that fills Perrin's chapters 29–40 ("Un Plagiaire Illustre: François Perrin du Lac," *Revue d'Histoire de l'Amérique Française*, VII [Septembre, 1953], 207–224). This *français de France* apparently had come to America to write a book about the territory which he thought was going to be retroceded to France; he knew good material when he saw it and, since the Truteau reports were in public archives, he gutted them with only the faintest of acknowledgment. It appears, however, that the visiting journalist[?] omitted or softened some of the trader's detail. There is much of interest in Truteau's manuscripts which is not now available in print.

1803–05

8. Tabeau, Pierre-Antoine

Tabeau's Narrative of Loisel's Expedition to the Upper Missouri. [Edited by Annie Héloise Abel, Norman, University of Oklahoma Press, 1939.]

Not strictly speaking a diary, but an on-the-spot account of the Upper Missouri. Tabeau divided his long report into sections on "The Missouri," "Animals," "Birds," "Fish," "Fruits," "Nations Which Roam over or Inhabit the Upper Missouri," "Concerning Trade," "Manners and Customs," "Religious Superstitions, etc.," "Savage Warfare," and "Description of Some Ceremonies." It covers the period 22 June 1803–20 May 1805.

1804–06

9. Lewis, Meriwether, *et al.*

The Original Journals of the Lewis and Clark Expedition, 1804–1806. [Edited by Reuben Gold Thwaites, 8 volumes, New York, Dodd, Mead and Co., 1904–05.]

The journals of Meriwether Lewis, William Clark, Charles Floyd, and Joseph Whitehouse.

10. Lewis, Meriwether, *et al.*

Letters of the Lewis and Clark Expedition with Related Documents, 1783–1854. [Edited by Donald Jackson, Urbana, University of Illinois Press, 1962.]

Includes letters written on the upriver voyage, 1804–05, and the return in 1806.

11. Gass, Patrick

A Journal of the Voyages and Travels of a Corps of Discovery under the Command of Capt. Lewis and Capt. Clarke . . . from the Mouth of the River Missouri, through the Interior Parts of North America to the Pacific Ocean, During the Years 1804, 1805, and 1806. [Pittsburgh, David McKeehan, 1807.]

12. Ordway, John

The Journals of Captain Meriwether Lewis and Sergeant John Ordway Kept on the Expedition of Western Exploration 1803–1806. [Edited by Milo M. Quaife, *Wisconsin Historical Society Collections,* XXII (1916), 31–402.]

Ordway's diary of the upriver trip begins at Camp Dubois above St. Louis 14 May 1804 and continues to 17 August 1805 (pp. 77–269); the account of the downriver voyage on return runs from 10 July 1806 until the arrival at St. Louis on 23 September (pp. 376–402). (The

Lewis diary is not Missouri River travel, for it is limited to the trip down the Ohio and up the Mississippi in 1803.)

1809

13. Thomas, Dr.

"Journal of a Voyage from St. Louis, La. to the Mandan Village, undertaken by the St. Louis Missouri Fur Company, for the purpose of conducting Shehekek the Mandan chief to his nation, and to establish trading houses on the head waters of the Missouri; by Dr. Thomas, Surgeon to the Party." [For the first part: St. Louis *Louisiana Gazette*, 30 November 1809. The concluding portion must have appeared in the next issue of the same newspaper; unhappily, however, no copy of this issue is extant. Clippings of the complete journal, however, have been found in the Liverpool (England) Library and will be published.]

The party left St. Louis in ten barges 17 May 1809 and arrived at the first Mandan village 21 September. The return journey "from the Company's trading house above the Gros Ventres" took forty days.

1811

14. Brackenridge, Henry Marie

"Journal of a Voyage Up the Missouri River, in 1811." [In his *Views of Louisiana* (Pittsburgh, Zadok Cramer, 1814), pp. 197–268; second edition (1816), a slightly enlarged text published alone.]

Brackenridge left St. Louis (i.e. St. Charles) with Manuel Lisa 2 April 1811; on 26 June he arrived at the Missouri Fur Company fort beyond the Mandan village. He set off on the return trip 6 July, and arrived with Bradbury (no. 15) "early in August" after a fourteen-day voyage from the Arikara to St. Louis.

15. Bradbury, John

Travels in the Interior of America in the Years 1809, 1810, and 1811; including a Description of Upper Louisiana. [Liverpool, by the author, 1817; second edition, London, 1819.]

Bradbury left St. Louis with Wilson Price Hunt's Astorians 18 March 1811, arrived at Reuben Lewis's fort (Missouri Fur Company) 22 June, met Brackenridge (no. 14) 25 June, started downriver with him 6 July, left the Arikaras 17 July, was at Boonslick 29 July, and arrived at St. Louis early in August.

1812

16. Luttig, John C.

Journal of a Fur-Trading Expedition on the Upper Missouri

1812–1813. [Edited by Stella M. Drumm, St. Louis, Missouri Historical Society, 1920. A new (facsimile) edition with additional notes and introduction by A. P. Nasatir has been published by the Argosy-Antiquarian Press Ltd., New York, 1964.]

The fur-trading party under Luttig's direction left St. Louis 8 May 1812 and reached Fort Manuel (Lisa) among the Arikaras 9 August (pp. 27–68). The last entry in the journal is dated 5 March 1813.

1813

17. Stuart, Robert

The Discovery of the Oregon Trail. [Edited by Philip Ashton Rollins, New York, Edward Eberstadt and Sons, 1935.]

This is the record of a brief downriver trip: Stuart's party of returning Astorians reached the Oto village on the Missouri 12 April 1813; there they made a canoe and came downriver to arrive at St. Louis 30 April (pp. 235–240).

Also in Kenneth A. Spaulding, editor, *On the Oregon Trail—Robert Stuart's Journey of Discovery* (Norman, University of Oklahoma Press, 1953), pp. 160–164.

1818–20

18. Gale, John

The Missouri Expedition, 1818–1820. The Journal of Surgeon John Gale with Related Documents. [Edited by Roy L. Nichols, Norman, University of Oklahoma Press, 1969.] The original manuscript (Western Americana Collection, Yale University Library) had been attributed to Lieutenant Thomas Kavanaugh.

This expedition, under the command of Colonel Henry Atkinson, left Fort Bellefontaine at Cold Water Creek on the Missouri near St. Louis to establish, on 18 October 1818, Martin's Cantonment near Isle des Vaches 380 miles above the mouth of the Missouri.

1819

19. Baldwin, William

Journal. [Torrey Correspondence, Columbia University Herbarium, New York.]

Dr. Baldwin, botanist on Long's western expedition (no. 21), kept a diary from the departure from St. Louis until his death at Franklin, Missouri, in mid-July.

20. [Biddle, Major John]

"Notes on the Missouri River, and some of the Native Tribes in its Neighborhood. By a Gentleman attached to the Yellowstone Expedition in 1819." [*Analectic Magazine*, n.s., I (Philadelphia, 1820), 293–375.]

Biddle was the appointed "journalist" on Stephen H. Long's western expedition; he resigned after his arrival at the winter camping ground.

21. James, Edwin

Account of an Expedition from Pittsburgh to the Rocky Mountains, performed in the Years 1819, 1820 . . . under the Command of Maj. S. H. Long. [2 volumes, Philadelphia, Carey and Lea, 1823. Reprinted in Reuben Gold Thwaites, editor, *Early Western Travels, 1778–1846* (Cleveland, Arthur H. Clark, 1905), Vols. XIV–XVII.]

The party left St. Louis aboard the steamboat *Western Engineer* 21 June 1819 (XIV, 121–129), was at Fort Osage 1 August, arrived at the mouth of the Platte 15 September, and wintered on the west bank of the Missouri three miles above Boyer's River, one-half mile above Fort Lisa, and five miles below Council Bluffs (p. 221).

22. Peale, Titian Ramsay

"The Journal of Titian Ramsay Peale, Pioneer Naturalist." [Edited by A. O. Weese, *Missouri Historical Review*, XLI (January and April, 1947), 147–163, 266–284.]

Peale left St. Louis 22 June 1819, going part of the way overland, but rejoined the steamboat 2 July (p. 269); the diary ends 1 August (p. 283) on arrival at Fort Osage.

1822

23. Paul Wilhelm, Duke of Wuerttemberg

First Journey to North America in the Years 1822 to 1824. [Stuttgart & Tübingen, J. B. Cotta, 1835. Translated by William G. Bek, *South Dakota Historical Collections*, XIX (1938), 7–474.]

Prince Paul left St. Charles, Missouri, 15 May 1823 (p. 237) by keelboat to arrive at Franklin, Missouri, 11 June (p. 288). He traveled overland to the mouth of the Kansas River, took water again 21 June (p. 302), reached the Platte River 29 July (p. 345), left Pilcher's fort above White River for return to Council Bluffs by boat 29 August (p. 410), was at Council Bluffs 9 September (p. 415), made a side trip to the Otos, finally left Council Bluffs by boat 2 October (p. 443), and arrived at St. Charles 23 October (p. 453).

1824

24. Kearny, Stephen Watts

Journal, 1824. [MS, Missouri Historical Society.]

From St. Louis to Council Bluffs, 17 September–2 November.

1825

25. Atkinson, Henry, and Benjamin O'Fallon

"Journal of the Atkinson-O'Fallon Expedition." [Edited by Russell Reid and C. G. Gannon, *North Dakota Historical Quarterly*, IV (1929), 5–56.]

The expedition left Fort Atkinson (Camp Missouri), nine miles north of Omaha, 16 May 1825 (p. 10), reached Red Water Creek below Porcupine River 24 August (p. 43), commenced descent 24 August (p. 43), and reached St. Louis 20 October (p. 54).

26. Atkinson, Henry

"Report of the Yellowstone Expedition of 1825." [Edited by Roger L. Nichols, *Nebraska History*, XLIV (June, 1963), 65–82.]

27. Kearny, Stephen Watts

Journal, 1825. [MS, Missouri Historical Society.]

Left Council Bluffs with Atkinson (no. 25) 16 May and returned there 19 September.

1832

28. Catlin, George

Letters and Notes on the Manners, Customs, and Conditions of the North American Indians written during eight Years of Travel Amongst the Wildest Tribes of Indians in North America in 1832, 33, 34, 35, 36, 37, 38, and 39. [2 volumes, London, by the author, 1841. Variant titles on later editions. 360 (i.e. 309?) illustrations.]

Catlin left St. Louis 26 March 1832 on the steamboat *Yellowstone* and arrived at Fort Union 16 June. He returned by canoe, accompanied by two men. The entire first volume and the first three chapters of the second are concerned with his story of his Missouri River experiences. The original letters written to the New York *Commercial Advertiser* have recently been collected and are being edited for publication. Since the sketches of Prince Paul (no. 23) were destroyed by bombing in World War II, Catlin's views of the Missouri River landscape remain the first extensive pictorial record of this region.

1833–34

29. Maximilian, Prince of Wied-Neuwied

Travels in the Interior of North America in the Years 1832, 1833, and 1834. [2 volumes and atlas, Coblenz, J. Hoelscher, 1839. Translated by H. Evans Lloyd, London, Ackermann and Co., 1843. Reprinted in Reuben Gold Thwaites, editor, *Early Western Travels 1748–1846* (Cleveland, Arthur H. Clark, 1906), Vols. XXII–XXV.]

Maximilian left St. Louis on the steamboat *Yellowstone* 10 April 1833. At Fort Pierre changed to the steamboat *Assiniboine* to arrive at Fort Union 18 June. Thence by keelboat 24 June to reach Fort McKenzie (Maria's River) 9 August. Left Fort McKenzie by mackinaw boat 14 September, wintered at Fort Clark (Mandans). Started descent in mackinaw 18 April 1834, reached Fort Leavenworth 18 May and St. Charles 26 May (XXII, 237–XXIV, 124).

30. Bodmer, Karl

The *Atlas* to illustrate the *Travels* of Prince Maximilian (no. 29) may be looked upon as a pictorial diary kept by the Maximilian's artist, Karl Bodmer. Plates 10–31, 36–71, 73–81 and many of the vignettes published in the volumes of text (Thwaites edition) picture a sequence of Missouri River landscapes and life along the river during the time covered by the prince's account. The entire collection of Bodmer sketches preserved by Maximilian (some four hundred pieces made on the American tour) are now owned by the Northern Natural Gas Company of Omaha and are on permanent loan to the Joslyn Art Museum of Omaha. Publication of the complete diaries and letters of Maximilian and the entire collection of Bodmer sketches is being planned. A small group of Bodmer field sketches is in the Ayer Collection of the Newberry Library, Chicago, and five other sketches are owned by the Baltimore Museum of Art.

1835

31. Parker, Samuel

Journal of an Exploring Tour beyond the Rocky Mountains . . . in the Years 1835, '36, and '37. [Ithaca, by the author, 1838; second edition, 1840.]

Parker left St. Louis on the steamboat *St. Charles,* Captain Shallcross, 7 April 1835 (p. 26). On 20 April the steamboat grounded twelve miles below Liberty, Missouri (p. 30).

32. Murray, Charles Augustus

Travels in North America during the Years 1834, 1835 & 1836. [2 volumes, London, R. Bentley, 1839.]

Murray left St. Louis on the steamboat *Hancock* for Fort Leavenworth in June 1835 (I, 237), landing at Liberty, Missouri, 2 July, after nine days of travel (p. 249). His return to St. Louis in September is reported in II, 82–88.

1837

33. Arese, Count Francesco

A Trip to the Prairies and the Interior of North America. [Translated by Andrew Evans, New York, Harbor Press, 1934.]

Arese traveled up the Missouri from St. Louis in the steamboat *St. Peters* in the spring of 1837 (pp. 66–73), reaching Council Bluffs in eleven days.

1838

34. De Smet, Pierre-Jean

Life, Letters and Times of Father Pierre-Jean De Smet, S.J. [By Hiram Martin Chittenden and Alfred Talbot Richardson, 4 volumes, New York, Francis P. Harper, 1905.]

In May De Smet traveled from the Kickapoo village to the Potawatomies by steamboat (I, 150–178).

This indefatigable traveler made at least five other trips up or down the Missouri during the years encompassed in this Checklist. The passages cited are all from his journals or letters. See also nos. 35, 37, 38, 55, 62.

1839

35. De Smet [no. 34]

Left St. Louis for the Sioux country 29 April aboard the American Fur Company steamboat (I, 179–192).

36. R——, H.

"Trip Up the Missouri in '39." [St. Louis *Western Atlas,* 14 May 1841.]

H. R. went as far as Fort Leavenworth.

1840

37. De Smet [no. 34]

Left St. Louis by steamboat for Westport 27 March (I, 198–201). Came downriver by canoe from Fort Vermillion to Council Bluffs 14 November (II, 638–652).

1841

38. De Smet [no. 34]

Left St. Louis on the steamboat *Oceana* 23 April to depart overland from Westport 10 May (I, 272–279).

39. Sire, Joseph

Logbook, American Fur Company steamboat *Trapper.* [Logbooks, American Fur Company Steamboats, 1841–46, MSS, French, Missouri Historical Society. See also nos. 40, 47, 49, 50, 52.]

The *Trapper* left St. Louis for Fort Union 7 April and returned 17 July.

1842

40. Sire, Joseph [no. 39]

Logbook, American Fur Company steamboat *Trapper*.

The *Trapper* left St. Louis for Fort Union 11 April and returned 19 August.

41. Anon.

"Trip Down the Missouri." [St. Louis *Missouri Republican*, 28 May 1842.]

Aboard the steamboat *Edna*, Captain Martin, from Weston, Missouri, 17 May, to St. Louis, 22 May.

42. G^xx de L^xx [Captain William Seaton Henry, U.S. Army]

"A Trip Up the Missouri." [New York *Spirit of the Times*, XV (1 November 1845), 423–424.]

Transfer of troops from Jefferson Barracks at St. Louis to Fort Leavenworth in the spring of 1842.

1843

43. Audubon, John James

"Missouri River Journals." [Maria R. Audubon and Elliott Coues, editors, *Audubon and His Journals*, 2 volumes, New York, Charles Scribner's Sons, 1897.]

Audubon and his party left St. Louis for Fort Union on the steamboat *Omega* 25 April (I, 455) and returned to St. Louis in a mackinaw boat 19 October (II, 175).

A portion of the original diary (16 August–6 November) is now in the Ayer Collection of the Newberry Library. For an interesting comment on the difference between it and the diary as published see Dwight L. Smith, "The Westward Traveler: Unexploited Manuscript Resources of the Newberry Library," pp. 92–94 below.

44. Audubon, John James

Audubon in the West. [Edited by John Francis McDermott, Norman, University of Oklahoma Press, 1965.]

Ten letters from Audubon to his family from various points on the Missouri, 25 April–17 June, are printed on pp. 69–120.

45. Harris, Edward

Up the Missouri with Audubon: The Journal of Edward Harris. [Edited by John Francis McDermott, Norman, University of Oklahoma Press, 1951.]

The St. Louis to St. Louis portion of this diary by Audubon's friend Harris is reported on pp. 54–184.

46. Spraguc, Isaac

Diary, 16 February–7 November 1843. [MS on deposit in the Boston Athenaeum.]

Sprague was employed by Audubon on the 1843 expedition to "draw plants and views for backgrounds." His diary, though interesting, is much slighter than those of Audubon and Harris. Isaac Sprague, Jr., the traveler's son, is planning to publish the diary.

47. Sire, Joseph [no. 39]

Logbook of the American Fur Company steamboat *Omega.*

The *Omega* left St. Louis 25 April and returned 29 June. A translation of this log, published in Hiram Martin Chittenden's *The American Fur Trade of the Far West,* has some inaccuracies (see reprint edition, edited by Stallo Vinton [2 volumes, New York, Press of the Pioneers, 1935], II, 956–973).

48. Field, Henry M.

"A Week on the Missouri." [St. Louis *Daily Evening Gazette,* 6, 7 July 1843.]

Field left St. Louis 20 June on the steamboat *Rowena,* traveling as far as Boonville.

1844

49. Sire, Joseph [no. 39]

Logbook of the American Fur Company steamboat *Nimrod.*

The *Nimrod* left St. Louis for Fort Union 30 April and returned 9 July.

1845

50. Sire, Joseph [no. 39]

Logbook of the American Fur Company steamboat *General Brooke.*

The *General Brooke* left St. Louis for Fort Union 22 May and returned 18 July.

1846

51. Lienhart, Heinrich

From St. Louis to Sutter's Fort, 1846. [Translated and edited by Erwin G. and Elisabeth K. Gudde, Norman, University of Oklahoma Press, 1961.]

Pages 5–8 are devoted to the five-day steamboat trip from St. Louis to Independence in May.

52. Sire, Joseph [no. 39]

Logbook of the American Fur Company steamboat *General Brooke.*

The *General Brooke* left St. Louis for Fort Union 23 May and returned 6 August.

53. Moore, Col. T. P.

Letter to S. Penn, Jr., dated Fort Pierre, 20 July 1846. [St. Louis *Missouri Reporter*, 8 August 1846.]

Described his voyage up the Missouri. He had left St. Louis 23 May in the steamboat *General Brooke*, reached Fort Union 5 July, and arrived once more at Fort Pierre 20 July.

54. Taylor, Daniel G.

Journal of the *Clermont*. [MS, four-page fragment, Missouri Historical Society.]

The steamboat *Clermont* started upriver from St. Louis 7 July.

55. De Smet [no. 34]

On 28 September De Smet left the Blackfeet Mission near Fort Lewis; he arrived at Westport 28 November and there took the stage for St. Louis (II, 600–612).

1847

56. Finch, D.

Logbook of the American Fur Company steamboat *Martha*. [MS, in English, at the close of the Sire logbooks, Missouri Historical Society.]

The *Martha* left St. Louis for Fort Union 15 May and returned 8 August.

57. Point, Nicolas

"A Journey in a Barge on the Missouri from the Fort of the Blackfeet [Lewis] to that of the Assiniboines [Union]." [Edited by Gilbert J. Garraghan, translated by Paul A. Barrette, *Mid-America*, XIII (1931), 236–254.]

Father Point left Fort Lewis 19 May and arrived at Fort Union 1 June. He traveled thence to St. Louis by the steamboat *Martha*.

This account is included in Joseph P. Donnelly, editor, *Wilderness Kingdom, Indian Life in the Rocky Mountains: 1840–1847; the Journals and Paintings of Nicolas Point* (New York, Holt, Rinehart and Winston, 1967), pp. 212–261—there entitled "A Stay at Fort Lewis and a Journey in a Barge down the Missouri." Father Point had arrived at Fort Lewis 24 September 1846. The great contribution of this volume is the publication of many sketches of Missouri River scenes and life, including, for example, the only known sketches of Fort Lewis and of the *Martha,* among many others. Point is far more important as a pictorial reporter of the Upper Missouri than as a diarist. A number of his sketches were used to illustrate the original publications of Father De Smet.

58. Palliser, John

Solitary Rambles and Adventures of a Hunter in the Prairies. [London, John Murray, 1853.]

The author left St. Louis by steamboat for Independence (pp. 78–82); there he met James Kipp of the American Fur Company and (2 September) traveled overland with him to Fort Union. Palliser returned to St. Louis a year later on the steamboat *Martha* (pp. 289–291).

1849

59. Decker, Peter

The Diaries of Peter Decker Overland to California in 1849. [Edited by Helen S. Giffen, Georgetown, California, Talisman Press, 1966.]

Decker arrived at St. Louis 9 April, left two days later by steamboat for St. Joseph, which he reached 16 April (pp. 47–54).

(Many of the California Gold Rush diarists of this and later years traveled by steamboat from St. Louis to one of the jumping-off places, but they seldom gave much space in their journals to this portion of the westward journey.)

60. Girardin, E. de

"A Trip to the Bad Lands in 1849." [*South Dakota Historical Review,* I (January, 1936), 50–78. Translated from the original French text as published in *Le Tour du Monde,* IX (1864), 49–68.]

Girardin left St. Louis on the steamboat *Iowa* as artist attached to John Evans' geological exploring party up the Missouri. The boat arrived at Fort Pierre after thirty-two days' travel. No specific dates given. Account illustrated with woodcuts after Girardin's sketches.

Of Girardin nothing is known. He was still (or again) with Evans on the Upper Missouri in 1853.

1850

61. Culbertson, Thaddeus

Journal of an Expedition to the Mauvaises Terres and the Upper Missouri in 1850. [Edited by John Francis McDermott, Washington, D.C., Smithsonian Institution (Bureau of American Ethnology *Bulletin 147*), 1952.]

Culbertson left St. Louis with his brother Alexander on the steamboat *Mary Blane* for St. Joseph 21 March and arrived there 26 March (pp. 15–21), thence traveling overland to Fort Pierre. From that place (5 June) he voyaged on the steamboat *El Paso* to Fort Union (16 June) and thence to Milk River, arriving 20 June (pp. 85–114). He left Milk River on the *El Paso* the same day and reached St. Louis 6 July (pp. 114–121).

1851

62. De Smet [no. 34]

Father De Smet this year went up the Missouri in the steamboat *St. Ange,* leaving St. Louis 7 June and arriving at Fort Union 14 July (II, 638–652).

1851–52

63. Kurz, Rudolph Friederich

Journal of Rudolph Friederich Kurz An Account of His Experiences among Fur Traders and American Indians on the Mississippi and the Upper Missouri Rivers during the Years 1846 to 1852. [Edited by J. N. B. Hewitt, translated by Myrtis Jarrell, Washington, D.C., Smithsonian Institution (Bureau of American Ethnology *Bulletin 115*), 1937. Illustrated with 94 plates of on-the-spot sketches.]

Kurz left St. Joseph, Missouri, for the Upper Missouri 16 June 1851 (p. 69), stayed principally at Fort Berthold and Fort Union, and left the latter establishment 18 April 1852 (p. 239) to begin his return to his native Switzerland. He arrived at St. Louis 25 May (p. 335).

This detailed account of his experiences in America was composed in German after his return from America; it was in effect an enlargement of diaries he had kept on the Missouri. One of these diaries (3 October 1851–25 September 1852, kept in English), recently discovered in Switzerland, is being prepared for publication in a new edition of the *Journal* to replace the long out-of-print BAE *Bulletin.* Kurz is of first importance not merely for his written text but for the hundreds of sketches he made during these years on the Missouri.

1853

64. Piercy, Frederick

Route from Liverpool to Great Salt Lake Valley Illustrated with steel engravings and wood cuts from sketches made by Frederick Piercy. [Edited by James Linforth, Liverpool, F. D. Richards, 1855.]

Piercy arrived at New Orleans from Liverpool 21 March 1853 on a visit to Salt Lake City. After a brief trip from St. Louis to Nauvoo, he traveled by steamboat from St. Louis to St. Joseph and thence overland by way of Kanesville. The narrative is thin, but the book is valuable for Piercy's Mississippi and western pictures.

65. Suckley, George

Diary on the Missouri River, 1853. [MS, Smithsonian Institution, Library of the Museum of Natural History. Note also Suckley letters in the Western Americana Collection, Yale University Library.]

Suckley, botanist and physician on the Isaac I. Stevens Pacific Railroad exploration expedition of 1853, traveled up the Missouri to meet the main party at Fort Union.

66. Stanley, John Mix

Official artist on the Isaac I. Stevens Pacific Railroad survey in 1853, Stanley contributed to this record of travelers' impressions a number of views along the Missouri River from Fort Union to Fort Benton published as lithographs in Vol. XII of the *Pacific Railroad Reports.*

1855

67. Cumming, Alfred

"Indians on the Upper Missouri." [34th Congress, 1st Session, *House Executive Document 65,* Serial 853.]

Journal of a trip from St. Louis 6 June 1855 to the Falls of the Missouri and return to St. Louis 5 January 1856. The fifteen-page report is dated St. Louis, 14 February 1856. Cumming's MS is in the Western Americana Collection (Coe No. 187), Yale University Library.

68. Hatch, Edwin A. C.

Journal, 6 June 1855–5 June 1856. [MS, Newberry Library. Being edited by Martin Ridge for publication.]

Hatch traveled up the Missouri on the steamboat *St. Mary* to spend the year 6 June 1855–5 June 1856 as U.S. agent to the Blackfeet.

1856

69. S——.

Accounts of the voyage of the American Fur Company steamboat *St. Mary* from St. Louis (7 June) to the Yellowstone. [Two letters from Nebraska Territory, dated Fort Pierre, June 1856, and Fort Union, 13 July 1856, in the St. Louis *Missouri Republican,* 29 July, 9 August 1856.]

70. H——.

"From the Upper Missouri." [St. Louis Tri-Weekly *Missouri Republican,* 12 November 1856.]

1857

71. "A Passenger"

Account in the St. Louis *Missouri Republican,* 17 June 1857, of a voyage on the steamboat *D. A. January,* leaving St. Louis 26 May and returning from Sioux City 7 June to arrive at St. Louis 13 June.

72. Anon.

"Steaming up the Missouri at Low Water or 'Astrea in Search of the New Atlantis.'" [*Cosmopolitan Art Journal,* II (December, 1857), 18–21.]

The unknown traveler left St. Louis on the steamboat *Arabia.* Not dated, but mentioned "damp spring wind." Five days to Brunswick, then to Kansas City, Leavenworth, Weston, St. Joseph; thence by stage to Council Bluffs. A second article, "Views from the Top of a Bluff; or, 'Astrea in search of the New Atlantis'" (II, 82–84), was concerned with Council Bluffs and Omaha but contained nothing to identify the author or to date his visit.

73. Anon.

"News from the Upper Missouri." [St. Louis *Missouri Republican,* 27 December 1857.]

74. Millington, J.

Log of the steamboat *Twilight,* Captain John Shaw. [St. Louis *Missouri Republican,* 22 July 1857.]

The *Twilight* had left St. Louis for the Yellowstone 31 May and returned 21 July.

1858

75. Anon.

Accounts of the voyage of the American Fur Company steamboat *Spreadeagle* from St. Louis to Fort Union and return, 15 May–28 June. [St. Louis *Missouri Republican,* 15, 16 May, 29, 30 June 1858; St. Louis *Missouri Democrat,* 29 September 1858.]

76. Boller, Henry A.

Among the Indians: Eight Years in the Far West, 1858–1866. [Edited by Milo M. Quaife, Chicago, Lakeside Press, 1959; original edition, Philadelphia, T. E. Zell, 1868.]

Boller left St. Louis on the steamboat *Twilight* 23 May 1858 for his post at Fort Atkinson at the Gros Ventres village (pp. 12–47).

77. Boller, Henry A.

Henry A. Boller, Missouri River Fur Trader: Letters and Jour-

nal. [Edited by Ray H. Mattison, Bismarck, State Historical Society of North Dakota, 1966.]

Letters by Boller to his family, reporting his voyage up the Missouri in the *Twilight* (no. 76), which left St. Louis 23 May 1858 (pp. 15–47).

78. Anon.

"Account of the Voyage of the steamboat *Twilight* up the Missouri." [St. Louis *Missouri Democrat,* 11 July 1858.]

79. Wimar, Charles

Account of his trip up the Missouri in the steamboat *Twilight,* originally published in the *Journal* of the Academy of Düsseldorf for 1858 (Perry Rathbone, *Charles Wimar, 1828–1862* [City Art Museum of St. Louis, 1946], pp. 18–24).

Wimar's value as a travel reporter lies primarily in the sketchbooks he filled on his Missouri River trips in 1858 and 1859, now in the City Art Museum of St. Louis and the Missouri Historical Society.

1859

80. Chouteau, Charles P.

"Early Navigation of the Upper Missouri River—Report of Charles P. Chouteau, to the Secretary of War [John B. Floyd] of a Steamboat Expedition from St. Louis to Fort Benton, 1859 [dated St. Louis, 1 November 1859]." [*Montana Historical Society Contributions,* VII (1910), 253–256.]

The American Fur Company steamboat *Spreadeagle* left St. Louis 28 May and arrived at Fort Union 1 July. Transferring to the accompanying smaller steamer *Chippewa,* Chouteau and others continued toward Fort Benton. At old Fort McKenzie, twelve miles below Fort Benton, fuel gave out on 17 July. The party was again at Fort Union 20 July.

81. Anon.

"Gatherings by the Way-side, or, a Trip to Fort Benton by Steam." [St. Louis *Missouri Republican,* 22 August 1859.]

Voyage of the *Spreadeagle* (no. 80).

82. C[rapster], M. H.

"From Fort Union and Yellowstone—Interesting Particulars of a Mountain Trip—Memoranda of Steamer Chippewa." [St. Louis *Missouri Republican,* 26 July 1859.]

83. Anon.

"Trip of the Chippewa from Fort Union to Fort Benton—Steam

Navigation on the Upper Missouri." [St. Louis *Missouri Republican,* 23 August 1859.]

84. A ——, R. B.

"Interesting Letter from the Upper Missouri–Steamer Carrier, July 23, 1859." [St. Louis *Missouri Republican,* 26 July 1859.]

85. Marsh, Elias J.

"Journal of Dr. Elias J. Marsh. Account of a Steamboat Trip on the Missouri River, May–August, 1859." [*South Dakota Historical Review,* I (January, 1936), 79–127.]

Voyage of the *Spreadeagle* (no. 80). On the return voyage the *Chippewa* overtook the *Spreadeagle* 2 August below old Fort Lookout; the passengers changed to the faster steamer and arrived at St. Louis 16 August.

86. Wimar, Charles

See no. 79. This year Wimar traveled on the *Spreadeagle.*

87. Maynadier, Henry E.

"The Journal of H. E. Maynadier. A Boat Trip from Fort Union to Omaha." [Edited by Elmer Ellis, *North Dakota Historical Review,* I (January, 1927), 41–51. Extracted from W. F. Raynolds, *Exploration of the Yellowstone* (Washington, 1868), pp. 147–152.]

The lieutenant's mackinaw left Fort Union 1 August and arrived at Omaha 3 October.

88. Raynolds, Captain W. F.

"Journal of the 1859–1860 Yellowstone Expedition." [40th Congress, 2nd Session, *Senate Executive Document* 77, Serial 1317, pp. 18–22.]

Raynolds had left St. Louis on the *Spreadeagle* 28 May 1859, arriving at Fort Pierre 18 June. His original MS is in the Western Americana Collection (Coe No. IV, 443), Yale University Library.

1860

89. Kautz, August V.

"From Missouri to Oregon in 1860. The Diary of August V. Kautz." [Edited by Martin F. Schmitt, *Pacific Northwest Quarterly,* XXXVII (July, 1946), 193–230.]

The diarist left St. Louis 3 May on the American Fur Company steamboat *Spreadeagle,* which was accompanied by the *Chippewa* and the *Key West.* On 7 June his company was transferred to the *Key West.* He arrived at Fort Benton 2 July.

90. Hays, William Jacob

Four letters to his family written on his way up the Missouri. [Robert Taft, "The Pictorial Record of the Old West: II, W. J. Hays," *Kansas Historical Quarterly*, XIV (May, 1946), 145–165, or his *Artists and Illustrators of the Old West, 1850–1900* (New York, Charles Scribner's Sons, 1953), pp. 36–52.]

The letters are dated 9 May, aboard the *Spreadeagle*; 11 May, aboard the *Spreadeagle*; 20 June, Fort Stewart, Upper Missouri; and 21 July, aboard the *Key West*. Taft also listed a number of sketches of Missouri River scenes made by Hays at this time.

91. Anon.

"Account of the Voyage of the *Spreadeagle* published on its return to St. Louis." [St. Louis Tri-Weekly *Missouri Republican*, 12 July 1860.]

92. Blake, [George]

Report of an Expedition Made by a Detachment of U.S. Recruits under the Command of Maj. [George] Blake, 1st Dragoons, from St. Louis, Mo. to Fort Benton, Nebraska Territory, via the Missouri River, during the Summer of 1860. [MS, National Archives.]

1861

93. Brown, John Mason

"A Trip to the Northwest in 1861. Part I." [Edited by John Mason Brown (grandson of traveler), *Filson Club Historical Quarterly*, XXIV (April, 1950), 103–136.]

Brown left St. Louis on the American Fur Company steamboat *Spreadeagle* (which was accompanied by the *Chippewa*) 1 May (p. 106); at Fort Union he and others transferred to the second boat, which blew up 23 June (p. 130) not far above Fort Union. Only Part I of Brown's diary is concerned with the Missouri River trip.

94. Anon.

"Accounts of the Voyage of the *Spreadeagle*." [St. Louis *Missouri Democrat*, 26 April 1861; St. Louis *Missouri Republican*, 2 May 1861.]

95. Cary, William de la Montagne

A number of sketches made by this artist on the 1861 voyage of the *Spreadeagle*, as well as a number of paintings after them, are in the collections of the Thomas Gilcrease Institute of American History and Art at Tulsa, Oklahoma.

FIGURE 1. *The steamboat* Yellowstone *at St. Louis, 1832. Oil by George Catlin. U.S. National Museum, Smithsonian Institution.*

FIGURE 2. *Mouth of the Missouri River about 1840. Lithograph by John Caspar Wild. Published February, 1842, in Lewis F. Thomas, ed.,* The Valley of the Mississippi Illustrated.

FIGURE 3. *The steamboat* Western Engineer *at Engineer Cantonment, February, 1820. Pen-and-ink sketch by Titian Ramsay Peale. Courtesy of the American Philosophical Society.*

FIGURE 4. *Mouth of the Platte River, 1832. Oil by George Catlin. U.S. National Museum, Smithsonian Institution.*

FIGURE 5. *Fort Pierre, with six hundred lodges of Sioux Indians encamped about it, 1832. Oil by George Catlin. U.S. National Museum, Smithsonian Institution.*

FIGURE 6. *Mandan Indian village, 1832. Oil by George Catlin. U.S. National Museum, Smithsonian Institution.*

FIGURE 7. *Indian women bathing, [1832]. Pencil sketch by George Catlin. Courtesy of the New York Historical Society, New York City.*

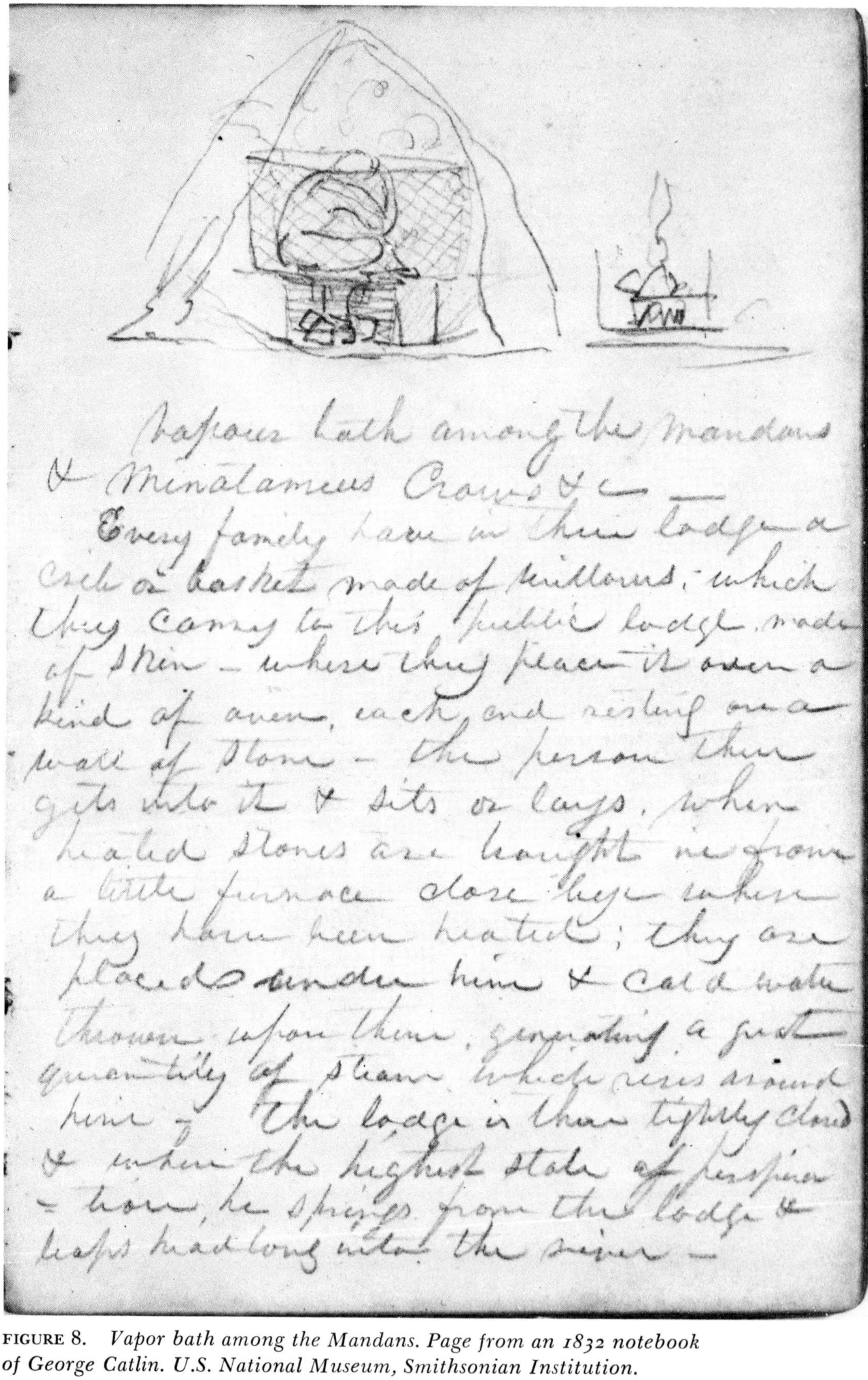

FIGURE 8. *Vapor bath among the Mandans. Page from an 1832 notebook of George Catlin. U.S. National Museum, Smithsonian Institution.*

FIGURE 9. *Lightening the steamboat* Yellowstone, *grounded on a sandbar near Fishing Creek, below Liberty, Missouri, April 19, 1833. Aquatint after a water color by Karl Bodmer. Courtesy of the City Art Museum of St. Louis. [Tableau 4, Maximilian,* Atlas, *1843; Plate 37, Thwaites edition.]*

FIGURE 10. *Buffalo herds on the Upper Missouri, 1833. Water color by Karl Bodmer. Northern Natural Gas Company Collection, Joslyn Art Museum, Omaha, Nebraska.* [*Tableau 40, Maximilian,* Atlas, *1843; Plate 73, Thwaites edition.*]

FIGURE 11. *Bear hunters on the Missouri, July 18, 1833. Pencil sketch by Karl Bodmer. The George A. Lucas Collection on loan from the Maryland Institute, The Baltimore Museum of Art, Baltimore, Maryland.* [*Tableau 36, Maximilian,* Atlas, *1843; Plate 69, Thwaites edition.*]

FIGURE 12. *Fort McKenzie, 1833. Water color by Karl Bodmer. Northern Natural Gas Company Collection, Joslyn Art Museum, Omaha, Nebraska.*

FIGURE 13. *Buffalo dance (Crow Indians), 1833. Pencil sketch by Karl Bodmer. The George A. Lucas Collection on loan from the Maryland Institute, The Baltimore Museum of Art, Baltimore, Maryland.*

FIGURE 14. *Fort Clark in winter, February, 1834. Aquatint after a water color by Karl Bodmer. [Tableau 15, Maximilian,* Atlas, *1843; Plate 49, Thwaites edition.]*

FIGURE 15. *Dance of Mandan women. Pencil sketch by Karl Bodmer. Courtesy of the Ayer Collection of The Newberry Library, Chicago, Illinois.* [*Vignette 28, Maximilian,* Atlas, *1843; Plate 28, Thwaites edition.*]

FIGURE 16. *Bivouac on the Missouri—Maximilian and Bodmer descending the Missouri, 1834. Water color by Karl Bodmer. Northern Natural Gas Company Collection, Joslyn Art Museum, Omaha, Nebraska. [Vignette 23, Maximilian,* Atlas, *1843; Plate 23, Thwaites edition.]*

FIGURE 17. *Fort Louis on the Missouri River above the Yellowstone, 1847. Water color by Nicolas Point, S.J. Courtesy of the Collège de Sainte-Marie, Montreal, Canada.*

FIGURE 18. *Interior of a trading store [Fort Union?], 1847. Water color by Nicolas Point, S.J. Courtesy of the Collège de Sainte-Marie, Montreal, Canada.*

FIGURE 19. *The steamboat* Iowa *passing Fort Berthold*[?], *1849. Woodcut after an original sketch by E. de Girardin in* Le Tour du Monde, *1864.*

FIGURE 20. *Blackbird's grave on the Missouri, June 20, 1851. Pen-and-ink sketch by Rudolph Friederich Kurz. From a photo in the Bureau of American Ethnology, Smithsonian Institution.*

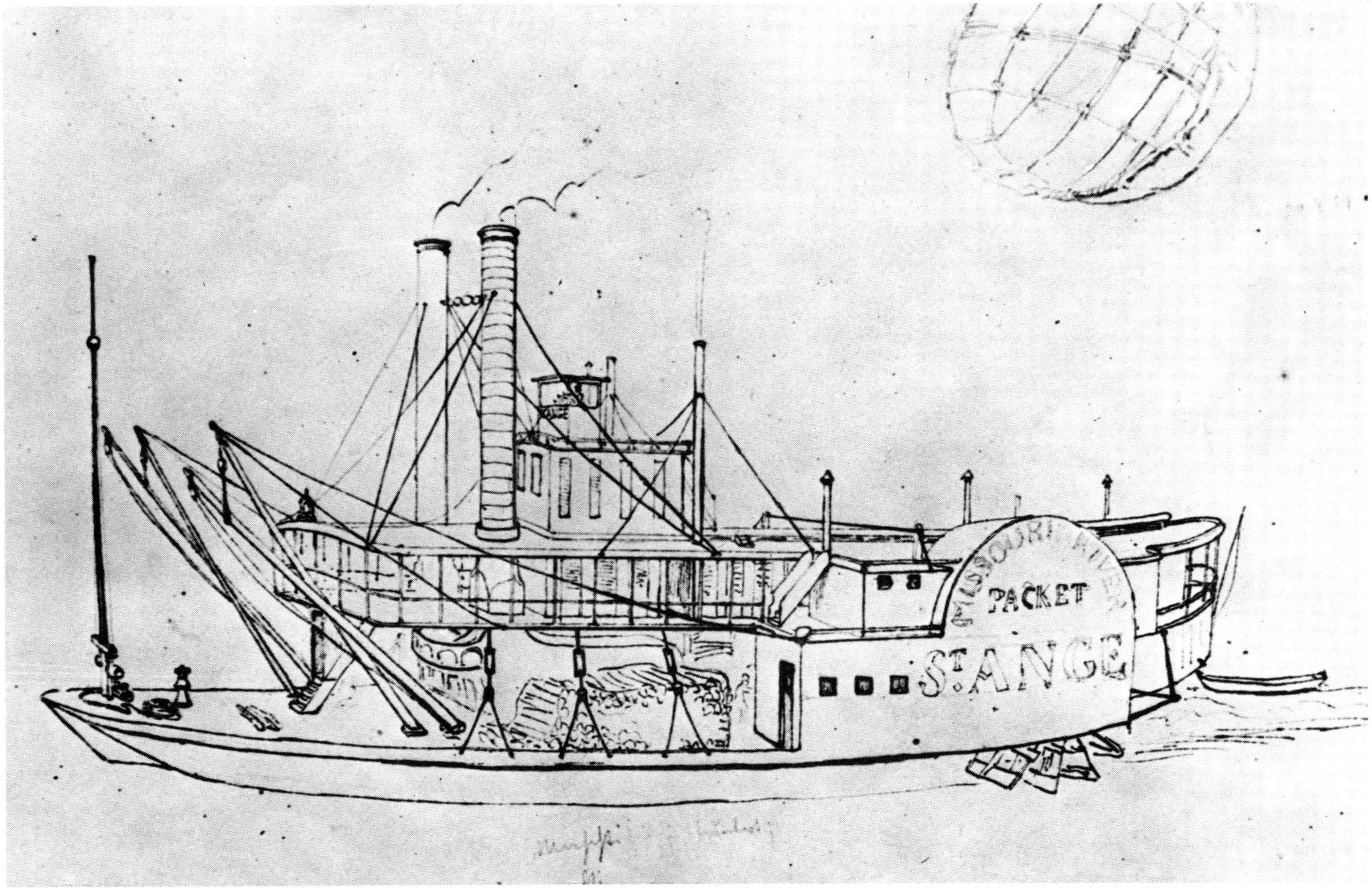

FIGURE 21. *The steamboat* St. Ange, *July 2, 1851. Pen-and-ink sketch by Rudolph Friederich Kurz. From a photo in the Bureau of American Ethnology, Smithsonian Institution.*

FIGURE 22. *Fort Pierre, July 4, 1851. Pen-and-ink sketch by Rudolph Friederich Kurz. From a photo in the Bureau of American Ethnology, Smithsonian Institution.*

FIGURE 23. *Interior of Fort Union, February 4, 1852. Pen-and-ink sketch by Rudolph Friederich Kurz. The Gilcrease Institute of American History and Art, Tulsa, Oklahoma.*

FIGURE 24. *Indian earth lodge, [1859?]. Pencil sketch by Charles Wimar. Missouri Historical Society, St. Louis.*

FIGURE 25. *Scenes near the mouth of Milk River, July 6, 1859. Pencil sketches by Charles Wimar. Missouri Historical Society, St. Louis.*

FIGURE 26. *The white castles on the Missouri, July 16, 1859. Pencil sketch by Charles Wimar. Missouri Historical Society, St. Louis.*

FIGURE 27. *The wreck of the* Kate Howard, *below the mouth of the Osage River, [sketched] August 15, 1859. Pencil sketch by Charles Wimar. Missouri Historical Society, St. Louis. [Wreck had occurred August 11.]*

FIGURE 28. *The steamboat* Chippewa, *1861. After a sketch by William de la Montagne Cary,* Recreation, *II (June, 1895), 395.*

Manuscript Resources in the Yale University Library for the Study of Western Travel

Archibald Hanna, Jr.

ONE OF THE MAJOR PROBLEMS which faces every librarian and curator is that of making known to the largest possible number of potential users the resources of his collection. As far as printed materials are concerned, the problem is more or less manageable. Subject bibliographies usually indicate holdings of at least the rarer books and pamphlets. The National Union Catalogue, for all its deficiencies, is, more often than not, able to show at least one location. A substantial number of card catalogues of outstanding subject collections in various fields have been published in book form.

For collections of manuscripts the problem is more difficult, both in scope and nature. With certain obvious exceptions, every manuscript is unique. This adds enormously to the labor of would-be bibliographers, since there is one and only one location for each diary or letter. There are comparatively few books which are owned only by individuals and not by any library, but I would not even venture to guess what percentage of manuscripts potentially useful to scholars are still in private hands, unlocated and unusable.

Even when manuscripts have been collected in libraries, there remain many and difficult problems before they can be made available to scholars. It is true that the authors of books often seem to ignore the neat little categories which libraries have designed to classify them, and the published work may refuse to fit tidily into an existing pigeonhole. But published materials in the field to which this conference is devoted—the literature of western travel—do not generally offer serious problems to either the cataloguer or the reader. A glance at the title page and the table of contents will usually give a fairly accurate idea of the scope and nature of the work.

With manuscripts the situation is not so simple. The papers of a single individual will deal with a great many different subjects over a long space of time. A collection of family papers will, of course, be even more varied. Yet the shortage of competent manuscript cataloguers is such that practically every research library has a large backlog of uncatalogued material. In time, at least some of the manuscripts get arranged, at least some entries appear in the catalogue, and with good fortune, some kind of calendar or list is made. Even then, most manuscript cataloguers are oriented toward persons rather than subjects, so that the subject index will tend to be skimpy. The scholar will then have to depend on the memory of the curator or the librarian rather than a catalogue in order to find the materials he wants. This can be a marvelously useful tool, but eventually librarians retire or move on to other positions.

This has been a long and perhaps digressive preamble. However, I think that it is a necessary one, for two reasons. The major one is that with the present rate of growth of graduate schools and the consequent increase in the demand for research materials, the situation of the research library is rapidly becoming critical. But if scholars will join forces with librarians in the attempt to bring about a more adequate level of staffing in their libraries, we may yet see the dawn of the millennium. On that happy day there will be no backlog of uncatalogued material, and manuscripts will be so well catalogued that the scholar will be able to spend his time utilizing his sources, rather than hunting for them.

The minor reason for the preamble is simply to explain why neither I nor anyone else can offer you an encyclopedic view of the resources of the Yale Collection of Western Americana. I can, however, erect a few signposts and point out certain major topographical features.

The gift to Yale, over a series of years beginning in 1943, of the William Robertson Coe Collection, represented more than simply a significant quantitative addition to the library's resources in books, maps, and manuscripts. Mr. Coe was, in many ways, the kind of donor whom libraries dream about. He continued for the remainder of his lifetime to add to his collection.

His initial endowment and subsequent bequest provided for a curator and for future acquisitions of material. He paid the entire cost of cataloguing the great collection he had so generously given. This made it possible for Yale to bring together in one place most of its rare source material relating to the trans-Mississippi West.

It also made possible the publication in 1952 by the Yale University Press of Mary C. Withington's *Catalogue of Manuscripts in the Collection of Western Americana Founded by William Robertson Coe,* a work which you will be glad to know is still in print. Its title is somewhat misleading, for the more than 9,000 items described under 542 headings include not only the manuscripts of the Coe Collection, but also those of the Winlock W. Miller Jr. Pacific Northwest Collection and manuscripts relating to the West to be found in Yale's Rare Book Room, Yale Memorabilia, and Historical Manuscript Collections.

The bulk of the materials described, however, are Mr. Coe's, and they reflect his collecting interests and tastes. These were wide-ranging and include the Canadian West and Alaska. There are, however, certain large gaps. Mr. Coe had little or no interest in the Spanish Southwest, or early California, though in later years he relented so far as to acquire a contemporary manuscript copy of the diary of the great Dominguez-Escalante expedition of 1776–77. He was not much concerned with the first tier of states west of the Mississippi. In general, he conceived his field as the Plains and the Rockies, the Pacific Northwest, and the Northwest Coast, from the earliest discovery until the end of the pioneer period. Although there are a few large collections of papers of individuals like Andrew J. Faulk, John W. Geary, Silas Reed, and James J. Strang, most of the entries are for individual diaries, journals, and small groups of letters. No less than 113 accounts of overland travel are included.

Miss Withington's entries are detailed and give excellent summaries of the materials. I regret to say, however, that the index leaves something to be desired. Personal names are fully indexed, but there are comparatively few entries under subjects. Scholars in search of material on a particular subject must therefore scan the whole text.

Two substantial groups of papers, both of interest to students of western history, were not included in Miss Withington's catalogue. The papers of Othniel C. Marsh, one of the fathers of American paleontology, include material on his many western expeditions in the period after the Civil War. They are, however, housed in the Peabody Museum of Natural History, rather than the University Library.

The manuscript portion of Henry R. Wagner's Texas Collection has now been transferred to the Western Americana Collection. The 900 or more manuscripts included span the years from 1690 to 1846. Though they deal mainly with the political and administrative problems of that remote province, they do include accounts of travel. Particularly noteworthy are a manuscript by Alonso de León which includes a diary of his expedition in 1690, and a group of Berlandier manuscripts, supplementary to those in the Library of Congress, relating to the travels of the Texas Boundary Commission of 1827.

In the sixteen years since the publication of Miss Withington's catalogue, the number of manuscripts in the Western Americana Collection has at least doubled. I wish I could tell you that a second and similarly inclusive volume was scheduled for publication in the near future. Unfortunately there is no such bright prospect.

We were, however, able to publish in 1965 a catalogue of the manuscript portion of the Frederick W. and Carrie S. Beinecke Collection, compiled by Jeanne M. Goddard and Charles Kritzler. This also is available from the Yale University Press. It is our hope to publish subsequent catalogues of the printed materials in this collection, especially those which have not been adequately described in existing bibliographies.

Mr. Beinecke's career as a serious collector began just as Mr. Coe's was drawing to a close. Although he came to collecting late in life, he had the imagination, tenacity, and resources necessary for success in this highly competitive field. Within a dozen years he brought together one of the major collections in the field of Western Americana.

Like Mr. Coe, Mr. Beinecke has been interested in the whole panorama of the trans-Mississippi West. As a member of a family of Yale men with a strong tradition of service to their alma mater, the major purpose of his collecting was to add to the strength of the research collections at Yale. Consequently, although his acquisitions have ranged far and wide over the whole sweep of western history, the major emphasis has been on those areas where Yale's collections were weakest. The Beinecke Collection thus possesses its greatest areas of strength in the Spanish Southwest down through the Mexican War and California history through the Gold Rush period.

The catalogue of the Beinecke manuscripts describes some 4,000 items listed under 285 individual entries. Like those in the Withington catalogue, these are mainly journals, diaries, and small groups of letters. The two collections complement each other not only geographically but also in other ways. For example, William Clark's day-by-day maps of the Lewis and Clark expedition are in the Coe Collection; his rough field notes are in the Beinecke Collection. John W. Geary's Mexican War correspondence is in the Beinecke Collection; his papers as Governor of Kansas are in the Coe Collection. There are not as many overland journals—only about a dozen as compared to more than a hundred in the Coe Collection—but there are twenty-two journals of voyages to the Pacific Coast by way of Cape Horn, Panama, or Nicaragua as compared to only nine in the Coe Collection. It may be worth mentioning that no less than sixteen named overland or shipborne mining associations can be identified in these journals.

Like the Coe Collection, the Beinecke Collection contains some material relating to Spanish exploration of the Northwest Coast. It adds to these a number of letters and reports from such early missionaries in the Southwest as Balthasar, Eymer, LaSuén, Osorio, and Ximénez.

A substantial portion of the Beinecke manuscripts relate to the Mexican War. While these are not, strictly speaking, travel accounts, they often contain accounts of travel through Texas and the Southwest, as well as in Mexico.

Also of interest to the subject of western travel is one of the few large groups of papers in the Beinecke Collection, consisting of some 7,500 pages relative to the U.S. Geographical Surveys west of the 100th meridian, usually known as the Wheeler Survey. Through a series of events too complicated to go into here, the records of this survey have been dispersed among several depositories throughout the country.

The group in the Beinecke Collection includes letterpress copies of outgoing letters, registers of incoming correspondence, topographical and meteorological notebooks, and photographs.

One more group of papers which should perhaps be mentioned is the Malaspina Papers. These are, in a sense, peripheral to the main theme of this conference. The Malaspina expedition of 1789 did explore portions of the Northwest Coast, but no reports of this are included. Their importance lies, rather, in the fact that they deal almost entirely with the problems of organizing, staffing, and equipping the expedition.

Yale is fortunate in that of the six individual collections which together form the Yale Collection of Western Americana, five have endowments of varying sizes. This means that at least a modest income is available each year for acquisitions. This income, however, must be used for such materials as books, maps, newspapers, and pictures, as well as manuscripts. For those of you familiar with the present state of the market in Western Americana, I need not point out that we have never yet seen a year when we were able to acquire more than a fraction of the desirable materials offered.

Obviously, our collections have not continued to grow at the same rate as when they were being formed by private collectors. But if the growth has slowed, it has not ceased. In the twenty years since Mr. Coe's gift, we have catalogued a number of manuscripts roughly equal to the combined total of those in the published Withington and Goddard catalogues. I regret to say that there are at least an equal number which have not yet been catalogued at all.

Since the two published catalogues already mentioned cover about one third of our manuscript collections, and our card catalogue only another third, it is plain that I can offer you no comprehensive guide to our holdings. I do not think that it would be particularly useful or inspiring if I were to devote the rest of this paper to a list of uncatalogued manuscripts in the Yale Library. Under the circumstances, I believe the most useful approach will be an outline of our acquisition policy, with some illustrative examples.

Let me state at the beginning that no such policy, no matter how logically conceived and elaborated, should ever be an iron-clad rule. There will always be occasions when exceptions can and should be made. The principal use of the policy is to insure that the time and money spent on acquisitions all contribute toward the building of a collection which will best serve the purposes of the sponsoring institution and be realistic in terms of available materials and means to acquire them.

Yale, like other universities, is engaged in running a Ph.D. factory, and the primary aim of the Yale Collection of Western Americana must be to provide the raw material for doctoral dissertations. This does not imply any exclusiveness; the same material can be and is used by graduate students of other institutions as well as by more mature scholars. But it does mean that the primary criterion in acquisition is simply the research value of the item under consideration. A single vivid letter of an unknown Iowa farmer is more to be desired that George A. Custer's commission as General of Volunteer Cavalry.

Even the largest institution must limit the scope of its collecting activities. While we realize at Yale that the history of the American West did not end with the hypothetical disappearance of the frontier in 1893, we have found that even that arbitrary date presents too long a time span for us. Instead, we have perhaps been even more arbitrary in saying that we will concentrate on the period of discovery, exploration, and first settlement of the West. If carried to its logical conclusion, this would mean selecting a different cut-off date for each state or even each region within a state.

Instead we simply use it as a rough rule of thumb, so that in scanning dealers' catalogues, for instance, we would pay much more attention to a group of letters from Dakota in the 1880's than a similar group from California. Essentially we believe that this represents a period of time large enough to be historically significant but limited enough so that over the course of years we will be able to bring together an adequate body of material for its study.

Geographically, we allow ourselves a rather wider scope, since we include not only all of the United States west of the Mississippi, but also the Canadian Northwest and Alaska. However, I must admit that we have not been very aggressive in our purchase of manuscript material relating to Canada. What strength we have in that area has come to us in the form of gifts, such as a group of daybooks from Fort Pelly.

Within this wide geographical area we have tried to concentrate on those events and experiences of a broad regional and national significance rather than collect materials for local history. This is more a matter of emphasis than of hard and fast rule. For example, we would try to acquire manuscripts relating to the Vigilantes of Montana or California not as material for the history of Virginia City or San Francisco, but rather as two local manifestations of a widespread western phenomenon. This may seem to be a distinction without a difference, but it does explain why you will find some materials in the collection while superficially similar materials are lacking.

With this in mind, it will be immediately understood why we stretched our financial resources to the limit to acquire the papers of William H. Emory of the Corps of Topographical Engineers and used every device of diplomacy to add the papers of James D. Graham, of the same illustrious corps. In the same category came the papers of Richard H. Pratt, founder of the Carlisle Indian School and a key figure in the whole Indian question during the last decades of the nineteenth century.

On the other hand, we would probably not even try to acquire the papers of a general, senator, or any other major political figure of any of the western states. We would feel fairly strongly that these more properly belong in a state university or a state historical society. We have a few such collections; for example, the papers of Governor Geary of Kansas, and of W. W. Miller, an important figure in early Washington Territory politics. These came to us as gifts, either as part of a larger collection or because of family associations with Yale. In general, we feel that most materials for state and local history belong in state and local repositories. As long as they are performing their functions with zeal and competence, as most of them now are, it is neither desirable nor possible for us to compete with them. There will be occasional heart-burnings about particular items, of course, but we hope no major battles.

The foregoing considerations also affect the form of the material that we acquire. We have comparatively few collections of an archival nature. It is true that we bought the whole of the papers of one Comstock silver-mining company. We are satisfied with that one as an example and a practice field, so to speak, for our economic historians, and desire no more. We would probably like, if it were of manageable size, a similar archive for one small western railway or stage company or freighter.

A few examples of recent acquisitions will point up the results of this policy. The T. J. Van Dorn Papers add to our Gold Rush material. The diary of his overland journey from Illinois to California in 1849 is not one of the most detailed in our collection, but it is admirably supplemented by some thirty-one letters to his wife, of which eight were written on the trail and most of the remainder from various mining camps in California.

A quite different view of California is given in the journal of Mary E. Clark. Accompanied by a brother, she went out to California via Panama in 1859. The journal extends from May, 1859, to September, 1860, and presents not only the feminine reaction to the journey but also an account of Sacramento society and customs.

Of special interest to ethnologists and ethno-historians would be the collection of sketches made by Sorrel Horse, a Sioux Indian, about 1877. The pictures, done with colored pencils on the pages of an account book, depict various incidents and phases of Indian life.

A group of fourteen letters by Lieutenant La Rhett L. Livingston give an account of Colonel Steptoe's expedition in 1854–55. Written from Fort Leavenworth, Salt Lake City, and points in between, they include information not only on Army life of the period but also on the Grattan massacre and affairs in Utah Territory.

Finally, a rather unusual series of diaries describe three successive journeys from Massachusetts to Colorado. Arthur W. Hoyt had mining interests in that state, and this is reflected in the daily entries. The journal of his first trip, if it ever existed, has disappeared, but we have acquired those for the second trip, June 13 to July 27, 1867; the third, between December 16, 1878, and February 16, 1879; and the fourth, which extended from November 9 to December 25, 1882.

In general, what we have been buying for the past twenty years, and what we will continue to acquire, are diaries, journals, and letters, either singly or in groups, whose contents can shed light on the great westward movement. What was the life of the common soldier in the Mexican War? In the Indian-fighting Army on the Plains? How did they view the conflict? What was the motivation and experience of the Boston shoemaker who joined the Salem Mechanics Mining and Trading Company and set sail for California in 1849? How did a wife and mother view missionary life in Oregon in 1840? Or a farmer in Kansas in 1860? What impression did the western scene make on the traveler from Ohio, or his more sophisticated fellow traveler from England?

It appears to us that in seeking such material we are achieving our aim of building a great research collection in the East without interference with the activities of western institutions. I must admit that the result of our policy makes certain difficulties for our scholars. We cannot turn over to them in a few tidy and concentrated bundles all the material they will need for their next epoch-making monograph. But given time and money enough, our cataloguing will reach a degree of perfection that will achieve the same end for them. In the meantime, we welcome them to our collections, and try to make up for any deficiencies in indexing by the fervor of our cooperation.

The Westward Traveler: Unexploited Manuscript Resources of the Newberry Library

Dwight L. Smith

WALTER LOOMIS NEWBERRY, a transplanted New Englander and pioneer Chicago merchant who died in 1868, left his considerable fortune in the form of a bequest for the founding of a private library. When the Newberry Library was established in 1887, it was decided that it would be reference in character. Its area of collection would be the whole field of knowledge. With the opening of the John Crerar Library in 1894 in the same city, however, in an effort to avoid needless duplication, it was agreed that Crerar would be limited to the natural sciences and technology and that Newberry would be concerned with the general field of the humanities. On the basis of special interests, specific strengths, and gifts of sometimes quite consequential specialized collections, Newberry has long since become renowned for holdings in specific areas.

In 1911 Newberry acquired one of its most noteworthy and valuable collections in the private library of Edward E. Ayer. The some 40,000 volumes, manuscripts, prints, maps, and other items were concerned primarily with native man in the New World. Today every period of American history is represented. The extensive collection of travel accounts into the interior of North America is superb. For certain topics the holdings are so extensive as to include practically everything that is available.[1]

Already rich by virtue of the Ayer and other collections, the New-

[1] *Handbook of the Newberry Library* (Chicago: The Newberry Library, 1938), *passim*.

berry Library leaped to the very front rank of depositories concerned with western history when in recent years the Everett D. Graff Collection was added. It consists of some 10,000 books, pamphlets, maps, broadsides, and manuscripts, primarily source materials, dealing in the main with the nineteenth-century exploration and settlement of the trans-Mississippi West.[2] No serious student of the American frontier can afford to overlook Newberry as a research library of major importance.

Although Newberry is not above all else a manuscripts repository, its manuscript holdings are extensive and its acquisitions are discriminating. Scholars are familiar with the checklist of the manuscripts in the Ayer Collection that was compiled by Mrs. Ruth L. Butler, the former long-time curator.[3] Parenthetically it should be mentioned that the office copy of this valuable checklist is so heavily annotated with subsequent additions to the holdings as to justify a new edition.

Within the prescribed framework of this session, manuscript resources of travel literature in the Mississippi Valley and the West before 1875, Newberry's holdings are consequential and exciting.

Rather than deal with statistics of numbers of manuscripts, size of shelf space, and the like, it is instructive to consider some specific manuscripts to determine the type and importance of Newberry's holdings to research in the particular area of present concern. To keep within manageable bounds, but certainly not to discredit or disparage their value to research, autograph copies, typescripts, or photocopies of manuscripts in other repositories are excluded from consideration. Also, except for a few, those manuscripts which have been published will not be considered, on the assumption that they are thus available elsewhere.

This is not to say, of course, that anything less than the original document or perhaps a photocopy or facsimile reproduction will satisfy the researcher. Occasionally a poor or imperfect copy, some-

[2] Colton Storm, "The Everett D. Graff Collection in the Newberry Library," *The Newberry Library Bulletin*, V (December, 1960), 190–213; Colton Storm, comp., *A Catalogue of the Everett D. Graff Collection of Western Americana* (Chicago: University of Chicago Press, 1968). For a descriptive and analytical essay of the guidebooks of the Graff Collection, see Ray A. Billington, "Books That Won the West: The Guidebooks of the Forty-Niners & Fifty-Niners," *The American West*, IV (August, 1967), 25–32, 72–75.

[3] Ruth L. Butler, comp., *A Check List of Manuscripts in the Edward E. Ayer Collection* (Chicago: The Newberry Library, 1937).

times badly mistreated under exercise of horrifying editorial license, is all that exists. The ubiquitous county history of yesteryear is regarded as invaluable today because it frequently contains copies of diaries, journals, letters, and other manuscripts which have long since disappeared.

In the Graff Collection, for example, is the 1858–59 journal of John W. Jones.[4] He was one of a party that journeyed from Minnesota to the Pacific Northwest. Lured by the accounts of Sir George Simpson, a Hudson's Bay Company administrator and explorer, Father Pierre-Jean De Smet, Jesuit "Blackrobe" missionary to the western Indians, and others, the party decided to go by way of Canada rather than the usual trails to the south. There were no guidebooks and well-established routes to follow. The journey was almost a trail-blazer itself. Indeed, in several instances, the Indian guides they employed were not really sure of things themselves or were hostile to the expedition.

Most of the country over which Jones traveled was literally wilderness, punctuated infrequently by a post or fort or Indian encampment. The journal is a vivid account of the vast prairies of southern Manitoba, Saskatchewan, and Alberta, and the southern Canadian Rockies, as these areas looked to any explorer or pathfinder. The journey was terminated at The Dalles in the Oregon country.

The pages of this manuscript are studded with interesting details of Red River carts, life in Hudson's Bay posts, Plains Indians, flora and fauna, travel across the desolate prairies, the prowess of mosquitoes, half-bloods, topography, and much of nature in the raw. The last appears particularly in the description of the winter struggle for survival amidst the Canadian Rockies where even the ingenuity of the Indians was taxed in the sub-zero heavy snows and total isolation.

By his own account, Jones kept the original journal in pencil. It deteriorated to the point where he decided to rescue its contents by rewriting them. While he did make some changes, the present copy seems essentially to be the verbatim account that he kept while on the

[4] John W. Jones MS journal, "Across the Plains. My Trip from Faribault, Minn., to Oregon, via Saskatchewan route, British America," 1858–59, Everett D. Graff Collection in the Edward E. Ayer Collection, Newberry Library. Unless otherwise indicated, all manuscripts cited hereafter are in the Ayer Collection of the Newberry Library.

trip. That it is a copy and not the original is beside the point, for without this copy of the lost original we have nothing. Perhaps what we have is better than the original.

A word of caution may be appropriate. While it does not apply to the Jones journal, sometimes when the keeper of an account rewrites he also revises. The new version is, therefore, substantially different from the original. Travelers have been known to dress up, to make textual alterations, to omit, and to add in the revision so as to put the journalist in the best light, to make the conditions or circumstances of travel more exciting, or to write for a potential audience rather than to report and record the expedition itself.[5]

Although most travel accounts that have already been published are excluded from this study, some highly significant exceptions must be made. No more striking way of illustrating this point can be offered than this passage from a Newberry manuscript. Note carefully the subject matter and detail.

> [Entry for August 22.] *Left early and travelled about 12 Miles* when we stopped for wind. *Went hunting Elks. Mr. C Killing a Dear and he and Squires brought the meat on their backs. I saw nothing but heard* four *shots* coming, *which I thought were from Harris. I ran for upward of a Miles hallowing the whole distance but nothing of him. Sent 3 Men who hunted for him but brought no intelligence.* The firing was at an Elk which was injured. *Bell shot a female and brought a portion of the meat. Mr. C. Squire & I walked to the little Missouri, and* I *shot the 4th Bull* I have Killed *this trip.* We crossed The Stream by Wading and brought The "Nerf"[.] *Saw four Ducks. We started in the afternoon and landed below the little Missouri* and *returned to the Bull and took* off *its horns &c. On returning to the Boat, Sprague* informed me that he thought he *had seen a* Grisley *Bear. We went toward the spot. The fellow had taken its path below the high Bank, and* we all fired at it in so quick a manner that it *was Killed in a few seconds. Mr. C. shot it firstly through the neck, Bell* 2 Balls elsewhere *and I* 1 *in the belly.* Sprague abused me greatly, but

[5] After returning home from an 1811 journey, John Watson, Jr., began to revise and rewrite the journal he had kept. The revision was primarily in the form of interlarding substantial chunks from the travel guide he had used on the trip. The original and revised manuscripts are in the Ohio Historical Society, Columbus. The journal with a fuller explanation of Watson's revision has been published. See Dwight L. Smith and S. Winifred Smith, eds., "The Journey of a Pennsylvania Quaker to Pioneer Ohio," *Cincinnati Historical Society Bulletin*, XXVI (January, 1968), 2–40; (April, 1968), 174–210.

let it pass! We had set about a dozen steel traps to catch *Prairie Marmots* as there was a large Village of them but *caught none*. These animals are extremely cunning and in all probability did not go out of their burrows that way. *The Wind was High and cold. Provost skinned the Bear* which [proved poor?] and about 3 or 4 years old. weighed probably 400 lb. Bell *shot 2 Prairie Marmots. Their notes resemble precisely those of the Arkansas Flycatcher. Left this afternoon and travelled about 10 Miles. Saw another Bear* on the Bank which was bent on swimming to a dead Bull fastened on a Log, he saw us, reared on his hind feat, gave a grunt & leaped on the upper bank and disappeared in a moment. *Several Wolves were also [disposed?] to go to the drowned Buffalo* but we frightened them all off. *We saw Wild Pigeons* and *encamped in a bad place with appearance of rain.*

Grisley Bear Male.—
Measurements of Do.

Nose to root of Tail	66 Inches
Tail vertebrae	3 "
Hair beyond	2 "
Nose to canthus	7½ "
Nose to root of ear.	16.
" " point of Do.	21½.
Width of Do.	3½
length of eye	1.
" " Mouth	5.
from top of shoulder to bottom of forefoot.	41.
length of palm of forefoot.	8.
Breadth of Do.	6.
length of palm of hind foot	9½.
Breadth Do. Do.	5½.
rump to bottom of hind foot	55.
around body behind Shoulders.	49.
between ears at root.	7½
between eyes at front canthus	4.
upper lip to top of nose	2¾
breadth of nose	2¼.
from fore to hind claws when extended	91.
around the head	28½.
Do. do. neck	30.

When Buffalo Bulls are in large herds their bel[l]owing may be heard probably for Miles. They below with the head enclining downward, pawing and tearing up the Earth all the While.—

[Entry for August 23.] Provost and Bell finished skinning the

Bear and its fine skin was put in a Barrell with strong pickle made of salt and water, an excellent method to preserve all the skins of larger animals. The wind continued high and cold[.] We left and only travelled about 10 Miles[.]

These two entries (italics added) are taken from the journal of a traveler who was on a fact-finding mission. The collection of data was for a projected multivolume study that was published some years later. The journals themselves were edited and published about forty years after that by the journalist's granddaughter.

A comparison of Newberry's manuscript journal with the published form is revealing. The italicized portions of the above quotation indicate, usually verbatim, all of the manuscript that was published in the entries for those two days. In other words, much of the manuscript for August 22 and all of it for August 23 did not appear in the printed journals.

This may be another example of the standards and practices of a former time when editorial license to edit out or alter without explanation was acceptable and common. Or, conceivably, since the manuscript here used is titled "Copy of my Journal," perhaps the journalist himself is responsible. He may also have made still another copy in an abridged form. The editor may have used this abridged form for her publication assuming that it was the original or at least a true copy of the original. Whatever happened and why, the discrepancy is considerable and significant.

At any rate from this and other travels came John James Audubon's three volumes on North American viviparous quadrupeds.[6]

Among the best-known western travelers were Meriwether Lewis and William Clark. Their expedition has long held the interest of

[6] John James Audubon and John Bachman, *The Viviparous Quadrupeds of North America* (3 vols., New York: V. G. Audubon, 1852–54). The particular journey here involved was taken from March 11 to November 6, 1843. The August 16–November 6 portion was lost until August, 1896, when two granddaughters found it "in the back of an old secretary." Until then, "no record of this part of the trip was known to exist, and none of the family now living had ever seen it" (Maria R. Audubon, *Audubon and His Journals* [2 vols., New York: Charles Scribner's Sons, 1900], I, 449). The discrepancies noted above are between this published version (II, 155–156) and the Newberry manuscript. John J. Audubon MS journal, "Copy of my Journal from Fort Union," August 16–November 6, 1843.

the American people as well as of historians. In 1904–05 Reuben Gold Thwaites published eight volumes of the original journals of the expedition.[7] He included the journal of Private Joseph Whitehouse, with entries from May 14, 1804, to November 6, 1805.[8] In the Newberry Library is the original manuscript which Thwaites used as the basis for his publication. It is in three notebooks. The third one is incomplete with pages torn from the end.[9]

Subsequently a foul autograph copy of the Whitehouse journal has been added to the Newberry collections. It contains a five-page Preface with a December 10, 1806, St. Louis dateline, a roster of personnel, and an entry for November 17, 1803. All of these occur before the initial entry of the Thwaites publication and the manuscript upon which it was based. But that is not all! After the final entry in Thwaites and its parent manuscript, the foul copy goes on with entries terminating on April 2, 1806, five months later. This takes the expedition to the mouth of the Columbia River.[10] Anything that sheds more light on the Lewis and Clark expedition, to say nothing of possible textual variations from previously known and published materials, is obviously important. What an exciting project for such a Lewis and Clark scholar as Donald Jackson.[11]

An earlier-day intrepid and remarkable traveler was Junípero Serra. When rumors reached Spain that the Russians were planning to push southward from their Alaskan trading posts, a Spanish expedition was sent northward to garrison San Diego and Monterey and to establish missions for converting and civilizing the natives. Fiery Franciscan Serra was the missionary on this expedition which ushered California into history.[12] Serra's diary with entries from March 28 to June 30, 1769, and some collateral materials, are in the Newberry Library.[13]

7 Reuben Gold Thwaites, ed., *Original Journals of the Lewis and Clark Expedition, 1804–1806* (8 vols., New York: Dodd, Mead and Co., 1904–05).

8 *Ibid.*, VII, 29–190.

9 Joseph Whitehouse MS journal, May 14, 1804–November 6, 1805.

10 Joseph Whitehouse MS journal (foul copy), November 17, 1803–April 2, 1806.

11 Donald Jackson, ed., *Letters of the Lewis and Clark Expedition with Related Documents, 1783–1854* (Urbana: University of Illinois Press, 1962).

12 John F. Bannon, ed., *Bolton and the Spanish Borderlands* (Norman: University of Oklahoma Press, 1964), pp. 270–274.

13 Junípero Serra MS diary, "Diario . . . Loreto to San Diego," March 28–June 30, 1769.

Although the diary has been published, most recently in 1936, for reasons suggested with previously discussed manuscripts it may be worthwhile to check out this important Serra diary.[14]

One of the interesting overland accounts at Newberry is that of Alden F. Brooks, a Winnetka, Illinois, portrait-painter.[15] Teaching in a country school in southwestern Wisconsin in the winter of 1858, Brooks contracted the "consumption" from overexposure in a snowstorm. Hearing that outdoor living was good for this ailment and that a neighbor was going to California in a prairie schooner, he contracted for board for $50 and proposed to walk along across the continent.

Brooks packed a large valise and "a small light rifle" and left in 1859 with the neighbor and several others for California. The initial entry in this account of a "Grand trip across the plains—" records the May 19, 1859, crossing of the muddy Missouri. Walking and sketching and portrait-painting his way westward, Brooks had his share of adventures.

Near a Pawnee Indian village, he stopped to buy some moccasins. "One large 6 ft. indian took my knife off of my belt to look at it & would not give it up I pounced him & took it by main strength & being barefooted had to make use of my legs as they all (some 15 or more) took after me but I out ran them & lucky for me for what they would have done I dont know."[16] In another way he was impressed by the Sioux, "the cleanest & hansomest looking tribe I have seen yet, almost fell in love with a beautiful squaw of 16 summers or at least I admired her symetry 'Witch of the Rockeys'."[17]

Appropriately, the party reached Independence Rock on July 4. There was a funeral shortly before their arrival, and a wedding after their departure. Brooks comments that although the Rock was "a grand foundation to get united on I had rather get married in the Devils Gate—which is in sight—for there the water makes such a noise one could not hear the 'ceremony' then if I did not like her [I] could excuse myself on those grounds—"[18]

14 Franciscan Missionaries of Mary, *Diary of Fra Junipero Serra . . . Documentary Preface to the History of the Missions of California* (North Providence, R.I.: The Franciscan Missionaries of Mary, 1936).

15 Alden F. Brooks MS diary, "Grand trip across the plains—," 1859.

16 Entry of May 22, 1859, *ibid.*

17 Entry of June 21, 1859, *ibid.*

18 Entry of July 4, 1859, *ibid.*

Relaxation as well as hard work and danger was a part of transcontinental travel. Camp was made one noon along the Platte. In the afternoon the tired herd of some fifty head of cattle was driven onto an island. After a good swim the party formed itself into a "Lyceum" for a debate. The topic of the evening was "Resolved that there is more pleasure or happiness in the pursuit than the possession." It was an affirmative victory. The question for the next evening was "Resolved that the love of money is greater than love for women." Unfortunately, Brooks does not say how this question was disposed of.[19]

Not all travelers who recorded their experiences and observations and comments did so in at-the-moment diaries, journals, or letters. As an example, in Newberry is the account of William Hillhouse, in the form of his reminiscences for 1840–44.[20]

Hillhouse journeyed on horseback from southern Ohio to Burlington, Iowa. There he found employment with an Indian trader and traveled among the Sauk and Fox. This gained him the confidence and friendship of these tribes and entrée to many of their customs and ceremonies. His fairly vivid accounts relate treaty negotiations, a hunting party which included future Vice-President John C. Breckinridge, experiences with pioneer settlers, annuity payments to the Indians, a drunken spree with the Indians, intervention which saved a white horse-thief from a burning at the stake by the Indians and made him run the gauntlet instead, frightening a renegade Mormon who wanted to become an Indian, and many other unusual things.

Although memoirs and reminiscences are often based on faulty memories and affected by the determinism of subsequent experiences, such accounts are still worthy documents for the use and consideration of the scholar. The Hillhouse manuscript would form the basis for an interesting study.

Round-trip accounts are harder to come by than one-way journals in travel narratives. Much of the travel literature concerns the westward movement where the final destination was the other end of the line. Among those returning home again, as in the case of some who participated in the gold rushes, were those who were ashamed of their failure to find the pot at the end of the rainbow. They wished to go

19 Entry of June 29, 1859, *ibid.*

20 William Hillhouse MS reminiscences, "Reminiscences of my Early Experiences in Iowa," 1840–44.

home with as little fanfare and publicity as possible. Perhaps those who returned to the East by the same route saw no use in repeating such travel details. Some made the return trip after a substantial time lapse and lacked the enthusiasm that motivated the record-keeping when they were heading westward. Also, since diaries and journals were sometimes kept to send back to home-based friends and relatives for vicarious informational purposes, the traveler may well have reasoned that he could relate the details and highlights of the return journey in person when he reached home.

In this vein, two of Newberry's round-trip accounts are appropriate. One is that of Josias Fendall Bell, who left Smithsboro, Pennsylvania, on April 19, 1841.[21] In simple prose, this twenty-six-year-old, somewhat deaf, club-footed journeyman shoemaker faithfully kept a diary of his journey. "Being of a sickly constitution having received some benifit during a tour to the western & Southern States," he writes, "I have made preparations for another & more lengthy Journey. my place of destination is across the Roucky [*sic*] Mountains to the mouth of the Columbia river."[22]

Having missed by three weeks the fur company party with which he planned to travel out of St. Louis, Bell obtained temporary employment in Peoria and Boonville. On July 20 he joined with James and Samuel Magoffin, who were freighting over the Santa Fe trail with a train of ten wagons and over a hundred mules. By plying his trade as a shoemaker and doing assorted jobs in the settlements en route, and by working with freighting companies and the like, he moved on farther westward. From Santa Fe to Chihuahua and on to the coast, with one two-week leg of the journey alone with a mule, Bell arrived in Guaymas in the early spring of 1842. By Spanish and American vessels to Mazatlán and up the California coast he eventually arrived in Monterey.

After working there for several months and having a variety of experiences, including the necessity to use his cane to defend himself—an incident which resulted in a court suit and his defense by Thomas Larkin—Bell signed on a New Bedford whaler as a cook and headed homeward via the Horn. His final entry, July 19, 1844, finds him in

21 Josias Fendall Bell MS diary, "Sketches Of a Journey From Smithsboro, Pa. to California and Return April 19, 1841–July 20, 1844 by Josias Fendall Bell."

22 Entry of April 19, 1841, *ibid.*

Albany, New York, soon to leave on the last leg by stage. Bell is not a Richard Henry Dana in literary ability, but his account is descriptive, readable, and sufficiently different in its approach, experience, and route of travel to make it useful and attractive.

Another round-trip illustration is that of John D. Young, who was one of a party of 1860 Pike's Peak hopefuls.[23] His journal is a straightforward account of a gold-seeker and his friends who failed to strike it rich. Spread on the pages is a detailed description of what it was like to be on a gold rush: the exigencies of travel across the Plains; Indians begging, attacking, trading; the Pony Express and how it worked; Denver buildings, newspapers, justice, gambling; a multitude of details about prospecting, claims, salting, placers, grubstaking; near-starvation; getting lost in the fastness of the Rockies; justice beyond the law; optimism *vs.* disappointment and reality; and the decision to return home.

Young was a failure since he did not return home laden with gold; but he was rich in experience. He returned to Illinois unashamed and happy for having had the adventure. Without apology and rationalization, he accepted the experience for what it was. The Young account is unusual and exciting.

Travel manuscripts at the Newberry Library, as at other institutions, are useful and important sources for any student of the westward movement. The few examples cited here are a sampling of those yet to be exploited. Many need competent editing and publication; some that are already published should be recast in the light of subsequent scholarship; others must be mined for the light they can throw on various aspects of the westward movement; and a few will modify or correct or add to already published versions. Finally, as Dale Morgan has pointed out in his discerning essay analysis of overland journals, manuscript travel accounts sorely need to become the object of some "energetic bibliographical studies as foundations upon which historians may build."[24]

[23] John David Young MS journal, "A trip to the gold regions of the Rocky Mountains in the summer of 1860."

[24] Dale L. Morgan, "The Significance and Value of the Overland Journal," in K. Ross Toole *et al.*, eds., *Probing the American West: Papers from the Santa Fe Conference* (Santa Fe: Museum of New Mexico Press, 1962), p. 33.

Western Travels and Travelers in the Bancroft Library

Dale L. Morgan

BEFORE WE LAUNCH upon our travels, we had better arrive at some understanding of that half-discovered country known as the Bancroft Library, the character of which has been markedly shaped by its unusual history. As a library primarily concerned with western North America, the Bancroft was the first of its kind in the world.

It is not just coincidental that such a library was brought together through the zeal of an energetic individual collector. Most of the institutions that we regard as Bancroft's peers have a similar tale to tell—the Huntington Library has evolved as an extension of the collecting passion of Henry E. Huntington; the Newberry Library owes its eminence in the western field primarily to Edward E. Ayer (now massively reinforced by Everett D. Graff's collection); and the Yale Western Americana Collection traces its origins and much of its abounding vitality to two great modern collectors, William Robertson Coe and Frederick W. Beinecke.

The Bancroft Library began in an extraordinarily offhand way. One day in 1860, the twenty-eight-year-old San Francisco bookseller, Hubert Howe Bancroft, brought together all the books in his store concerned with California, Oregon, Washington, and Utah—this for the convenience of William H. Knight, who was preparing a Pacific states "handbook almanac" for the Bancroft publishing house. Surprised that his array of western books totaled some fifty or seventy-five titles, young Bancroft began to amuse himself by adding to the collection. His doom was sealed. Before long, he was collecting historical materials, including manuscripts, for the whole of western North America, from Panama to Alaska; and before much more time passed, he was embarking upon that gigantic publishing enterprise of which the principal result was a thirty-nine-volume, partly staff-written "History of the Pacific States." H. H. Bancroft gathered in collections of source materials made by others, family archives, and the like; he sent agents to state and ecclesiastical archives to copy documents he could not purchase; and with his lively awareness of the recency of much of California's history, embarked upon an exhilarating program of collecting memoirs and dictations from living informants.

After his own period of productive scholarship ended in the 1890's, Bancroft was anxious that his library, now a virtual living entity in its own right, be preserved intact, preferably in California; he was also shrewd enough to know that "practical" men mainly value things they have to pay through the nose to acquire. Protracted negotiations led to purchase of the library by the Regents of the University of California in 1905. Of the finally agreed price, which was $250,000, H. H. Bancroft himself contributed $100,000. The library had not yet been removed to Berkeley at the time of the Great Earthquake of 1906, but it was housed outside the fire area—not without foresight on H. H. Bancroft's part—and was the only San Francisco library of any moment to survive intact, 60,000 books and almost countless manuscripts, maps, and newspapers. From that time to the present, all associated with the Bancroft Library have had an abiding interest in fire; and every now and then we take a fresh look at Bancroft's transcripts from the Hispanic California archives, our only means of access into whole areas of California history that lie back of the holocaust of 1906.

At this point I should like to draw attention to something that has been largely forgotten in the long-sustained excitement over H. H. Bancroft's massive library. Since 1897 the University of California had owned a nuclear library of Californiana, the Robert E. Cowan Collection, formed between 1891 and 1895 by the bookseller afterward so famous as a California bibliographer. This collection was purchased from Cowan for presentation to the university by the cordially detested railroad magnate, Collis P. Huntington. The price, $3,000, would not suffice today to purchase dozens of individual items in the collection, but the uncle of Henry E. Huntington got scant public acclaim for a gift described by the knowing as "mere trash."

The "litter" comprised 600 bound books (many of them rare even in 1897), 3,300 pamphlets, and some 4,000 manuscripts, including papers of most California governors from 1782 on, a fine copy of Father Pedro Font's diary of Anza's 1775–76 colonizing expedition to San Francisco Bay, and like things.

The University of California combined the Cowan Collection with the larger Bancroft holdings, and since 1906 has gone on adding to the library, which by stipulation retained H. H. Bancroft's name. For many decades, money was very hard to come by (in a ceaselessly changing world, this one thing never seems to change), and especially through the 1920's and 1930's growth was slow.

During that same era, prime attention was focused upon foreign archives, which a system of annual fellowships financed by the Native Sons of the Golden West made it possible for Herbert E. Bolton's graduate students to exploit, always to Bancroft's profit. The Bancroft Library by no means had a proprietary interest in foreign archives, as those who have spaded the collections of the Library of Congress and the Missouri Historical Society are aware, but no other institution worked at the job so long and so conscientiously. It was thus a very logical development, when university funds became available after World War II, that the Bancroft Library jumped head over heels into a foreign microfilming program.

In the twenty years since the program was inaugurated, a vast amount of microfilming has been done in the archives of France, Germany, Portugal, and the Netherlands, as also in England, Mexico, and Spain, where work is still in progress. Altogether, over a twenty-year span, the Bancroft Library in behalf of the University of California has invested $200,000 in this work—money that might otherwise have gone into the procurement of the books, manuscripts, maps, and so forth which are more usual objects of collecting zeal. Any becoming survey of the resources for the study of western travel in the Bancroft Library must take account of the immense new availability of the diaries and other documents described in such works as Bolton's *Guide to Materials for the History of the United States in the Principal Archives of Mexico* (Washington, D.C.: Carnegie Institution, 1913), and Charles E. Chapman's *Catalogue of Materials in the Archivo General de Indias* [at Seville, Spain] *for the History of the Pacific Coast and the American Southwest* (Berkeley: University of California

Press, 1919). Even the monolinguals among us find it profitable to wade into these microfilms, with Chapman or Bolton as guide. I would add that the Bancroft Library has not been neglectful of our own treasure house, the National Archives in Washington; at frequent intervals we have ordered films of individual items and blocks of records, a very high proportion of which in one way or another concern travelers in the West.

On becoming Director of the Bancroft Library in 1946, George P. Hammond backed off to take a fresh look at the library—its strengths, its inadequacies, its needs, and its potential for growth and adjustment to change. He saw the imperative necessity of a vigorous new acquisitions program and the direction it should take. The library's holdings of what we describe as "Old Bancroft dictations" were unique, impossible of duplication by any institution, the only remote parallel being the Draper Collection in the State Historical Society of Wisconsin, which is primarily concerned with the Midwest. To adopt modern terminology, the dictations were oral history, presented while it could be; from one point of view, these thousands of dictations were the life histories of almost as many travelers to and across the face of the West. Students of history return to them unceasingly, particularly the longer dictations recorded in California and the Pacific Northwest; for lack of diaries, they are often the only record of the activities they describe. George Nidever's account of his adventures in the fur trade, his coming to California with Bonneville's men, and his subsequent adventures hunting sea otter, is one famous example. Another is Joel Walker's dictation of his experiences on the Santa Fe Trail in the 1820's, and his overland journey to Oregon in 1840; still another is Isaac Given's account of his journey to California via Santa Fe and the Spanish Trail in 1841. I could list dozens of others; some have been published, but more have not, like the extended dictation by John Bidwell of the Bartleson party.

Still, there existed a serious need for contemporary documentation which would provide hard skeletal frameworks for the sometimes flabby reminiscences. H. H. Bancroft himself had done much along this line; his acquisition of the Larkin and Vallejo papers, to name two examples, gave archival scope to his collection. But much more could and should be done. The doing would involve finding new sources of funds, since many desirable manuscripts were finding their way to the marketplace, after a long epoch during which western manuscripts played second fiddle to printed works. If Bancroft had no book budget, Dr. Hammond would have to obtain one; and means would have to be found for Bancroft to acquire its proper share of the magnificent books and manuscripts that are offered for purchase every now and then—usually when an institution's bank account is most depleted. All these things got done, and during Dr. Hammond's nineteen-year tenure as Director, the Bancroft Library became a force to reckon with in the disposition of manuscripts offered for sale.

At the same time, and I wish to lay particular stress upon this phase of the library's recent history, Dr. Hammond redoubled Bancroft's efforts to find manuscripts at the source, to learn where they were and promote their acquisition—sometimes by purchase, but more often by gift. Collecting of this kind is truly creative, not just a matter of waiting with endless patience for someone to come in and plunk down a collection of letters or a diary: "Thank you very kindly, we're glad to have it." Such collecting, moreover, creates its own momentum; other things are swept along in the train of the prime object sought, and may end up alongside it in the stacks. Examples within my personal recollection are the Jedediah Smith Family Papers, which led to acquisition of the Samuel Parkman Papers; and the John Marsh Family Papers, which brought in the Eisner and Lyman collections. The Charles Weber Family Papers comprise so extensive an archive that Dr. Hammond and I have described them in detail in a substantial book. We prize the relations with family members that have developed along the way. But the point is that we in Bancroft remain constantly aware of the possibility that opportunity may knock upon our door, and we will go to any amount of trouble to help opportunity get within a long arm's length of our door.

Consider the bearing of what I have just been saying on the overland literature of the 1840's, antedating the Gold Rush. The Bancroft Library has an astonishing group of manuscripts relating to the Bartleson party of 1841, the first emigrants from the Missouri frontier to cross the Sierra Nevada into California. In H. H. Bancroft's day, dictations were obtained from John Bidwell, Joseph B. Chiles, Charles Hopper, and Josiah Belden; and for good measure Bancroft acquired the only copy of Bidwell's printed diary that has ever been found, down to the present day. I have already remarked the acquisition of the Charles Weber Papers; within the past decade Bancroft has also been given the surviving personal papers of Josiah Belden and a rich collection of the papers of Nicholas ("Cheyenne") Dawson, including a terse itinerary kept en route, a description of California made on the spot in 1842, the original manuscript of his memoirs as published in Texas in 1901, and an array of correspondence dating back to 1839, when he left his native Ohio for Missouri. (With these came a diary Dawson kept on the trail when returning to California by the Gila route in 1849.) All of these were gifts to the library.

There was no overland emigration to California by the northern route in 1842; but it is a challenge to us that we have found no diaries for the years 1843–45 except those by Pearson B. Reading (1843, via southeastern Oregon) and Jacob R. Snyder (1845), both held by the Society of California Pioneers. Some patient further search among descendants of the overlanders of these years is clearly indicated. At Bancroft we are quite as interested in what we do *not* have as in what we do, particularly since California is our immediate cultural heritage, our historical back yard.

Come 1846 and we are entitled to feel rich again. H. H. Bancroft obtained from George H. McKinstry, in 1871, two documents beyond price, the compelling diary kept in the Sierra Nevada by Patrick Breen of the starving Donner party—surely the most famous single diary in the record of overland emigration—and also McKinstry's own journal, which unfortunately breaks off soon after leaving Fort Laramie. Among the dictations H. H. Bancroft obtained from 1846 emigrants was one by Nicholas Carriger; by happy coincidence, fourteen years after Bancroft's own death, Carriger's trail diary of 1846 joined his dictation in the library's collections. Only three other manuscript diaries by 1846 California emigrants are known; one, by James Mathers, is on deposit at Bancroft; and two are in the Sutter's Fort Historical Museum Collection at Sacramento.

If we advance to 1847, we are confronted by another desert. Neither Bancroft nor any other library has a manuscript journal by a California emigrant of this year, though several Oregon diaries are known. In fact, one is a recent addition to the Bancroft collections, Isaac Pettijohn's ingratiating record of his journey to Oregon in 1847 and return to the States via the Applegate Cutoff next year. Pettijohn's is an especially welcome acquisition because of his return record in

1848, another drought year for overland chronicles. Two printed 1848 journals of travel to Oregon were known, but none to California by the South Pass route. So it is highly exciting that Bancroft has been able to locate and acquire the diary of Richard Martin May, who in 1848 came to the Golden Shore in the party led by Joseph B. Chiles (making his third California trek in eight years). Still more recently, Bancroft has obtained a typed copy of a fragmentary diary kept by Edward L. B. Smith for the first three weeks of the journey—as far as the Big Blue River of Kansas.

I mentioned a *typed* copy. Like most great libraries, Bancroft cherishes the original manuscripts which in their own way are final authorities; but realistically, in our long quest after the materials of our history, we often settle for what we can get—some owners will permit the making of photographic or typed copies of manuscripts, but cannot be budged on possession of the originals. In other cases—as with the Edward Smith journal of 1848 just mentioned—no one is even sure whether the original still exists; a copy made long ago has been the instrument of its survival. As another instance, Simon Fraser's rough diary of 1808, recording his exploration of the raging Fraser River in British Columbia, we preserve in the form of a transcript H. H. Bancroft made in 1878—the original has disappeared without trace, and so have seven out of eleven Fraser letters that Bancroft copied. So we offer no apologies when we serve up to scholars secondary versions of manuscripts; we congratulate ourselves—and are sometimes congratulated—on a successful holding action against the destructive forays of time.

Much as I would enjoy doing so, I cannot undertake to discuss in any detail the mass of overland journals we preserve in Bancroft for the Gold Rush period and after, on to the 1860's. Nine years ago, in editing *The Overland Diary of James A. Pritchard,* I appended a descriptive list of the 134 known diaries or collections of letters (published or unpublished) written by gold-seekers who took the South Pass route to California in 1849. For that year, interested students are referred to my book, and they will find that Bancroft has its full share. Since the book was published, another dozen 1849 diaries have emerged to view, about half of these being Bancroft acquisitions.

It has been my hope that other students will take up where I left off, treating in detail the overland emigration of each succeeding year, and recording all the known diaries for that year, wherever found; the same job needs to be done for those who took southern trails to California. In general, I can say that Bancroft has a diary kept on practically every one of the various trails used by overland emigrants, from 1849 on. We do not have a diary kept on the Hastings Cutoff in 1849—but neither does anybody else; and we keep a vigilant eye on the possibility that such a diary may turn up. We also poke around in likely places, knowing whom the Lord helps.

So far, I have been speaking rather exclusively about diaries kept by overland emigrants, though the emphasis seems desirable in view of the nature of this conference. I shall discuss other areas of the Bancroft collecting empire, but I want to point out to students who may be only now entering the field, or who missed earlier announcements, that the library has in progress a very large *Guide* to its manuscript collections. The first volume appeared in 1963, and described what we term "Pacific and Western Manuscripts"—that is, those pertaining to all the western states other than California. The volume has a very extensive index, and one subject entry is "Diaries." Another is "Emigration & overland travel," with subentries for the years 1834, 1846, 1861, or whatever. Far advanced in preparation are similar volumes describing the Bancroft Library's Mexican and colonial Spanish-American manuscripts, and our California manuscripts.

Bancroft's reference staff finds most inquiring students to be interested not so much in travel, generally speaking (let us say overland travel in the year 1853), as in particular travelers. Here the Bancroft Library has extraordinary resources in information, resources that are less than widely known. We have a modern "Information File," a species of corporate memory constantly enlarged as staff members inquire into this subject or that (and including also citations to brief biographies in the innumerable California county histories). But we also have something beyond compare, a mine of information dating back to H. H. Bancroft's day that was effectively reopened in the 1950's by Robert H. Becker, now the library's Assistant Director. I refer to the ultimate manuscript source of H. H. Bancroft's well-known "Pioneer Register," which undertook to list all residents in, or visitors to, California between 1542 and 1848.

H. H. Bancroft's staff formed the practice of breaking down biographical information by the use of slips of paper which could be alphabetized by name, then sorted out chronologically for each name. The printed "Pioneer Register" (originally appended to four volumes of Bancroft's *History of California,* but republished in 1964 as a separate compilation) was in effect a severely condensed version of the manuscript notes, now arranged within 128 looseleaf binders of the springback variety, and given the general name, "California Biography." This larger mine of information is by no means limited to Californians of pre-1849 vintage, for it contains clippings and notes relative to many later comers. Even for persons listed in the "Pioneer Register," fuller and more adequately documented information is to be found in the "California Biography" notes. And what has not been generally realized, these biographical notes constitute another means of access into the Spanish and Mexican archives which burned in the San Francisco fire. I have found that when H. H. Bancroft's workers were formally abstracting the California Archives, they made only the barest reference to men and their affairs in such areas as passports, licenses, naturalizations, and so on. The reason was that fuller notes were being made for Bancroft's biographical file. And now these grubby-looking slips of paper solely preserve vital information once afforded by the California Archives. No one trying to pursue an early traveler through the labyrinths of time should ignore the possibility of finding his track in our "California Biography" file.

Our concern here is with manuscript resources, but some may not be aware that a twenty-two-volume *Catalogue of Printed Works in the Bancroft Library* was published in 1964 by the G. K. Hall Company (besides another volume called *Index to Printed Maps*). Sets of this extensive work are available in the larger libraries; and since the Bancroft dictionary card catalogue was reproduced, much off-trail information may be obtained there—for instance, articles analyzed as being in various periodicals, obscure and otherwise.

The original Bancroft Library was not especially rich in pictorial materials, though it included some interesting drawings and lithographs, especially of Gold Rush vintage. A picture file built up over the years was vigorously expanded after John Barr Tompkins joined the library as head of its reference services in 1950; one especially interesting acquisition was the Zelda Mackay Collection of daguerreotypes, which includes a number of good views of Gold Rush scenes.

One of the last great services of Dr. Hammond, prior to his retirement in 1965, was his engineering the acquisition of the Honeyman Collection of Early Californian and Western American Pictorial Material. The collection formed by Robert B. Honeyman would go far to fill an ever more apparent void in the library's documentation of the past; at the end of a half-million-dollar fund-raising campaign, we found this to be the fact. Almost 2,000 pictorial items, including oil paintings, water colors, drawings, lithographs, engravings, and etchings, plus photographs, illustrated lettersheets, maps, manuscripts, and other diversities, have pre-emptive interest for scholars concerned with travel or travelers in the West, and the range is exciting. There are, for example, drawings by Spanish artists of the Malaspina expedition of 1791—the earliest surviving drawings of any scene in California —as also water colors dating back to the first visit by Vancouver in 1792. Other drawings and water colors by G. H. von Langsdorff, Louis Choris, and others depict scenes from California to Alaska recorded in 1805 and 1816. The Beechey expedition of 1826–27 made further contributions to the record of life on the Pacific littoral—and so the catalogue goes, to and beyond the turbulent era of the Gold Rush. Pictorial materials are not the answer to every scholar's necessities, but sometimes nothing can take their place.

Having entered so dramatically upon this new collecting field, the Bancroft Library has continued with high enthusiasm; one outstanding recent acquisition I should like to mention as unique: a group of twenty-three scenes by George Catlin, hand-colored on glass. This came to us almost simultaneously with an imposing cache of Catlin family letters, unknown to his biographers, which had been preserved in a Berkeley attic. I might say that working in a great library, and participating in the action, is made worthwhile many times over by developments of this sort!

By way of making more enticing to scholars our invitation to come out to Berkeley and investigate someone or something other that the late lamented hippies of Telegraph Avenue, let me point to some areas of history, and special items or collections, which might render a visit more memorable.

You are interested in fur trade or mountain men? Our Kit Carson Papers, Jedediah Smith Family Collection, or Andrew Drips Papers are for you, and so are the Alexander Barclay Papers, with the unique diary Barclay kept between 1845 and 1850 at the Hardscrabble Settlement on the upper Arkansas, and at Fort Barclay in New Mexico. You prefer missionaries? We have a whole slew of the Spanish variety, from Eusebio Kino to Junípero Serra and beyond. We also have Marcus Whitman's fragmentary diary of 1835, and the copy of her diary of 1836 that Narcissa Whitman made for her mother-in-law, besides some valuable letters. We have Mormons in good supply, too, that being an old specialty of the house. Among the later California divines, Thomas Starr King seems especially notable in the Bancroft collections.

If your taste runs to voyages in the Pacific Ocean, again you may find Bancroft a spiritual home. The library has any number of diaries or logbooks kept on voyages around Cape Horn, especially after the discovery of gold in 1848, but earlier records deserve attention. Some concern the Hawaiian Islands, which may not fit the usual definition of "western" but nevertheless are vitally "western" to a scholar based in Oregon or California. Eliab Grimes (1820–22), William Sturgis Hinckley (1823), Francis Mellus (1838–40), and J. B. R. Cooper (1839–44), all well-known figures in the early mercantile history of California, may (with their journals) serve as type specimens. U.S. naval history in the Pacific is also by no means unrepresented, particularly the role of the Navy in the occupation (or conquest) of California during the Mexican War. One work of boundless fascination is the lavishly illustrated journal of William H. Meyers, another quite recent gift. (Within the past year we have acquired another dozen sketches by Meyers.)

The John Charles Frémont Family Papers, to the extent that they have survived, are preserved in Bancroft, and so are those of many other Army officers, E. O. C. Ord and Henry Naglee, for example. H. H. Bancroft would heartily have applauded these acquisitions, as also journals kept by such vigorous and eloquent women as Evaline M. Alexander, who as the wife of an Army officer traveled extensively in New Mexico and Colorado in 1866–67; and Anne W. Booth, a ship arrival of 1849. A few lady travelers more highly seasoned, like Lola Montez, have a place in the Bancroft scene, too. Although in his own day H. H. Bancroft must have felt that his collecting tastes embraced everything, he might have been surprised at the vigor with which the modern library has enlarged the Bancroft domain, literary history being as much our concern as political, social, or military history; I may cite, as examples within our time-range, the papers of Bret Harte, including a diary of 1857–58, and the papers of the famous Comstock chronicler, Dan DeQuille, whose real name was William Wright. It seems appropriate to add that the Mark Twain Papers are now housed under the same roof with Bancroft, though not technically in the Bancroft Library.

Even with Bancroft's enormous range, the library cannot expect to be, and is not, equally strong in all areas of western history. Significant Lewis and Clark manuscript materials are conspicuous by their absence, and we are not notable for collections relating to the Plains states; we also have only incidental source material for what we might call the "Bad Man's West." We are philosophic about our deficiencies, recognizing, for one thing, that there has been a cultural revolution in the West since H. H. Bancroft's day, with state historical societies and state universities now actively collecting the materials of their own history. But in few libraries, perhaps, may so satisfactory an overview of the West be obtained as in Bancroft. For the advantages of that overview, as well as for the delights of working in our collections, we invite all interested scholars to do some traveling in the West and knock upon our door in Berkeley.

Postscript

After this paper was prepared, just prior to publication, the University of California greatly enlarged the Bancroft Library's sphere of usefulness by expanding it to incorporate the Department of Rare Books and Special Collections and the Mark Twain Collection, heretofore units of the main University Library. A notable scholar in the field of Americana, Dr. James D. Hart, was appointed Director of the expanded library, effective January 1, 1970. Scholars may anticipate that these developments will make even more rewarding their pilgrimages to the Bancroft Library.

The Documents and Reports of the United States Congress: A Primary Source of Information on Travel in the West, 1783-1861

Herman R. Friis

SETTLEMENT, land use, and successful movement or transit through a region generally are a response to the reading of an account, a record, describing the cultural and physical landscape. The verbal account, which is transient and subject to frequent modification, is not normally a reliable record. This has been as true of the American West as of most settled regions of the world. The record takes many forms, such as a journal, a diary, survey field notes, a map, a magazine article, correspondence, a report, a landscape painting, and a photograph. These forms are a record of observation by man of a landscape at a moment in time. The accuracy of this record may be good or it may be bad, depending to a large degree upon the qualifications of the observer and the motives that stimulated him to record his thoughts.[1]

Travel and geographical exploration are not, strictly speaking, synonymous, but each includes a large element of observation and interpretation of the landscape. Geographical exploration is perhaps a more precisely planned activity, the end product of which usually is a prescribed form of written record. Both are the movement of man through a region. There is, of course, a substantial body of material in this subject field and its value as a written record ranges widely

[1] Alan Gregg, "Travel and Its Meaning," *Scientific Monthly*, LXX (1950), 151–156.

from the ridiculous to the sublime.[2] Yet it is this very large body of information that tantalized so many of our forebears and stimulated them to move west to take up new homes, often in a substantially different environment for which they generally were ill-prepared. The surprising thing about it all is that so many settlers quickly and successfully modified the environment to fit their needs and made the requisite adjustments to it.[3]

There is extant a very large body of information on the geographical exploration of our West that has been so infrequently tapped by historians, geographers, and others who are interested in successive changes in the landscapes, from initial observation, through settlement, to intensive land use. I refer here to the treasure trove of reports, journals, accounts, and the like that were prepared by civilians and especially by military personnel in response to an official request and as part of a prescribed obligation to the federal government. It is important to point out that in most instances these accounts

2 This literature includes accounts in magazines, travelogues, newspapers, and books. For examples of some of these see: Percy G. Adams, *Travelers and Travel Liars, 1660–1880* (Berkeley: University of California Press, 1962); Emmett H. Anderson, "Appraisal of American Life by French Travelers, 1860–1914," University Microfilms *Publication 9630* (Ann Arbor, Mich., 1954); Max Berger, *The British Traveller in America, 1836–1860* (Gloucester, Mass.: Peter Smith, 1964); Samuel T. Chambers, *Observations and Opinions of French Travellers in the United States from 1790 to 1835* (Georgetown University thesis, Washington, D.C., 1949); Thomas D. Clark, ed., *Travels in the New South, a Bibliography [1865-1955]* (2 vols., Norman: University of Oklahoma Press, 1962); Seymour Dunbar, *A History of Travel in America* (4 vols., Indianapolis: Tudor, 1915); James R. Eckman, *The British Traveller in America, 1875–1920* (Georgetown University thesis, Washington, D.C., 1946); Robert R. Hubach, *Early Midwestern Travel Narratives, an Annotated Bibliography, 1634–1850* (Detroit: Wayne State University Press, 1961); Robert R. Hubach, "Unpublished Travel Narratives on the Early Midwest, 1720–1850: A Preliminary Bibliography," *Mississippi Valley Historical Review*, XLII (1955), 525–548; Frederick A. Palmer, "Westerners at Home: Comments of French and British Travelers on Life in the West, 1800–1840," University Microfilms *Publication 1557* (Ann Arbor, Mich., 1957); Henry R. Wagner, *Henry R. Wagner's The Plains and the Rockies; a Bibliography of Original Narratives of Travel and Adventure, 1800–1865, Revised and Extended by Charles L. Camp* (3rd ed., Columbus, Ohio: Long's College Book Co., 1953); and Edward S. Wallace, *The Great Reconnaissance: Soldiers, Artists and Scientists on the Frontier, 1848–1861* (Boston: Little, Brown and Co., 1955).

3 Some of the best references are Dorothy A. Dondore, *The Prairie and the Making of Middle America: Four Centuries of Description* (Cedar Rapids, Ia.: Torch Press, 1926); W. Eugene Hollon, *The Great American Desert Then and Now* (New York: Oxford University Press, 1966), with an excellent bibliography; G. Malcolm Lewis, "Early American Exploration and the Cis-Rocky Mountain Desert: 1803–1823," *The Great Plains Journal*, V (1965), 1–11; G. Malcolm Lewis, "Changing Emphases in the Description of the Natural Environment of the American Great Plains Area," *Transactions and Papers of the Institute of British Geographers*, XXX (1962), 75–90.

were prepared by trained observers whose reporting was in response to specified needs for information. These needs were for an objective record of the observable features of the landscape.

The more important, exciting, and "famous" of these were privately published, many others have never been published, and a surprising number have been published as official documents of the U.S. Senate and of the House of Representatives.[4] The official documents are published in what often are referred to as the Congressional Serial Set or Congressional Documents. This fundamental source of information is available in published form as volumes in a large number of libraries in the United States, but surprisingly they are infrequently used and referred to. The large volume of the official manuscript or "original" accounts may be found among the records of various agencies of the federal government, especially of the Office of the Chief of Engineers, the Bureau of Topographical Engineers, the Office of the Secretary of War, the General Land Office, and the Office of Indian Affairs. Annually, the officer in charge of each of these bureaus prepares a report of accomplishments, which report normally is transmitted through channels and is included in the President's annual message to the Congress. The House of Representatives and the U.S. Senate often have requested and received specific reports and other

[4] The following are references of particular value to the researcher interested in the extent and the potential use of publications of the U.S. government. De Alva S. Alexander, *History and Procedure of the House of Representatives* (Boston: Houghton Mifflin Co., 1916); Ernest S. Bates, *The Story of Congress, 1789–1935* (New York: Harper and Brothers, 1936); Anne M. Boyd, ed., *United States Government Publications* (New York: H. W. Wilson Co., 1949); Martin P. Claussen and Herman R. Friis, comps., *Descriptive Catalog of Maps Published by Congress, 1817–1843* (Washington, D.C.: privately published, 1941); Paul L. Ford, ed., *Some Materials for a Bibliography of the Official Publications of the Continental Congress, 1774–1789* (Boston: by order of the Trustees, 1890); Oscar Handlin *et al.*, comps., *Harvard Guide to American History* (Cambridge, Mass.: Belknap Press, 1954); Adelaide R. Hasse, *Reports of Explorations Printed in the Documents of the U.S. Government. A Contribution Toward a Bibliography* (Washington: G.P.O., 1899); George H. Haynes, *The Senate of the United States, Its History and Practice* (2 vols., Boston: Houghton Mifflin Co., 1938); James L. and Julia B. McCamy, *Government Publications for the Citizen; a Report of the Public Library Inquiry* (New York: Columbia University Press, 1949); Floyd M. Riddick, *The United States Congress; Organization and Procedure* (Manassas, Va.: National Capitol Publishers, 1949); Laurence F. Schmeckebier and Roy B. Eastin, eds., *Government Publications and Their Use* (Washington, D.C.: Brookings Institution, 1961), the best single source—see esp. pp. 119–177; and Dorothy L. C. Tompkins, *Materials for the Study of Federal Government* (Chicago: Public Administration Service, 1948).

communications and have ordered them printed as congressional documents.[5] It is those that cover travel and exploration that concern us in this paper. Frequently, the maps, illustrations, and related materials have not been reproduced because of the considerable expense. In some instances these too may be found among the official records of the Senate and of the House and normally are among the records of the originating agency now in the National Archives.[6]

In the preparation of this paper I have examined the thirty-eight volumes comprising the *American State Papers,* which include many of the published documents for the period prior to 1817 and the first 1,110 numbers of the Congressional Serial Set prior to 1861.[7] Time and space preclude the presentation of more than a representative selection of the journals and similar accounts of official geographical explorations that have been published within these volumes. I shall illustrate this paper with reproductions of maps, landscape views, portraits, and the like that accompany the printed document, or of the corresponding official record in the National Archives. Each is a remarkable source of on-the-spot objective observation of the landscape along the route of travel by a trained observer. The Congressional Serial Set, these numerous published documents in orderly

[5] For excellent comprehensive finding aids to these official records see Buford Rowland, Handy B. Fant, and Harold E. Hufford, comps., "Records of the United States House of Representatives, 1789–1946, Volume 1," *The National Archives, Preliminary Inventory,* No. 113 (Washington, D.C., 1959), pp. 1–292; and Harold E. Hufford and Watson G. Caudill, comps., "Records of the United States Senate [1789–1946]," *The National Archives, Preliminary Inventory,* No. 23 (Washington, D.C., 1950), pp. 1–284.

[6] Unfortunately, many of these original illustrations have been lost or were not returned by the engraving or lithographing firms to which they had been sent for estimates as to cost and for use in making reproductions for publication. There is evidence, for example, that many of these illustrations were stored in the lithographic establishment of August Hoen and Company in Baltimore when it was destroyed by fire about the turn of the century. There is also evidence that this lithographic firm retained a good many of the original illustrations; but a search by Mr. Albert B. Hoen, the son, in the late 1940's turned up very few. The two firms of August Hoen and Company and Julius Bien of New York City during the second half of the nineteenth century produced a large quantity of lithographic work for the federal government that was recognized as the hallmark of excellence. The A. Hoen Company to this day continues to produce maps of the highest quality.

[7] For a list of the volumes of the *American State Papers* see Superintendent of Documents, *Checklist of United States Public Documents, 1789–1909 . . .* (Washington, D.C., 1911), pp. 3–4; for a list of the volumes comprising Congressional Serial nos. 1–1110 (1817–61) see *ibid.,* pp. 5–38.

arrangement, is a fundamental source of "travel" information.[8] This presentation is essentially chronological in sequence and is divided into four periods.

The Formative Period: 1783–1817

During the latter half of the eighteenth century geographical exploration of western North America advanced at a rapid pace and led to a surprising fund of knowledge, some of which has only recently come to light (Figure 1).[9] England, France, Spain, and Russia were the principal participants in the drama, the main themes of which were the search for the Northwest and Northeast passages to the Orient and for the vast riches thought to exist there. By the end of the century the advances on all fronts had proved rather conclusively that the North American continent was indeed a tremendous land mass, a barrier to a direct water route to Asia, though perhaps through it there might be found that conveniently located waterway making transcontinental

[8] Works cited in footnote 4 and John G. Ames, ed., *Comprehensive Index to the Publications of the United States Government, 1881–1893* (2 vols., Washington: G.P.O., 1905); Adolphus W. Greely, comp., "Public Documents of the Early Congresses," *Annual Report of the American Historical Association for 1896* (Washington: G.P.O., 1897), pp. 1109–1248; Adolphus W. Greely, comp., *Public Documents of the First Fourteen Congresses, 1789–1817. Papers Relating to Early Congressional Documents* (Washington: G.P.O., 1900); and Benjamin P. Poore, comp., *A Descriptive Catalogue of the Government Publications of the United States, September 5, 1774–March 4, 1881* (Washington: G.P.O., 1885).

For specific references see particularly Hasse, comp., *Reports of Explorations,* and Claussen and Friis, comps., *Descriptive Catalogue of Maps* (see footnote 4).

[9] Many good references are available on the general subject of exploration of our American West. Among the most helpful are: Ray A. Billington, *Westward Expansion. A History of the American Frontier* (New York: Macmillan, 1967); Herbert E. Bolton and Thomas M. Marshall, *The Colonization of North America, 1492–1783* (New York: Macmillan, 1936); John B. Brebner, *The Explorers of North America, 1492–1806* (New York: Macmillan, 1933); Edmund W. Gilbert, *The Exploration of Western America, 1806–1850; an Historical Geography* (Cambridge: Cambridge University Press, 1933); William H. Goetzmann, *Army Explorations in the American West, 1803–1863* (New Haven, Conn.: Yale University Press, 1959); LeRoy R. Hafen and Carl C. Rister, *Western America: The Exploration, Settlement, and Development of the Region beyond the Mississippi* (New York: Prentice-Hall, 1941); Savoie Lottinville, ed., *The American Exploration and Travel Series* (55 vols., Norman: University of Oklahoma Press, 1938–67); Reuben Gold Thwaites, ed., *Early Western Travels, 1748–1846* (32 vols., Cleveland: Arthur H. Clark, 1904–06); and Carl W. Wheat, *Mapping the Transmississippi West* (6 vols., San Francisco: Institute of Historical Cartography, 1957–63).

passage possible. To those who wanted to believe it there appeared to be sufficient proof that the several wide water entrances (Puget Sound, Columbia River, and San Francisco Bay) led far inland to meet with the rivers, such as the Missouri, draining eastward across the Great Plains and into the Mississippi.

The presumed limitless wealth in furs and in minerals as well as the anticipated brisk trade with the Indians served to spirit exploring expeditions and individuals into this "unknown region" from all approaches along the periphery. Terrain information acquired during exploratory surveys by government-sponsored parties, by the padres and friars of religious orders, and by the field representatives of commercial interests often was carefully recorded and preserved, although frequently it was jealously guarded as secret information. The numerous treks into the interior by parties of intrepid traders and by free-lance individuals in search of traffic with the natives generally went unrecorded; such information about the "lay of the land" as was acquired was passed on verbally and often assumed fantastic proportions of untruth.

Information about the landscape that was acquired by individuals whose travels took them into familiar and unfamiliar regions often was recorded in journals, diaries, survey field notebooks, letters, and reports. The veracity of much of this information was open to question and often led to gross inaccuracies in cartographic representations, as for example the mythical rivers of the West.[10] By the end of the eighteenth century the more objectively compiled maps of the North American continent, such as Aaron Arrowsmith's "Map Exhibiting all the New Discoveries in the Interior Parts of North America . . ." (Figure 2), published in London in 1802 on a scale of one inch to seventy miles, gave a reasonably accurate view which was derived from travel accounts and to a limited extent from field surveys.

10 See for example: Aubrey Diller, "Maps of the Missouri River before Lewis and Clark," in Montague F. Ashley-Montague, ed., *Studies and Essays . . . in Homage to George Sarton* (New York: Henry Schuman, 1946), pp. 505–519; and Diller's "A New Map of the Missouri River Drawn in 1795," *Imago Mundi*, XII (1955), 175–180. An excellent discussion of Humboldt's map of the river systems is C. Gregory Crampton, "Humboldt's Utah, 1811," *Utah Historical Quarterly*, XXVI (1958), 269–281; and C. Gregory Crampton and Gloria G. Griffin, "The San Buenaventura, Mythical River of the West," *Pacific Historical Review*, XXV (1956), 163–171.

It was apparent to the intelligent observer that much of the North American West was a vast and uncertain void.

United States interest in these *terrae incognitae* that spread Pacific-ward seemingly without end prior to 1803 was limited to a few sporadic forays.[11] The young nation was too intimately involved in defining and marking its exterior boundaries and in responding to the development of a plan for much-needed internal improvements for its rapidly expanding population. We should note that there is paltry little information in the Congressional Documents about the first four attempts by the United States to explore the American West, namely those proposals of George Rogers Clark,[12] John Ledyard,[13] Andre Michaux,[14] and John Armstrong.[15] The sketch map by John Armstrong with the Harmar Papers in the Clements Library is one of the earliest official U.S. maps of the hydrographic pattern of the Mississippi Valley (Figure 3).

The amount of terrain information in the form of descriptive accounts of travels and exploration and of cartographic results that Thomas Jefferson had in his possession and that served to spark his relentless drive to discover the "West" we may never know. It is perhaps safe to conclude that in his extensive library, through his wide personal acquaintances at home and abroad, and during his periods of service to the government in positions of trust, he acquired a mass of information about western America that placed him in a unique position of intelligence and made possible the ultimate success of the first official U.S. expedition into the region and of a number of others that blazed trails and made historic observations across the full extent of the plains west of the Mississippi River (Figure 4). Strangely, the records of these expeditions were not fully published

[11] See for example the excellent scholarly publications by Donald Jackson, ed., *Letters of the Lewis and Clark Expedition with Related Documents, 1783–1854* (Urbana: University of Illinois Press, 1962), pp. 654–672; and A. P. Nasatir, ed., *Before Lewis and Clark* (2 vols., St. Louis Historical Documents Foundation, 1952).

[12] See in the George Rogers Clark Papers in the State Historical Society of Wisconsin Library, Madison, and the Virginia Historical Society Library, Richmond.

[13] Jackson, ed., *Letters of the Lewis and Clark Expedition*, pp. 656–661.

[14] *Ibid.*, pp. 667–672.

[15] *Ibid.*, pp. 661–667. See also correspondence in the Records of the Office of the Secretary of War (RG 77) in the National Archives, and the Josiah Harmar Papers in the William L. Clements Library, Ann Arbor, Mich. A good published reference is Colton Storm, "Lieutenant Armstrong's Expedition to the Missouri River 1790," *Mid-America*, XXV (1943), 180–188.

under government auspices but found a ready public response through private printing.[16]

In his communication to Congress dated Washington, January 18, 1803, President Thomas Jefferson at some length developed his thoughts on the need for exploration of the vast *terrae incognitae* that spread tantalizingly through the continent of North America between the Mississippi River and the Pacific Coast. Jefferson justified his motives in part because, he said,

> While other civilized nations have encountered great expense to enlarge the boundaries of knowledge, by undertaking voyages of discovery and for other literary purposes, in various parts and directions; our nation seems to owe to the same object, as well as its own interest, to explore this [the Missouri River], the only line of easy communication across the continent, and so directly traversing our own part of it. The interests of commerce place the principal object within the constitutional powers and care of Congress; and that it should, incidentally, advance the geographical knowledge of our continent, cannot but be an additional gratification. . . .[17]

As we know, the Congress supported Jefferson. The saga of the Lewis and Clark expedition from the time of its departure from St. Louis on May 14, 1804, to its return to St. Louis on September 13, 1806, has been recounted by many. It is distressing to learn that there is only occasional brief notice of this and related expeditions in official published records of the Congress.[18]

16 There is a wide variety of publications. See for example *Henry R. Wagner's The Plains and the Rockies* (see footnote 2), pp. 1–27; Wheat, *Mapping the Transmississippi West*; Thwaites, ed., *Early Western Travels*; and Goetzmann, *Army Explorations in the American West* (see footnote 9).

17 "Communication on Trade," submitted by President Thomas Jefferson to the Congress, January 18, 1803, 7th Congress, 2nd Session, in *American State Papers, Indian Affairs*, Vol. I, Doc. 102 (Washington, 1832), pp. 684–685.

18 Herman R. Friis, "Cartographic and Geographic Activities of the Lewis and Clark Expedition," *Journal of the Washington Academy of Sciences*, XLIV (1958), 338–351. For excellent descriptive accounts see especially John Bakeless, *Lewis and Clark; Partners in Discovery* (New York: William Morrow and Co., 1957); Nicholas Biddle, ed., *History of the Expedition under the Command of Captains Lewis and Clark* (2 vols., Philadelphia: Paul Allen, 1814); Nicholas Biddle and Elliott Coues, eds., *History of the Expedition under the Command of Lewis and Clark* (4 vols., New York: Francis P. Harper, 1893); Elliott Coues, "An Account of the Various Publications Relating to the Travels of Lewis and Clark," *Bulletin of the Geological and Geographical Survey of the Territories*, No. 6, Ser. 2 (Washington, 1876), pp. 417–444; and particularly

On February 19, 1806, President Thomas Jefferson sent to the Congress a very lengthy communication in which he summarized the geographical accomplishments of the Lewis and Clark expedition to its winter quarters at the Mandan villages on the Upper Missouri to April, 1805;[19] John Sibley's exploration of the Red River; and William Dunbar and Dr. George Hunter's exploration of the Washita River, all in the newly acquired Louisiana Territory.[20] Jefferson includes the lengthy letter of Meriwether Lewis dated April 7, 1805, in which he recounts in remarkable detail his travels up the Missouri to the Mandan villages, and describes the geographical landscape and Indian populations.

Lewis notes that "The map which has been forwarded to the Secretary of War, will give you the idea we entertain of the connexion of these rivers. . . ."[21] Apparently, at least three copies of this map were made by the cartographer-surveyor Nicholas King in Washington (Figure 5). One was retained by the Secretary of War, quite possibly the map we view here, and two copies were sent forward by Jefferson with his communication to Congress. Neither of these are with these documents today, nor can they be found. Indeed, they appear never to have been reproduced in the Congressional Documents.

The rich source of geographical information available in these abstract journals and in other accounts of these pioneer explorers is well illustrated by Sibley's remarks about a small section of the Red River (Figure 6): "The country is interspersed with prairies, resembling, as to richness, the river bottoms, and in size from five to five thousand acres. The hills are a good grey soil, and produce very well, and afford beautiful situations. The creek called Bayou Pierre (Stony creek) passes through the settlement, and affords a number of good

---

Reuben Gold Thwaites, ed., *The Original Journals of the Lewis and Clark Expedition, 1804–1806* (8 vols., New York: Dodd, Mead and Co., 1904–05).

19 Ernest S. Osgood, ed., *The Field Notes of Captain William Clark, 1803–1805* (New Haven, Conn.: Yale University Press, 1964).

20 "Communications on Lewis and Clarke's Expedition [and others]," submitted by President Thomas Jefferson to the Congress, February 19, 1806, 9th Congress, 1st Session, in *American State Papers, Indian Affairs*, Vol. I, Doc. 113 (Washington, 1832), pp. 705–743.

21 *Ibid.*, p. 706. For discussion of the role of this map see Jesse S. Douglas, "Lewis' Map of 1806," *Military Affairs*, V (1941), 68–72; Arnold Hague, "An Early Map of the Far West," *Science—an Illustrated Journal*, X (1887), 217–218; and Samuel L. Mitchill, "Lewis's Map of the Parts of North America," *Medical Repository*, 2nd Hexade, III (1806), 315–318.

mill seats, and its bed and banks lined with a good kind of building stone; but no mills are erected on it. . . ."[22]

In the lengthy extract from the journals of William Dunbar and Dr. George Hunter are numerous detailed descriptions of the landscape of the Washita River valley (Figure 7),[23] for example:

> Above the Isle de Mallon, the country wears another aspect; high lands and rocks frequently approach the river. The rocks, in grain, resemble free stone, and are hard enough to be used as hand-mill stones, to which purpose they are frequently applied. The quality of the land improves, the stratum of vegetable earth being from six to twelve inches, of a dark brown color, with an admixture of loam and sand . . . and in many situations, on both sides of this river, there are said to be salines which may hereafter be rendered very productive, and from which the future settlements may be abundantly supplied.[24]

It is perhaps surprising that these invaluable journals and accounts and those of other explorers such as Zebulon Montgomery Pike during the period were not published by the federal government.[25] Only abstracts and excerpts were included in official publica-

22 "Communications on Lewis and Clarke's Expedition," p. 728. See also Isaac J. Cox, *The Early Exploration of Louisiana* (Cincinnati: University of Cincinnati Press, 1906); Thomas Jefferson, *Message from the President of the United States Communicating Discoveries Made in Exploring the Missouri, Red River and the Washita, by Captains Lewis and Clark, Doctor Sibley, and Mr. Dunbar* (Washington: A. and G. Way, Printers, 1806); and Annie Héloise Abel, ed., "A Report from Natchitoches in 1807, by John Sibley," *Indian Notes and Monographs. Miscellaneous*, No. 25 (New York: Museum of the American Indian, Heye Foundation, 1922), pp. 1–102.

23 For an excellent scholarly documented edition of Hunter's journal see John Francis McDermott, ed., "The Western Journals of Dr. George Hunter, 1796–1805," *Transactions of the American Philosophical Society*, n.s., LIII, Pt. 4 (1963), 1–133.

24 "Communications on Lewis and Clarke's Expedition," p. 736.

25 Recently scholars with special competence in the field have gathered together the critical documents and edited them for publication. See for example the excellent work by McDermott (see footnote 23) and Jackson (see footnote 11) and Jackson's recent *Journals, with Letters and Related Documents. Zebulon Montgomery Pike* (2 vols., Norman: University of Oklahoma Press, 1966).

For a good review of these explorations and the manner of their publication see Max Meisel, *A Bibliography of American Natural History, the Pioneer Century, 1769–1865* (3 vols., New York: Premier Publishing Co., 1926), Vol. I; for the role of the American Philosophical Society in sponsoring certain of these explorations and in serving as a depository for the records see its *Transactions*, Vols. II–VI (1786–1809), and its *Proceedings*, Vol. XXII (1744–1838); and *The Medical Repository of New York City*, Vols. I–XVIII (1797–1817).

tions of Congress prior to 1818. But then, for the period prior to 1818 there was no systematic attempt to arrange these publications,[26] and there was but a faint interest by Congress in the lands beyond the Mississippi River.

The Period 1818–42

Establishment of a Topographical Bureau and a rekindled interest by the War Department in the continent beyond the Mississippi River, the pressure of a never-ceasing restiveness by citizens to move ever farther west, the federal government's growing awareness of the need to establish and maintain lines of circulation (roads and paths) in the West, and a contagious curiosity to find out precisely what the geographical composition of these newly acquired lands comprised, stimulated the government to launch a succession of geographical exploring expeditions (Figure 8).[27] A primary end product was a remarkable treasure trove of journals, diaries, reports, and related records that give the reader a reasonably objective view of the landscape immediately prior to the era of the Great Migrations beginning in the 1840's. Many of these accounts were published in brief and had wide circulation; some were published in the Congressional Documents and have generally been lost to view.

It is perhaps surprising that very few if any of the journals and reports of official geographical explorations of our American West prior to about 1830 were requested for and published as or in a Con-

26 Greely, comp., *Public Documents of the First Fourteen Congresses* (see footnote 8).

27 Helpful references to this and the following periods are James T. Adams, ed., *Atlas of American History* (New York: Charles Scribner's Sons, 1943); Leonard J. Arrington, *Great Basin Kingdom: An Economic History of the Latter-Day Saints, 1830–1900* (Cambridge, Mass.: Harvard University Press, 1958); Henry P. Beers, *The Western Military Frontier, 1815–1846* (Philadelphia: privately published, 1935); Ralph H. Brown, *Historical Geography of the United States* (New York: Harcourt, Brace and Co., 1948); Leland H. Creer, *The Founding of an Empire; the Exploration and Colonization of Utah, 1776–1856* (Salt Lake City: Bookcraft, 1947); Grant Foreman, *Advancing the Frontier, 1830–1860* (Norman: University of Oklahoma Press, 1933); Frederic L. Paxson, *History of the American Frontier, 1763–1893* (Boston: Houghton Mifflin Co., 1924); and W. O. Scroggs, "Early Trade and Travel in the Lower Mississippi Valley," *Mississippi Valley Historical Association, Proceedings*, II (1910), 235–256.

gressional Document.[28] For example, one searches in vain for the official published reports of such a significant exploration as Stephen Harriman Long's in 1819–20 into the northern Plains.

One of the earliest reports and journal accounts published in the Congressional Serial Set is "Lieutenant [James] Allen and Henry R. Schoolcraft's visit to the Northwest Indians in 1832."[29] A principal product was a map of the headwaters of the Mississippi (Figure 9). In his journal entry for July 24 Allen noted: "We arrived at the falls of St. Anthony at 1 p.m. and at Fort Snelling at 3 p.m., distance of ninety miles from our encampment. The river and country we passed to-day have the same character as yesterday, the country being uneven prairie on both sides, and the river filled with islands, but becoming wider continually, from its numerous tributaries. . . ."[30]

Apparently the first government-sponsored geotopographical survey in our West was made in 1834[31] and 1835[32] by the English geologist

28 Forrest G. Hill, *Roads, Rails, and Waterways; the Army Engineers and Early Transportation* (Norman: University of Oklahoma Press, 1957); Harlow Lindsay, "Western Travel, 1800–1820," *Mississippi Valley Historical Review*, VI (1919), 167–191; and Warren S. Tryon, ed., *A Mirror for Americans: Life and Manners in the United States, 1790–1870, as Recorded by American Travellers* (Chicago: University of Chicago Press, 1952).

29 "Letter from the Secretary of War, Transmitting a Map and Report of Lieut. Allen and H. B. [*sic*] Schoolcraft's Visit to the Northwest Indians in 1832," 23rd Congress, 1st Session, *House Doc. 323*, Serial 257 (Washington, 1834), pp. 1–68. Schoolcraft's report was published in his *Summary Narrative of an Exploratory Expedition to the Sources of the Mississippi River, in 1820; Resumed and Completed by the Discovery of Its Origin in Itasca Lake in 1832* (Philadelphia: Lippincott, Grambo, and Co., 1855). He also published a *Narrative of an Expedition through the Upper Mississippi to Itasca Lake, the Actual Source of This River, Embracing an Exploration through the St. Croix and Burntwood (or Brule) Rivers in 1832, under the Direction of H. R. Schoolcraft* (New York: Harper and Brothers, 1834). See also his *Personal Memoirs of a Residence of Thirty Years with the Indian Tribes on the American Frontiers . . . AD 1812 to AD 1842* (Philadelphia: Lippincott, Grambo, and Co., 1851); William T. Boutwell, "Schoolcraft's Exploration Tour of 1832," *Minnesota Historical Society Collections*, I (1902), 121–140; and Henry R. Schoolcraft, *Narrative Journal of Travels through the Northwestern Regions of the United States, 1820*, Mentor L. Williams, ed. (East Lansing: Michigan State University Press, 1953).

30 "Letter from the Secretary of War," pp. 54–59.

31 "Geological Report of an Examination Made in 1834, of the Elevated Country between the Missouri and Red Rivers. By G. W. Featherstonhaugh, U.S. Geologist," 23rd Congress, 2nd Session, *House Doc. 151*, Serial 274 (Washington, 1835), pp. 1–97. *Senate Doc. 153*, Serial 269, in the same Congress and Session is essentially the same report, but there are some minor differences.

32 "Report of a Geological Reconnoissance [*sic*] Made in 1835, from the Seat of Government, by the Way of Green Bay and the Wisconsin Territory, to the Coteau de

George W. Featherstonhaugh (Figure 10). The area was between the Missouri and Mississippi rivers. One of his several manuscript maps in the Records of the Office of the Chief of Engineers was printed with his report and journal account for 1835. His journal is one of the earliest "scientific descriptions" of the region. His record of his march up the St. Peter's to its source includes much detailed description of the landscape, as, for example, ". . . the stream is about one hundred yards broad, and runs for some distance through low, well-wooded banks, forming a very pleasing country. About twelve miles up the river, the slopes are covered with large boulders, near which the river narrows . . . and gradually becomes shallow, its sandy bed being covered with very beautiful unios of various species, the beaks of which were not at all decorticated. . . ."[33]

During the summer of 1835 Colonel Henry Dodge made a comprehensive reconnaissance of the "Indian Frontier," the area of the plains between Fort Leavenworth and the Rocky Mountains (Figure 11).[34] Dodge's journal report includes much landscape description; for example, on July 28 he recorded:

> From this we ascended one of the peaks to the distance of about a mile above the plain. From the top of this we had a beautiful and extensive view of the country for many miles; we saw the timber upon the Arkansas and the Platte, and a large extent of waving prairie

---

Prairie, an Elevated Ridge Dividing the Missouri from the St. Peter's River, by G. W. Featherstonhaugh, U.S. Geologist," 24th Congress, 1st Session, *Senate Executive Doc. 333*, Serial 282 (Washington, 1836), pp. 1–168. See also "A Report of the Mineralogical and Geological Investigations Made by [Featherstonhaugh]," 23rd Congress, 2nd Session, *Senate Executive Doc. 153*, Serial 269 (Washington, 1835), pp. 1–43, for his earlier reconnaissance. As for Featherstonhaugh's geological analyses see George P. Merrill, "Contributions to the History of American Geology," *U.S. National Museum Annual Report for 1904* (Washington, 1906), pp. 323–325. Merrill remarked that it was "about as much worthless rubbish as could be put together."

33 The quotation is from "Report of a Geological Reconnoissance," p. 145. In his "Report from the Topographical Bureau, Washington, November 2, 1835 to Lewis Cass, Secretary of War," in "Message from the President of the United States," 24th Congress, 1st Session, *House Executive Doc. 333*, Serial 282 (Washington, 1835), p. 218, John J. Abert says: ". . . but he [Featherstonhaugh] has to contend with the difficulties of an unknown and Wilderness country, and in a climate affected early in the season with the inclement weather of winter. . . ."

34 "Journal of the March of a Detachment of Dragoons, under Command of Colonel Dodge, during the Summer of 1835," in "Report of the Secretary of War, dated February 27, 1836," 24th Congress, 1st Session, *House Doc. 181*, Serial 289 (Washington, 1836), pp. 1–37.

> country lying between the two rivers. To the right, at an immense distance we could see the feathery and indistinct outline of the Spanish peaks just rising above the visible horizon; while in our rear there lay a long succession of high ranges of mountains, until the snowy summits of the last and highest appeared to meet and mingle with the clouds. Nature appears to have thrown aside her wild and sportive mood, and to have given to the whole scene her deepest impress of grandeur and sublimity. . . .[35]

One of the important and valuable land surveys, topographical maps, and detailed descriptions of the landscape was that made by the French topographer-geodesist, Joseph Nicolas Nicollet, whose explorations of the extensive Missouri River drainage basin during 1836–40 were made for the U.S. Topographical Bureau (1838–43).[36] A significant product of his surveys were two large maps of the region; the one on a smaller scale (1:1,200,000) is published with his report (Figure 12).[37] In his lengthy report and journal he described the prairie at length.

> . . . and, finally, to reach the vast interminable low prairie that extends itself in front,—be it for hours, days, or weeks, one never tires . . . so vast is the extent which the eye takes in; a far-spreading verdure,

35 *Ibid.*, p. 22.

36 For biographical notes on this important scientist of the nineteenth century see Ruth A. Gallaher, "J. N. Nicollet, Map Maker," *The Palimpsest*, XXVI (1945), 289–302; A. Quetelet, "Joseph Nicolas Nicollet, 1786–1843," *Academie Royale des Sciences, des Lettres . . . Belgique, Annuaries*, X (1844), 133–137; N. H. Winchell, "Joseph Nicolas Nicollet, 1786–1843," *American Geologist*, VIII (1891), 343–352; "Joseph Nicolas Nicollet, 1786–1843," *Association of American Geologists and Naturalists, Report for 1840–42* (Boston: the Association, 1843), pp. 32–34; and Martha Coleman Bray, "Joseph Nicolas Nicollet, Geographer," in John Francis McDermott, ed., *Frenchmen and French Ways in the Mississippi Valley* (Urbana: University of Illinois Press, 1969), pp. 29–55. Most of Nicollet's manuscripts are in the National Archives and the Manuscript Division in the Library of Congress.

37 "Report Intended to Illustrate a Map of the Hydrographical Basin of the Upper Mississippi River, Made by I. [*sic*] N. Nicollet, While in Employ under the Bureau of the Corps of Topographical Engineers," 26th Congress, 2nd Session, *Senate Doc. 237*, Serial 380 (Washington, 1843), pp. 1–237. A copy of the same report is *House Doc. 52*, Serial 464, pp. 1–170, with map. See also J. N. Nicollet, "Some . . . Remarks upon the Geology of the Region of the Upper Mississippi, and the Cretaceous Formation of the Upper Mississippi," *Association of American Geologists and Naturalists, Report for 1843* (Boston: the Association, 1850), pp. 32–34; and his article "[Nicollet] Exhibited His Original Map of the Northwestern Territory of the United States, Made from Personal Observations, and Read an Account of His Geographical Exploration of the Sources of the Mississippi," *Proceedings of the American Philosophical Society*, III (1843), 140–142.

> relieved by a profusion of variously colored flowers; the azure of the sky above, or the tempest that can be seen from its beginning to its end; the beautiful modifications of the changing clouds. . . . In the summer season, especially, everything upon the prairies is cheerful, graceful, and animated. . . .[38]

The report is filled with a wealth of information about the physical and cultural features of the landscape by a scientist with a keen sense for analytical description.

The Period 1842–49

This was the short decade during which the United States extended its area to the Pacific Coast and marked its southwestern boundary to the western sea (Figure 13).[39] Significantly, it was a period during which the federal government interlaced the American West with a wide variety and a large number of military and scientific exploring expeditions. One of the most important products of these reconnaissances were the journals, reports, and similar records of on-the-spot observations of a landscape still so little tarnished with the changes of "modern man."[40] Many of these expeditions included scientists,

38 "Report Intended to Illustrate a Map," p. 52.

39 Charles Oscar Paullin and John K. Wright, eds., *Atlas of the Historical Geography of the United States* (Washington, D.C., and New York: Carnegie Institution and the American Geographical Society, 1932).

40 For examples of helpful secondary sources see Roland H. Alden and John D. Ifft, "Early Naturalists in the Far West," *California Academy of Sciences, Occasional Papers*, XX (1943), 1–59; Frederick Brendel, "Historical Sketch of the Science of Botany in North America, 1840–1858," *American Naturalist*, XIV (1880), 25–38; Samuel F. Emmons, "The Geology of Government Explorations," *Science*, n.s., V (1897), 1–15, 42–51, 105–106; Kate L. Gregg, *The Road to Santa Fe, the Journal and Diaries of George C. Sibley and Others* (Albuquerque: University of New Mexico Press, 1952); Amos W. Hartman, "The California and Oregon Trail, 1849–1860," *Oregon Historical Quarterly*, XXV (1924), 1–35; William J. Heffernam, *Edward M. Kern, the Travels of an Artist-Explorer* (Bakersfield, Calif.: Kern County Historical Society, 1953); Robert V. Hine, *Edward Kern and American Expansion* (New Haven, Conn.: Yale University Press, 1962); William T. Jackson, *Wagon Roads West: A Study of Federal Road Surveys and Construction in the Trans-Mississippi West, 1846–1896* (Berkeley: University of California Press, 1952); Rogers McVaugh, *Edward Palmer, Plant Explorer of the American West* (Norman: University of Oklahoma Press, 1956); Donald W. Meinig, "The Mormon Culture Region: Strategies and Patterns in the Geography of the American West," *Association of American Geographers, Annals*, LV (1965), 191–220; and Ellen C. Semple, *American History and Its Geographic Conditions* (Boston: Houghton Mifflin Co., 1933), a fundamental source.

geologists, geographers, botanists, zoologists, and others whose remarkable talents of observation have left us a priceless record of a natural landscape little modified by man. Let us review several of those that were published as Congressional Documents.

One of the most important and remarkable explorers of this period was John Charles Frémont, whose passion for geographical observation and analysis has left an invaluable heritage. He was the leader of three expeditions that surveyed much of the West during this period. With the published report and journal of his first expedition, in the country lying between the Missouri River and the Rocky Mountains, is a relief map of the region on a scale of 1:1,000,000 (Figure 14).[41]

With Frémont's published report and journal are some five lithographic illustrations, simple, perhaps even crude, and among the first to appear in the Congressional Documents. These sketches, possibly

---

For examples of contemporary published guidebooks, geographies, and similar references based to a large extent on government sources see Philip St. G. Cooke, *Scenes and Adventures in the Army: Or, Romance of Military Life* (Philadelphia: Lindsay and Blakiston, 1859); Edmund Dana, *Geographical Sketches on the Western Country* (Cincinnati: Looker, Reynolds and Co., 1819); William Darby, *The Emigrant's Guide to the Western and Southwestern States and Territories* (New York: Kirk and Mercein, 1818); Timothy Flint, *A Condensed Geography and History of the Western States, or the Mississippi Valley* (2 vols., Cincinnati: E. H. Flint, 1828); James Hall, *Notes on the Western States; Containing Descriptive Sketches of Their Soil, Climate, Resources, and Scenery* (Philadelphia: H. Hall, 1838); Lanford W. Hastings, *The Emigrants Guide to Oregon and California . . . Reproduced in Facsimile from the Original Edition of 1845* (Princeton, N.J.: Princeton University Press, 1932); Ethan A. Hitchcock, *A Traveler in Indian Territory; the Journal of Ethan Allen Hitchcock, Late Major General in the United States Army* (Cedar Rapids, Ia.: Torch Press, 1930); Fitz Hugh Ludlow, *The Heart of the Continent; a Record of Travel across the Plains and in Oregon* (Cambridge: Riverside Press, 1870); and Randolph B. Marcy, *The Prairie Traveler. A Hand-book for Overland Expeditions* (New York: Harper and Brothers, 1859).

41 "A Report on an Exploration of the Country Lying between the Missouri River and the Rocky Mountains, on the Line of the Kansas and Great Platte Rivers," from John C. Frémont to John J. Abert, Chief of the Corps of Topographical Engineers, dated Washington, March 1, 1843, in "Report from the Secretary of War," 27th Congress, 3rd Session, *Senate Doc. 243*, Serial 416 (Washington, 1843), pp. 1–207. See also in 28th Congress, 2nd Session, *House Executive Doc. 166*, Serial 467 (Washington, 1845), pp. 7–101, and in *Senate Doc. 174*, Serial 461, pp. 7–101, same Congress and Session. For non-government publications see John Charles Frémont, *Narrative of the Exploring Expedition to the Rocky Mountains in the Year 1842, and to Oregon and North California in the Years 1843–44* (New York: A. S. Barnes and Co., 1848); and his *The Exploring Expedition to the Rocky Mountains, Oregon and California; to Which Is Added a Description of the Physical Geography of California* (Buffalo, N.Y.: Miller, Orton and Mulligan, 1854). Dr. Donald Jackson is preparing a definitive edition of Frémont's publications and manuscripts.

by the German topographer of the expedition, Charles Preuss, include a view of Fort Laramie in July, 1842 (Figure 15). In his entry for July 16, 1842, Frémont records a vivid detailed description of the fort and vicinity, which reads in part: "I walked up to visit our friends at the fort, which is a quadrangular structure, built of clay, after the fashion of the Mexicans. . . . The walls are about fifteen feet high, surmounted with a wooden palisade, and form a portion of ranges of houses, which entirely surround a yard of about one hundred and thirty feet square. Every apartment has its door and window, all, of course, opening on the inside. . . . ."[42] Here is one of the best contemporary descriptions of this fort and its environs that straddled so important a site on the path of migration to the West over which so many travelers moved in their relentless trek to the dreamed-of El Dorado.[43]

During 1843 and 1844 Frémont extended his surveys from the Rocky Mountains to Oregon and California.[44] He pioneered the surveying and mapping of much of the Oregon Trail and defined and described with surprising clarity and accuracy the primary physiographic regions of our American West. Accompanying his report are several maps; one of them, of the Great Salt Lake, on a scale of 1:1,000,000, shows not only the primary physiographic features but the triangulations for mapping, and "original" toponymics (Figure 16).[45]

Farther west near the base of the Sierra Nevada Mountains in present-day Nevada, Frémont discovered a large playa lake (Figure 17). In his journal entry for January 13, 1884, he remarked that "we encamped on the shore, opposite a very remarkable rock in the lake, which had attracted our attention for many miles. It rose, according to our estimate, 600 feet above the water; and from the point we

42 "A Report on an Exploration," p. 36.

43 Ralph H. Brown, "Trans-Montane Routes in Colorado," *Economic Geography*, IV (1930), 412–424; Edmund W. Gilbert, "South Pass: A Study in the Historical Geography of the United States," *Scottish Geographical Magazine*, XLV (1929), 144–154; and LeRoy R. Hafen, *Fort Laramie and the Pageant of the West, 1834–1890* (Glendale, Calif.: Arthur H. Clark, 1938).

44 "A Report of the Exploring Expedition to Oregon and North California in the years 1843–'44, by Brevet Capt. J. C. Fremont," 28th Congress, 2nd Session, *House Executive Doc. 166*, Serial 467 (Washington, 1845), pp. 103–583. See also the same report in *Senate Doc. 174*, Serial 461, pp. 1–693, same Congress and Session.

45 *Ibid.* (Serial 467), map opp. p. 154.

viewed it, presented a pretty exact outline of the great pyramid of Cheops. The accompanying drawing presents it as we saw it. . . . This striking feature suggested a name for the lake; and I called it Pyramid Lake. . . ."[46]

James W. Abert's reconnaissances and topographic delineations of the little-explored regions of New Mexico in 1846–47 were described in elegant detail in his journal account.[47] His journal, published as a Congressional Document, is liberally illustrated with excellent lithographic reproductions, possibly of his own sketches, as for example of the Indian settlement of Acoma No. 1 perched high atop a large mesa-like feature in the headwaters of the Río de San José west of Albuquerque (Figure 18). He described this remarkable feature in part when he viewed it on October 21, 1846: "After a journey of 15 miles we arrived at 'Acoma'. High on a lofty rock of sandstone such as I have described sits the city of 'Acoma'. On the northern side of the rock, the rude boreal blasts have heaped up the sand, so as to form a practical ascent for some distance; the rest of the way is through solid rock. . . ."[48]

Early in 1849 Howard Stansbury of the Topographical Engineers was ordered on an expedition to survey accurately the Great Salt Lake and to explore its valley. His report and journal must rank with the major contributions to our objective knowledge of our West at mid-century. His account gave the large number of travelers west a reliable source of terrain information in cartographic, textual, and graphic form.[49] His report is liberally illustrated with sketches of landscape,

46 *Ibid.*, p. 217.

47 "Report of Lieut. J. W. Abert of the Examination of New Mexico in the Years 1846–'47," 30th Congress, 1st Session, *House Executive Doc. 41*, Serial 517 (Washington, 1848), pp. 416–548. See also the same report in *Senate Executive Doc. 23*, Serial 506, pp. 1–132, same Congress and Session. In the Foreword to his report he notes that he became delirious and violently ill at Bent's Fort en route to New Mexico and was left "harassed with the thoughts of having come thus far, and having been stopped just as I was entering upon a field full of interest to the soldier, the archeologist, the historian and the naturalist. On the 26th of August I had recovered sufficiently to resume my diary; this, with a copy of Horace, a Greek testament, and my sketch book, served to make the hours of confinement pass pleasantly" (Serial 517, p. 419).

48 *Ibid.*, pp. 470–471.

49 "Exploration and Survey of the Valley of the Great Salt Lake of Utah, Including a Reconnaissance of a New Route through the Rocky Mountains, by Howard Stansbury, Captain Corps of Topographical Engineers, U.S. Army," 32nd Congress, Special Session, March, 1851, *Senate Executive Doc. 3*, Serial 608 (Philadelphia, 1852), pp. 1–487. In his preparation of Appendix C of this report, "Zoology," Professor Spencer F. Baird wrote:

botany, geology, zoology, and paleontological subjects. Stansbury's account of his first view (Figure 19) of the Great Salt Lake on August 27, 1849, is a good example of his writing. It includes in part the following comments: "Descending the pass through dense thickets of small oak-trees, we caught the first glimpse of the GREAT SALT LAKE, the long-desired object of our search, and which it had cost us so many weary steps to reach. A gleam of sunlight, reflected by the water, and a few floating, misty clouds, were all, however, that we could see of this famous spot, and we had to repress our enthusiasm for some more favourable moment. . . ."[50]

The Period 1850–61

Survey for the most practicable route for a railroad between the Mississippi River and the Pacific Ocean, development of a system of public and military roads between military bases, settlements, and mines, discovery of precious minerals in California, Colorado, Montana, and Idaho, migration of a continuous succession of Mormons to Utah Territory and of others to Oregon and California, and establishment of successful agricultural communities especially in the high Plains and in numerous oases in the West, required considerable exploration by the federal government (Figure 20).[51] One of the primary

"In fact, no Government expedition, since the days of Major Long's visit to the Missouri [in 1819–20], has ever presented such important additions to Natural History. Of the great advancement of geographical knowledge, the reports of the officers will speak for themselves" (p. 307).

50 *Ibid.*, p. 83.

51 For examples of publications by commercial publishers of journal and diary accounts see especially John R. Bartlett, *Personal Narrative of Explorations and Incidents in Texas, New Mexico, California, Sonora and Chihuahua* (2 vols., New York: D. Appleton and Co., 1854); Grant Foreman, *Marcy & the Gold Seekers; the Journal of Captain R. B. Marcy* (Norman: University of Oklahoma Press, 1939); Andrew B. Gray, *Survey of a Route on the 32nd Parallel for the Texas Western Railroad, 1854: The A. B. Gray Report* (Los Angeles: Westernlore Press, 1963); Gwinn H. Heap, *Central Route to the Pacific, from the Valley of the Mississippi to California* (Philadelphia: Lippincott, Grambo, and Co., 1854); John Mullan, *Miners and Travellers' Guide to Oregon, Washington . . . via the Missouri and Columbia Rivers* (New York: W. M. Franklin, 1865); and Nolie Mumey, *John Williams Gunnison (1812–1853), the Last of the Western Explorers: A History of the Survey through Colorado and Utah* (Denver: Artcraft Press, 1955).

Additional examples of official reports in the Congressional Documents are Osborne Cross, "A Report, in the Form of a Journal to the Quartermaster General, of the March of the Regiment of Mounted Riflemen to Oregon, from May 18 to October 1849," 31st

results were journals, diaries, correspondence, and reports by members of the expeditions. Many of these are in the National Archives.[52] Some have been published as Congressional Documents.

For example, William H. Emory's report and journal accounts, illustrations, and maps covering his survey of the United States and Mexican Boundary in 1854–55 comprise three numbers of the Congressional Serial Set.[53] Within the reports, journals, scientific appendices, and many black-and-white and color illustrations is a wealth of information about the landscape. Some of the illustrations are perspective landform sketches (Figure 21).

There is much information about Indian culture, as for example the account and illustrations of the Papagos by John Michler, Emory's assistant (Figure 22).[54]

> Nature supplies them [the Papagos] with numerous useful plants which grow spontaneously; from the suwarrow (Cereus Giganteus) and pitaya they make an excellent preserve by simply boiling the

---

Congress, 2nd Session, *Senate Doc. 1,* Serial 587 (Washington, 1850), pp. 126–231; George H. Derby, "A Report on the Tulare Valley," 32nd Congress, 1st Session, *Senate Executive Doc. 110,* Serial 621 (Washington, 1852), pp. 1–17; Randolph B. Marcy, "Report of an Expedition to the Sources of the Brazos and Big Witchita Rivers, during the Summer of 1854," 34th Congress, 1st Session, *Senate Executive Doc. 60,* Serial 821 (Washington, 1856), pp. 1–48; Randolph B. Marcy, "Exploration of the Red River of Louisiana in the Year 1852," 32nd Congress, 2nd Session, *Senate Executive Doc. 54,* Serial 666 (Washington, 1853), pp. 1–320; Gouverneur K. Warren, "Explorations in Nebraska [1855–57]," 35th Congress, 2nd Session, *Senate Executive Doc. 1,* Serial 975 (Washington, 1859), pp. 620–670; and Adolph Wislizenius, "Memoir of a Tour to Northern Mexico, Connected with Col. Doniphan's Expedition, in 1846 and 1847," 30th Congress, 1st Session, *Senate Miscellaneous Doc. 20,* Serial 511 (Washington, 1848), pp. 1–121.

For a brief review of the principal geographical and surveying and mapping activities of the American West during the period see Herman R. Friis, "The Image of the American West at Mid-Century (1840–60): A Product of Scientific Geographical Exploration by the United States Government," in John Francis McDermott, ed., *The Frontier Re-examined* (Urbana: University of Illinois Press, 1967), pp. 49–63.

52 In the National Archives see especially the Records of the Office of the Chief of Engineers (RG 77), the Records of the Boundary and Claims Commissions (RG 76), and the General Records of the Department of the Interior (RG 48).

53 "Report on the United States and Mexican Boundary Survey, Made under the Direction of the Secretary of the Interior, by William H. Emory, Major First Cavalry and United States Commissioner," 34th Congress, 1st Session, *Senate Executive Doc. 108,* Serial nos. 832–834 (3 vols., Washington, 1857–58). See also William H. Goetzmann, "The U.S. Mexican Boundary Survey, 1848–1853," *Southwestern History Quarterly,* LXII (1958), 164–190.

54 "Report on the United States and Mexican Boundary Survey," I (Serial 832), 101–125.

fruit down without sugar, and a candy of the same material. They collect from a low bush growing wild seeds called 'Chie', which are coated with a gummy substance. . . . The women are better dressed than most Indian women; they all wear skirts of manta or calico, covering the body from the hips down. . . .[55]

Many of the collections of stuffed animals, plants, minerals, and artifacts were examined, identified, and described in detail and with accompanying beautiful color lithographs in reports appended to the basic document by the leading scientists, specialists in the field. For example, Dr. Spencer Fullerton Baird's report on the birds collected includes a color lithographic rendering of three birds obtained in the Rio Grande valley of Texas, which is appended to Emory's report (Figure 23).[56]

The call for a transcontinental railroad between the Mississippi River and the Pacific, a whisper in the 1830's, a promise and a hope in the 1840's, became a national issue of formidable proportions by the early 1850's.[57] By now the question was not so much shall a railroad be constructed; rather, it was how and where. In 1853 Congress authorized the Secretary of War to undertake a systematic survey along each of four east-west routes to determine the best, most practicable route for a railroad (Figure 24). A fifth route was to be run in California. In order to achieve the prescribed goals the Secretary wisely established an Office of Explorations and Surveys. Operating out of this office were the field parties who periodically reported back to it with a wide variety of scientific, cartographic, and pictorial information. Here indeed was a remarkable account of the observations, records, and interpretations of so much of the geographic landscape of the West at mid-century.[58]

55 *Ibid.*, p. 123.

56 *Ibid.*, III (Serial 834), "Birds of the Boundary by Spencer F. Baird, Assistant Secretary of the Smithsonian Institution, with Notes by the Naturalists of the Survey," pp. 1–32, Plate 15.

57 Perhaps the best over-all reference is George L. Albright, *Official Explorations for Pacific Railroads* (Berkeley: University of California Press, 1921).

58 The *Reports of Explorations and Surveys to Ascertain the Most Practicable and Economic Route for a Railroad from the Mississippi River to the Pacific Ocean* are a bit of a bibliographic problem because they were published over a period of six years as Senate and House Documents comprising twelve (in thirteen) volumes. An excellent list of provenance is appended to Robert Taft, "The Pictorial Rcord of the Old West: XIV. Illustrations of the Pacific Survey Reports," *Kansas Historical Quarterly*, XIX (1951),

Selected portions of this large fund of information, often in the form of journal accounts, were published over a period of several years as a series of twelve volumes (in thirteen), surely one of the best, if not the best, single source of objective on-the-spot landscape description of our West during the 1850's. These publications comprise official documents of the House and of the Senate and so generally are readily available.[59] Many maps, profiles, and graphs accompany the documents, as for example the large-scale topographic "Map of Passes in the Sierra Nevada," compiled from field surveys in 1853 (Figure 25).[60]

Surely one of the most remarkable products of these surveys are the numerous black-and-white and sepia lithographic landscape, botanical, zoological, geological, anthropological, and other sketches that illuminate the volumes and elucidate the descriptions in the journal and narrative accounts (Figure 26). With these sketches are descriptive remarks such as A. W. Whipple's comments about the activities at Fort Smith, Arkansas, in 1853, on the eve of the reconnaissance party's departure from that site for its traverse across the West. "We arrived at Fort Smith on the 2d of July [1853]. . . . Nothing but the Quartermaster's stores from Philadelphia were wanting to enable us to proceed with the reconnaissance. While awaiting these, astronomical and meteorological observations were made, as a basis for future operations; and the geologist, the botanist, and the zoologist employed themselves in examining the surrounding country to obtain collections in their various departments. . . ."[61]

One of the more challenging, certainly pioneering, explorations

---

379–380. The Senate edition includes Serial nos. 758–768 and 992; the House edition includes Serial nos. 791–800 and 1054–55.

59 These and of course many of the other Congressional Serial volumes are available in designated depository libraries throughout the United States. For a list of these depositories as of August 1, 1960, see Schmeckebier and Eastin, eds., *Government Publications and Their Use* (see footnote 4), pp. 445–456.

60 Many of the manuscript compilations and a few of the field survey maps are with the General Records of the Department of the Interior (RG 48) in the National Archives. Not all of these were printed and included with the published volumes. Related materials will be found with the Records of the Office of the Chief of Engineers (RG 77) in the National Archives.

61 "Route Near the Thirty-fifth Parallel, under the Command of Lieut. A. W. Whipple, Topographical Engineers, in 1853 and 1854. Itinerary," 33rd Congress, 2nd Session, *Senate Executive Doc. 78*, III, Pt. 1, Serial 760 (Washington, 1854), p. 4.

of the 1850's was Joseph Christmas Ives's survey of the little-known Colorado River of the West.[62] His journal account includes much valuable information on the archeology and Indian culture of the region and is well illustrated with lithographic reproductions, as for example the "Interior of a Moquis House," which he visited on May 11, 1858 (Figure 27), noting in his journal: "Everything was clean and tide. . . . I noticed, among other things, a reed musical instrument with a bell-shaped end like a clarionet, and a pair of painted drum-sticks tipped with gaudy feathers. . . ."[63]

Surely one of the best contemporary sketches of the famous *U.S. Explorer*, a steamboat carried in parts by ship from the East Coast and assembled at the mouth of the Colorado by the expedition to "ascertain how far the [Colorado] river was navigable for steamboats," is the lithograph that illuminates the introduction to Ives's report (Figure 28).[64] But Ives was not convinced of the boat's practicability; he emphasized that "The transportation of the steamer was, to the parties concerned, a source of more trouble than profit. . . ."[65]

We have neither the time nor the space for a recitation of the accounts of the other expeditions in the 1850's, except one, the exploration by James Hervey Simpson across the Great Basin of Utah to Carson Valley in 1859. Simpson was commissioned to find a usable shortcut south of the treacherous Humboldt River route.[66] He succeeded and he described it in considerable and lively detail in a report submitted in 1861.[67] Unfortunately, the Civil War postponed its pub-

62 "Report upon the Colorado River of the West, Explored in 1857 and 1858 by Lieutenant Joseph C. Ives, Corps of Topographical Engineers, under the Direction of the Office of Explorations and Surveys," 36th Congress, 1st Session, *House Executive Doc. 90*, Serial 1058 (Washington, 1861), pp. 1–130.

63 *Ibid.*, p. 121, "Camp 93, Moquis pueblos, May 11, [1858]."

64 *Ibid.*, p. 21. Ives noted that "a boat of suitable construction had, therefore, to be built on the Atlantic coast and transported to San Francisco, and then to the mouth of the [Colorado] river . . . the kind offices of the agents of the Panama Railroad Company, and of the captains of the steamships on both the Atlantic and Pacific coasts, united to the careful supervision of Mr. Carroll, enabled the awkward mass of freight to reach San Francisco in safety by the first of October."

65 *Ibid.*

66 For an excellent account of the historical background see Dale L. Morgan, *The Humboldt, Highroad of the West* (New York: Farrar and Rinehart, 1943).

67 See the letter of Captain J. H. Simpson submitting a report to Col. J. J. Abert, Chief of the Corps of Topographical Engineers, dated Washington, February 5, 1861, in the Records of the Office of the Chief of Engineers, National Archives.

lication until 1876,[68] despite the urgings of Congress in 1865,[69] and then as a U.S. Engineer publication. With his comprehensive manuscript report and journal in the Records of the Office of the Chief of Engineers are the manuscript maps, illustrations, profiles, and graphs which were not published by Congress, though they were so intended. In the Foreword to his printed report he notes: "To Mr. von Beckh I am indebted for the original sketches of the scenery, and to Mr. John J. Young, of this city (Washington) for the very handsome manner in which they have been elaborated and perfected in the office for my report. . . ."[70]

They were responsible for the beautiful water-color sketch of "Carson Lake from the East, Sierra Nevada in Distance," which was one of the landscape sketches that were prepared to accompany Simpson's official report (Figure 29). In his journal he records: "June 6, Camp No. 31, North end of Carson Lake. We retrograde today in our course, southerly direction, and skirt the east shore of Carson Lake. Air balmy and throwing a blue veil over the near and distant mountains. The snowy peaks of the Sierra Nevada seen on our right; the water of Carson Lake beautifully blue; lake margined with rushes; the shores are covered with muscle shells; pelicans and other aquatic fowl a characteristic. . . ."[71]

It is of interest to note that on this expedition Simpson had several photographers and photographic apparatus but he considered the results a failure because "the camera is not adapted to distant scenery. . . ." He then emphasized that "In my judgment, the camera is not adapted to explorations in the field, a good artist, who can sketch readily and accurately, is much to be preferred."[72]

68 James Hervey Simpson, *Report of Explorations across Great Basin of Utah for Direct Wagon-Route from Camp Floyd to Genoa in Carson Valley, in 1859* (Washington, 1876). This is an Engineer Department publication.

69 *Journal of the House of Representatives of the United States: Being the First Session of the Thirty-ninth Congress; Begun and Held at the City of Washington, December 4, 1865*, Serial 1243 (Washington, 1866). Page 432 includes Mr. Garfield's resolution: "*Resolved*, that the Committee on Printing be directed to inquire into the expediency of publishing the report of exploration across the great basin of Utah to San Francisco in 1859 by Captain J. H. Simpson, of the corps of engineers."

70 Simpson, *Report of Explorations* (see footnote 68), p. 8.

71 *Ibid.*, p. 186.

72 *Ibid.* For an excellent study of the background of this intriguing subject see Robert Taft, *Photography and the American Scene; a Social History, 1839–1889* (New York: Macmillan, 1938).

In this brief space I have attempted to show by selective illustration and description the rich source of firsthand observation of successive physical and cultural landscapes of our West through time by qualified observers that appears in the published Congressional Documents. The footnotes have been expanded to include references to many of the works not included in this discussion. These are a substantial treasure trove that has been infrequently used. It is a resource that bears review for selective republication as primary studies of the changing landscapes of our American West, and as a generally available source of on-the-spot observations.

Descriptive List of Illustrations

FIGURE 1. "Principal Routes of Geographical Exploration in the United States Prior to 1803," by Herman R. Friis, on a U.S. Geological Survey base map of the United States. Scale 1:7,000,000. Dimensions 20 x 32 inches. Annotated printed map in color, National Archives (hereafter NA).

FIGURE 2. "Map Exhibiting All the New Discoveries in the Interior Parts of North America . . .," published in London with additions to 1802 by Aaron Arrowsmith. Scale approx. 1 inch to 70 miles. Dimensions 48½ x 57 inches. Printed map in color on paper. Reference Collection in the Cartographic Branch, NA.

FIGURE 3. Sketch map of the rivers of the Mississippi Valley. Copy by Herman R. Friis from printed reproduction of map in Colton Storm, "Lieutenant Armstrong's Expedition to the Missouri River 1790," *Mid-America,* XXV (1943), 180–188, from a copy in the Josiah Harmar Papers in the William L. Clements Library, Ann Arbor, Mich.

FIGURE 4. "Routes of Principal Geographical Exploration: 1803–1817," by Herman R. Friis, on a U.S. Geological Survey base map of the United States. Scale 1:7,000,000. Dimensions 20 x 32 inches. Annotated printed map in color, NA.

FIGURE 5. "A Map of part of the Continent of North America . . . Copied by Nicholas King. 1806." Scale approx. 1 inch to 35 miles. Dimensions 43⅛ x 30 inches. MS map in ink on paper. Records of the Office of the Chief of Engineers, Map Ama 21, NA.

FIGURE 6. "Map of the Red River in Louisiana from Natchitoches to the Coashatay Village. Protracted from the Courses and Distances given in Mr Thos Freeman's Journal of a Survey thereof made in June 1806, by Nich^{s} King." Scale 1 inch to 1 mile. Dimensions 33 x 101½ inches. MS map in ink and color on paper. Records of the Office of the Chief of Engineers, Map M 33–1, NA.

FIGURE 7. "Map of the Washita River in Louisiana . . . Laid down from the Journal and Survey of M[r] Dunbar, in the year 1804 by Nich[s] King." Scale 1 inch to 4 miles. Dimensions 39½ x 79½ inches. MS map in color on paper. Records of the Office of the Chief of Engineers, Map M 35, NA.

FIGURE 8. "Routes of Principal Geographical Exploration and for Trade 1818–1842," by Herman R. Friis, on a U.S. Geological Survey base map of the United States. Scale 1:7,000,000. Dimensions 20 x 32 inches. Annotated printed map in color, NA.

FIGURE 9. "Map of the Route passed over by an Expedition into the Indian Country in 1832 to the Source of the Mississippi by Lieut. J. Allen U.S. Inf." Scale 1 inch to 5¾ miles. Dimensions 15½ x 19 inches. Printed map in ink on paper. With Allen's report in 23rd Congress, 1st Session, *House Doc. 323*, Serial 257 (Washington, 1834), opp. p. 1, NA.

FIGURE 10. Map of "A Reconnoissance of the Minnay Sotor Watapah; or St. Peter's River, to its sources: Made in the Year 1835," by G. W. Featherstonhaugh. Scale 1 inch to 15 miles. Dimensions 34 x 17 inches. MS map in ink on paper. Records of the Office of the Chief of Engineers, Map Misc. 14–1, NA.

FIGURE 11. Relief map of "Western Territory" showing Indian reservations and land west of Missouri and Arkansas. Scale 1 inch to 20 miles. Dimensions 19½ x 32½ inches. Printed map on paper with color annotations. With Dodge's journal report in 24th Congress, 1st Session, *House Doc. 181*, Serial 289 (Washington, 1836), opp. p. 36, NA.

FIGURE 12. "Hydrographical Basin of the Upper Mississippi River . . . by J. N. Nicollet, in the years 1836, 37, 38, 39, and 40 . . ., 1843. Published by Order of the U.S. Senate." Scale 1:1,200,000. Dimensions 38 x 33 inches. Printed map in ink on paper. With Nicollet's report in 26th Congress, 2nd Session, *Senate Executive Doc. 237*, Serial 380 (Washington, 1843), opp. p. 96, NA. This is the northwest quadrant of the MS map in Records of the Office of the Chief of Engineers, US 131, NA.

FIGURE 13. "Routes of Principal Geographical Explorations and Roads and Traces: 1842–1849," by Herman R. Friis, on a U.S. Geological Survey base map of the United States. Scale 1:7,000,000. Dimensions 20 x 32 inches. Annotated printed map in color, NA.

FIGURE 14. "Map to Illustrate an Exploration of the Country, lying between the Missouri River and the Rocky Mountains, on the line of the Nebraska or Platte River [1842]. By Lieut. J. C. Fremont, of the Corps of Topographical Engineers." Scale 1:1,000,000. Dimensions 14½ x 33 inches. Printed map in color on paper. With Frémont's report in 27th Congress, 3rd Session, *Senate Doc. 243*, Serial 416 (Washington, 1843), opp. title page, NA.

FIGURE 15. "Fort Laramie." Lithographic engraving with color wash.

Dimensions 9 x 5½ inches. With document cited for Figure 14 above, opp. p. 36, NA.

FIGURE 16. Map of "The Great Salt-Lake." Scale 1:1,000,000. Dimensions 8½ x 5½ inches. Printed map in ink on paper. With Frémont's report in 28th Congress, 2nd Session, *House Executive Doc. 166*, Serial 467 (Washington, 1845), opp. p. 154, NA.

FIGURE 17. "The Pyramid Lake." Lithographic engraving. Dimensions 9 x 5½ inches. With document cited for Figure 16 above, opp. p. 217, NA.

FIGURE 18. "Acoma No. 1." Lithographic engraving in ink on paper. Dimensions 9 x 5½ inches. With Abert's report in 30th Congress, 1st Session, *House Executive Doc. 41*, Serial 517 (Washington, 1848), opp. p. 470, NA.

FIGURE 19. "First View of Great Salt Lake Valley, from a Mountain Pass." Lithographic engraving with color wash. Dimensions 9 x 5½ inches. With Stansbury's report in 32nd Congress, Special Session, March, 1851, *Senate Executive Doc. 3*, Serial 608 (Philadelphia, 1852), opp. p. 268, NA.

FIGURE 20. "Routes of Principal Geographical Explorations and Traces and Roads: 1850–1859," by Herman R. Friis, on a U.S. Geological Survey base map of the United States. Scale 1:7,000,000. Dimensions 20 x 32 inches. Annotated printed map in color, NA.

FIGURE 21. Landscape views 13 and 14. Lithographic engravings in black ink. Dimensions 11½ x 8¾ inches. With Emory's report in 34th Congress, 1st Session, *Senate Executive Doc. 108*, Serial nos. 832–834 (3 vols., Washington, 1857–58), I, on one plate following p. 100, NA.

FIGURE 22. "Papagos." Lithographic engraving in color. Dimensions 11½ x 8¾ inches. With document cited for Figure 21 above, I, opp. p. 122, NA.

FIGURE 23. "1. Lophophanes wollweberi. 2. Aegithalus flaviceps. 3. Psaltriparus melanotis." Lithographic engraving in color. Dimensions 11½ x 8¾ inches. With document cited for Figure 21 above, III ("Birds of the Boundary by Spencer F. Baird," Serial 834), Plate 15, NA.

FIGURE 24. "Principal Routes of Surveys and Explorations for a Railroad from the Mississippi River to the Pacific Ocean: 1853–1857," by Herman R. Friis, on a U.S. Geological Survey base map of the United States. Scale 1:7,000,000. Dimensions 20 x 32 inches. Annotated printed map in color, NA.

FIGURE 25. "Map of a Survey of the Passes in the Sierra Nevada . . . By Lieut. R. S. Williamson U.S. Top. Engrs . . . 1853. Drawn by Charles Preuss." Scale 1:240,000. Dimensions 34½ x 25¼ inches. MS map in ink and color on paper. Records of the Office of the Secretary of the Interior, Pacific Railroad Surveys, Routes in Southern California, NA.

FIGURE 26. "Fort Smith, Arkansas." Lithographic engraving in color. Dimensions 11½ x 9 inches. With Whipple's report in 33rd Congress, 2nd

Session, *Senate Executive Doc. 78,* III, Pt. 1, Serial 760 (Washington, 1854), opp. p. 5, NA.

FIGURE 27. "Interior of a Moquis House." Lithographic engraving in color. Dimensions 11 x 8½ inches. With document cited for Figure 26 above, opp. p. 121, NA.

FIGURE 28. "Steamboat *U.S. Explorer.*" Lithographic engraving in black and white. Dimensions 11½ x 8¾ inches. With Ives's report in 36th Congress, 1st Session, *House Executive Doc. 90,* Serial 1058 (Washington, 1861), frontispiece, NA.

FIGURE 29. "Carson Lake from the East, Sierra Nevada in Distance ... [By] J. J. Young from a Sketch by H. V. A. v. Beckh." In James Hervey Simpson, *Report of Explorations across Great Basin of Utah . . . 1859* (Washington, 1876), Plate IX. MS water-color sketch on paper. Dimensions 11½ x 24 inches. Records of the Office of the Chief of Engineers, No. Misc. 120–8, NA.

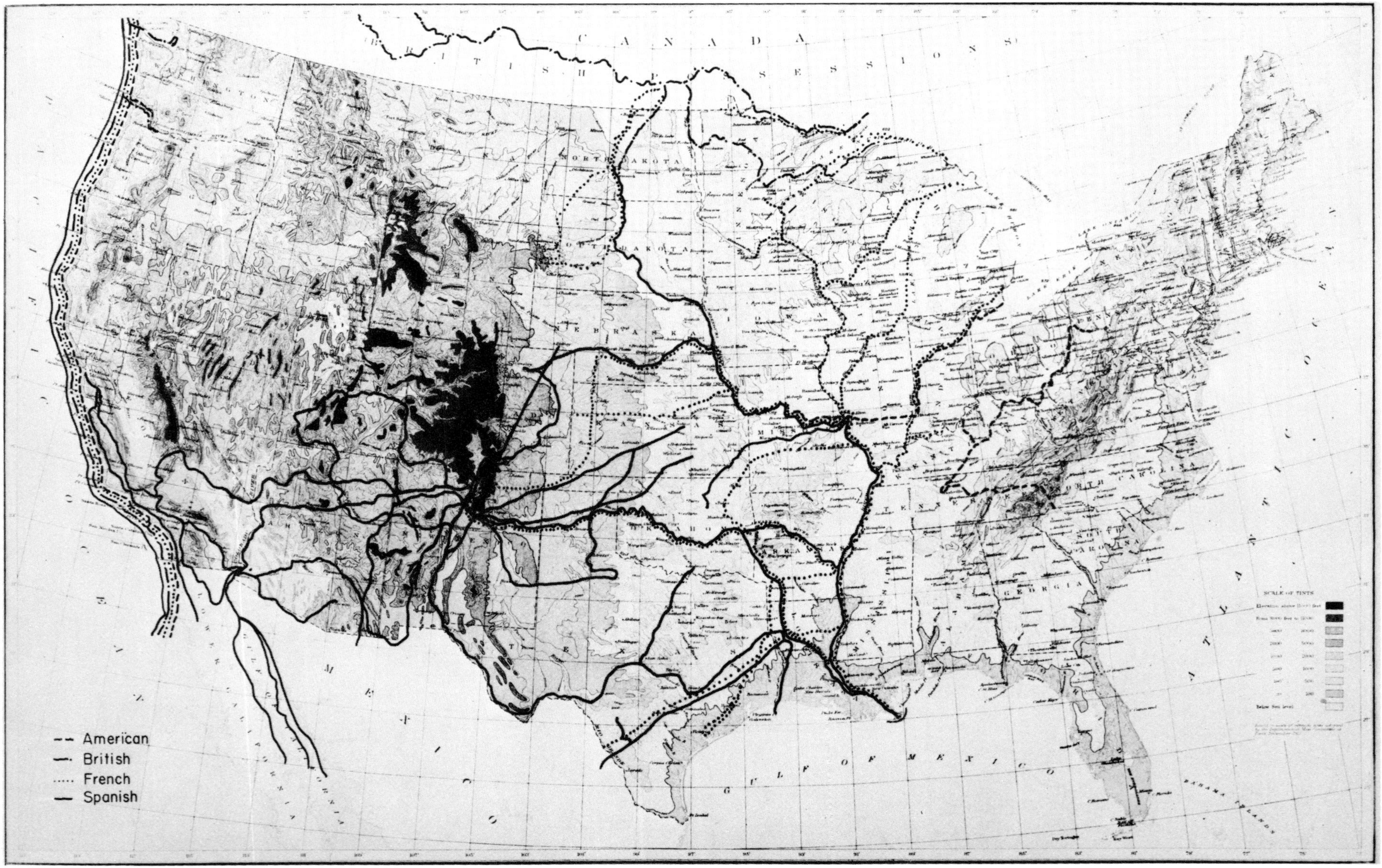

CANADA
(BRITISH POSSESSIONS)
NORTH DAKOTA
SOUTH DAKOTA
NEBRASKA
KANSAS
IOWA
TENNESSEE
NORTH CAROLINA
SOUTH CAROLINA
GEORGIA
GULF OF MEXICO
SCALE OF TINTS
Below Sea level
American
British
French
Spanish

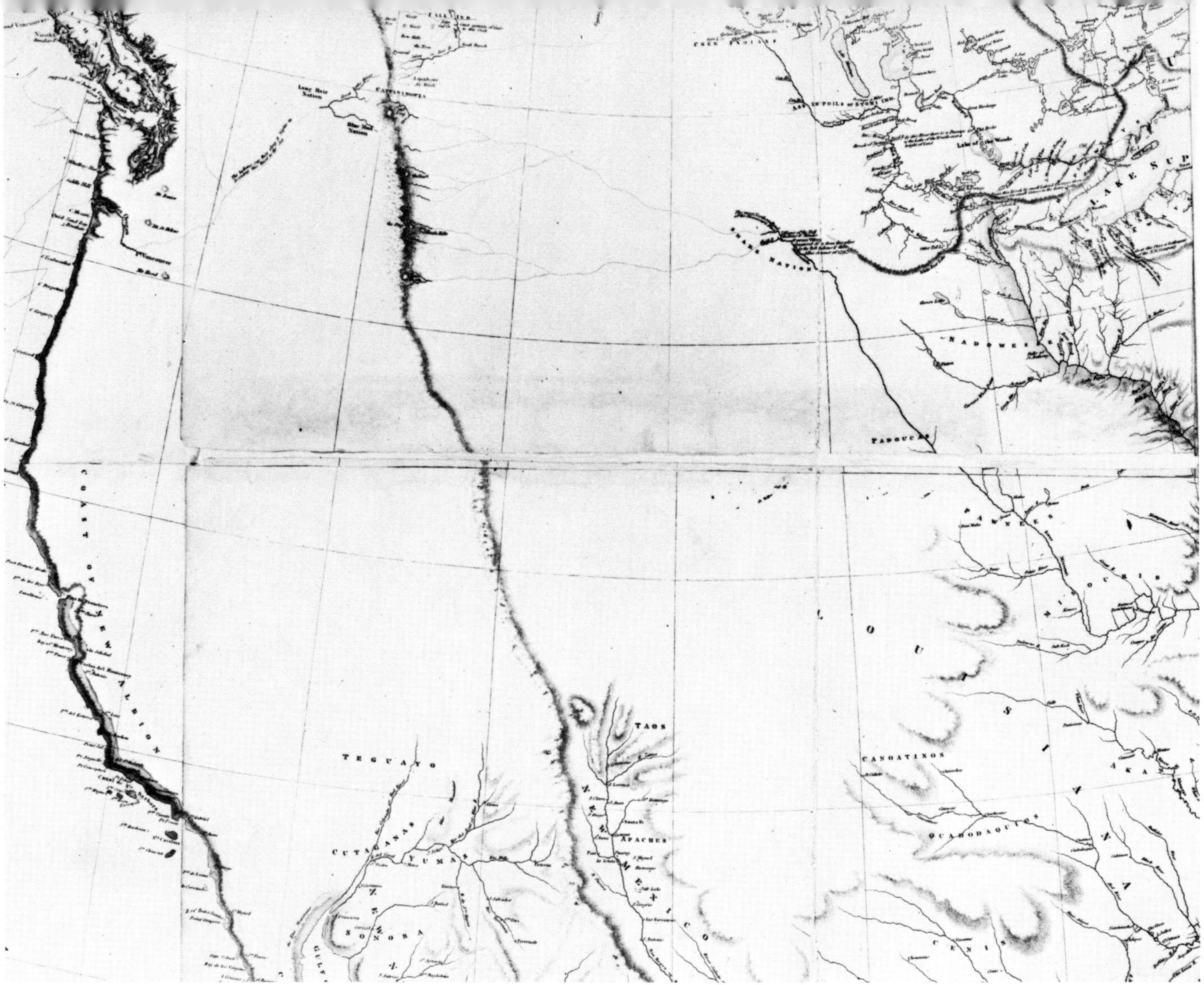
LAKE SUP
NADOWESSI
PADOUCAS
PAWNEES
MISSOURIS
CANOATINOS
QUADODAQUIOS
CENIS
TAOS
TEGUAYO
APACHES
NEW MEXICO
CUTAGANAS
YUMAS
NEW SONORA
COAST OF NEW ALBION
CREE INDIANS
SNAKE NATION

FIGURE 2

Missouri River
Sta Fe
Ohio
Gulf of Mexico
Del Norte
20 40 60
Leagues

FIGURE 3

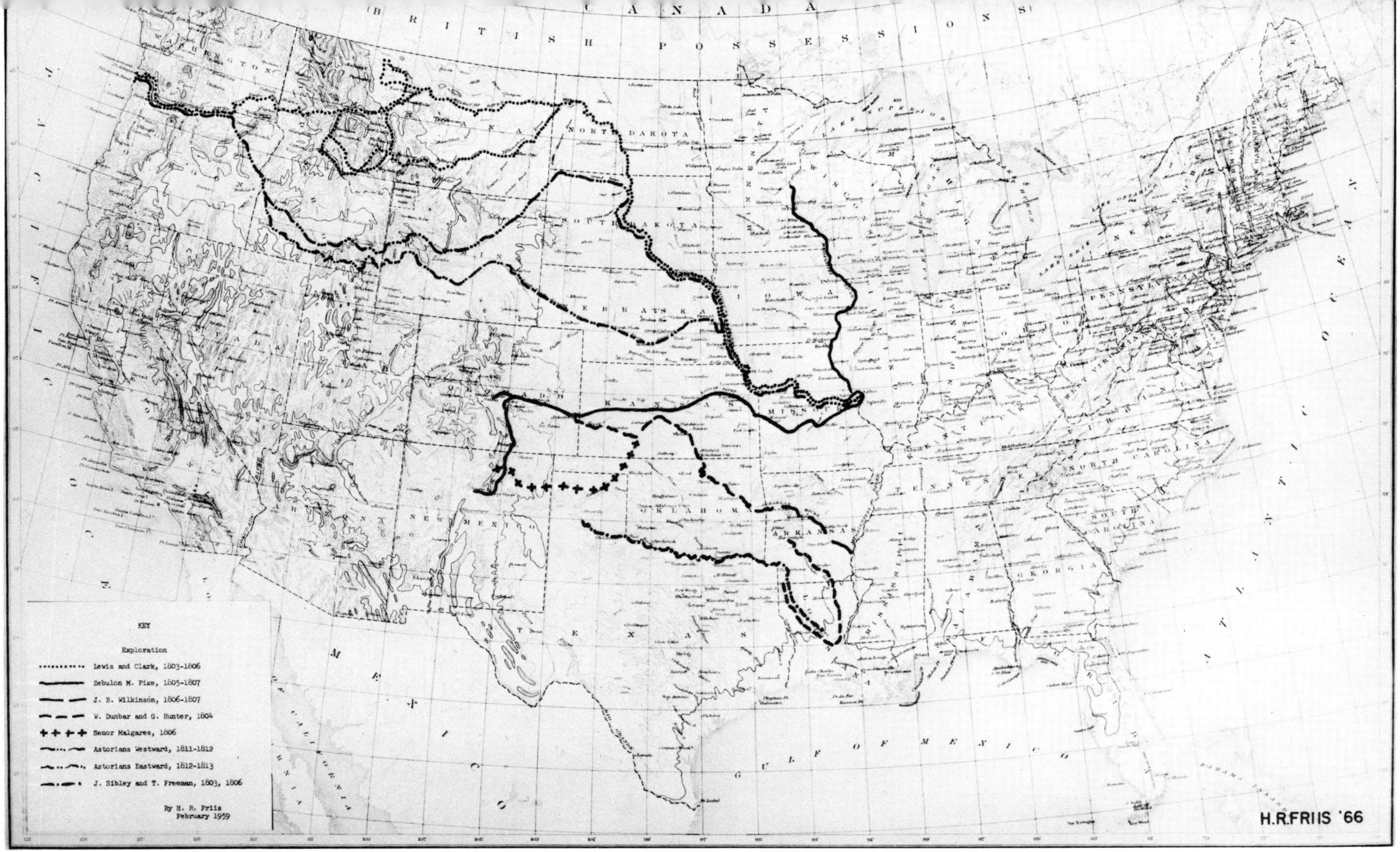
(BRITISH POSSESSIONS)
CANADA
NORTH DAKOTA
SOUTH DAKOTA
NEBRASKA
IOWA
KANSAS
OKLAHOMA
ARKANSAS
TEXAS
NEW MEXICO
GEORGIA
NORTH CAROLINA
SOUTH CAROLINA
GULF OF MEXICO
KEY
Exploration
Lewis and Clark, 1803-1806
Zebulon M. Pike, 1805-1807
J. B. Wilkinson, 1806-1807
W. Dunbar and G. Hunter, 1804
Senor Malgares, 1806
Astorians Westward, 1811-1812
Astorians Eastward, 1812-1813
J. Sibley and T. Freeman, 1803, 1806
By H. R. Friis
February 1959
H.R.FRIIS '66

FIGURE 4

A MAP
North America
LAKE MICHIGAN
LAKE SUPERIOR
LAKE WINNIPIC
NORTH PACIFIC OCEAN

[FIG]URE 6

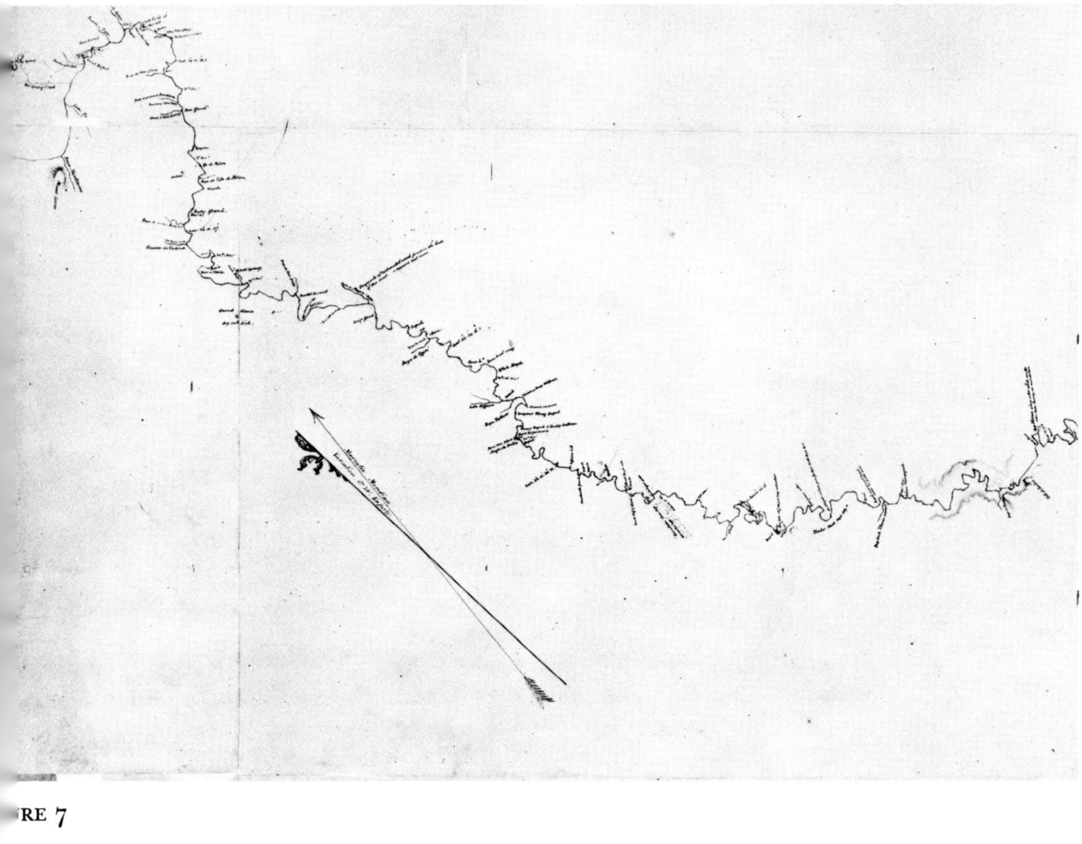

[FIG]URE 7

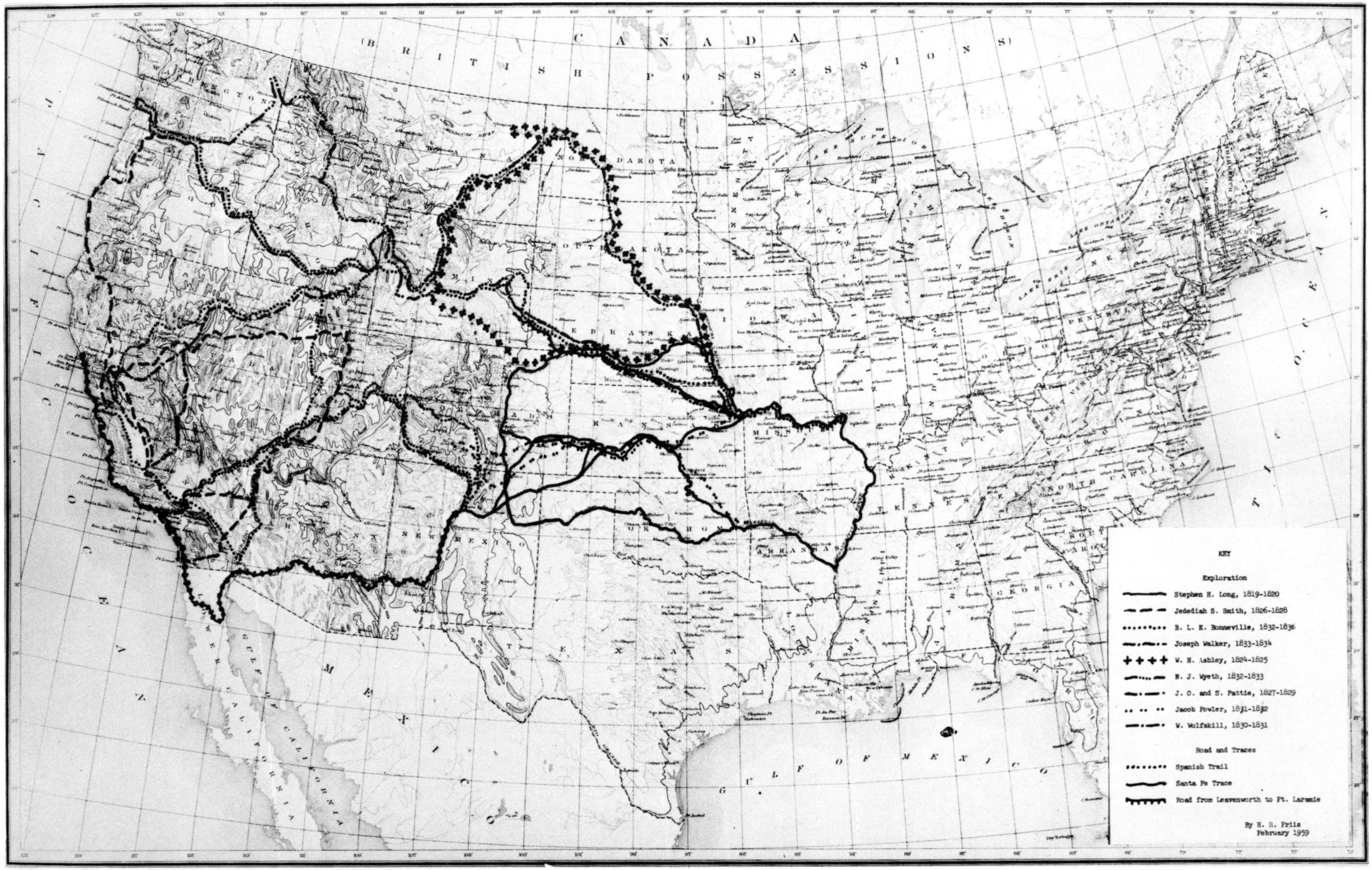

CANADA
(BRITISH POSSESSIONS)
PACIFIC OCEAN
ATLANTIC OCEAN
GULF OF MEXICO
MEXICO
GULF OF CALIFORNIA
LOWER CALIFORNIA
KEY
Exploration
Stephen H. Long, 1819-1820
Jedediah S. Smith, 1826-1828
B. L. E. Bonneville, 1832-1836
Joseph Walker, 1833-1834
W. H. Ashley, 1824-1825
N. J. Wyeth, 1832-1833
J. O. and S. Pattie, 1827-1829
Jacob Fowler, 1821-1822
W. Wolfskill, 1830-1831
Road and Traces
Spanish Trail
Santa Fe Trace
Road from Leavenworth to Ft. Laramie
By H. R. Friis
February 1959

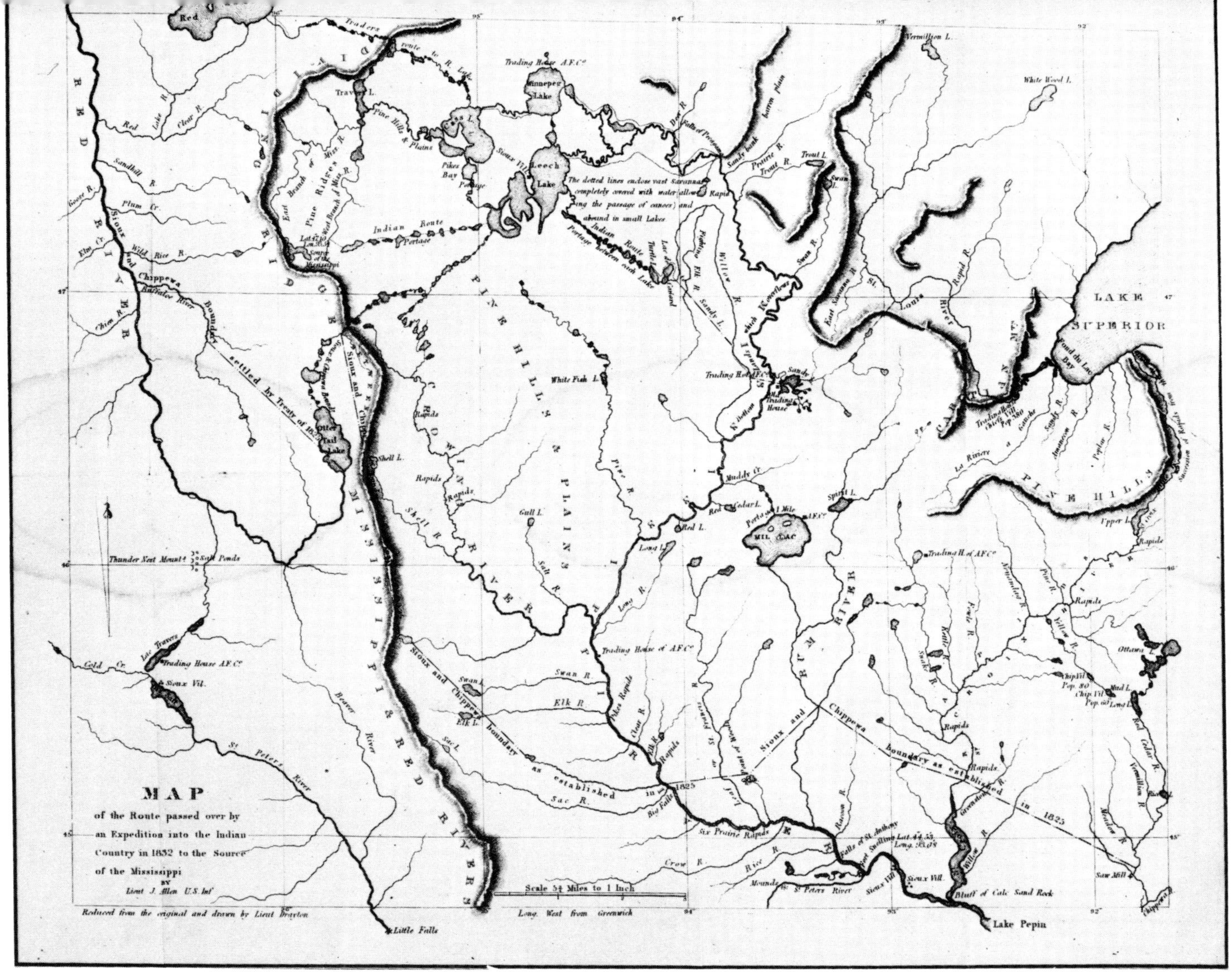
MAP
of the Route passed over by
an Expedition into the Indian
Country in 1832 to the Source
of the Mississippi
BY
Lieut J. Allen U.S. Inf
Reduced from the original and drawn by Lieut Drayton
Scale 5¼ Miles to 1 Inch
Long. West from Greenwich
LAKE SUPERIOR
Fond du Lac Bay
Leech Lake
Lake Pepin
Little Falls
MISSISSIPPI & RED RIVERS
PINE HILLS & PLAINS
Sioux and Chippewa boundary as established in 1825
The dotted lines enclose vast Savannas completely covered with water (allowing the passage of canoes) and abound in small Lakes

FIGURE 9

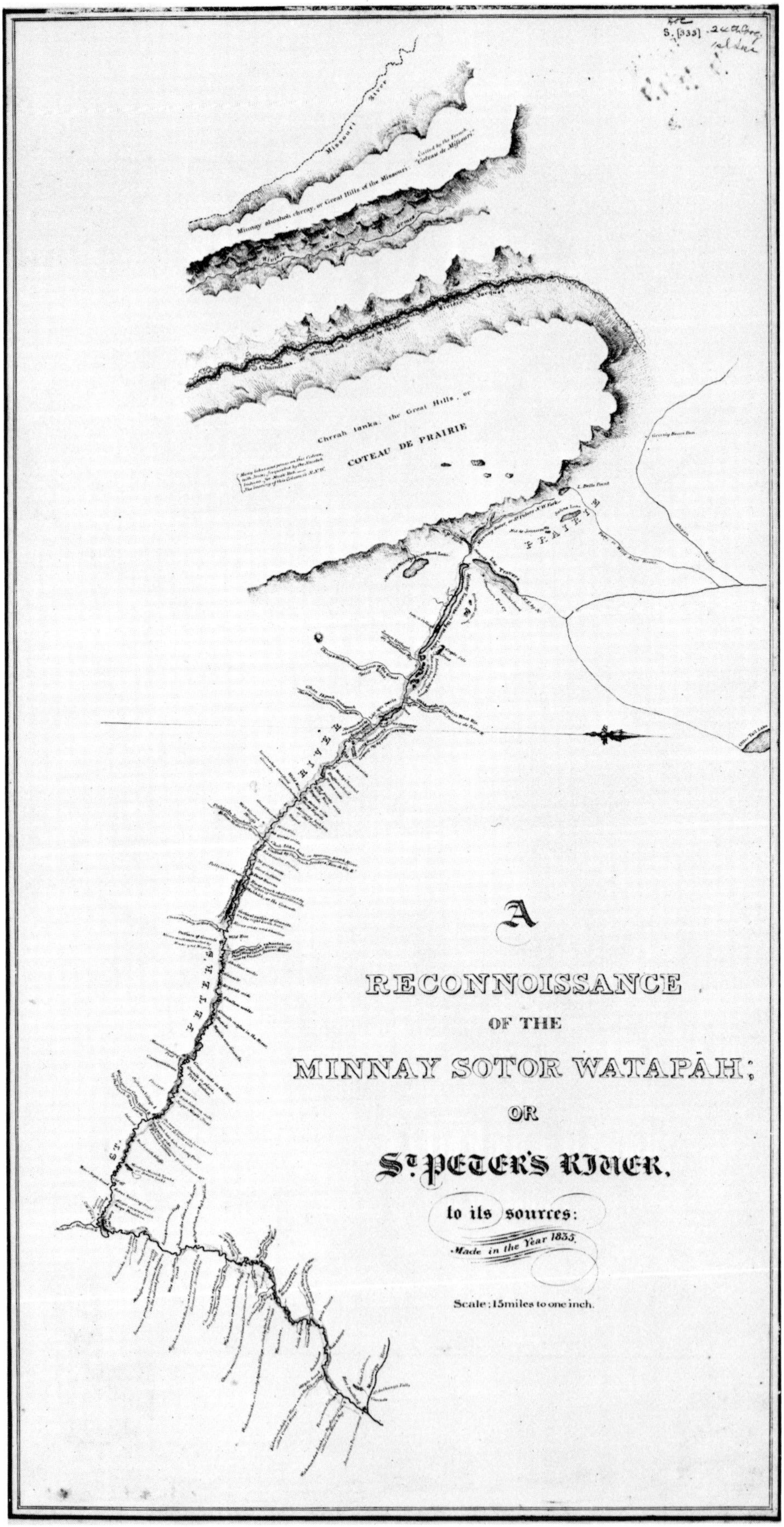

Minnay shoshoh chray, or Great Hills of the Missouri: Called by the French "Coteau de Missouri."
Missouri River
Chreah tanka, the Great Hills, or
COTEAU DE PRAIRIE
PRAIRIE
RIVER
ST. PETER'S
A
RECONNOISSANCE
OF THE
MINNAY SOTOR WATAPĀH;
OR
St. PETER'S RIVER,
to its sources:
Made in the Year 1835.
Scale: 15 miles to one inch.

FIGURE 10

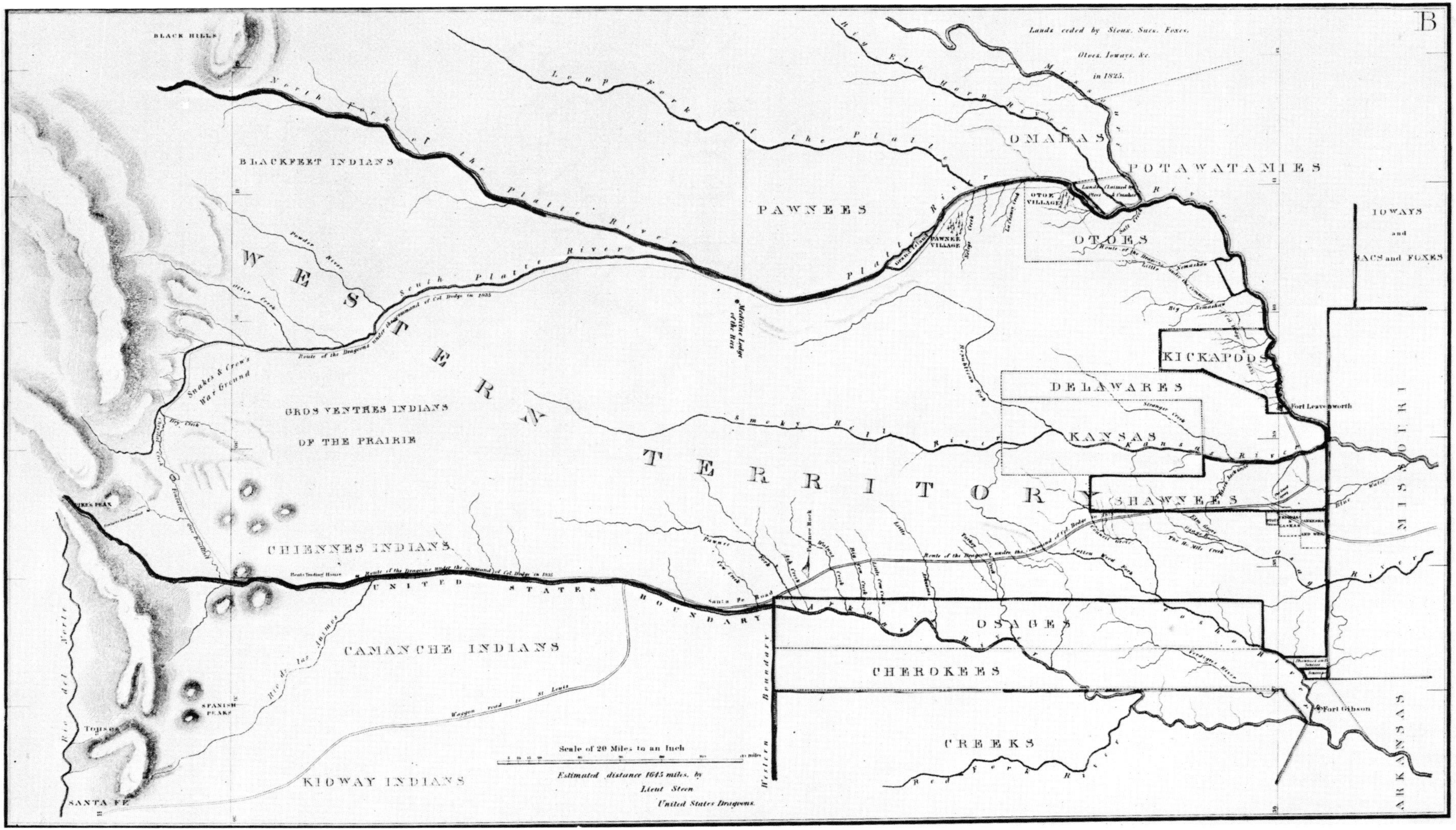
B
Lands ceded by Sioux, Sacs, Foxes, Otoes, Ioways, &c. in 1825.
BLACK HILLS
BLACKFEET INDIANS
PAWNEES
OMAHAS
POTAWATAMIES
IOWAYS and SACS and FOXES
OTOES
OTOE VILLAGE
PAWNEE VILLAGE
KICKAPOOS
DELAWARES
KANSAS
SHAWNEES
Fort Leavenworth
MISSOURI
WESTERN TERRITORY
GROS VENTRES INDIANS OF THE PRAIRIE
Snakes & Crows War Ground
Medicine Lodge of the Rees
CHIENNES INDIANS
UNITED STATES BOUNDARY
OSAGES
CHEROKEES
CREEKS
Fort Gibson
ARKANSAS
Western Boundary
CAMANCHE INDIANS
KIOWAY INDIANS
SPANISH PEAKS
PIKES PEAK
SANTA FE
Waggon road to St Louis
Scale of 20 Miles to an Inch
Estimated distance 1645 miles, by Lieut Steen United States Dragoons.

FIGURE 11

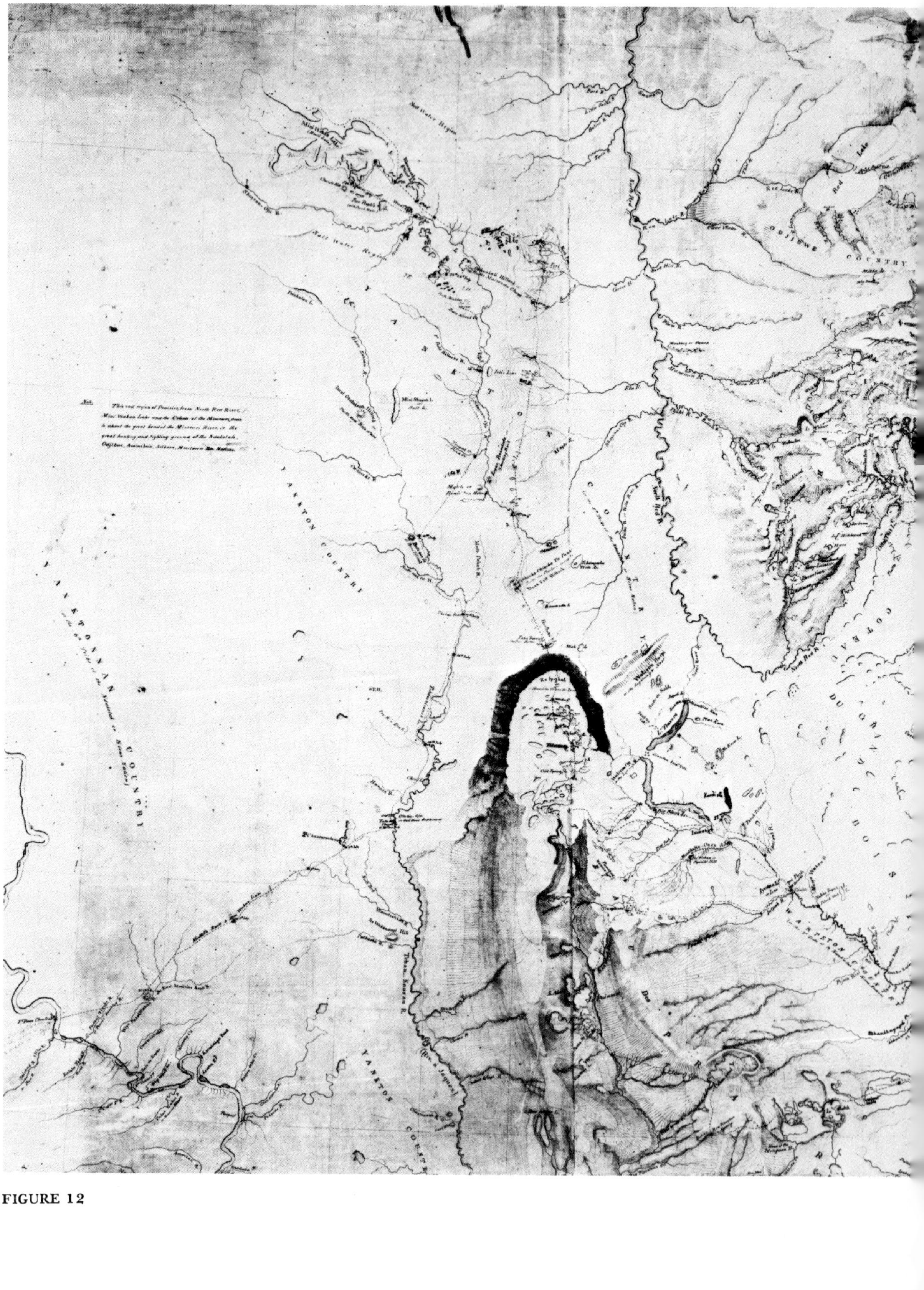

FIGURE 12

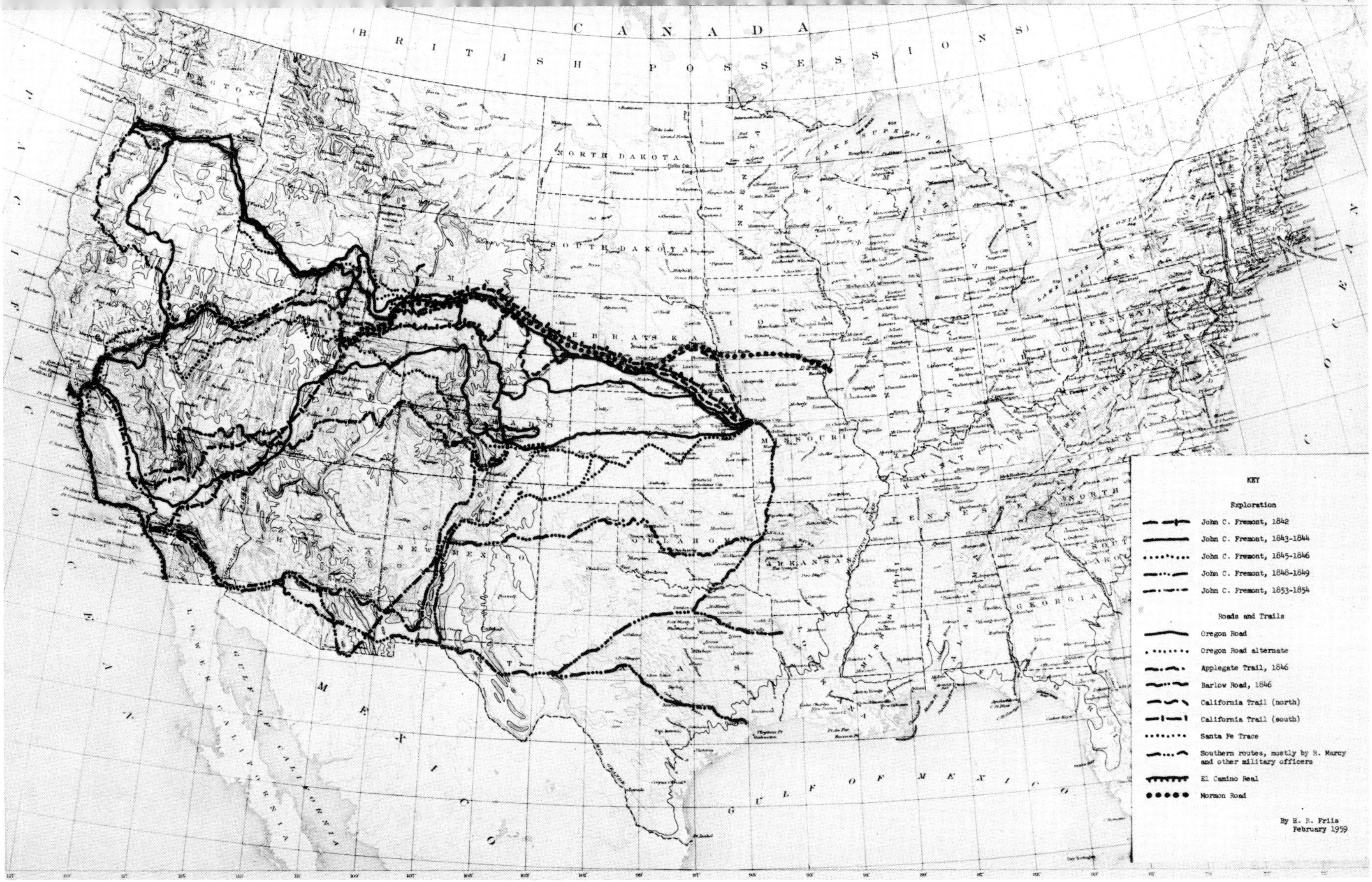
(BRITISH POSSESSIONS)
CANADA
NORTH DAKOTA
SOUTH DAKOTA
NEBRASKA
IOWA
MISSOURI
OKLAHOMA
ARKANSAS
NEW MEXICO
GEORGIA
PENNSYLVANIA
LAKE SUPERIOR
LAKE ERIE
LAKE ONTARIO
GULF OF MEXICO
GULF OF CALIFORNIA
LOWER CALIFORNIA
MEXICO
KEY
Exploration
John C. Fremont, 1842
John C. Fremont, 1843-1844
John C. Fremont, 1845-1846
John C. Fremont, 1848-1849
John C. Fremont, 1853-1854
Roads and Trails
Oregon Road
Oregon Road alternate
Applegate Trail, 1846
Barlow Road, 1846
California Trail (north)
California Trail (south)
Santa Fe Trace
Southern routes, mostly by R. Marcy and other military officers
El Camino Real
Mormon Road
By H. R. Friis
February 1959

FIGURE 13

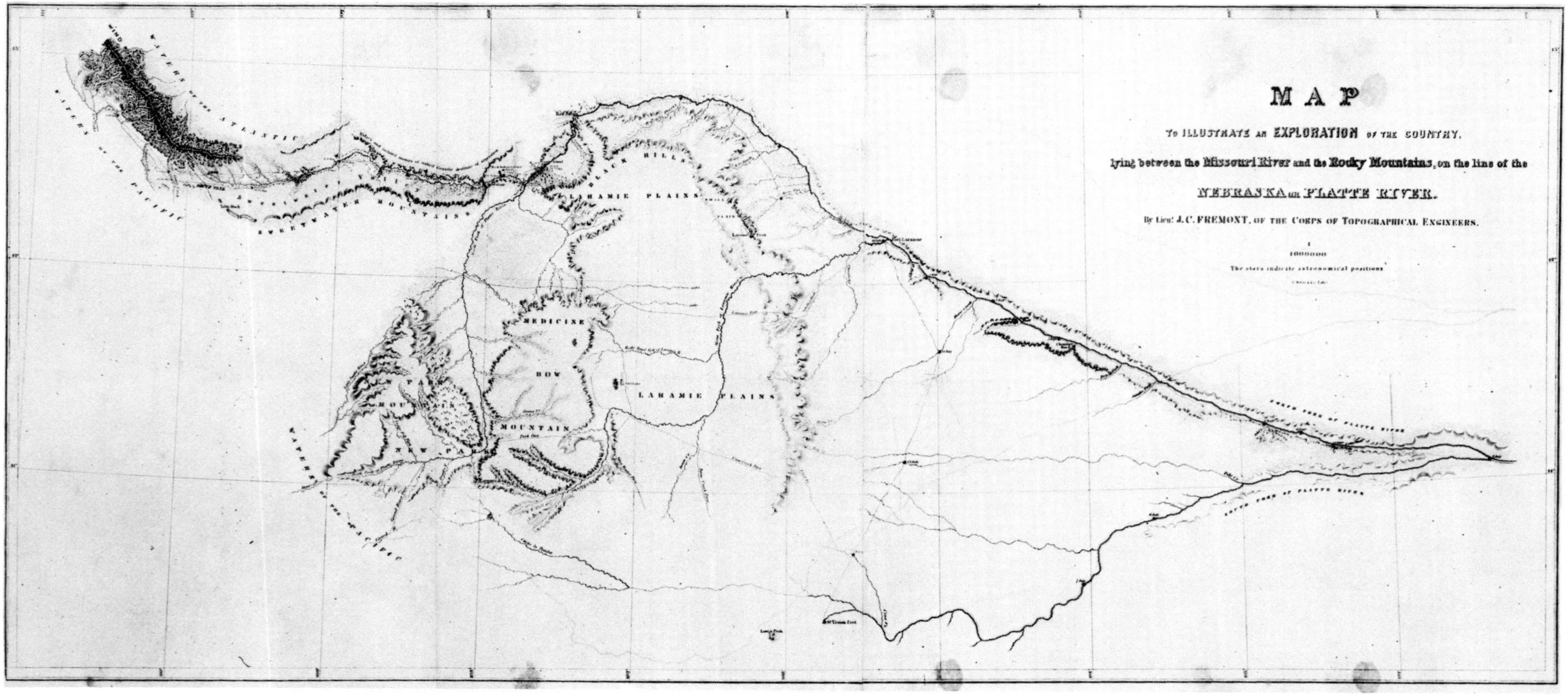
MAP
To ILLUSTRATE AN EXPLORATION OF THE COUNTRY,
lying between the Missouri River and the Rocky Mountains, on the line of the
NEBRASKA OR PLATTE RIVER.
By Lieut. J. C. FREMONT, OF THE CORPS OF TOPOGRAPHICAL ENGINEERS.
The stars indicate astronomical positions
WATERS OF THE ATLANTIC
WATERS OF THE PACIFIC
SWEETWATER MOUNTAINS
BLACK HILLS
LARAMIE PLAINS
MEDICINE
BOW
MOUNTAIN
LARAMIE PLAINS
NORTH FORK OF PLATTE RIVER
SOUTH FORK OF PLATTE RIVER

FIGURE 14

FIGURE 15

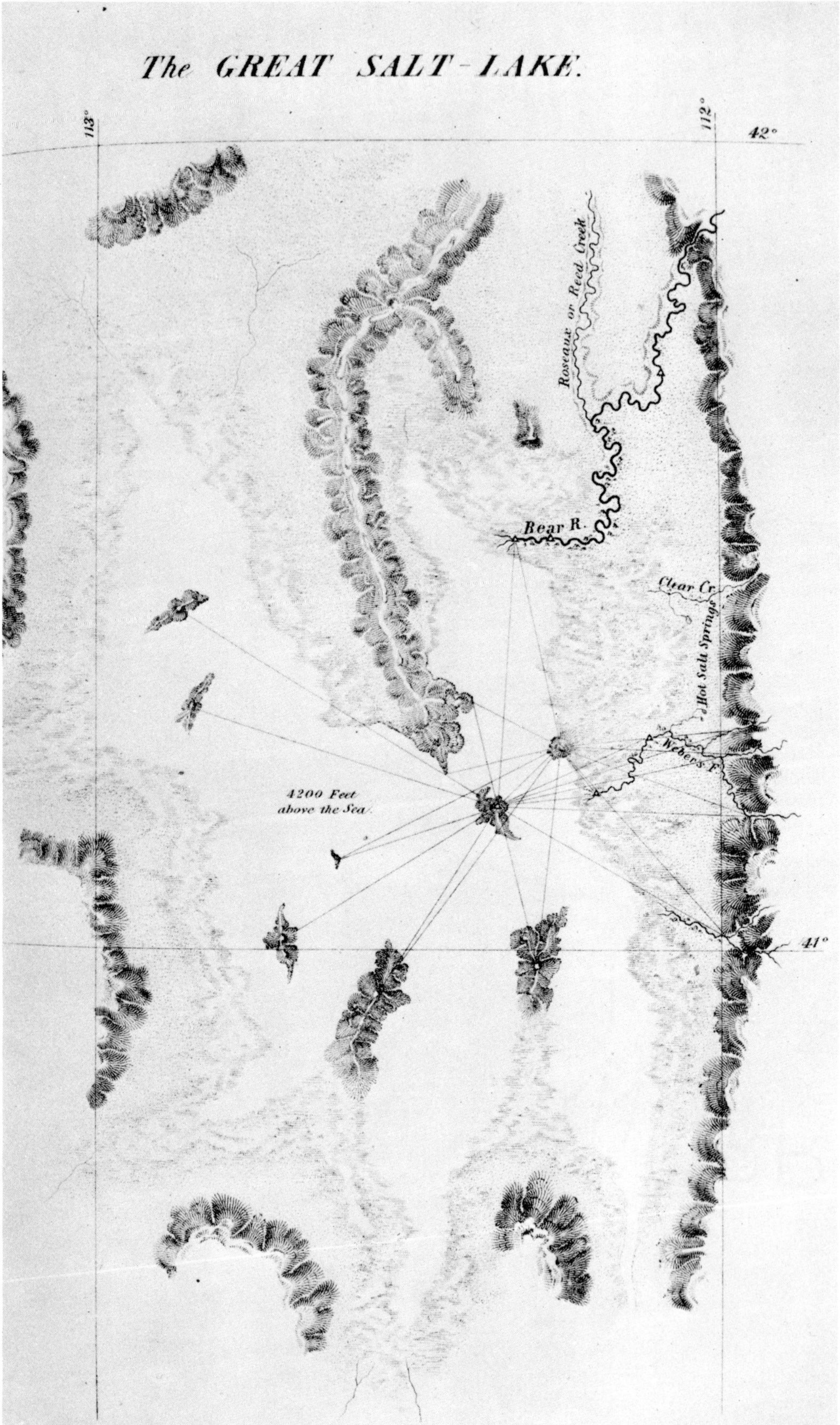
The GREAT SALT-LAKE.
113°
112°
42°
Roseaux or Reed Creek
Bear R.
Clear Cr.
Hot Salt Springs
Weber's F.
4200 Feet
above the Sea
41°
SCALE 1: 1000000.

FIGURE 16

FIGURE 17

FIGURE 18

FIGURE 19

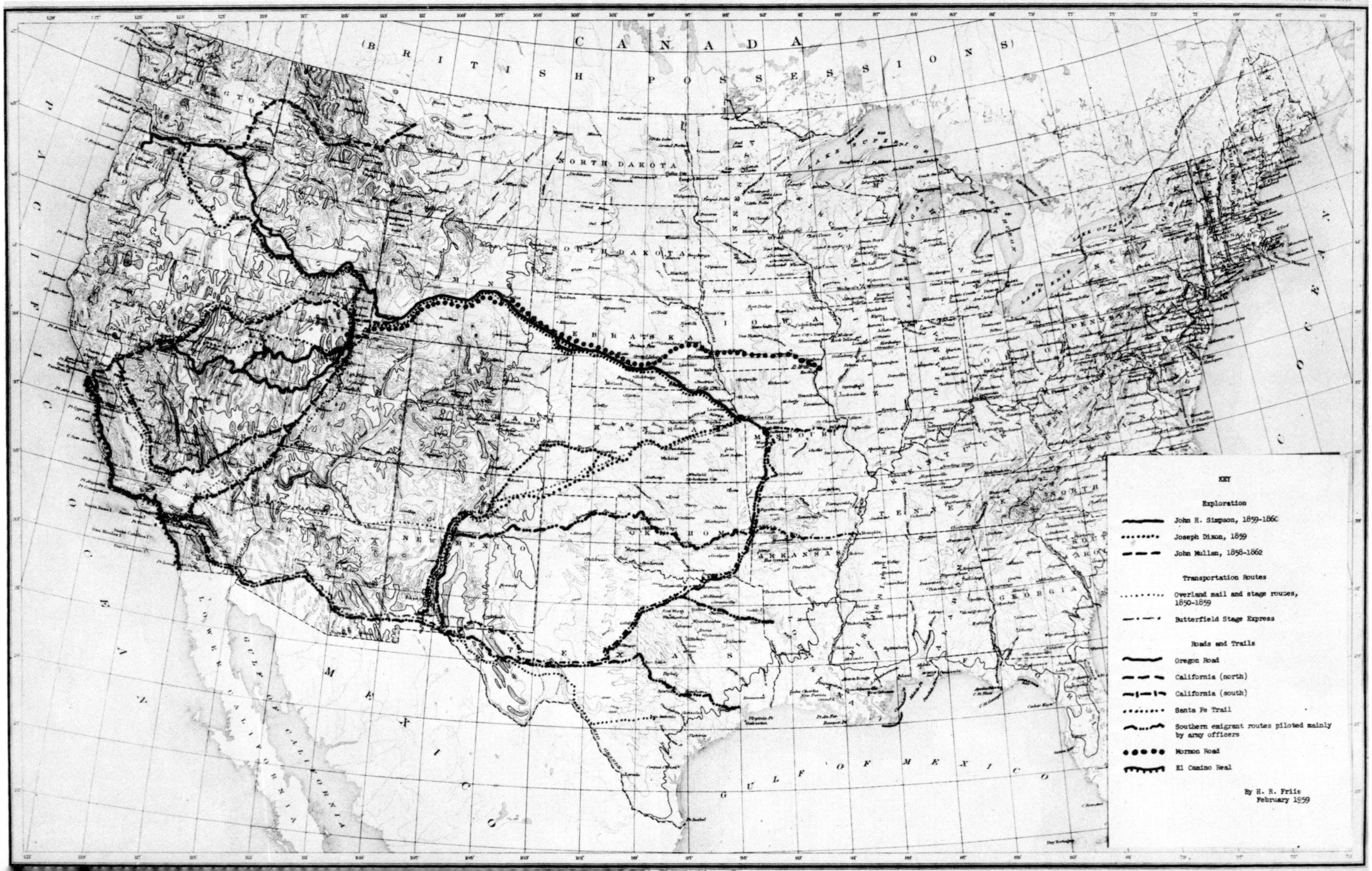

CANADA
(BRITISH POSSESSIONS)
PACIFIC OCEAN
GULF OF MEXICO
MEXICO
LOWER CALIFORNIA
GULF OF CALIFORNIA
NORTH DAKOTA
SOUTH DAKOTA
NEBRASKA
IOWA
KANSAS
MISSOURI
OKLAHOMA
ARKANSAS
TEXAS
NEW MEXICO
TENNESSEE
GEORGIA
KEY
Exploration
John H. Simpson, 1859-1860
Joseph Dixon, 1859
John Mullan, 1858-1862
Transportation Routes
Overland mail and stage routes, 1850-1859
Butterfield Stage Express
Roads and Trails
Oregon Road
California (north)
California (south)
Santa Fe Trail
Southern emigrant routes piloted mainly by army officers
Mormon Road
El Camino Real
By H. R. Friis
February 1959

VIEW FROM HILL RANGE REFERRED TO IN No 13 BACK TO INTERSECTION

FROM INTERSECTION OF MERIDIAN AND PARALLEL OF 36°20' LOOKING WEST ALONG THE PARALLEL TO THE FIRST RANGE OF HILLS

RE 21

FIGURE 22

1. LOPHOPHANES WOLLWEBERI 2. AEGITHALUS FLAVICEPS 3. PSALTRIPARUS ME[illegible]

FIGURE 23

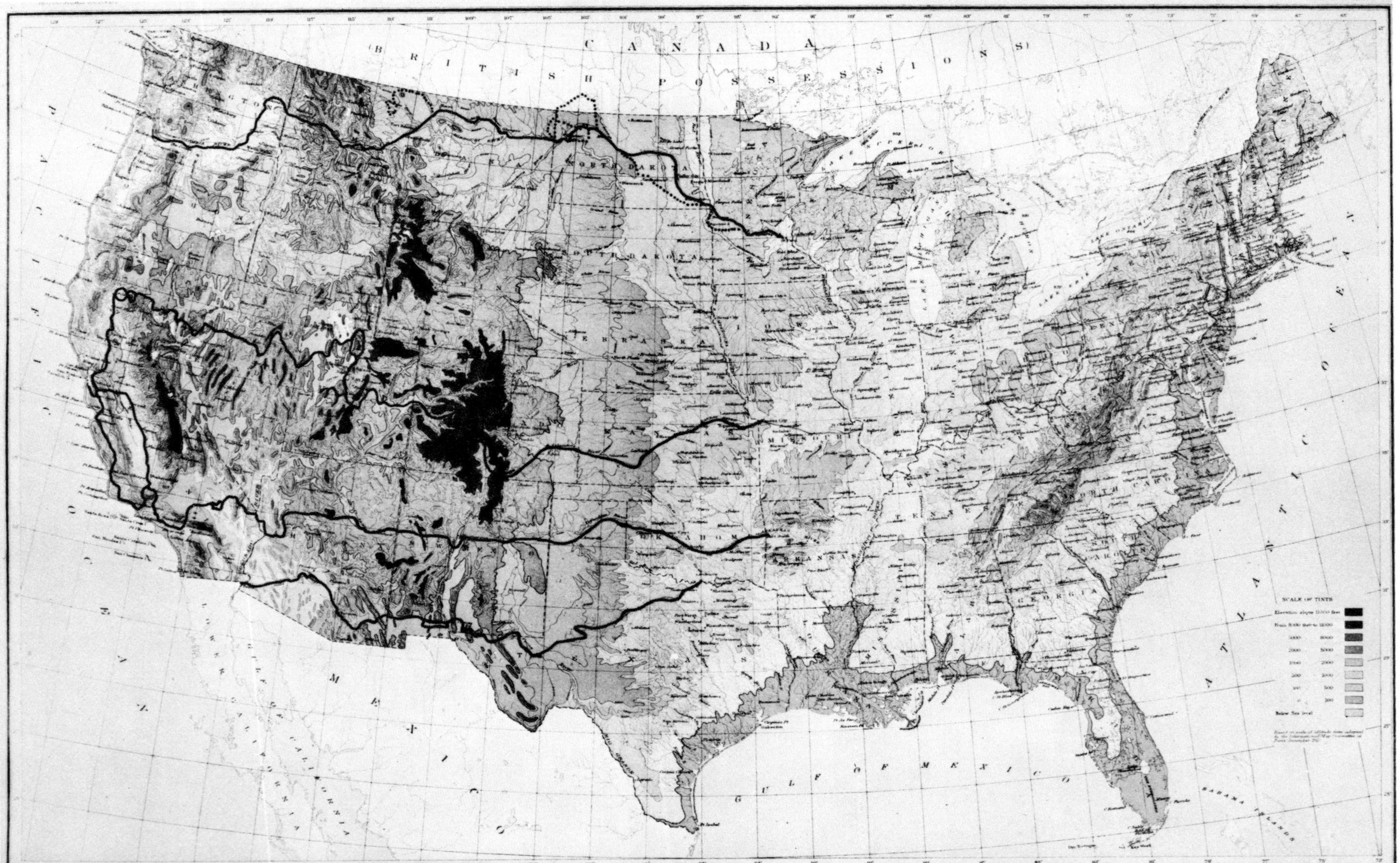
CANADA
(BRITISH POSSESSIONS)
PACIFIC OCEAN
ATLANTIC OCEAN
GULF OF MEXICO
MEXICO
LOWER CALIFORNIA
GULF OF CALIFORNIA
BAHAMA ISLANDS
NORTH DAKOTA
SOUTH DAKOTA
NEBRASKA
KANSAS
IOWA
MISSOURI
ARKANSAS
TENNESSEE
NORTH CAROLINA
SOUTH CAROLINA
GEORGIA
LAKE SUPERIOR
LAKE ONTARIO
SCALE OF TINTS
Below Sea level

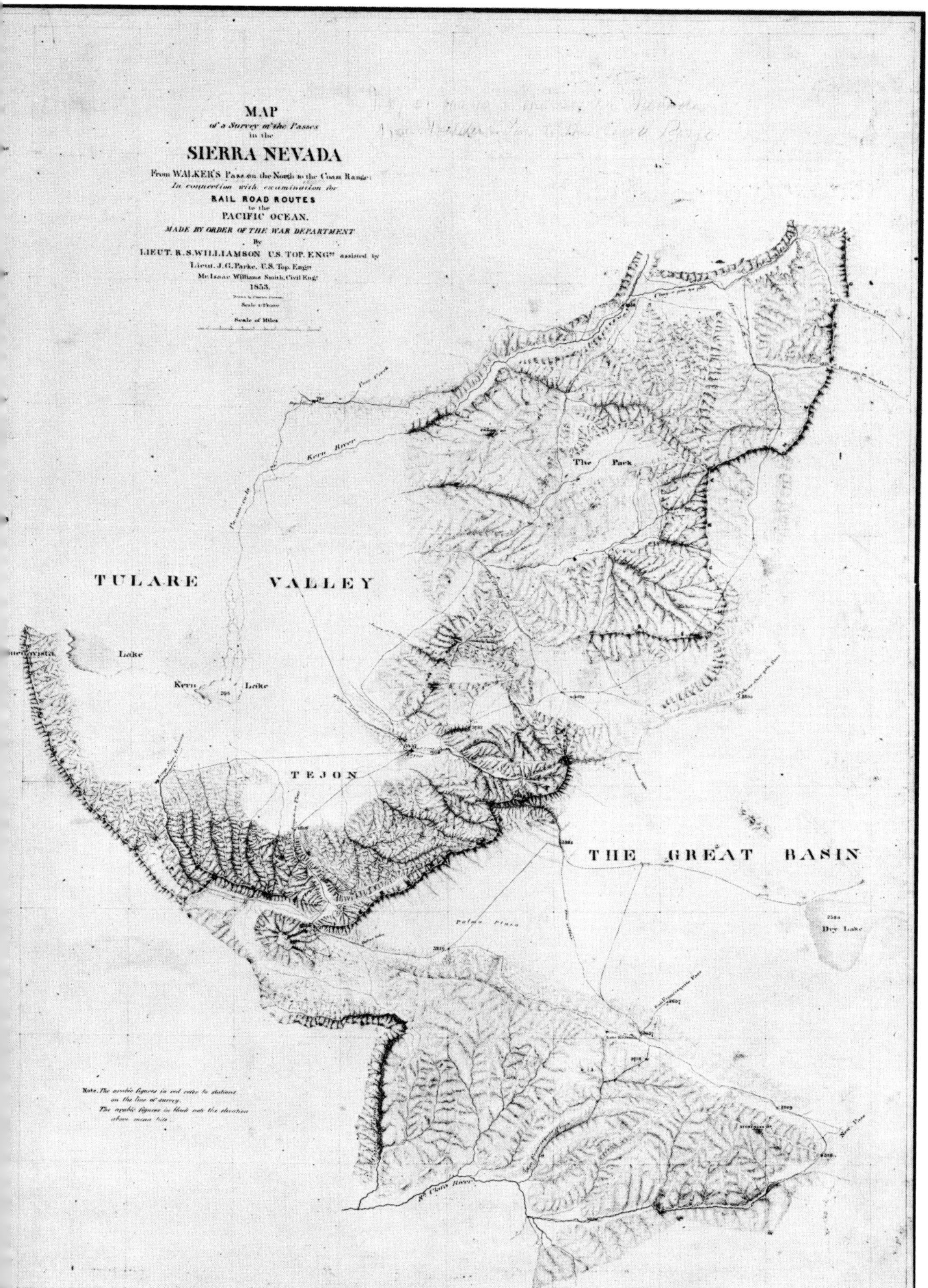
MAP
of a Survey of the Passes
in the
SIERRA NEVADA
From WALKER'S Pass on the North to the Coast Range:
In connection with examination for
RAIL ROAD ROUTES
to the
PACIFIC OCEAN.
MADE BY ORDER OF THE WAR DEPARTMENT
By
LIEUT. R. S. WILLIAMSON U.S. TOP. ENGRS assisted by
Lieut. J. G. Parke, U.S. Top. Engrs
Mr. Isaac Williams Smith, Civil Engr
1853.
Scale of Miles
Kern River
The Park
TULARE VALLEY
Lake
Kern Lake
TEJON
THE GREAT BASIN
Dry Lake
St. Clara River

RE 25

FIGURE 27

FIGURE 28

FIGURE 29

Western Sportsmen Travelers in the New York *Spirit of the Times*

John T. Flanagan

ONE OF THE MOST SIGNIFICANT periodicals published in nineteenth-century America was the *Spirit of the Times,* edited in New York by William T. Porter, the Tall Son of York, from 1831 to 1856.[1] Although essentially a sporting magazine, it was both diversified and lively, and it probably enjoyed as large a national readership as many journals with greater intellectual pretensions. Porter many times defined his purpose in editing such a periodical, which he called "A Chronicle of the Turf, Agriculture, Field Sports, Literature and the Stage." By including material about books and the theater, foreign and domestic intelligence ranging from social events to shipping news, and eventually sketches of life from the hinterland, the *Spirit* was intended to avoid monotony. Porter eventually drew much of his original material from Mississippi and Louisiana, while his subscribers included devotees of the green room, enthusiasts of the turf, plantation owners, and officers stationed at frontier military posts. He boasted in 1836 that "We have a subscriber so far up the Missouri river he says he is 60 miles from Franklin and 300 from any where else."[2]

True to his editorial policy Porter opened his columns to poetry,

[1] Porter dissociated himself from the *Spirit of the Times* in the summer of 1856 and began *Porter's Spirit of the Times,* which he edited until his death in 1858. The University of Illinois Library has a substantial run of both these magazines, acquired with the purchase of the Franklin J. Meine Collection.

[2] *Spirit of the Times,* VI (June 25, 1836), 148. The periodical will be cited henceforth simply as *Spirit.*

essays, and fiction. Since he rarely paid his contributors he borrowed much of his material, from both English and American sources. Thus he reprinted Irish novels by Charles Lever and Samuel Lover, he serialized the *Pickwick Papers* and *Barnaby Rudge* by Charles Dickens, he gave space to the Yellowplush Papers of Thackeray and to the prose of Thomas Hood, N. P. Willis, and Washington Irving. Nor did he neglect the theater. Column after column was devoted to news of the metropolitan stage, to theatricals in New Orleans or St. Louis, to gossip about actors and repertory companies. Even amateur performances of Shakespeare at isolated Army posts attracted his attention.[3] No student of the nineteenth-century American theater can afford to ignore the *Spirit* even though it was less a medium for the reviewing of plays than a clearing house for theatrical information.

But Porter's great love was the world of sport; here his interests were eclectic and his information encyclopedic. Any aspect of the turf fascinated him: the pedigrees of race horses, the purses offered, the records of various tracks and races, the formation of jockey clubs from Baltimore to Peoria. He welcomed details about fox- and wolf-hunting and solicited reports from an army of unpaid but loyal correspondents. One of them, Charles F. M. Noland of Batesville, Arkansas, who wrote either as "N. of Arkansas" or as "Pete Whetstone," contributed over two hundred items to the *Spirit*, ranging from accounts of backwoods horse races to dialect sketches. In addition Porter printed descriptions of cockfighting (which he once elegantly called a "poultry quarrel"), fishing for trout or pike or bass, hunting deer or elk, shooting waterfowl or such upland birds as quail, grouse, and woodcock, marine sports like rowing and sailing, rifle and pistol marksmanship, turtle racing, and even pedestrianism. Riffling through the pages of the *Spirit*, one is as likely to find an account of shooting tigers in Bengal or pursuing giraffes in Africa as bagging woodcock by flares at night in Louisiana.[4]

Porter's passion for the world of the outdoors and his determina-

3 "G** de L**" (William S. Henry) described a theater at Fort Jesup, Louisiana, in 1845, in which resident civilians, officers' wives, and military personnel played Shakespeare. See *Spirit*, XV (July 12, 1845), 227.

4 A recent anthology of southwestern genre and humor sketches, *Men with the Bark On*, edited by John Q. Anderson (Nashville, Tenn.: Vanderbilt University Press, 1967), reprints many items from the *Spirit*. An earlier collection, *Tall Tales from the Southwest*, edited by Franklin J. Meine (New York: Alfred A. Knopf, 1930), also drew extensively from the *Spirit* and has been an influential model for such gatherings.

tion to improve the breeding of the horses and dogs participating in field sports are perhaps most clearly indicated in the fascinating notes to contributors and subscribers which appear below the masthead in nearly every issue of the *Spirit*. Porter was not only an editor but a banker, a shipping agent, an entrepreneur. He was ready to procure a pair of bull terriers or a brace of gamecocks or even a quarter horse for unidentified subscribers; he supplied the rules for a bear-baiting contest, settled disputes about the shuffling and dealing of cards, published equine pedigrees, and provided data about prize fights. On request he searched for rare sporting volumes, procured a sulky, or gave advice on how to train pointers or cure the bots. Once he advised Charles Noland that he was sending him hooks, flies, and a trout line. Only rarely did he demur or express annoyance about the nature of the requests with which he must have been besieged, as when he got in the same mail a demand for a clergyman's robe and a false tail for a horse.

Although the bulk of the *Spirit* contained announcements, long excerpts from previously published books, and the usual filler paragraphs (which he called *on dits* or *olla podrida*), its reputation grew and was sustained by Porter's receptiveness to reports of sporting events all over the world and eventually to genre stories of life in the South, Southwest, and trans-Mississippi West. Porter reprinted sporting material from such English periodicals as *Blackwood's*, the *Dublin University Magazine*, the *Athenaeum*, and *Bentley's Miscellany* but also from native periodicals like the *Southern Literary Messenger*, the *Knickerbocker*, and the New York *Mirror*. Yet far more important was the editor's awareness of and his willingness to use items from the regional press, the New Orleans *Picayune*, the Concordia (Louisiana) *Intelligencer*, and the St. Louis *Reveille* (articles written for the *Reveille* by Sol Smith and Joseph M. Field frequently reappeared in the *Spirit*). In such sources Porter found the material which appealed to him and which made it possible for him to issue for twenty-five years a twelve-page weekly paper which at one time sold for $10 a year and reached forty thousand subscribers.

It has been remarked by Norris Yates, the author of the best study of Porter and his journal, that the contributors to the *Spirit* were generally amateurs who wished to communicate their delight in local activities or to submit certain records of the turf or the field for others to judge.[5] Oddly enough, the best-known writers about life in the South and West did not contribute to the *Spirit*; no original contribution by James Hall, Timothy Flint, John James Audubon, George Catlin, John Mason Peck, or Daniel Drake appeared in Porter's columns although some of their work was reprinted from other sources. Moreover, many contributors relished anonymity or took refuge behind curious pseudonyms. Research has established the identity of the "Turkey Runner" as Alexander G. McNutt, once Governor of Mississippi; of "Obe Oilstone" as Phillip B. January, a Mississippi planter; and of "Falconbridge" as Jonathan Falconbridge Kelley, a journalist. But "Azul" and "Ruff Sam" and "Skyscraper of Iowa" (an interesting nom de plume in 1848) defy identification.

Nevertheless, gifted writers did contribute to the *Spirit* and some of their work is central to this discussion. The "Pete Whetstone" papers of Charles Noland of Arkansas, if heavy in dialect, are readable and interesting.[6] "G** de L**," the odd-looking pseudonym of Cap-

5 Norris W. Yates, *William T. Porter and the "Spirit of the Times"* (Baton Rouge: Louisiana State University Press, 1957).

6 A good example of "N. of Arkansas's" epistles to the *Spirit* is the following colloquy between Old Sense and Dan Looney in backwoods Arkansas (*Spirit*, XIII [May 13, 1843], 127):

[OLD SENSE]: "Good morning, sir, are you well?"
[LOONEY]: "If you call a man well that has run twenty miles, I am *that*."
"Did you see any bear?"
"If you call a big black thing about the size of PETE WHETSTONE'S black mar, or hoss, I did."
"Had you a gun?"
"Now you hit me."
"Did you draw blood?"
"Do you call my double, double handsfull of brains, *blood*?"
"Had you a dog?"
"Is *Old Bose* a dog?"
"Did you skin him?"
"Well, if you call a man in his shirt sleeves, with a knife 17 inches in the blade among ribs and meat, skinning, I was *thar*."
"Was he fat?"
"Do you call cutting 18 inches on the ribs, *fat*?"
"Did you pack him in?"
"If you call four poney loads packing, why I packed some."
"Light loads, I reckon."
"If *four hundred pounds* to a poney is a light load, they were light."
"Did you eat any of it?"
"Do you call drinking *a quart of bars ile*, eating?"
"You must have meat."
"If you call *two thousand seven hundred pounds* of clean meat, without a bone, safe inside a smoke house, *meat*, we have got *some*."

tain William Seton Henry, was often affixed to interesting epistles about hunting on the western prairies; Henry also contributed factual material about his experiences with General Taylor's army in the Mexican War which later appeared in book form.[7] Lieutenant J. Henry Carleton described the expedition of the dragoon regiment to the Pawnee villages in Nebraska in 1844 and later the tour to the Rocky Mountains. "Hal, a Dacotah" was the appellation chosen by Henry Hastings Sibley, later the first Governor of Minnesota, to append to his vigorous narratives of big-game hunting between the Mississippi and Missouri rivers. Solon Robinson contributed sketches of border life localized in early Indiana, and George W. Harris wrote vivid tales of backwoods life among the Tennessee knobs. Above all, Thomas Bangs Thorpe, gifted painter and editor, first printed in the *Spirit* not only "Tom Owen, the Bee-Hunter," but one of the immortal American tall tales, "The Big Bear of Arkansas," which appeared in the issue of March 27, 1841.

The reader of the *Spirit* during its first decade quickly discovers that horse racing, Porter's special sporting interest, easily dominated the early columns given over to field sports. Throughout the life of the periodical information about cups, meets, equine names, breeding, and jockey clubs was given space, together with the results of races at such cities as Mobile, Natchez, Louisville, New Orleans, and Chicago. But toward the mid-century interest in horse racing seems to have declined slightly, coincident perhaps with a decrease in the purses offered and a reduction in the money available even to plantation owners for the maintenance of racing stables. Stories about fishing and hunting then began to assume unusual prominence. These stories, moreover, often transcended mere reports of the slaughter of game to become dramatic accounts of encounters with animals or incidents of backwoods life in which both dialogue and dialect were employed. Columns of the *Spirit* in the 1840's are full of reports of excursions or adventures in the Mississippi Valley states.

Inevitably, of course, one finds examples of the ring-tailed roarer

---

"They must be fat at your house."

"Do you call a *candle* fat?"

At this point Old Sense squealed and vowed that he had found the man he was in quest of.

[7] William S. Henry, *Campaign Sketches of the War with Mexico* (New York: Harper and Brothers, 1847).

familiar to readers of the exploits of Mike Fink or Davy Crockett, often couched in a language which was once dubbed by Bernard De Voto as the Big Bear school of literature. The following example, entitled "A Riproarious Fight on the Banks of the Mississippi," is more vivid than most such melees.

> One day as I was sitting on the starn of my broad horn, the old Free and Easy, on the Mississippi, taking a horn of midshipman's grog, with a tin pot in each hand, first a draught of whiskey, and then one of river water, who should float down past me but Joe Snag; he was in a snooze as fast as a church, with his mouth wide open; he had been ramsquaddled with whiskey for a fortnight, and as it evaporated from his body it looked like steam from a vent pipe. Knowing the feller would be hard to wake, with all his steam on, as he floated past me I hit him a crack over the knob with my big steering oar. He waked in a thundering rage. Says he, hallo stranger, who asked you to kill off my live stock? Said I, shut up your mouth, or your teeth will get sunburnt. Upon this he crooked up his neck and neighed like a stallion. I clapped my arms, and crowed like a cock. Says he, if you are a game chicken, I'll pick the pin feathers off of you. For some time past I had been so wolfy about the head and shoulders, that I was obliged to keep kivered up in a salt crib to keep from spiling, for I had not had a fight for as much as ten days. Says I, give us none of your chin music, but set your kickers on land, and I'll give you a severe licking. The fellow now jumped ashore, and he was so tall that he couldn't tell when his feet were cold. He jumped a rod. Says he, take care how I lite on you, and he gave me a real stopdologer, that made my liver and lites turn to jelly. But he found me a real scrouger.—Broke three of his ribs, and he knocked out five of my teeth and one eye. He was the severest colt that I ever tried to break. I finally got a bite hold of his posteriors that he couldn't shake off. We were now parted by some boatmen, and we were both so exorsted, that it was more than a month before either of us could have a fight. It seemed to me a little eternity. And although I didn't come out second best, I took care not to wake up a ringtailed roarer with an oar again.[8]

Steamboat travel, especially between New Orleans and St. Louis, with side trips up the tributary rivers, produced many interesting comments. Indeed a note from Vicksburg in 1837 suggests that river

[8] *Spirit*, VIII (April 14, 1838), 72.

traffic was heavy long before Mark Twain's day. "The Mississippi is rising very fast, and alive with steamboats," one correspondent wrote. "They make such a noise with their puff, puff, puff, that it is almost impossible to sleep at nights."[9] Four years later another writer described a trip up the river on a steamboat loaded with four hundred Seminole Indians bound for a new reservation. The warriors were depicted as lethargic and sleepy. "The girls were possessed of little or no personal charms, while the women, the laborers of the tribe, were as hideous as any hags that can be imagined." Heat, illness, and the refusal of the Indians to take medicine made the voyage nightmarish, until the steamboat veered toward the shore and the passengers suddenly espied a bear in the water. The deck churned into activity with some braves endeavoring to launch a canoe in pursuit while others impulsively leaped with knives into the river. But a lethal shot from a white hunter's gun ended the chase. Questioned about his temerity in firing during such confusion, the hunter remarked: "My old shooting iron never misses, but if it had hit a red skin, by accident, I should not have been ashamed of the shot—for the Bear is the best of the two, and a perfect Christian, compared with the best copper skin in the tender thar."[10]

In 1848 a traveler embarked on the steamboat *Mohawk* at Vicksburg bound for St. Louis and eventually the Falls of St. Anthony. He was assured of a berth on the floor of the cabin if he retired at nine o'clock in the evening, but if he remained up until ten o'clock he would have to sleep on the boiler deck. The three hundred passengers included many women and children but also broken-down ministers of the gospel, blacklegs, and pickpockets, the last seeking to levy public or private contributions. The traveler pictured Cape Girardeau as "a pretty little town, famous for corn, marble, and boatmen." At St. Louis he found a hundred steamboats along the levee, which was piled with barrels, sacks, and piles of lead. "The river streets are narrow, crooked, and excessively dirty," he observed, and he added that Irish touts besought passengers to come to the Planters House, the Virginia House, or the City Hall.[11]

Steamboats sometimes terrified the squatters of the back country.

[9] *Spirit*, VII (April 15, 1837), 70.
[10] *Spirit*, XI (September 4, 1841), 320.
[11] Ginger, "Trip to the Falls of St. Anthony," *Spirit*, XVIII (May 27, 1848), 158–159.

Two Arkansas brothers arrived at the river just as the *General Jackson* reached the small levee, "puffing, and paddling, and jerking cotton bales and negroes over her bow, and looking for all the world like an infernal big frame house with the kitchen wall knocked out." One of the brothers ventured upon the boiler deck just as a cloud of steam emerged from the pipe; positive that an explosion was imminent, he jumped toward the shore and got thoroughly drenched.[12] More sophisticated passengers were less frightened than scornful of the vessels that plied the smaller streams. A contributor who identified himself as a backwoods lawyer embarked at St. Louis for a trip up the Illinois River to Peru and Peoria; he found the Peoria prairie lovely but had only scorn for the Illinois—"a sluggish, dirty stream of water, precisely resembling a stagnant pool, covered with long trails of dusty filth, and creeping seaward at the rate of half a mile an hour."[13] The description makes one wonder if the backwoods lawyer had read Dickens' description of the Mississippi at Cairo.[14]

T. B. Thorpe was equally disdainful about some of the river packets, notably those that traversed the ponds and bayous carrying mail and needed supplies. He once described a vessel which was small, noisy, and cramped. The lady's cabin had one berth, about as wide as a shelf, and the male passenger found himself with his feet on the lower deck and his head halfway up the stairs. "The machinery was tremendous," Thorpe observed ironically; "two large kettles firmly set in brick, attached to a complicated looking coffee mill, two little steam pipes, and one big one." At squatters' settlements, where the captain stopped to buy wood, the only inhabitants seemed to be a seedy father, a brood of squalid children, and some invalid hens. The main ports of call were dreary-looking townsites which once had ambitions and which were now grateful for a sagging pouch of mail or a hogshead of whiskey.[15]

Indeed, accounts of fluvial or overland travel in the *Spirit* are full of allusions to ghost towns or hamlets which never quite justified

12 Guguscutus, "An Arkansas Original," *Spirit*, XVI (February 28, 1846), 1.

13 "Sketches of Western Travel," *Spirit*, XIII (September 2, 1843), 314.

14 Cf. Charles Dickens, *American Notes* (1842), chapter 12, where he describes the Mississippi as "an enormous ditch, sometimes two or three miles wide, running liquid mud six miles an hour."

15 T. B. T[horpe], "The Little Steamboats of the Mississippi," *Spirit*, XIV (March 9, 1844), 19.

their promoters' aspirations. The sketch entitled "A New Town in Arkansas" describes Belleair on the Arkansas River, pictured by its promoters in glowing terms as cool, healthy, and close to some of the most fertile regions of the state. But when the visitor finally emerges from his mired stage and reaches the supposed center of town he finds only one log cabin, both leaky and filthy, inhabited by a slatternly family. Instead of properly marked lots, he discovers "stakes marking tier on tier of streets, and on an old gum stump, some ten feet high, was stuck a white-washed board on which was scrawled with charcoal, 'Broadway'; it was unnecessary for us to look for the 'Park'—it was around and about us."[16] Depressed and angry, the visitor has to make do for dinner with corn pone, coffee compounded of the washings of half-grown Irish potatoes, and black, dirty, wild honey for sweetening.

In 1845 a letter from Callum Beg at Honey Creek, Missouri, urged the editor of the *Spirit* to sample the fishing and hunting in that community. Even the girls, while not exactly city belles, would attract the stranger. "The[y] wear neither bustles nor breeches, and are not much encumbered with shoes or stockings, except when they have their 'Sundays on'; but they can play the fiddle, call a cotillion, and dance a double shuffle to your satisfaction. They will also give and take a joke without being particular, and will ride or run a race without choice of ground."[17]

Throughout the early issues of 1846 ran a series entitled "Scraps from the Note-book of a Missouri Lawyer," which gave revealing vignettes of life in the "Show Me" state. The first installment described St. Louis as the author knew it when it was a small city of five thousand in 1830. "The streets were narrow and filthy; the buildings were mean and generally of an ancient appearance." But the population was active and enterprising, and among the transient visitors were familiar western types: river boatmen eager to fight or to frolic; half-naked Indians daubed with paint and waiting for their bounty payments; Rocky Mountain trappers with the skin on their faces and hands like smoked parchment; polite Frenchmen constantly smoking and chattering; dark-eyed Spaniards, dignified and quiet; loose-jointed backwoodsmen in town to trade peltries for lead and powder or for "fixens" for their womenfolk; and smartly dressed Yankees bustling around

[16] *Spirit*, XIV (March 9, 1844), 14.
[17] *Spirit*, XV (April 5, 1845), 59.

and devoted to their occupation of "picking up the loose change afloat." The St. Louis of fifteen years later, the lawyer added, was nearly nine times larger and an impressive city which had lost some of its earlier color.[18]

The same writer subsequently filled in his portrait of the backwoodsman by stressing the crudity and solitariness of the man at the same time that he credited him with shrewdness and a fondness for jokes which were often broad and unsparing.[19] In another sketch he drew attention to the prominence of Yankee clock peddlers in Missouri, their persistence and their success. Frequently a Yankee clock was the only furnishing in a primitive cabin not made by the settler himself. The peddler would sell a clock if he could, rent it, leave it as a demonstrator, or ask the reluctant settler to store it while he moved around the vicinity. In one instance when the peddler returned after an absence of six months and asked to replevin his clock, the action produced such a commotion in the household that the settler gathered together all the cash he had in the world—$30—in order to retain the timepiece.[20]

Another aspect of backwoods life, the fondness for rough sports, can best be represented by an account of a gander-pulling on a Missouri farm. An old settler named Hinkle had left a solitary tree standing on a prairie with a protruding lateral branch. A deep furrow circled the tree and marked the limits of a ring for the seven mounted competitors. Then a gander whose head and neck had been carefully plucked and coated with grease was hung upside down to the branch, its legs tied together. The horsemen drew lots and in sequence rode under the gander, each trying to grasp the bird's head and wrench it off. While the gander retained vitality and the horses plunged past, the efforts of the horsemen were futile. But eventually, though the gander had been regreased, its gyrations stopped, and young Joe Hinkle managed to grab its head, leaving the decapitated fowl swinging from the limb.[21]

Backwoods trials and ignorant justices of the peace occasioned many amusing reports. A correspondent from Benton County, Min-

18 *Spirit*, XVI (July 18, 1846), 247–248.

19 *Spirit*, XVI (September 5, 1846), 331.

20 *Spirit*, XVI (August 29, 1846), 314.

21 "A Gander Pulling at 'Old Man Hinkle's,'" *Spirit*, XVI (September 26, 1846), 361–362.

nesota, described a magistrate who fled across the county line to avoid issuing a write of habeas corpus but could not evade the performance of a marriage ceremony so easily. He asked everyone for some book to be used as a manual but turned up nothing but a copy of Ike Marvel's *Reveries of a Bachelor,* which was clearly of no use. So reluctantly he performed the ceremony with a terse admonition: "You, T—— P——, take this *young woman,* whom you hold by the right hand, to be your lawful wife, and you now promise to cleave unto her, and *all other women,* so help you God." The writer added that after three months the young wife besought the territorial legislature for a divorce.[22] An even stranger marriage scene took place in Arkansas, according to "Skyscraper." In the first place, the parson was in a hurry because in an hour he had to be five miles away to judge a horse race. Also, the groom was what might be described as overeager. Attendants dragged the red-haired, barefooted swain before the clergyman where "he came a pawing and squealing, and nickering and snorting like a four year old." As soon as the ceremony was over, the groom and his bride plunged beneath a bearskin. Four months later, the correspondent asserted, twins had already arrived.[23]

In all the trans-Mississippi states, overland travel was slow and tedious, with common problems such as fording streams, extricating wagons from the prairie gumbo, and putting corduroy supports over sloughs. But even in 1845 the Iowa farms, especially in the eastern part of the territory, were impressive. One farmer had two hundred acres under cultivation and reported crops of wheat and corn of twenty-five to thirty bushels and sixty to seventy bushels to the acre respectively. Moreover, a correspondent claimed that a comfortable house could be provided for $400. The farmer, hospitable to strangers, also set a good table for there was a profusion of food: "pork cut up in small pieces, and baked in a spider, smearcase, short biscuits, loaf bread, stewed black-berries, maple molasses, coffee, cucumbers, and thickened milk."[24]

Occasional contributions from the frontier forts described the life of the Plains Indians as they came in contact with the garrisons, but much of this material was imbedded in the reports of diplomatic

22 Winne Shik, "Anecdotes of a Western Judge," *Spirit,* XXII (July 17, 1852), 254.
23 Skyscraper, "A Wedding Frolic in Arkansas," *Spirit,* XVIII (July 15, 1848), 247.
24 *Spirit,* XV (March 8, 1845), 16–17.

or punitive expeditions to the land of the hostiles. In 1842 a detachment of dragoons marched north from Council Bluffs along the Missouri Valley in an effort to keep the peace between the Sioux and the Potawatomies. A correspondent noted the luxuriant prairie grass and the abundance of small game; he also described how one trooper climbed a bee tree with only a large handkerchief around his face and neck for protection and dug out wild honey with a hunting knife while the bees swarmed around him. But he also watched the Indians in camp. "For the whole evening the Indians were in high glee, some dancing, some singing, some playing a queer game of their own with straws, the stakes being their silver and brass ornaments, which were lost and won without their betraying any more emotion than so many gamblers carved in stone."[25] A little later, eighteen numbers of Lieutenant Carleton's "Prairie Log Book" appeared in the *Spirit* from November 9, 1844, to April 12, 1845, a detailed account of the journey of five companies of dragoons from Fort Leavenworth to the Pawnee villages in Nebraska. Carleton described the route and its physical obstacles, various hunting episodes, bouts with heat and illness, and particularly encounters with such tribes as the Kickapoos, Potawatomies, and Pawnees. The author's eye for salient detail makes these sketches still highly readable.[26]

Henry H. Sibley frequently accompanied the Sioux hunting parties in their quest of elk and buffalo and wrote many comments about his aboriginal companions two decades before he led a federal army in pursuit of the hostiles after the massacre at New Ulm. In a sketch entitled "Three Dacotahs" he told the story of three braves who engaged in a hunting and scalping expedition against their hereditary enemies, the Ojibwas. Eager to win fame, they rashly penetrated far into enemy country and killed two Ojibwas before they were surrounded in a thicket on the open prairie. But their coolness and fleetness of foot enabled them to return safely to their village despite their foolhardy tactics and they contributed two scalps to the commemorative dance.[27]

25 *Spirit,* XII (September 10, 1842), 331.

26 These accounts were not collected in book form until Louis Pelzer edited *The Prairie Logbooks* in 1943 for the Caxton Club of Chicago.

27 Hal, a Dacotah [Henry H. Sibley], "The Three Dacotahs," *Porter's Spirit of the Times,* I (January 31, 1857), 345–346. The sketch was presented as a chapter in an unfinished novel of the frontier; actually Sibley was making use of an episode in the life

Fascinating accounts of frontier justice, social life, and travel fill many a column of the *Spirit*. Fishing stories too had their place. One vivid narrative from Jefferson City tells how eight men in two skiffs floated down the Missouri River watching twenty-four half-gallon jugs bob up and down in the current. Each jug had a stout cord attached to it equipped with fishhooks baited with fresh beef. In this way catfish weighing from twenty to fifty pounds were caught and a monster of two hundred pounds was not unknown.[28] Such stories make Huck Finn's references to giant Mississippi catfish more real.

But it is the hunting stories which impart a special flavor to the *Spirit* and which confirm Porter's assertion that his paper was read throughout the western country, on plantations and presidios, and in many foreign lands as well. For the mid-century was the heyday of the hunter. Equipped with improved fowling pieces and accurate rifles, carrying the Colt revolver for close-range work, riding well-trained horses and often accompanied by greyhounds, the nimrods found the western prairies a utopia for shooting long before Buffalo Bill Cody began to decimate the herds of bison so that the workers for the Kansas Pacific Railroad could be assured of their daily rations. Many a "venerable venator," to use the euphemism of Cooper's Obed Bat, pursued elk, bear, and buffalo, or coursed after prairie wolves. Greenhorns from the East, young English noblemen, itinerant land hunters, settlers weary of the plough and the axe, professional men who liked guns, all preyed on the game of the prairies, but it was the Army officers who made hunting almost a profession and who wrote long letters to the *Spirit* about their feats. It is time to sample some of these reports.

T. B. Thorpe contributed several articles about bird-shooting in Louisiana. He praised the wild turkey and ranked it with the buffalo and the Indian as "the three most remarkable living productions of the Western world." Like Franklin, he thought that the turkey was the most proper emblem for the American nation. He called attention to the turkey's remarkable ground speed and commented that the birds often miscalculated the width of a stream and fell into the water,

---

of a half-blood scout named Jack Frazer, who was one of the three Dacotahs involved. See Theodore C. Blegen and Sarah A. Davison, eds., *Iron Face* (Chicago: Caxton Club, 1950), pp. xvi, 44.

28 " 'Jug' Fishing in the Missouri," *Spirit*, XX (November 2, 1850), 439.

thus becoming the easy prey of squatters living along the banks.[29] Thorpe also described woodcock-hunting at night on the edge of the Mississippi River where a ridge separated the water from interior swamps. No dogs were used, but a Negro equipped with a warming pan which had holes in its bottom and carrying pine-knot splinters provided illumination. Thorpe reported that two hunters working under these conditions once shot thirty birds in two hours, while a toll of a hundred *becasse* during one nocturnal hunt was not unusual.[30]

In 1840 a correspondent from Quincy commented on the excellence of night fishing along the Mississippi and the abundance of bass, perch, and pike (his party had speared one pike almost four feet long). But the prairie hunting in that vicinity was even more profitable. In two days two men killed eighty grouse before they became tired of their slaughter. The writer commented: "This, however, I think will suffice me after this kind of game, as there is a great deal of sameness in the pursuit of it, and one can hardly congratulate oneself upon doing any great things in knocking down so large a bird which gets up under your feet in open ground, and goes off with an even steady flight."[31] Such a note of tedium, incidentally, is rare in these chronicles of field sports. Generally the hunter was jubilant over the amount of his toll.

Thorpe also reported a hunt near the headwaters of the Arkansas and Black rivers in which he pursued antelope, deer, and buffalo. But the most interesting aspect of his story is his account of the numerous wild horses in the vicinity, which he described as sleek, agile, and mettlesome. He commented that the Osage Indians near whom he camped demonstrated superior horsemanship but that only white hunters could really gentle a wild stallion.[32]

Fort Gibson in the Arkansas valley was the scene of many a horse race, chase after wolves, and hunting expedition. One Army officer garrisoned at this remote post told of chasing wolves with greyhounds and for variation tracking wild cats. "The Branch is alive with cats, and in half an hour we have three of them treed, dead, and slung behind us. A smart gallop soon brought us home, and a breakfast of wild

29 T. B. T[horpe], "Wild Turkey Shooting," *Spirit*, X (August 1, 1840), 253.

30 T. B. T[horpe], "Woodcock Fire Hunting," *Spirit*, XI (May 1, 1841), 103.

31 "Sports on the Prairie," *Spirit*, XI (March 13, 1841), 18.

32 T. B. T[horpe], "The Wild Horses of the Western Prairies," *Spirit*, XII (April 9, 1842), 61.

duck and buckwheat, softened down with a good whiskey toddy, soon brought all things straight."[33] Another writer traveling with a troop of dragoons commented on a big-game hunt in conjunction with the Potawatomies north of Council Bluffs. The combined booty amounted to 57 buffalo, 20 elk, and 104 deer, with too much small game to be inventoried. But the exploit of one trooper deserves quotation.

> After chasing the elk about six miles, he overtook an immense buck, who, on account of his being very fat, could not keep up with the herd. As soon as he got abreast, he aimed his carbine at his most vital part, and pulled the trigger. The cap alone exploded. The soldier, being determined not to be foiled in his purpose, drew his bayonet, *seized the elk by his horns* with his left hand, and stabbed him through the back and neck until he dropped dead. All the Indians considered this the most extraordinary piece of daring, and skill in the management of horse and arms, they had ever seen or heard of.[34]

Hunting possibilities around Burlington, Iowa, were described by "Short Pete," who reported that deer were common and that prairie chickens, quail, snipe, and woodcock were numerous. The variety of birds also brought wolves, who provided the quarry for many a mounted party. One wolf which "Short Pete" claimed was twenty years old eluded his pursuers for almost a whole day and covered eighty miles before he was overtaken. Another writer reported on prairie sports just west of Chicago in 1847. Only a few miles from the city, in temperatures which reached 102°, he killed 54 woodcock, 4 snipe, and 2 ducks during an afternoon's outing. Sometimes there were even rival groups of sportsmen, such as the Peoria nimrods in 1846 who organized themselves into teams for one day's slaughter; the total take was 412 ducks (including teal, wood ducks, and grey ducks but mostly mallards), 5 turkeys, a small number of geese, crane, and brant, 95 squirrels, minor numbers of quail, snipe, and prairie chickens, 14 hawks and owls, and a swan.[35] One can only remark one's amazement that these trigger-happy fanatics were able to refrain from shooting each other.

33 "A Hunt in the West," *Spirit*, XII (July 2, 1842), 216.

34 Reginald Melton, "Hunting Adventures in the Far West," *Spirit*, XII (September 10, 1842), 331; (September 17, 1842), 344.

35 Short Pete, "Sport in Iowa," *Spirit*, XIV (May 11, 1844), 127; XVII (August 7, 1847), 278; XVI (November 14, 1846), 450.

In 1845 Captain Henry described a three-day hunt along the Nueces River in Texas in which five officers from Corpus Christi accounted for an impressive amount of game: 10 deer, 51 geese, 69 snipe, plus ducks, turkeys, 2 sandhill cranes, and 4 bitterns. The inclusion of bitterns in one's game bag is singular indeed, since they are inedible and certainly as targets for expert shots they leave much to be desired. More worthy of the party's marksmanship was a panther, described by Henry as seven feet eight inches in length, four feet in height, and weighing 160 pounds.[36] Another Army officer hunting in the same general area claimed that his party had bagged seventy-one turkeys, many of the gobblers exceeding twenty pounds in weight. More interesting, perhaps, was the sight of some forty wild horses, varying in color from white and bay to sorrel, gray, and black; they "presented a beautiful motley as they rushed in a mass down the slope." The officer added that the animals were clean of limb and had short backs and powerful muscles. "The manes of some of the older horses were of extravagant length, and flowed in the wind like a woman's hair." Such a herd on the Texas prairies was not uncommon since groups of several hundred mustangs were subsequently reported.[37]

While most of these hunting tales were soberly factual, if one allows for a slight inflation of the amount of game bagged, some definitely had tall-tale or even comic elements. "Skyscraper," for example, told of an Arkansas bear hunt involving a backwoodsman named Long Jim or Tussle Jim. "His stock wasn't very large, only an old cow and a sow, but the sow littered every month or so, and the old cow had a calf every year—she never failed but once. One winter it was so cold that she concluded to hold over, and not have a calf in the spring, but she made it up afterwards, for the next spring she had a calf and a yearling."[38] Jim once killed a bear cub in a hole in a tree root. Crawling in to get his game, he found his egress suddenly blocked by the arrival of the mother bear. He shot her with a bullet right down her throat but then couldn't get past the body and couldn't employ his knife to cut her apart. So, according to the narrator, Jim just ate his

36 G** de L** [William S. Henry], "A Three Days' Hunt in Texas," *Spirit*, XV November 22, 1845), 459.

37 *Spirit*, XVI (February 28, 1846), 1.

38 Skyscraper, "An Arkansas Bear Story," *Spirit*, XIX (March 17, 1849), 43.

way through the bear. A similarly fantastic story was reported from Missouri in 1853. An old man, tired of an employee who was always borrowing his shotgun, loaded the weapon with a generous handful of powder and thirty-five buckshot in each barrel. When the young man fired both barrels at geese in a cornfield, the discharge was lethal; four geese were killed instantly, two were winged, and the recoil was so violent that the hunter broke his collarbone.[39]

A correspondent who signed himself "Okawania" and gave his location as "Okaw, Pecan County, Illinois," wrote frequently to the *Spirit* about fishing and hunting expeditions in the American Bottom, especially in Monroe and St. Clair counties. "Okawania" ranged widely and reported anecdotes of steamboat travel, backwoods justice, horse races, and fishing under difficulties. His epistles tend to be diffuse and incoherent but Porter apparently appreciated their lighter mood.

One of the most reliable correspondents in the upper Mississippi Valley was Henry Sibley, who did extensive hunting in Minnesota Territory during the 1840's. Sibley was a resident agent of the American Fur Company with a professional interest in the taking of furs and pelts, but his delight in shooting was unmistakable. Accompanied by Alexander Faribault and the half-blood scout Jack Frazer (known as Iron Face) in 1842, he took part in a safari in the buffalo country two hundred miles west of Fort Snelling. In twenty-two days of prairie hunting the men accounted for 16 buffalo, 3 elk, 244 ducks, 80 grouse, besides, as Sibley put it, "sundry other snaps not worth recording."[40] Sibley kept careful records of the game he killed and claimed that in a three-year period he had shot 1,798 ducks![41] It is interesting that only a few years later he began to have second thoughts about such wanton slaughter since he lamented the gradual disappearance of elk and buffalo from the Minnesota prairies and was vituperative in his scorn for the market hunter. In a letter to Porter he claimed that game should be killed only in season when

39 Jo. Bird, "Wild-Goose Hunting in Missouri," *Spirit*, XXII (January 22, 1853), 579.

40 Hal, a Dacotah [Henry H. Sibley], "A Buffalo and Elk Hunt in 1842," *Spirit*, XVI (April 11, 1846), 73. This sketch was reprinted in *Minnesota History*, XV (December, 1934), 382–394; and also in John T. Flanagan, ed., *America Is West* (Minneapolis: University of Minnesota Press, 1945), pp. 150–157.

41 Cf. Theodore C. Blegen, *Minnesota, a History of the State* (Minneapolis: University of Minnesota Press, 1963), p. 138.

the flesh was in good condition and that pot hunters who killed deer from canoes or dugouts aided by flares were not legitimate hunters.[42] But it must be added that this suggestion of conservation of game birds and animals is rare in the hunting reports of the mid-century.

The discovery of gold in California and the dispatch of military expeditions to the West Coast brought many reports to the *Spirit* of hunting beyond the Rockies. Here the seasonal flights of waterfowl and the presence of undiminished numbers of grouse, quail, deer, and elk delighted nimrods and prolonged the destruction of North American wildlife for an additional decade or two. A goose hunter on the San Joaquin River reported incredible numbers of birds and claimed that in one day he killed fifty-seven geese (including five brant) as the flocks moved back and forth from the mud flats to the tule patches along the river.[43] Another sportsman hunting in the same vicinity two years earlier killed several elk, two bucks having a total weight of 1,165 pounds.[44] One of the sports peculiar to California was the lassoing of bears by mounted hunters, often for the purpose of capturing the bears alive and bringing them back to the ranch. "El Muchacho" described such a feat in 1852.

Some fourteen vaqueros spotted a grizzly in open country and with great dexterity threw ropes around him which the well-trained cow ponies daringly tightened. Eventually the bear was tied up and carried to a corral. Here a wild bull was introduced and the animals confronted each other. The bull rushed and tried to gore his ursine opponent. The bear scratched and slashed and bit. Once the bull knocked the bear over in a wild charge only to have his flanks raked by the bear's claws. Finally the bull, his sides bleeding and one eye ripped out, gave up the fight and leaped over the side of the corral. A vaquero then shot the bear.[45] One need not comment on the cruelty of such an entertainment. Recent events in our own time do not suggest that the twentieth century can assert a morality superior to that of the nineteenth.

William T. Porter would have no truck with articles dealing with religion or politics; he rejected many contributions simply be-

42 Hal, a Dacotah [Henry H. Sibley], "Game in the West," *Porter's Spirit of the Times*, I (October 25, 1856), 126.

43 "California Geese and Greener's Guns," *Spirit*, XXII (August 7, 1852), 295.

44 "Elk Hunt on the San Joaquin," *Spirit*, XXI (February 22, 1851), 6–7.

45 El Muchacho, "Bull vs. Bear," *Spirit*, XXII (May 1, 1852), 122.

cause they touched on these *verboten* topics. Likewise, he objected to material which, as he put it, was too "rich," too "highly seasoned." Oaths and profanity were generally interdicted, and even a mild "hell" was usually spelled "h--l." Obscenity, not to speak of mild indecency, never reached print in the *Spirit*. But such censorship aside, he welcomed vivid, sprightly, specific accounts of travel and sport, no matter what their genesis or location. News of jockey clubs and hunting excursions fascinated him, he had a genuine liking for tall tales, as evidenced by the frequent appearance of T. B. Thorpe and George Washington Harris in his journal, and frontier sports, however rough and brutal, always commanded space in his columns. If the *Spirit* does not provide information about missionary activities or the squabbles of political parties, it is inexhaustible as a source for details about social life, popular entertainments, and the pursuit of game on the frontier. The Tall Son of York enjoyed the devotion of his contributors and the affection of his subscribers (half of whom, he often boasted, he knew personally). As a consequence, the *Spirit* remains a rich mine which formal history can neglect only at its peril.

Sources for Western History in The American Turf Register and Sporting Magazine, 1829-44

John Porter Bloom

BROWSING AMONG the early magazines published in the United States can give one valuable insights into a way of life considerably different from our own of today. Editors of these pioneers of the magazine field were closer to their readers than our contemporary editors are, who may surgically excise such parts of their readership as may be guilty of residing in the "wrong" postal zones. Readers of early magazines might be carried as subscribers for years without paying a penny. Their letters, when received, were likely to be seized upon eagerly by editors, and more likely then than now to be published, excerpted, and noted. If such an editor were especially interested in the West, his publication would naturally be a good prospect as a source for western American history.

Such, indeed, was the case with the leading personality behind *The American Turf Register and Sporting Magazine*, John Stuart Skinner (1788–1851), whose career deserves some attention.[1] Skinner

[1] The two basic sources of information on Skinner by contemporaries are Ben Perley Poore, "Biographical Sketch of John Stuart Skinner," in *The Plough, the Loom, and the Anvil* (1854), reprinted privately by John L. O'Connor with a Foreword by Fred E. Pond dated at New York City, January 7, 1924; and "Memoir of John S. Skinner," *The American Farmer*, Ser. 4, VII (April, 1852), 325–326. The latter is anonymous, but said to be by "one who knew him well and loved him." Careful recent sketches are in Albert L. Demaree, *The American Agricultural Press, 1819–1860* (New York: Columbia University Press, 1941), pp. 23–38; Harry Worcester Smith, *A Sporting Family of the Old South* (Albany, N.Y.: published for private subscription, 1936), pp. 7–35; Herbert Anthony Kellar, "John Stuart Skinner," *Dictionary of American Biography*, XVII (New York: Charles Scribner's Sons, 1943), pp. 199–201; and Myrtle Helfrich, "A Baltimore Pioneer of Farm and Turf," Baltimore *Sun*, February 17, 1935, magazine section, pp. 10–11.

was reared on a Maryland plantation traceable in his family back to the earliest colonial days. He came into some prominence at the time of the War of 1812, when he served the federal government in several capacities. He was the Paul Revere of the War of 1812, riding in the night to warn the City of Washington of the coming British land attack, and he was Francis Scott Key's companion on the night when the "Star Spangled Banner" was composed—also its first publisher according to some accounts.

After the war Skinner soon launched into his twofold career, first as Postmaster of Baltimore beginning in 1816, later as Assistant Postmaster General in Washington, 1841–45. Skinner's simultaneous second career was as a magazine publisher, which is to say editor, writer, business manager, printer, salesman, and just about everything else. He entered the magazine business in 1818 with a short-lived publication called *The Censor,* of a political nature. Less than a year after it started, the first issue of *The American Farmer* appeared—April 2, 1819—converted from an earlier magazine which he bought out. It was a notable success and established Skinner as "the pioneer and father of American farm journalism."[2] The magazine endured until 1897, through several changes and interruptions, and inspired many imitators.

Skinner's lifelong interest in scientific agriculture was genuine and productive. His contacts with seafaring men, especially naval officers both American and British, eased the way for him in obtaining thoroughbred animals, seeds, guano, and other farm-related items from abroad. He distributed two barrels of guano among Maryland farmers in the 1820's for testing as fertilizer, but this experiment did not catch on and twenty years were to pass before the substance became popular. He was one of the earliest persons to champion the idea of introducing camels for use in the arid West. Skinner was interested in improvements to the internal transportation system of the nation as well, and as a member of the Maryland House of Delegates in 1827 he participated in chartering the Baltimore and Ohio Railroad Company, which he promoted eagerly in the pages of *The American Farmer.*

Skinner is known to have gone into the West at least once. Following his summary dismissal from the Baltimore postmastership by

2 Demaree, *Agricultural Press,* p. 23.

President Martin Van Buren, he engaged in a variety of activities, including editing foreign books for publication in the United States. He invested in a spasmodic attempt to start a silk industry in Maryland, and purchased some land in the Southwest, which he visited. The itinerary and duration of his visit are not known, but the fiscal results of both investments were unhappy. Skinner's work for Lafayette and the Lafayette heirs was presumably more conservative and more successful. After becoming quite friendly with the aged Frenchman during his visit to the United States in 1824–25, Skinner was named agent in charge of the twenty thousand–acre estate in Florida which Congress presented to Lafayette in recognition of his services to the nation.[3] Following his term in the Post Office Department, 1841–45, Skinner was again at loose ends, and on this occasion determined to go to New York City. He worked with Horace Greeley and others on various publishing ventures, and then in 1848 moved to Philadelphia, where he started another new monthly magazine, *The Plough, the Loom, and the Anvil.* It proved to be a huge success,[4] and he was still editing it when an accidental fall downstairs in the Baltimore Post Office ended his life.

Skinner's interests naturally included field sports such as were commonly associated with agricultural pursuits and country life. Field sports were "regularly spoken of" in *The American Farmer* by 1825,[5] and a few years later Skinner established a new magazine to satisfy needs he felt to exist in this area: *The American Turf Register and Sporting Magazine,* Volume I, Number 1, September, 1829, with purposes stated as follows: ". . . an account of the performances on the American turf, and the pedigrees of thorough bred horses, will constitute the *basis* of the work, [but] it is designed, also, as a Magazine of information on veterinary subjects generally; and of various rural sports, as RACING, TROTTING MATCHES, SHOOTING, HUNTING, FISHING, &c. together with original sketches of the natural history and habits of American game of all kinds. . . ."[6] Skinner invited all readers to communicate freely with him, asking especially for "curious anecdotes and interesting facts."[7]

3 Poore, "Biographical Sketch," reprint ed., p. 17.
4 Smith, *Sporting Family,* p. 35.
5 Poore, "Biographical Sketch," reprint ed., p. 20.
6 I (September, 1829), 1. Italics and capitalization in original.
7 *Ibid.,* p. 3.

The fifteen-year existence of the new publication may be divided conveniently into three periods of ownership and management. The first six years were Skinner's, and they were the most productive of West-related material. Skinner sold the magazine in August, 1835, for $10,000—half the price he had received five years earlier for *The American Farmer*—and it came into the hands of Robert Gilmore, Jr., Gideon B. Smith, and Allen Jones Davie, all apparently of Baltimore. Gilmore (1774–1848), the owner, was a successful merchant and banker, chiefly notable as the first significant collector of art in Baltimore. Smith, sometime editor but more important as business manager of the magazine, had been associated with Skinner in running *The American Farmer*. His main distinction was as a zealous advocate of silk culture in Maryland in the 1830's and 1840's. He was the inventor of a "silk reel" and the leading figure in the American Silk Society, with headquarters in Baltimore and Smith as editor of its publication, *Silk Journal*.[8]

During the three years comprising the second period in the history of *Turf Register* one has the impression that there was little new editorial initiative, that the new staff merely coasted along on the momentum provided by the very energetic Skinner. It is true that the country suffered severe financial straits during this period, and the magazine along with the country. Several delays in publication resulted in the last issue of Volume IX appearing in December rather than August, 1838. But the unaggressive philosophy of the editor was clearly revealed in the scolding note included in that issue, headed "To Our Patrons":

> It will have been observed by all our readers that there has been a great falling off in the work, particularly in respect to original matter, and engravings. Will our readers bear with us when we tell them that this is *their* fault, *not ours*. Original matter can only be furnished by contributors; there never was an editor that could supply it for a periodical such as this. It would require an omnipresent being to perform such a task. All that can be expected from the editor and publisher is to receive, collate and publish such matter as the various individuals in different parts of the country find it convenient to communicate, and to add such other matter as they are able to collect

[8] Notes and clippings on Gilmore and Smith are found in the Biographical File, Maryland Department, Enoch Pratt Free Library, Baltimore.

> from their own observation. This is a practical and plain view of the case. Now if these correspondents cease to furnish this matter, the editor is left without any other resource than that of selections from other publications; and this has been our case.[9]

Editor Smith continued, complaining of the many subscribers who were not paying for the magazine, and that many who did pay sent their letters without postage and enclosed depreciated currency that could be negotiated only at a substantial loss to the magazine. Although this note did not announce it, the magazine was in fact suspended for several months at this juncture.

William T. Porter, editor of the popular newspaper *Spirit of the Times,* now took over and moved *Turf Register* to New York.[10] Although a younger publication than *Turf Register, Spirit of the Times* had built up a large nationwide circulation and attracted much favorable attention among sportsmen because of its considerable coverage of their interests. Porter's broad scope was indicated by his newspaper's subtitle, "A Chronicle of the Turf, Agriculture, Field Sports, Literature and the Stage." Porter believed correctly that *Turf Register* would complement his own publication. First he had to get it back into operation, however, and it was not until the July, 1839, issue that it resumed the regular monthly schedule. The first six months of the year were covered by three combined issues, which came out tardily. Some improvements were immediately apparent under Porter's editorship, such as an increase in the number of illustrations, but Porter suffered financial reverses with *Spirit,* seeing ownership of it and probably of *Turf Register* also pass into other hands although he remained as editor. Finally, in the December, 1844, issue, the conclusive "Notice to Subscribers" appeared:

> The present number of "*The American Turf Register and Sporting Magazine*" completes its fifteenth volume, and, at the same time, its existence.
>
> With a list of subscribers amply sufficient to defray the expenses of its publication, the Publisher is imperiously obliged to discontinue it, upon the sole ground of their neglect to pay their subscriptions.

9 IX (December, 1838), 529–530.

10 Francis Brinley, *Life of William T. Porter* (New York: D. Appleton and Co., 1860), is a basic source for this interesting personality. See also Nelson F. Adkins, "William Trotter Porter," *Dictionary of American Biography,* XV, 107–108.

Hundreds of the "*patrons*" of this magazine have paid no subscription for years![11]

The contents of the magazine, in general terms, remained much the same over its fifteen-year existence and were outlined well by the editorial announcement in the first issue. Horses were the major preoccupation—registering thoroughbreds, listing pedigrees, and clarifying confusion due to duplicate names and other reasons; describing famous horses and races, American and foreign, current and historic; and giving instructions on handling, feeding, and healing horses. Most issues had engraved frontispieces—most often of a distinguished horse. The magazine had a real impact on the market value of horses, whose lineage could now be substantiated by published data. Thoroughbred prices jumped by as much as from $100 to $5,000 or even $10,000. Gratified owners presented Skinner with a silver dinner service in recognition of this result.[12]

"There is nothing that can so well give to this Magazine the character for it that we covet, as descriptions of sports and of game in the far west," wrote Skinner in an early issue,[13] commenting on a communication from St. Louis which he published under the head, "Sports of Missouri." This specific statement was repeated in effect by Skinner at two later occasions.[14] It must be weighed in light of the plain fact that his primary preoccupation was with the turf, but, in addition to the initial general invitation to all readers to write to him, it did evoke some interesting responses.

Of 159 items in *Turf Register* listed as pertaining to the American West,[15] 52 involved horses in a leading way. This was twice as many as the next category, birds (26), although if all of the "hunting" category (such as birds, buffalo, deer, horses, wolves, etc.) are taken together that total is much larger. Dealing further in terms of numerical analysis, we note that in the six years of Skinner's editorship the western items per volume averaged 14.7, of which only 7 percent were copied from other publications. During the next three years

[11] XV (December, 1844), 706.

[12] Poore, "Biographical Sketch," reprint ed., p. 25.

[13] I (February, 1830), 296.

[14] VI (January, 1835), 240; (April, 1835), 411.

[15] "American West" here means with minor exceptions the Mississippi Valley and parts west of it. Routine notices of race results from St. Louis, etc., are not included in the count cited here, but only material with narrative or descriptive value.

the average volume had 12 western items, of which 14 percent were copies. The number of western items per volume dropped to 5.7 during the last six years, when the magazine was published in New York City, and of them 35 percent were copies from other publications. The proportion of nonoriginal material in the other parts of the last issues (except routine race reports) was closer to 100 percent. Other categories of items relating to the West, in addition to ones on horses and the hunting and description of animals, included the categories of Indians (20 items), travel description (14), fishing (8), and miscellaneous (20). In the last category were pieces on such things as gambling in the West, painting, marksmanship, game laws, a Davy Crockett anecdote, and a story about an alleged petrified buffalo.

The American Turf Register and Sporting Magazine was a special-interest magazine, as the two-part title clearly indicates, but it did attract some contributions in the genre of "travel-writing"—i.e., narratives based on a trip and offering general comments on places and people that were observed and experiences that resulted. The special interests of the editor almost always predominated. An otherwise unidentified Mr. J. C. L. of Cincinnati had taken a tour of Texas, for example, as he wrote in a letter published in the sixth issue of the magazine.[16] The thing he gave most attention to, however, as far as the *Turf Register* account indicates, was the impression made upon the Mexicans by his friend's method of breaking a horse to saddle. Another Texas item, "Extracts from a Journal Kept in the Spring of 1835, in a Ramble on the Prairies,"[17] contains quite a bit about the countryside and people, including some Indians encountered near the Brazos River, but the main concern was hunting buffalo. Two more Texas travel items appear in the last year of the magazine's publication. They were by a British naval officer, Piercy B. St. John, who had been in the Texas Navy about 1841 and described something of the people and countryside while recounting hunting exploits. The first was entitled "Wild Sports in the West" and the second "A Walk amongst the Wild Turkeys." Both were copied from London sporting publications.[18]

An original and more significant contribution ran in the eighth

[16] I (February, 1830), 285–286.
[17] VII (February, 1836), 263–268; (March, 1836), 310–314.
[18] XV (February, 1844), 80–84; (April, 1844), 232–236.

volume of the magazine.[19] The writer, William Marshall Anderson, commenced as follows: "I accept the invitation to occupy a few pages of your Register with a description of my horseback adventures to and beyond the Rocky mountains. . . ." He described outfitting himself and going in 1834 from Louisville, Kentucky, to St. Louis, where he became part of a company of thirty-seven men, "headed by a good trapper and a brave man—all in all, just such a one as you would like to know—gods what a country this would be, if every man was such as he. This tall Jackson-faced, raw-boned brave is W. L. Sublette, with as quick an eye and steady a hand as ever lead [*sic*] company or shot a Blackfoot. When in camp, he resembled an old bruin in one respect, and that was, that you could touch in no place, that he was not ready to fend off." Anderson continued, describing an encounter with Pawnee Indians, the appearance of the Platte River, buffalo, mirages and looming, and other phenomena of interest. Also original, apparently, and of some interest, is an account published in May, 1843, of an excursion to hunt buffalo undertaken by a group of Canadian or British Army officers who set out from Montreal.[20] Some accounts of expeditions by the military, or men accompanying them, may be classed as travel writings. "A Reader," writing from Fort Gibson, August 1, 1833, found his way into print in the October issue of *Turf Register*, describing an expedition into the "Grand Prairie, southwest of us" during the previous May and June.[21] The next issue of the magazine contains another account of the same expedition by a rather frequent contributor who is signed only by the number "33."[22]

In addition to the naval officer's travel pieces already mentioned, there were several others in the magazine borrowed from other publications. One is a review from the London *(New) Sporting Magazine* of a book by John Kirk Townsend, *Sporting Excursions in the Rocky Mountains*.[23] A fourteen-stanza poem by "Phazma," who was Matthew

19 VIII (May, 1837), 409–412; (July, 1837), 454–457; (November, 1837), 549–552. The articles have been described and reprinted several times, most recently by Dale L. Morgan and Eleanor Towles, eds., in *The Rocky Mountain Journals of William Marshall Anderson: The West in 1834* (San Marino, Calif.: Huntington Library, 1967).

20 XIV (May, 1843), 249–251.

21 V (October, 1833), 70–75.

22 V (November, 1833), 141–143.

23 XI (May, 1840), 235–240. *Turf Register* gives the author's name as J. R. Townsend. The book, with title as given here, was published in two volumes in London in 1840 by H. Colburn. It was derived from the author's *Narrative of a Journey across the*

(Matt) C. Field, printed first in the New Orleans *Picayune,* was reprinted twice in *Turf Register,*[24] the second time in conjunction with an account of "The Hunted Buffalo" copied from George Catlin's *Letters and Notes on the Manners, Customs, and Condition of the North American Indians.* Other borrowings are from J. J. Audubon,[25] something called *The City Journal and Ladies' Daily Gazette,*[26] and a piece mostly on wildcats in the South by Thomas Bangs Thorpe, credited also to the London *(New) Sporting Magazine.*[27]

> How little is the public aware [exclaimed Skinner] of the privations experienced by the officers of our army, with mental cultivation and qualities to enjoy all the social refinements that are the growth of dense and opulent population; yet, called by duty to stand sentinel on distant outposts in the west, far beyond the utmost limit of civilized life. . . . Happily, this want of the means of social amusement is, in some measure, supplied by *abundance of game,* the pursuit of which refreshes at once the body and the spirits. Hence we hear of feats of horsemanship and marksmanship by our officers . . . unequalled in the sporting annals of any country.[28]

With some due allowance for patriotic hyperbole, certain it was that Army officers provided the mainstay of contributions to *Turf Register* on the West. Major (after 1836 Lieutenant Colonel) Richard Barnes Mason, both a writer to the magazine and written about in it, was easily the most prominent officer in its pages. Others included Lieutenant Reuben Holmes, Lieutenant John Gano Furman (who died in 1830), Major Richard M. Coleman (a surgeon), Lieutenant Joseph Van Swearingen, Lieutenant Dixon Stansbury Miles, Lieutenant S. W. Moore (whose real name was Stephen Moore Westmore), Lieutenant Forbes Britton, Lieutenant Theodoric Henry Porter, Lieutenant Abraham Robinson Johnston, and Captain Martin Scott.

Rocky Mountains, published in Boston in 1839. Townsend's trip was with the Wyeth party to Oregon in 1834.

24 XI (December, 1840), 648–649; XII (May, 1842), 240–241. See it also on pp. 93–96 of *Matt Field on the Santa Fe Trail,* collected by Clyde and Mae Reed Porter, edited and with Introduction and Notes by John E. Sunder (Norman: University of Oklahoma Press, 1960).

25 XII (January, 1841), 46–49.

26 XIII (May, 1842), 280–283.

27 XIII (September, 1842), 518–521.

28 III (February, 1832), 296. See another exclamation, III (September, 1831), 42.

Fort Gibson, far southwestern bastion of the nation from its establishment in 1824 until the annexation of Texas, was the most heard-from single place, followed by St. Louis (Jefferson Barracks) and Chicago (Fort Dearborn). Also notable were Prairie du Chien (Fort Crawford), Green Bay (Fort Howard), Fort Leavenworth, and even Fort Vancouver.

The western preoccupation with horses manifested itself in two main and connected concerns, first with racing and next with breeding. Soldiers and civilians alike, in the West, regarded the establishment of clubs as one of the marks of the struggle to promote civilization. Jockey clubs required somewhat more in stability and investment than a transient military population could sustain, but the period while *Turf Register* was being published witnessed the creation by civilians of many new western jockey clubs. The racing of horses at far western military posts was likely to be on an informal basis. Officer contributors to the magazine provided more than their share, however, concerning an issue that filled many pages of the magazine from June, 1833, until January, 1836: could the qualities of American horses be improved by breeding them with wild or Indian horses from the West?

The issue was opened when a letter from "A Subscriber," dated at Cantonment Jesup, Louisiana, on July 15, 1832, was published belatedly almost a year later.[29] The writer had visited an Osage village on the Verdigris River in 1829 with a party of gentlemen, and had been greatly impressed to find the Indians with a splendid stock of "horses possessing good wind, great powers of endurance, and hardy constitutions, with fine bony, sinewy limbs." He urged that American breeders obtain the finest possible examples of Indian horses in order to engage in careful, extensive experiments. The same writer, "33," in later published pieces from Fort Gibson, pushed the matter further. "There appeared to be two breeds of the wild horse," he wrote under the date of July 29, 1833: "a small, inferior, or pony breed; and a large, fleet, and majestic race, which was usually seen in rocky ground" and seemed impossible to capture. Colts which were taken, on the recent expedition into the Osage country, did not survive.[30]

29 IV (June, 1833), 501–503.
30 V (November, 1833), 141–143.

The next year, 1834, was the Year of the Wild Horse in *Turf Register*. The editor led off in January with an open "Letter to Gen. [Charles] Gratiot, On the Importance of Procuring the best Wild Stallion from our Prairies."[31] He believed that the general, the Chief of the Corps of Engineers, and the other important persons whose names he threw in, would be interested in faster, more durable horses not only for cavalry duty but also for sport. Skinner was even willing to pay all the expenses of obtaining breeding stock and transporting it wherever necessary—as long as the expenses were kept low. There followed a flurry of excitement over a horse in Tennessee called Camancha Chief—doing a profitable business at stud—but four months later the stallion, valuable and former property of Sam Houston though he was, was exposed as possessing a domesticated ancestry.[32] Enthusiasm in the project was maintained, however, by letters from a self-styled former dragoon, Colonel H. C. Brish of Ohio, who had "never met with any thing of the horse kind that possessed strength, action, and wind equal to the 'mustang' horses"; from Lieutenant Dixon S. Miles at Fort Gibson reporting that Lieutenant S. W. Moore [*sic*] had bought two "prairie studs" from Osages on the Blue River; and by an essay-letter from "33," published in two consecutive issues of the magazine under the somewhat misleading title, "On the Origin and Qualities of the Wild Horse of the Prairies of the South-West."[33] Then the sky fell in. "All Aback—Wild Horses" was the head given a letter from Dragoon Major R. B. Mason, written from "Camp near Ft. Gibson," August 19, 1834. He stated: ". . . they are not what they are cracked up to be. . . . I have a wild mare that I bought from a Camanchie Indian the day after he caught her, she is decidedly the very best I have seen, and I believe equal to any in the prairie, and she is such a nag as you can buy any where for fifty or sixty dollars."[34]

Editor Skinner kept a stiff upper lip, we may assume, and perhaps congratulated himself that his impulsive offer to pay the expense of procuring "wild horse" studs had not cost him, say, $5,000. Skinner's successor exhibited less interest in the subject, perhaps, but found that the sutler at Fort Gibson, E. B. Nowland, thoroughly disagreed

[31] V (January, 1834), 221–224.

[32] V (April, 1834), 409; (August, 1834), 609.

[33] V (May, 1834), 463–464; VI (September, 1834), 30–31; (October, 1834), 61–66; (November, 1834), 118–124.

[34] VI (December, 1834), 166.

with the renowned Mason, explaining that the latter had been "immediately on the Spanish or Texas frontier" whence the Indians stole the scrubs that disappointed him. "I am in hopes when the Major again returns from the Prairie, he will have seen more of the true wild horse, and less of the cat-hammed, ewe-necked, spindle-shanked Spanish breed. . . ." Nowland announced at length that he himself had acquired a horse, named Neosho, "of the pure native blood," whom he hoped to breed back home in Tennessee. "I prize him so highly," he stated, "that nothing less than three thousand dollars can purchase him. . . ."[35] One more major contribution on the subject appeared in the magazine, in January, 1836, written by an unidentified man in Little Rock, Arkansas. This letter was also critical of Mason's knowledge of the prairie. The author claimed himself to have traveled widely, and pointed out that the best wild horses always escaped their pursuers.[36]

If Fort Gibson could not support a jockey club, the sportsmen there decided in 1835 that at least they could organize a hunting club, and they did so. Major Mason was president, Lieutenant Britton secretary, and nine members were listed also (including Brevet Brigadier General Mathew Arbuckle). It was a publicity-conscious group, apparently, but the *Turf Register* seemed willing enough to cooperate. The report of the club's organization concluded by quoting two formal resolutions:

> That this Club subscribe for the American Turf Register and Sporting Magazine from its commencement, and its Editor be elected an honorary member.
>
> That the formation of this Club and the proceedings thus far be published in the American Turf Register and Sporting Magazine.[37]

Most of the other contributions to the magazine that can be identified as from military men in the West consist of reports of the excitements and successes of hunting. Wolves, deer, birds, and of course buffalo were their primary interests. They were interested not only in their own exploits but also in describing the hunting methods of Indians, especially in pursuit of buffalo. Some writers

[35] VII (October, 1835), 60–62.
[36] VII (January, 1836), 204–205.
[37] VI (June, 1835), 511–512.

were obviously single-minded and dedicated, such as A. H. P., who was probably a young lieutenant stationed at Fort Crawford, Prairie du Chien. He had his horse shod "with sharp heels and steel toes in his shoes" in order to run down wolves on the frozen Mississippi River. He got thirteen in the month of January, 1831, by himself, and denounced his associates who would not join him, even though they all owned good mounts. "They are dunghills, and show no blood," he fumed.[38] Rather more pleasantly, indeed with real charm, Lieutenant A. R. Johnston described the appearance and behavior of two captive prairie dogs whom he had with him for several weeks. "Billy [the name given one of them] took a fancy to my dogs, and amused himself searching for fleas on them: to this the dogs would doubtless have had no objection, but he being equally fond of horny substances, would attack their nails, which always broke up the party."[39]

Of fishing there was very little in *Turf Register*, from civilian or military sources, but one such item did mark a farthest west extreme touched by the magazine. This was a letter from "Dr. Gardener," presumably young Dr. Meredith Gairdner of the Hudson's Bay Company, who wrote from Fort Vancouver in November, 1834, describing the salmon on the Columbia River, their muscular power "truly astonishing."[40] What may have seemed a "fish story" came from H. O. L. of Manchester, Mississippi, who described using the entrails of a pig for bait to catch a gar, which he called "alligator gar," eight feet two inches in length and weighing 114 pounds.[41] Two of what certainly were "fish stories" came from "Sigma," a correspondent on several subjects, from Kaskaskia, Illinois.[42]

Fish stories and prairie dogs, however, were diversions from the main burden of discussion in *Turf Register*, and so may be out of the main path of the present description. The horse was the thing, and it seems even more evident when one turns to concentrate upon western contributions to the magazine by civilians. Jockey clubs were announced in several places and, as in the case of the Fort Gibson

38 III (December, 1831), 182.

39 XV (May, 1844), 282–286.

40 VII (January, 1836), 221. See A. G. Harvey, "Meredith Gairdner: Doctor of Medicine," *British Columbia Historical Quarterly*, IX (April, 1945), 89–111.

41 VI (October, 1834), 95.

42 IV (June, 1833), 527–528.

Hunting Club, some with the evident intention of advertising themselves through *Turf Register*. Little Rock, Batesville, Pine Bluffs, and Fayetteville in Arkansas,[43] Vicksburg and Port Gibson in Mississippi,[44] and Natchitoches in Louisiana[45] were among the ones mentioned most.

A continuing discussion, somewhat reminiscent of the question of getting wild Indian or prairie horses to improve the American breed, developed during the second period of editorship of the magazine. "Sigma," mentioned above, described a stranger who had come to Kaskaskia about 1833 and performed amazingly in "Taming wild horses," as the printed letter was entitled. After demonstrating his success he sold the secret of his method to several persons for $5 each and departed, and the purchasers found his procedure "a perfect panacea for all the wickedness and 'deviltry' which many of the horse kind possess." The writer speculated that some sort of drug might be involved.[46] Responding to pressure from the editor,[47] "Sigma" could announce in a letter printed later in the year that he had bought the secret from someone in Kaskaskia, and the editor announced that now he had it also, and would test it as thoroughly and quickly as possible.[48] By the following spring he and an East Coast friend had tested the method on stubborn horses and also on mules and a bull, with entire satisfaction. But the secret had been bought and sold, with solemn pledges exchanged of not reselling it, and so it could not then be published. But as soon as previous owners could be found and indemnified, wrote the editor, it would be published in *Turf Register*. "We pledge ourselves to the public that we shall omit no effort to accomplish the object," he asserted.[49] But a new editor moved the magazine to New York in a few months, and the subject does not appear again in its pages.

Interest in horses contributed to the first appearance in *Turf Register* of the work of a notable western artist, Peter Rindisbacher, who had moved to St. Louis from Wisconsin and Canada, and gained

43 Esp. VII (December, 1835), 182; VIII (October, 1836), 63; IX (September, 1838), 386.

44 VIII (November, 1836), 124–125.

45 XIV (December, 1843), 728–731.

46 VIII (February, 1837), 261–263.

47 VIII (March, 1837), 316–319.

48 VIII (September, 1837), 500–501.

49 IX (May, 1838), 193–196.

the favorable attention of patrons who sent samples of his work to Skinner in Baltimore. The frontispiece of the second issue of the magazine was engraved from one of Rindisbacher's drawings and entitled "Sioux Warrior Charging." It was accompanied by a rather turgid essay on the "Horsemanship of the North American Indians," and praising Rindisbacher's work—perhaps written by the editor, although signed "Don Alphonso."[50] Eight more engravings and a woodcut appeared in succeeding issues of *Turf Register*, down to December, 1833, and one more engraving in the October, 1840, issue. The artist's work was superior and well merited publication, and had he not died so soon (1834) and so young (twenty-eight) this exposure of his work in a high-quality publication of national circulation would no doubt have contributed to his reputation over the years.[51] While the hope was expressed in 1836 that the magazine would soon present some of the artistry of George Catlin, this did not come about until six years later and under another editor. The frontispiece of the May, 1842, issue was an Indian portrait entitled "A Patrician of the New World," engraved after a drawing by Catlin, and accompanied by a "description of it . . . from his recently published 'Letters and Notes on the Manners, Customs, and Condition of the North American Indians.' "[52] The quality and number of illustrations in the magazine were an indicator of its health. Volume IX, the last of the three years of the magazine's second editorial phase, did not contain a single illustration. Under Porter as editor of the last six volumes there was a strong effort at improvement at first, but this fell off as more and more was copied from English and other publications, and at least once an engraving from an earlier volume was repeated. Finally, in the last four months of the magazine's existence, there was no illustrative material at all.

If the *Turf Register* did not offer much in the way of art, it offered less in the way of original literature. Aside from material copied from published works such as those of Washington Irving, John J. Audubon, "Lewis and Clark's Journal," John Tanner's *Narrative*, and Dr. John Davidson Godman's *American Natural History*, there

50 I (October, 1829), opp. 73 and 73–74.

51 See John Francis McDermott, "Peter Rindisbacher, Frontier Reporter," *Art Quarterly* (Spring, 1949), pp. 129–144, and "Further Notes on Peter Rindisbacher," *Art Quarterly* (Spring, 1963), pp. 73–76.

52 XIII (May, 1842), opp. 239 and 239–240.

were several items by Thomas Bangs Thorpe but in no case was the first printing in *Turf Register*. Thorpe's famous "Big Bear of Arkansas" story had an early printing here, but it had appeared a few weeks earlier in Porter's *Spirit of the Times*.[53] The magazine contained almost nothing by way of intended humor. Perhaps this had a bearing on its ultimate failure.

In sum, *The American Turf Register and Sporting Magazine* was a publication of limited interest regarding the history of western America, but one of real value within its designated scope. It would be well if it could be made more readily accessible to scholars by the indexing of its original contributions.

[53] XII (May, 1841), 274–280.

Reveille in the West: Western Travelers in the St. Louis *Weekly Reveille*, 1844-50

Nicholas Joost

ON MONDAY MORNING, July 15, 1844, the busy citizens of that gateway to the West and center of the fur trade, the Mound City, St. Louis, could purchase for ten cents a copy—or, if they preferred, could subscribe for the coming year, for $3, "*favorably, in advance*"—the first issue of the St. Louis *Weekly Reveille*.[1]

[1] There was also announced the St. Louis *Daily Reveille*, for $5 a year. The *Daily Reveille* was the parent journal, and one guesses that a major reason for its weekly offspring was the convenience with which a weekly packet of news, gossip, verse, and light fiction could be mailed to outlying areas and frontier settlements, especially by river steamer. The various advertisements in the *Weekly Reveille* must also have been pertinent to the relatively isolated settlers dependent on St. Louis as a major entrepot of the western frontier. The consecutively dated columns of news and statistics and gossip in the *Weekly Reveille* (hereafter abbreviated in these notes as *WR*) were, of course, reprinted from its daily parent—occasionally with confusing results, as when under the heading "Letters from the Pacific," *WR*, V (May 14, 1849), 2106, an unsigned editorial piece informs the reader that "We give on our first page a letter from a gentleman now on his way to the Pacific—one among many whom we have made particular arrangements with for a regular and useful correspondence." As no such letter appears on p. 2105, the first page of the *WR* under discussion, the editor's reference is obviously to the particular daily edition of the *Reveille*. And the letter in question—under the heading "Letters from the Emigration" and signed S.—appears not on p. 2105 but on p. 2106, along with the item referring to it. As substantially consecutive files of the *Daily Reveille* are not extant, this paper will necessarily concern itself with files of the *WR*, I (July 15, 1844), 1, to VII (September 23, 1850), 4364. A warning: pagination of the *WR* is continuous but not always accurate.

The files consulted are those of the Missouri Historical Society, St. Louis. For advice and help in the research of this paper at the society, I thank Mr. George Brooks, Director; Mrs. Ernst Stadler, Archivist; and Mrs. Fred C. Harrington, Librarian, and her staff. Also I thank my colleague, Professor John Francis McDermott, for guidance and for providing me with certain materials; and Mr. Dale Morgan, for valuable suggestions for the improvement and completeness of the paper.

According to the Prospectus of the *Reveille,* the paper was "a sheet of eight pages, of the largest quarto size." Throughout its publication, the *Reveille* indicated the symbolism of its title by means of the vignette carried on its masthead title. The first of these was a drummer boy between lines of Army tents, the national flag flapping bravely beside him; behind his back flowed the Mississippi, beyond which rose the crudely depicted levee business district of St. Louis, buildings and warehouses and towering courthouse dome, with a river steamboat tied up at the quay. This charming but fuzzy and crudely cut woodblock print was discarded at the beginning of the third year of publication, when the *Reveille* substituted a more sophisticated wood-engraved title and vignette, which it procured from the New York *Spirit of the Times.* Now little comic male figures writhed around and climbed upon the letters of "Weekly Reveille"; and a more naturalistic representation of the St. Louis waterfront was attempted, with the important addition of the cathedral spire complementing the dome of the federal courthouse.

The *Weekly Reveille* (which for convenience will be hereafter called the *Reveille*) published a great deal that was not only topical but newsworthy, yet it was much more than a newspaper. As the Prospectus asserted, "A *light* and *agreeable* news sheet is what we design—noticing all local events, paying special attention to all matters connected with the interests of the glorious West." Variety, said the proprietors, was the sauce of their newspaper as it was the spice of life, and they proposed to steer clear of "all those wrangling jealousies and bitter recriminations which too often render an editorial life one of incessant vexation"; the road the *Reveille*'s drummer boy proposed to travel was a sunnier one, independent of political squabbles and things "ornate." "It cannot be," concluded the Prospectus, that "the great West, in its giant strides to wealth and power, can be entirely indifferent to those way-side flowers of fancy, and sprigs of merriment, which *will* arise to seek the sun, however unimportant they may be deemed when compared with the more marketable produce surrounding them. The march of empire, with us, is the march of intelligence, which embraces in its train as well the arts that amuse as those which refine; and while that march is onward, be it ours to beat the 'Reveille.' "[2]

2 *WR*, I (July 22, 1844), 24.

Calling themselves Keemle & Field, the three proprietors—Colonel Charles Keemle, Joseph M. Field, and their "junior" editor, Joseph's younger brother Matthew C. Field—adhered to the policy outlined in their Prospectus. Mat Field soon became ill and left the paper to travel for his health; aboard ship, he died en route from Boston to Mobile (and eventually St. Louis), aged thirty-two years, on December 15, 1844. Joe Field and Colonel Keemle became Keemle & Field and saw to it that their *Reveille* remained lighthearted.[3] It did print news, usually rather scrappily: the news items appeared, along with other items, in consecutively dated columns; that is to say, after a front page of wit and humor and *belles lettres*, there appeared a series of consecutively dated columns, six sets for each day of the week, Tuesday through Sunday (Monday's news was undated), with the latest news thus published in the rear pages in the columns for Sunday, the day preceding issuance of each weekly number of the *Reveille*. There was, as one might expect, a good deal of local news and correspondence, whether of the cholera epidemic of 1848–49, or the rising level of the Missouri above St. Louis, or the Great Fire of 1849, or the results of a city election.

The *Reveille*, in an equally scrappy and piecemeal fashion, con-

3 For Joseph M. Field see Oral S. Coad, "Joseph M. Field," *Dictionary of American Biography*, III, Pt. 2 (New York: Charles Scribner's Sons, 1931), 366. For Matthew C. Field see "Death of M. C. Field," *WR*, I (December 23, 1844), 185 (this front page wore its columns bordered in black): "After a severe attack of sickness, during the past summer, still presuming upon his youth and repeated returns of partial strength," Matthew ("Mat") Field thought "that a sojourn among eastern friends—perhaps, a long sea voyage, if his strength still improved, might be of service. But, too late:—still failing, he embarked at Boston, at the 13th ultimo, for Mobile, to rejoin his family, who were there to meet him; but on the second day out, as we learn from the report of Capt. Linnell, of the barque Huma, in the Pensacola Gazette, he bade us all farewell! He had nearly completed his thirty-second year, and has left a widow, with two children. He had, also, left his gentle memory in the hearts of those who knew him. Heaven's will be done." Two memorials that M. C. Field received in the *Reveille* are noteworthy in the present context: John Brown, "A Tribute to the Memory of Matthew C. Field, Who Died at Sea," *WR*, I (March 31, 1845), 2, reprinted in Elliott's autobiographical *Notes Taken in Sixty Years* (St. Louis: R. P. Studley and Co., 1883), p. 196 (and concluding: "Yet death's last crowning triumph more appals / The soul, when genius falls!"); and the actor and artist, George Jamieson, "The Late Matthew C. Field, 'Phazma' at Niagara," *WR*, I (March 24, 1845), 294, reported "*From the Knickerbocker, for March*." See also: W. G. B. Carson, "The Diary of Mat Field, St. Louis, April 2–May 16, 1839," *Missouri Historical Society Bulletin*, V (January, 1949), 91–94; Matthew C. Field, *Prairie and Mountain Sketches*, Kate L. Gregg and John Francis McDermott, eds. (Norman: University of Oklahoma Press, 1957), *passim*; John E. Sunder, ed., *Matt Field on the Santa Fe Trail* (Norman: University of Oklahoma Press, 1960), esp. pp. xvii–xxix.

trived to give its readers much national and international news and comment. It presented such items, more often than not, as fillers, as when on the front page of the issue for July 29, 1844, the printer's sort of a small hand with index finger pointing indicated the single sentence: "John Quincy Adams was 76 years old on the 12th of July inst." At the end of the *Reveille*'s life, a more international item pointed out: "An Italian and a Frenchman, who had just returned from California with $18,000 in gold dust, were recently robbed in London, while they were 'spreeing it' at Vauxhall Gardens." Shades of *Evelina*![4]

The *Reveille* was more original, however, and retains considerable interest for the student of American culture, in two major categories of the copy it printed. First, as its Prospectus professed, its stock in trade was humor, the novel "American" humor that, arising recently on the old Southwest frontier of Georgia and Alabama, had by the 1840's found raucous expression all along the Mississippi Valley by means of the river traffic, and that would rapidly spread during the 1840's to the emigrant settlements and mining camps of Oregon and California. Here the *Reveille* constitutes—to use one of its own clichés—a veritable El Dorado for the scholar who is willing to dig.[5]

Second, and appropriately for the theme of "Travelers on the Western Frontier," the *Reveille* contains many letters and journals written by travelers in the western regions. It is to be expected that a St. Louis newspaper would regularly print these materials concerned with a topic then of local, national, and international importance: the nation's westward expansion. The subscribers to the *Reveille* were spread over the entire United States east of the Mississippi, to judge by its list of agents in Boston, New York, Philadelphia, Baltimore, Pittsburgh, Memphis, and Mobile (there was even a representative, J. B. Washbourne, Esq., in Van Buren, Arkansas). Undoubtedly subscribers were held by the wit and humor of the contributions in the *Reveille*, but it is obvious that potential emigrants, land speculators, businessmen (both manufacturers and entrepreneurs), politicians,

[4] *WR*, I (July 29, 1844), 17; VII (September 23, 1850), 4363.

[5] See, e.g., John S. Robb, *Streaks of Squatter Life and Far-West Scenes*, John Francis McDermott, ed. (Gainesville, Fla.: Scholars' Facsimiles & Reprints, 1962), pp. v–xvi *passim*.

and soldiers continued to read the *Reveille* because it was a compendium of information about the West. The *Reveille* was on the spot to use this information where it all collected in the great emporium of the West. Familiar to most people are the advantages of the geographical location of St. Louis, at the confluence of three great rivers, the Mississippi, Missouri, and Illinois, and with the confluence of the Ohio and the Mississippi conveniently nearby. Perhaps less familiar is the fact that for the railways, highways, and even the telegraph, these rivers constituted major barriers.

In the early 1840's, letters carried no stamps and still had to be sealed with sealing wax. As late as the start of Frémont's fateful expedition to the Pacific region, from Kansas Landing, on May 30, 1843, the only way in which Jessie Benton Frémont could expedite an urgent message to her husband was by special courier from St. Louis: he must leave immediately before an order reached him to return to Washington to explain why he was taking along a howitzer. "It was," wrote Mrs. Frémont later, "in the blessed day before telegrams. . . ."[6] By the late 1840's the *Reveille* was beginning to rely on telegraphic dispatches for news from the states east of the Mississippi, as being quicker, more reliable, possibly more accurate. The letters from eastern correspondents become relatively fewer—and less interesting. Comparison of the reporting of the 1844 election returns with the similar reporting of the election returns of 1848 shows a definite divergence in repertorial techniques.[7]

6 As quoted in Fredrika Shumway Smith, *Frémont: Soldier, Explorer, Statesman* (Chicago: Rand McNally and Co., 1966), p. 74. See also footnote 41 below.

7 See *WR*, I (November 11, 1844), 138–142, and V (November 12, 1848), 1901, 1907 ("The Political Future"). In 1844 the paper—which, to repeat, reported all its items day by day under a series of consecutively dated and printed columns—gave the news as it dribbled in, beginning with the preceding Tuesday and concluding with the Sunday the paper went to press. Under Wednesday, November 6, 1844, the first news about the election printed local results in St. Louis, St. Louis County, and in Illinois, Alton, Upper Alton, and Monticello (now Godfrey; all three Illinois towns voted majorities for the Whig candidate, Henry Clay). Further returns were printed in Friday's columns, and Saturday's columns gave final results for seven states, but as late as Sunday, November 10, the *Reveille* printed returns, in this case those for Pennsylvania. In 1847 the telegraph lines reached St. Louis. Techniques of reporting changed in consequence. In 1848 the "Telegraphic Despatches for the *Reveille*" giving returns on the presidential election were all collected on one page devoted mostly to incoming, incomplete election returns, for Sunday, November 12. The exception was that the columns dated Thursday, November 16, 1848, published the city and county returns for St. Louis, accompanied by an editorial on the election, "The Political Future."

By contrast, the way west of St. Louis remained in its primitive stage to the end of the decade—as Jessie Frémont wrote, at the mercy of fog and snag. That is to say, travelers were ferried across the Mississippi to St. Louis and then embarked on river steamer up the Missouri as far as Independence, Westport, or St. Joseph. These places were the debarkation points for most river traffic in the 1840's and in them one pulled himself and his family and possessions together before setting out across the Plains on one of the main trails west. In 1849, under the aegis of Senator Thomas Hart Benton, the first real estate firm in St. Louis, Hiram Leffingwell and Richard S. Elliott, called a "National Convention to meet in St. Louis in October, to consider the subject of a *Pacific Railroad*."[8] But the iron horse did not replace Old Paint, the Conestoga wagon, or the river steamboat as a means of transportation westward until the 1850's. These facts are generally known but perhaps not appreciated as pertinent to the publication in St. Louis and by the *Reveille* (and of course other papers) of contemporary, firsthand documents by travelers in the West. It is in the context of these facts of publication that one grows to a greater awareness of how that information was disseminated in the journals of the time.

And now to recount something of this early literature of the West. Whom among its correspondents did Keemle and Field especially prize? From time to time they indicated the answer, as, for example, in the front-page masthead column of the issue of May 18, 1846:

> Our arrangements for the future will render the REVILLE WEEKLY issue more attractive than ever before, and we have no scruple in spending time and money upon it, encouraged as we daily are, by a swelling subscription list.
>
> Mr. SOL SMITH, we take great pleasure in stating, will continue from time to time, his inimitable stories. [An actor-manager in partnership with Joe Field, Solomon Smith is important to the *Reveille* for his humorous contributions but not for his writing about the

[8] Elliott's *Notes*, p. 263. The railroad came to Alton in 1852 (*ibid.*, p. 270). "As railroads and telegraphs were yet new in 1850, and we were just beginning to use self-sealing envelopes, and had not attained to postage stamps, if I recollect aright, the reader will see that I was not wrong in looking forward to 'improved means of transit and correspondence' " (*ibid.*, p. 266).

West, and one thus eliminates him from further consideration here.]

Mr. JOHN S. ROBB, ("Solitaire,") whose skill and humor, as a sketcher of Western Life, is acknowledged over the whole country, is engaged to devote his time, henceforth, exclusively to the paper.

A young writer from Europe, "THE SCOTCH EMIGRANT," whose talent as an *Etcher* is most remarkable—dashing off caricatures of life with a spirit worthy of Cruikshank—is preparing a series of *illustrations*, which will appear from time to time, accompanied by extra pages of humorous letter press. [As with Sol Smith, "The Scotch Emigrant" (whose real name was J. T. Gaugain) eliminates himself, by his choice of subject (dialect humor of the newly arrived European-American), from further consideration here.]

Mr. GEORGE L. CURRY, late of this paper, is engaged to furnish a *California Correspondence*, and this feature alone will render the paper of high and peculiar interest, especially throughout the west.

"JOHN BROWN'S" PAPERS are not yet exhausted, and "EVERPOINT" has hardly yet begun; and these, with the host of clever *occasionals* who favor us, must certainly give a spirit and life to whatever they may be engaged upon. [One also eliminates "Everpoint"—one of Joseph M. Field's pen names—from further consideration as a western correspondent.][9]

Three of these six contributors to the *Reveille* are of considerable importance: John S. Robb, or "Solitaire"; George L. Curry, or "Laon" (his pen name in the *Reveille*); and Richard S. Elliott, or "John Brown." To these one adds a fourth name, Matthew C. Field, who like Robb, Curry, and Elliott used a pseudonym, "Phazma"; Mat, as he was familiarly called, also contributed anonymously to the *Reveille*. In fact, he was most important to the paper as the anonymous contributor of a group of western travel sketches that the *Reveille* serialized in its early months of publication.

9 *WR*, II (May 18, 1846), 851. For one of Sol Smith's contributions, "*Written for the Reveille*," see "A Brag Boat, and a Brag Captain," *ibid.*, I (October 14, 1844), 105. For "Everpoint" see his comic dialect story, "A 'Sucker' in a Warm Bath," *ibid.*, II (May 4, 1846), 842. For a piece by "The Scotch Emigrant" see *ibid.*, p. 848. Also see Sol Smith's autobiographical *Theatrical Management in the West and South for Thirty Years*, Arthur T. Tees, ed. (New York: Benjamin Blom, Inc., 1968). See also William G. B. Carson, *The Theatre on the Frontier: The Early Years of the St. Louis Stage* (Chicago: University of Chicago Press, 1932), and its sequel by Carson, *Managers in Distress: The St. Louis Stage, 1840–1844* (St. Louis Historical Documents Foundation, 1949). J. T. Gaugain, "The Scotch Emigrant," left St. Louis in 1846 for parts west, according to an item in *WR*, III (August 17, 1846), 967.

Field's anonymous sketches were scattered among the numbers of the *Reveille* during the latter half of 1844 under the general title of *Prairie and Mountain Life.* As is well known among specialists in the lore of western travel literature, Matthew C. Field excerpted the sketches the *Reveille* published from his much longer manuscript of his adventures on the famous western expedition of Sir William Drummond Stewart from late April until early November, 1843. A major portion of *Prairie and Mountain Life* was first printed in the New Orleans *Picayune.* Also in the *Picayune* he published many letters from the Stewart party during its progress. Most of these, together with the extant diaries of Field, have been collected by Kate L. Gregg and John Francis McDermott as Field's *Prairie and Mountain Sketches.*

The *Picayune* published those selected sketches from Field's *Prairie and Mountain Life* because he had already published successfully in the paper. On doctor's orders, Mat Field had gone on his first trip west in 1839 from St. Louis to Santa Fe and back; then, going to New Orleans, he joined the staff of the *Picayune* and wrote up his travels for the readers of that paper. A little later, the Scottish traveler Sir William Drummond Stewart met Field in New Orleans, invited the journalist along on an expedition to the Rockies, and thought well enough of him to equip the young writer at his own expense; Stewart even proposed to make any arrangements necessary for the care of Field's new family during their safari of 1843.[10] One guesses that out of Field's travels with Stewart emerged plans for something besides the manuscript of *Prairie and Mountain Life.* To be sure, a sizable portion of the manuscript was, as we know, serialized in the *Picayune*; but Field soon left that paper and New Orleans. Within a year after returning to St. Louis at the end of October, 1843, from the trip west, he returned again to St. Louis to settle there for the few months remaining to him. Colonel Keemle and Mat's elder brother Joseph brought the younger man into the *Weekly Reveille*; as had the *Picayune,* so did the *Reveille* serialize portions of *Prairie and Mountain Life.* Mat Field also wrote poems and pieces in prose for the paper under the pseudonym of "Phazma," a pen name he had already made well known among American periodicals. After his death at sea on November 15, 1844, the *Reveille* published two more sketches. In the

10 *Prairie and Mountain Sketches,* p. xxvi.

issue for November 18, 1844, appeared Mat Field's set piece of the famous "petrified forest," and in the issue for December 2 appeared his theatrical, romantic, consciously Byronic picture of the Wind River Mountains:

> Thick forests covered the mountain, half the trees standing, half of them prostrate, and every one *dead*. Not a particle of bark remained among all these ghost-like remnants of a gigantic, but now blasted and extinct vegetation. The huge rocks were swept bare of earth, by the violent winds from which this chain derives its name. Nothing met the eye, in any direction, but naked granite and blasted trees. A feeling of intense awe chilled through our veins, and crept into our hearts, as we gazed round upon a scene that forced into the mind a new and vast conception of desolation in sublimity! Big rain drops were still beating against us, with the force of hail-stones, as they were driven almost horizontally across the bleak mountain top by the screaming wind. The tall pines, leafless, barkless and branchless, stood in gaping clefts and fissures pointing their spires into the sky, like ghostly fingers upbraiding their destroyer! Many were pulpy with rottenness, though still standing, upheld by the firm twining of their roots among the rocks. Those that had fallen, seemed as though they had crumbled to their descent without a crash, so silent was every thing, except the fierce wind, to which the white spectres appeared listening, in desolate grandeur, as it flew over the mountains, screaming the requiem of giants gone! We had never before seen and only once read, of a spectacle so singularly wild and strange as this. It was darkness in day! It was midnight without moon, stars, or obscurity! It was the hush of death over nature, and the sun yet rolling! It seemed all that should be vague, and nothing that could be real! It was something resembling an actual presentment of Byron's appalling conception of the death of motion:
>
> "Ships, sailorless, lay rotting on the sea,
> And their masts fell down piece-meal; as they dropp'd
> They slept on the abyss without a surge!"
>
> Just so these rotten pines seemed to have fallen, "piece-meal," and without a sound.[11]

[11] For these seven sketches see *WR*, I: "Camp William—Methodist and Catholic Missions—A Young Rogue Arrested—Rockwell, the Mormon—The Jail at Independence—Frightful Accident at Camp, &c." (August 19, 1844), 45; " 'Approaching'—Turn out in the Morning—Starting from the Picket—FLYING BUFFALO!" (August 26, 1844), 54; " 'Ap-

At about the same time that the *Reveille* was desultorily serializing Mat Field's *Prairie and Mountain Life*, it was beginning to print the contributions of another correspondent, "Solitaire," the pen name of John S. Robb, a "typo" printer from Philadelphia (most probably), who had worked his way to the Mound City and who first contributed a piece in the new vein of American humor to the *Reveille* for October 21, 1844: "Not a Drop More, Major, Unless It's Sweetened." In his medley of contributions to the *Reveille*, 1845–47, and printed by Carey and Hart's Library of Humorous American Works in 1847, with illustrations by F. O. C. Darley, as *Streaks of Squatter Life and Far-West Scenes*, Robb in his subtitle described the miscellany as "a series of humorous sketches descriptive of incidents and characters in the wild West." The general tenor of the collection is indicated by Robb's assertion in his Preface that the "west abounds with incident and humor, and the observer must lack an eye for the comic who can look upon the panorama of western life without being tempted to laugh."[12]

John S. Robb was promoted out of the printing shop of the *Reveille* to the post of Assistant Editor in April, 1846, when George L. Curry left the paper to go to California; Robb thus assumed a new importance for the *Reveille*, although his writing had for some time been one of the attractions of the paper. As early as July, 1845, the proprietors waggishly noted: "The Mobile Tribune desires us, of all things, to send that way our 'Solitaire,' but it would be a downright *Robb*-ery."[13] Robb remained, as Professor McDermott has pointed

---

proaching'—The Phanton Bear—The Three Bulls" (September 9, 1844), 70; "Ogling a Buffalo Bull" (not in any issue of *WR* but extant in a clipping: see *Prairie and Mountain Sketches*, pp. 118–121); "The Petrified Forest" (November 18, 1844), 150; "The Wind River Mountains" (December 2, 1844), 166. See also "Santa Fe, by the Late M. C. Field," III (October 19, 1846), 1039, reprinted from the *Picayune*. The excerpt quoted in the text was not reprinted in *Prairie and Mountain Sketches*.

12 For "Not a Drop More, Major, Unless It's Sweetened" see *WR*, I (October 21, 1844), 113 (an unsigned contribution). For the quotation from Robb's Preface see p. viii. See McDermott's Introduction, p. ix, for an account of the circumstances of the publication by Carey and Hart, out east in Philadelphia, of Robb's first book.

13 *WR*, II (July 14, 1845), 417 (the first issue of the second volume). For the notice that Curry was leaving and that Robb would be the replacement, see *WR*, II (May 4, 1846), 842: "Mr. George L. Curry, late assistant editor of the St. Louis Reveille, has left on a trip to California. He intends furnishing sketches of his trip, which will, no doubt, add much to the interest of that sheet." Taken from the Louisville *Courier* by the editors of the *Reveille*, this was followed by a second paragraph: "Mr. John S. Robb, who has written many admirable and lively sketches under the signature of *Solitaire*, has taken Mr. C.'s seat. His connection will make the already popular Reveille even more popular than ever."

out, on the staff until January, 1849, when as the special correspondent for his paper he left with a group of St. Louis men for the California gold fields. Once in California he started a newspaper in Stockton, California, as its publisher and editor and thus outlived the *Reveille*, which ceased publication in 1850.[14]

Robb expanded his creative range with an occasional piece of more serious fiction; for example, his story "Mo-Kah; or, Night. (Sequel to Ka-Am; or, Daylight.) A Tale of the Rocky Mountains" combines melodrama and documentation in the *Reveille* for July 10, 1848. More important for the present purpose, Robb was the roving reporter for his paper, and, for example, in the issue of August 7, 1848, he is represented—as "Solitaire"—by a set of three lengthy letters, the first pair entitled "Letters from Indian Land" and subheaded "Lake Pepin —No. 1: *Its Entrance—Dinner under a Mosquito Bar—Point-no-Point —A Lively Supper*" and "*Lake Pepin—No. 2: An Active Morning—A Fair Breeze—The Maiden's Leap—An Indian Family—Safe upon the Beach.*" These were dated respectively July 24 and 25, 1848, and were written during the trip downriver. The third letter, "Progress Northward," was dated July 27 by the industrious correspondent and was a retrospective look at the progression of settlement to the northwest in which Robb comments on the general topic of the removal of the Indians westward and the consequent shifting of the western frontier. His special concern is with the region of central Minnesota, around the Falls of St. Anthony. "Settlers are taking up sites even above the Falls of St. Anthony, around the St. Croix, and indeed, at every point, from Fever river upwards, which either promises mineral treasures, or productive soil for culture. The Indian's foot has no sooner departed from his old home than the white man plants his in the track." "Solitaire" forecast the abandonment in the near future of the military posts of Fort Atkinson and Prairie du Chien, "as the tribes for whose subjection they were constructed, have departed. . . . The new Indian post will be built at 'Crow Wing' Island, on the Upper Mississippi, some one hundred and thirty miles above the Falls of St. Anthony." Such letters as Robb's give, as no other documentation could, a vivid notion of the shifting of the western frontier. His chief companion on the return voyage as far as Keokuk was the artist Henry Lewis, whom Robb depicts sketching with pencil in hand, "complete-

[14] McDermott, Introduction, p. vii.

ly wrapt up in the beauty of the scene before him," on the waters of Lake Pepin.[15]

Such adventures were mild indeed in contrast to those of the western emigrants. One of the better known of these was George L. Curry. The *Reveille* for April 20, 1846, identified him as having been "connected with this paper since its commencement" and as now being on "his way to Independence, to join the California company there collecting."

> Mr. C. is a gentleman of intelligence and enterprise; his object is to obtain a full acquaintance with a region which more than any other upon the Pacific coast, is destined to be the seat of commerce, wealth and political importance; and his letters, (to be published in the *Reveille*) replete as they will be with shrewd observation, intelligent calculation, and dashed, moreover, with the spice of novelty and adventure, may be fairly looked for with interest. He will write us by every opportunity, and no point, whether connected with the present welfare of the emigrants, or the prospective changes of the country, will be neglected by him.[16]

Curry was only one among the swarms of emigrants; the *Reveille* in that eventful spring of 1846 noted: "A perfect fever appears to pervade the whole section where they are clustering, and many Missourians, it is expected, will pull up stakes and join the tide."[17] In the same issue appeared Curry's poem "The Missouri," written at "Arrow Rock, April 23, 1846" and concluding:

[15] "Progress Northward," *WR*, V (August 7, 1848), 1785; the other two letters mentioned in the text of this essay appear on the same page of the *WR* as does "Progress Northward." For an edition of other letters by Robb in the *WR* and describing his stay at Fort Snelling, see John S. Robb ("Solitaire"), "A Journalist at Old Fort Snelling," John Francis McDermott, ed., *Minnesota History*, XXXI (December, 1950), 209–221. This article reprints six letters by Robb as "Solitaire": *WR*, IV (July 10, 1848), 1756; V (July 31, 1848), 1777 (four letters, three of them dated Fort Snelling on, respectively, July 4, 5, and 8, 1848, and a fourth dated "On Board the Mini-Ha-Ha, Below Lake Pepin," on July 15, 1848); *ibid.*, p. 1778 (dated "On the 'Mini-Ha-Ha,' Raccoon Slough," on July 17, 1848).

[16] "Upper California," *WR*, II (April 20, 1846), 831. For an unsigned contribution by Curry—admittedly this is a guess based on his activity as a youth among the "Boston mechanics' guild"—see "Dr. Channing. The Mechanic's Friend," *WR*, I (November 25, 1844), 152, on William Ellery Channing. For a biographical sketch see Robert C. Clark, "George Law Curry," *Dictionary of American Biography*, II, 604–605.

[17] "California Emigration," *WR*, II (May 4, 1846), 845.

What carest thou for man and his high sway?
Thy sand-bars, snags and rocks are all thy own,
And from thy depths fair commerce still must groan.

The fair commerce that groaned from the river's depths was a "noble steamer" that "like an untamed horse" had ridden the bosom of the river but that had foundered: "She lieth now beneath thy murky wave."[18] The poem—a thirteen-line attempt at a sonnet—seems to have been written aboard the river steamer Curry took to get to Independence, which, as he later remarked, was the last of civilization before the barbarism of the plains and the mountains. Not all of Curry's correspondence for the *Reveille* was so literary, but that scarcely mattered, for what counted with Curry's readers were the factual information he could give them and the impressionistic verbal sketches of the scenes he journeyed through. As the *Hancock Eagle* (of Nauvoo) said, the columns of that "sprightly paper," the *Reveille*, were "to be enriched by the contributions of a California correspondent, Mr. George L. Curry, who is now on his way to join an expedition destined for that 'land of promise.' If this is not 'carrying the war into Africa,' it is pushing it into the 'bowels of the earth' quite as far; and we shall not now be surprised if Keemle announces a *Canton* correspondent."[19]

Under the name of "Laon," Curry sent a flurry of correspondence back to the *Reveille*; but as his party, under the command of "Colonel" William H. Russell, proceeded ever more deeply into the wilderness, the letters back to St. Louis grew fewer, were printed more sporadically (one must realize that the only mail service was that furnished by trappers, mountain men, returning emigrants, and the military making for the focal point of St. Louis), and finally stopped. His later career as Governor of Oregon Territory gives additional piquancy to these letters of a printer twenty-six years old.[20] Dale Mor-

18 *WR*, II (May 4, 1846), 843.

19 Quoted in "St. Louis Reveille," *WR*, II (May 11, 1846), 855.

20 Dale Morgan has collected Curry's letters to the *Reveille* in the second of two volumes he has compiled and edited, entitled *Overland in 1846: Diaries and Letters of the California-Oregon Trail* (Georgetown, Calif.: Talisman Press, 1963): two letters dated April 23, 1846 (*WR*, II [May 4, 1846], 845), pp. 503–505; April 28 (*WR*, II [May 11, 1846], 856), pp. 509–510; April 29 (*WR*, II [May 11, 1846], 856), pp. 510–511; May 6, 1846 (*WR*, II [May 25, 1846], 869), pp. 513–515; May 11, 1846 (*WR*, II [May 25, 1846], 871), pp. 520–

gan, who has edited Curry's letters to the *Reveille*, concludes of him that his "notable series of letters to the *Reveille* from the California-Oregon Trail was long forgotten" and that their reprinting "restores a lost chapter to his life."[21]

The feats of reportage performed by the *Reveille* are impressive, even when they are not completely achieved, as in the case of George Curry's letters on the overland trail. For the paper not only reported much news of the westward emigration but did so during two years when its most important space usually had to be devoted to news of the Mexican War. The *Reveille* was not a jingoist paper in these years, 1846–47, but it was a patriotic one and not only reported the vicissitudes of the war in detail—as became a journal published from a great entrepot of the Mexican trade from New Mexico and Chihuahua—but also published dozens of letters from the volunteers in the Laclede Rangers from St. Louis (attached to the First Regiment of U.S. Dragoons) and the Regiment of Missouri Mounted Volunteers. The latter group, surely one of the most justly famed of all American military regiments, in June, 1846, elected Alexander Doniphan as their Colonel. Under Doniphan's command the Missouri regiment executed a march through country not only hostile but largely unknown to these Americans, a feat often favorably compared to the march to the sea of Xenophon's Ten Thousand.

The reporting of much of that feat by Richard Smith Elliott, a lieutenant in Doniphan's regiment, and its publication in the *Reveille* constitute a major reason for the importance of the paper, even though Elliott's letters have never been reprinted as a body of comment and reportage of the Mexican War. Elliott, moreover, was the most voluminous and the most important of the *Reveille* correspondents in these years.

There is still a further reason for Elliott's importance, one that, so far as I am aware, has not been printed: Elliott has a good claim to

---

523; May 19, 1846 (*WR*, II [June 1, 1846], 874), pp. 539–540; May 17, 1846 (*WR*, II [June 1, 1846], 881), pp. 544–546; June 12, 1846 (*WR*, III [July 27, 1846], 939), pp. 552–554; June 16, 1846 (*WR*, III [July 20, 1846], 931), pp. 563–564; June 25–26, 1846 (*WR*, III [August 10, 1846], 955), pp. 572–576; and July 12, 1846 (*WR*, III [September 14, 1846], 997), pp. 609–611. Mostly these letters bear the title "The Californians" with an occasional subtitle indicating the chief topic of a particular letter, e.g., "The War News Received" (June 1, 1846).

21 Morgan, Introduction, II, 464. Morgan's biographical sketch of Curry is on pp. 461–464.

be considered—along with the famous George W. Kendall of the New Orleans *Picayune*—as one of the earliest American war correspondents. Frank Luther Mott has said that Kendall is usually called the "first" American war correspondent, but it is a matter of record that Elliott should share in the title along with other correspondents who also regularly reported the events of the Mexican War.[22] It is true that Elliott, unlike Kendall, did not have behind him the resources of a paper as important as the *Picayune*, eight years older than the *Reveille* and with a more stable record of publication; but as often as the trains of teamsters toiled up the Santa Fe Trail to Independence, Elliott faithfully sent his detailed reports of the epic campaign of the First Missouri Mounted Volunteers, with, naturally, a special emphasis on the parts played by the St. Louis soldiers. It is interesting that Frank Luther Mott, not only a distinguished scholar but also a man interested in Missouri history, should dismiss such a repertorial achievement as that of Richard S. Elliott by burying it in anonymity: "Many soldiers wrote letters from time to time to their home papers. Some of these were carried eastward over the Santa Fe Trail or up the Mississippi to St. Louis and Cincinnati."[23] Besides Kendall, Mott cites only two other reporters of the Mexican War by name: Kendall's partner, Lumsden, and James L. Freaner of the *Picayune*, who signed his letters pseudonymously as "Mustang," after killing a Mexican officer and taking his horse at the Battle of Monterey.

One reason that Elliott's dispatches from Doniphan's command have never received their due is that he signed himself pseudonymously, like Freaner; but Elliott's pseudonym was the humdrum and colorless one of "John Brown," and as he never collected these letters as a book and never owned to writing them in his autobiography, *Notes Taken in Sixty Years* (published in 1883 in St. Louis), posterity understandably has passed them by. True, Bernard De Voto may well have read Elliott's letters in the *Reveille* when he used the resources of the Missouri Historical Society for writing *The Year of Decision* (1943),

22 Frank Luther Mott, *American Journalism, a History: 1690–1960* (New York: Macmillan, 1962), pp. 249–250, n. 33. Mott adds that "there were probably as many as a score of other war correspondents in the field in 1846–47," and that although Kendall was a combatant (unlike the modern war correspondent), he was nevertheless recognized "as a war correspondent, and was the first outstanding regular reporter of military movements and action."

23 *Ibid.*

but De Voto's acknowledgment of his research materials is so eccentric as to be largely useless, and thus one can merely guess that some knowledge of the *Reveille* entered into the composition of *The Year of Decision.* Robert Lewis Taylor does acknowledge in the Principal Bibliography appended to his novel about the First Missouri Mounted Volunteers, *Two Roads to Guadelupe,* the use of "Letters from New Mexico, published in the St. Louis *Weekly Reveille* (1847) by Richard S. Elliott."[24] And at least one attempt has been made in recent years to interest a university press in the publication of a collection of Elliott's Mexican War correspondence. Undoubtedly the time will come when some scholar will locate a suitable publishing outlet for these full-blooded, lively, important letters.

As was appropriate in the context of the *Reveille,* "John Brown" first appeared there as an exponent of the new American humor. In the issue for August 12, 1844, he wrote a letter addressed from High Creek, Holt County, Missouri, on August 9, which the *Reveille* printed under the title of "What's in a Name?"

> At the present writing, I have not seen *The Reveille.* I may never see it. I am only mortal, like its editors (the paper, too, perhaps!) and may die, as others have done. But I am assured by good authority, that *The Reveille* is seen and felt every morning, Sundays not excepted, by the good people of St. Louis, and that its rub-a-dubs are directed by good *Field* officers. Seen and felt! *Reveille*! But there's no telling what will come next, as the old lady said when told of the new way to hatch eggs by steam. "Dear me," says she, "I suppose the next thing"—and here she muttered something—"but, for my part, I would prefer the old way!"

"John Brown" added a postscript to the effect that if the editors thought his letter worth a place in their columns—"your name is so military that I can't keep war-like thoughts down"—they should "place it among the *rank* and *file.* Just *say* if you please, it is very humorous and good, or your readers may not discover its merits."[25]

At the time of writing, Richard Elliott was a young newspaperman from the farm country near Harrisburg, Pennsylvania, and very

24 (New York: Doubleday, 1964), p. 427; Principal Bibliography, pp. 425–428.
25 *WR,* I (August 12, 1844), 41.

newly transplanted to Missouri.[26] When he was twenty, in 1837, he had enlisted in the army of the struggling young Republic of Texas; but he "deserted" in Louisville, paid out his debt of $6, and returned home to Pennsylvania, to help run once again his father's rural paper and engage himself as a "jour. printer" and then as an editor to sundry employers. Elliott married a local girl in 1838 and read for and was admitted to the bar; also he dabbled in Whig party politics with the pleasing result that through President Tyler's help early in 1843 he secured from his "old friend, Mr. Potts, chief clerk of the Indian Bureau . . . 'a little sub-agency' at Council Bluffs, $750 salary." Mr. Potts kindly explained the difference between an agency and a sub-agency: the latter was an "agency, except in title, salary, and mode of appointment. Same duties as those of an Agent, who gets $1,500. The Council Bluffs sub-agency is east of the Missouri river, and disburses over $40,000 a year. The bond is $20,000. The Secretary of War appoints the sub-agents—the President appoints the agents." Because the prospective subagency might lead to something, Elliott decided to go west: "I had a vague idea that something might come of it."

Lured by the bright promise of the western frontier, Elliott made his way out to the primitive encampment of his subagency on the site opposite present-day Omaha in the late spring and early summer of 1843. How he got in touch with Colonel Keemle and the Fields, Elliott fails to say in his *Notes*, and one guesses that as a printer, editor, and one-time bit player during his youthful vicissitudes, he easily and naturally fell in with these like-minded men, who also had gone west to advance themselves. As Elliott and his wife and little boy spent the winter of 1843–44 in St. Louis, he probably met the Fields then. Again, one guesses that when the *Reveille* began publication, its weekly issues were mailed to Elliott out on his frontier post, most probably with an invitation to write for the paper.

As "John Brown," Elliott's first dispatch—he also contributed much verse, with which I am not concerned—to the *Reveille* was dated from Council Bluffs, September 10, 1844, and was about his Indian charges. "Movements among the Red Skins" deals with the peculiar relationship between the federal government and the Indian tribes of the Otos, Pawnees, and Potawatomies. "They receive from the Gov-

[26] This account of Elliott is taken from his *Notes*, pp. 1–190 *passim*; for his autobiographical relation of the Doniphan expedition, see pp. 216–257 *passim*.

ernment a small cash annuity of about $2,500, and are, in every respect, a poor and degraded people. Their number is about 1,000," wrote Elliott of the Otos. The Pawnees, about 6,500 in number, were not much better, being "yet wild and primitive in their habits." But the Potawatomies were "a well-disposed people . . . considered to be very respectable Indians." Most of the dispatch was devoted to Elliott's description of the annual council these tribes had just concluded with the Superintendent of Indian Affairs west of the Mississippi.[27]

From his post on the Missouri, John Brown was able to send the *Reveille* some excellent and vital advice for its issue of March 24, 1845 (his letter is dated February 22): "Please order the whole Regiment of Emigrants for Oregon, to shape their course for this point [Council Bluffs] if they wish to make a fair start." The emigrants must not make for the spot on "the map" marked "Council Bluffs" (the old bluff, "where Lewis and Clark held a council with the Indians, some forty years ago") but to another point marked "Bellevuc."

> If the *Regiment* march up this way, they can cross at Bellevue, where there is a new ferry boat about being launched, and will have a good route on the north side of the great Platte, or "Nebraska," clear to Fort Laramie, in the great "South Pass" of the Mountains. The distance from Independence to Fort Laramie, by this route, is about the same as by the direct northwest route from Independence, and the road is much better. By the other route, the way is agreeably diversified by hundreds of streams, with steep banks—deep ravines—sloughs, occasionally, and other little circumstances of prairie travelling; but to go from here to Fort Laramie, there is, on the north side of [the] "Nebraska," but one stream difficult to cross—the Elkhorn—and this, unless when swollen by rains, can be forded, as the banks and bottom are good.[28]

For Elliott, 1845 was largely taken up with various negotiations for the Potawatomies in Washington, and he was away from Council Bluffs and St. Louis part of the year. But he continued to report back to the paper, in much the same manner as John S. Robb was doing. For example, in April, 1845, he sent the proprietors of the *Reveille*

27 *WR*, I (October 7, 1844), 97. For Elliott's years as an Indian subagent, 1843–45, see the relevant papers in the Archives of the Bureau of Indian Affairs.

28 *WR*, I (March 24, 1845), 289.

his "Hibernian Log-Book—A Trip to Galena," of which they published three entries. The second day out, as "John Brown" sat on the guard of the *Hibernian* contentedly smoking his after-breakfast cigar and admiring the forested banks of the Mississippi, "touched with the pencil of the great artist until they shone with ten thousand beautiful tints," Captain Miller joined him and entered into reminiscent and philosophical converse.

Said Brown: "A beautiful river, too, Cap'n—ain't it?"

"Yes—but I prefer the Missouri—I like that old *creek* the best, with all its snags and bars."

"Can't say much for your taste, Cap'n. But let's have your reasons."

"Why it's not so beautiful a stream as this I admit. It hasn't the picturesque scenery—it hasn't the pretty islands, and sloping banks, which we see along this stream, especially as you get higher up—and the water ain't so clear, either—some little danger, perhaps, but we have the pleasure of surmounting its perils." And, continued the Captain, "When a man runs into the Missouri and out again, he feels as if he had done something! . . . I tell you what, to cross a bar where there are but four feet of water, with a boat drawing four and a half, is something to think of—it's the heroism of steam boating!"[29]

Some life, excitement, danger, "doing something," heroism were all in the offing. Leaving the subagency of the Potawatomies, early in 1846 Elliott set himself up in St. Louis as an attorney-at-law, in an office on the second floor of a building opposite the "old Court House"; but immediate prospects of a peaceful career amid judges and litigants were soon out of the question. In April of that year fighting on a large scale broke out between American and Mexican forces, and the next month President James K. Polk declared war on Mexico. War came as no surprise, but it did come to the United States as a bitterly decisive event. Yet, as Elliott rhetorically asked in his memoir, for Missourians, "How can patriotic impulses be kept down?" Accordingly the first piece on the front page of the *Reveille* for May 18, 1845, was a "Volunteers' Song" concluding:

And when age creeps apace to the sundown of life,
Shall your deeds be rehearsed 'mid the joys

[29] *WR*, I (April 28, 1845), 334.

Of freedom's firesides, won in liberty's strife,
By the gallant Missourian boys!
Then equip ye right handy, and cross Rio Grande,
And send, double quick, to Old Scratch,
Arista, the nigger, Ampudia and Vega,
And their bandy-legged Mexican batch!

The rest of the front page of the issue was devoted to war news, "Glorious News!!!" of General Taylor's victory over "The Mexican Hawks" at Matamoros. The requisition for troops was then announced, among them two regiments from Missouri, totaling twelve hundred men. Most of the last two columns of the front page were taken up with a lengthy letter from Santa Fe, dated February 9, 1845, "delayed, unfortunately, some weeks," and written to "one of our oldest and most respectable citizens" by "an old resident of New Mexico—one possessed of great influence, and intimately versed in the affairs of the country"; the *Reveille* withheld his name, as was only prudent in the case of one who advised that "All that is required by New Mexico, to make it a wealthy, productive and flourishing province, is a good form of Government to encourage enterprise and industry, and a majority of the body of the people—the laboring and producing classes—are evidently looking forward with anxiety for annexation to the United States. The military, office-holders, clergy, and a few of the wealthy citizens, are the only opponents, being aware that under a Government protecting all alike, their importance and power will be lost."[30]

During May and June, Elliott, as a first lieutenant, was active in forming the Laclede Rangers, a hundred men from St. Louis. During June the volunteers met at Fort Leavenworth, and by July 1 "John Brown" was able to report:

> The "Laclede Rangers," Capt. Hudson, are now fairly on the march. On the 29th of June we left Fort Leavenworth, about one o'clock P. M., and marched out some nine miles, where we made our first camp, which we called, in honor of a distinguished friend, whom, perhaps, you know—"Camp Keemle." Everything was done in a soldierly style, you may depend—horses and men all in good order. The Quartermaster had allowed us two teams of six mules each to haul our

[30] *WR*, II (May 18, 1845), 851.

> provisions and camp equipage—in addition to which the company have purchased a wagon and three yoke of oxen to transport the saddle-bags of the men, so as to relieve the horses of part of their load.

The *Reveille* duly printed his newsletter in its issue of July 20, 1846.[31] In all as "John Brown," Richard Elliott sent back upwards of seventy dispatches printed in the columns of the *Reveille* between June, 1846, and July, 1847, when he returned to St. Louis at the disbanding of the Regiment of Mounted Volunteers, to the resumption of his law practice, and to writing on other topics for the *Reveille*.

Elliott's letters were more often than not entitled by the *Reveille* "Letters from New Mexico." In them he reported the usual griping of officers and ranks; the rumors endemic in war; various skirmishes and forays; the very real hardships of the Missouri Volunteers, who were not paid during their entire stay in New Mexico; the deaths among the soldiers, and their causes (he emphasized particularly that one should have been in good health back home in Missouri before starting down the trail to Santa Fe); and the life of the occupation forces in New Mexico. "I have no doubt," he wrote in a dispatch dated November 7, 1846, and published in the *Reveille* for January 4, 1847,

> that there prevails, among many of the New Mexicans, a very bitter feeling towards our Government and people; and that our presence here, as their conquerors, is but illy relished, especially by the more weighty of them, who, of course, see that they will not figure so largely in comparison with Americans, as they have heretofore done among their own countrymen. Often in conversation I have inquired if they were well satisfied with the present condition of things—a rather impertinent question, I admit. The upper classes invariably tell me yes—assure me they never were so happy, and that they expect to enjoy a delightful time under American rule. But the answer made to me by a Mexican teamster, whom I had with me to Bent's Fort, tells the whole story. I asked him if the people generally were contented. "*Los pobres, si—los Ricos, no*"—(the poor, yes—the rich, no)—was the answer, after which he went on to assure me, that the reason why the rich were dissatisfied was, that they could not oppress the poor as they had heretofore done—frequently requiring the laboring classes to toil from early dawn until dark, for two or three dollars per month,

[31] *WR*, III (July 20, 1846), 933.

and giving them scarcely food sufficient to keep body and soul together.[32]

Early in December, 1846, Elliott wrote about Doniphan's attempt to come to terms with the Navajo:

> The Colonel left here [Santa Fe] on the 27th of October, marched southward some distance, and then turned westward into the country of the Nabajo Indians. On the 23rd of November, at "Ojo Oso," or Bear Spring, about 250 miles south-west of Santa Fe, he met the Nabajoes, (all the chiefs being present, in person or by proxy) and made a treaty with them, stipulating for an exchange of prisoners between the Nabajoes and Mexicans, and for a peace, to embrace the Mexicans and Pueblo Indians, as well as the Americans. At this treaty some presents were exchanged, and among others the Indians gave the Colonel three blankets, of rare workmanship, which, I understand, he intends to send to the Department at Washington for the National Museum.

The treaty, added Elliott (he termed it "Col. Doniphan's treaty"), had been much discussed:

> It is said to be very defective, and not likely to effect any very substantial peace. Gentlemen here, well acquainted with the Nabajoes, expect every day to hear new outrages being committed by them. The achievement of this treaty does not, therefore, seem to confer many laurels; but we ought to remember that making Indian treaties is a new business to the Col., and if he has not made a very good one on the first trial, he may do infinitely better next time. But the Nabajoes, it is here thought, will continue to steal sheep and commit other outrages, until they are well whipped a few times; but, unfortunately, like the Seminoles or Comanches, they are not easily caught, and, for that reason, are difficult to whip.[33]

Despite strict discipline, unpaid soldiers, and shifty Mexicans, Christmas of 1846 in Santa Fe was pleasant enough for the American occupying forces, with a round of parties and that usual recreation of occupation troops and military prisoners, theatrical performances,

[32] *WR*, III (January 4, 1847), 1123–24.

[33] *WR*, III (February 22, 1847), 1185–86; John Brown's letter is dated from Santa Fe, December 6, 1846.

which for the sake of the *Reveille* Elliott reported in detail.[34] "John Brown's" letter dated from Santa Fe, December 5, 1846, added as a postscript: "I send you the 'poster' (two foolscap sheets, written off in 'printing hand.'—*Eds.*) of a grand performance which is to come off on Christmas night, and which, no doubt, will attract 'a full and fashionable audience.' " The "tragedy" to be performed was *Barbarossa.* After *Barbarossa* came performances of "LA POLKA! By an American Gentleman and *Spanish Lady*"; the farce of *Fortune's Frolic!*; and concluding the whole, the Virginia Minstrels singing "The old colored Gentleman," "Get along home, you Spanish Gals," "Blue Tail Fly," and "You ain't good looking and you can't come in."

But there were also the grimmer businesses of actual fighting and of dying soldiers, which Elliott bravely and dutifully reported back home for the families who read the *Reveille.* His "Letters from New Mexico" reported what the *Reveille* called the "First Battle of the Army of the West." "John Brown's" brief dispatch is dated from Santa Fe, January 5, 1847, and as printed in the paper, it precedes the more detailed accounts sent on to Keemle and Field by J. W. Folger and Edmund Chadwick. Folger and Chadwick were writing for "Lieut. Elliott (your 'John Brown')," who had "been unwell for some time, and is now confined to his room." So poor Elliott was to be balked in his ambition to go to Mexico as a field correspondent for the *Reveille.* Following the letter from Folger and Chadwick the *Reveille* printed the brief "official account . . . a queerly printed handbill from the Santa Fe Press"; and then came, finally, a firsthand relation of the action, Lieutenant C. H. Kribben's report to Major M. L. Clark, the son of the explorer, dated from the "Camp below Bracito Rio Grande," on December 26, 1846, the day after the battle. While the occupation forces back in Santa Fe were rollicking about as Virginia Minstrels, their companions down near El Paso were blooded. It was fitting that Kribben should thus appear as the *Reveille*'s historian of the fighting at Brazito, for he had announced himself and had been accepted as the official historian for the German detachment from St. Louis and was preparing to write a history, in German, of Doniphan's campaign. Kribben concluded: "We lost not a single man, and had but seven slightly wounded;—we took eight prisoners, six of whom died last night. Thus ended the battle of Bracito, the first battle of the army of

34 *WR*, III (March 1, 1847), 1187.

the west, and as bravely fought by our men as ever men fought at any engagement."[35]

"John Brown" never followed Doniphan into old Mexico; instead he continued to send the *Reveille* reports from Santa Fe, telling of the vicissitudes of the American occupation, as, for instance, his "Circumstantial Narrative of the Late Insurrection and Atrocities in New Mexico," printed in the issue for April 12, 1847, but dated from Santa Fe, February 15, 1847, and detailing the mutiny, as his letter termed the small rebellion, at Taos in which Governor Charles Bent was murdered. Loyal as ever to its correspondent, the *Reveille* gave the report a prefatory puff:

> The narrative of our able correspondent at Santa Fe, "John Brown," is a bold and faithful one of the late events in New Mexico, and it will be read with deep interest through the State—the volunteers being all our own. We have a letter from Mr. Robert Carey, who was supposed to have been killed at Taos. He mentions that his office, house, &c., were robbed of everything. The misguided wretches have been taught a lesson, and it is to be hoped that they will not again attempt an outrage. No trust, however, should be placed in them. The escape of Elliott Lee, as described by "John Brown," is sufficiently thrilling. The whole story of the atrocities committed by the murderers is terrible.

To his account of the insurrection, "John Brown" appended a brief note that Doniphan and his men had left El Paso del Norte for Chihuahua on February 1.[36] A report of the events there came to the *Reveille* from one of Doniphan's officers, Thomas B. Hudson, one of the original organizers of the Missouri Volunteers. Dated March 14, 1847, the letter was printed in the *Reveille* for May 24.[37]

But the fighting by the boys from Missouri was nearly over. Late in April Doniphan's men left Chihuahua to join with Taylor's major force; and late in May, by General Taylor's orders, they made for the coast, where at Brazos they took ship for New Orleans and then home. Meantime the Santa Fe contingent, under the command of Colonel Sterling Price, was also preparing to return home, back across the

[35] *Ibid.*, p. 1192.
[36] *WR*, III (April 12, 1847), 1235–36.
[37] *WR*, III (May 24, 1847), 1284.

mountains, the rivers, up to Council Grove, then on to Independence. Riding ahead of Price, Lieutenant Elliott led his Laclede Rangers on the return journey, sending as always his letters about the expedition to Keemle and Field. By July 7, 1847, he told his readers in the *Reveille* for July 19, he had arrived at Council Grove (his letter was dated July 8), "having left Santa Fe on the 12th June." Under the rule of Colonel Price, all had been quiet; and Elliott then reviewed the "condition of things in the Mexican country," which he said was "critical enough, but not entirely desperate." One detects a note of wistfulness when Elliott remarks that he had "read with pleasure the account of the reception of the volunteers in St. Louis"; Doniphan's boys had received the first roaring welcome home, upon their arrival up the river from New Orleans.[38] But there was still another letter, "Travelling on the Plains," dated from Independence, July 13, 1847, a casual account of happenings on the return journey, when Elliott and his companions were in a train of about seventy men under the command of a Mr. Houck. Written in the manner of Mat Field's prairie sketches, Elliott's "Travelling on the Plains" lacks the romantic flair of Field's writing.[39]

I find it astonishing that in his autobiographical *Notes* of 1883, Elliott never once refers to his having written for the *Reveille*; he reprints from it several of the poems he wrote for Keemle and Field, some sentimental, some comic, some merely horrifyingly bad. The only time he mentions his "Letters from New Mexico" he does so very obliquely—indeed so obliquely that the uninitiated would miss the point of Elliott's little private joke. Writing of the march over the prairies to Santa Fe in the summer of 1846, he remarks that "Life on the prairies had little novelty for me except in military events and duties, as I had been on the frontier long enough to be familiar with out-door life. From old notes taken on the march, I might, if I had the ability required, write out a story of more diversity and interest than Irving's Crayon Miscellany; but the day for prairie sketches has gone by, as every one can now go out in a Pullman car and see for himself. A century hence, some future Sir Walter may work up long gone

38 *WR*, IV (July 19, 1847), 1351; the two letters from John Brown on this page are dated July 8 and 13, 1847.

39 *WR*, IV (July 26, 1847), 1355; John Brown's letter bears the date of July 13, 1847, an indication that he now had leisure—and that his material was running thin.

events into romance, but we are now too near the past and too busy."[40] In sum, Richard S. Elliott seems to have been that rarest of persons, a man too modest and too lacking in ambition to care about going down in history. Four days after leaving Independence, he was back with his family in St. Louis; a few days later he shaved off the fierce military mustache he had brought home with him. The rest of his life is, for all its busyness and prosperity, an anticlimax for the reader of his autobiography, mostly because the author of *Notes Taken in Sixty Years* clearly regarded the decades of dabbling in the law, real estate, insurance, and railroads as anticlimactic to those four years spent with the Potawatomies and the Mexicans.

Besides "John Brown's" "Letters from New Mexico" there were many other dispatches and communications from the American Army of the West. Not only did Elliott have his friends substitute for him on occasion, not only did he extend his coverage by forwarding to the *Reveille* letters written by the combatants at Brazito and Chihuahua, he also usually appeared in the paper with other correspondents; and when Keemle and Field had no letters from Elliott and his fellow soldiers in Santa Fe, they printed the letters of other men concerned in the war. For example, at the beginning of the war the *Reveille* printed a lengthy set of extracts headed "Upper California. Extracts from a letter from Captain Fremont, U.S. Army," dated from the "Bay of St. Francisco, *Yerba Buena, Upper California*," on January 24, 1846, and published in the *Reveille* for June 1, 1846. Although the *Reveille* did not specify the person addressed by Frémont, she obviously was his wife Jessie, for he began by telling his correspondent that "Now, as rapidly as possible, I will tell you where I have been, and where I am going," and also directed her to "Tell your father that with a volunteer party of fifteen men, I crossed" what Frémont had just termed "the great basin" between "the parallels of 38° and 39°." After escaping with the howitzer, because of Jessie's cleverness about the mails, Frémont made sure that the world would be apprized of his side of the story of his expedition (that combination of exploring party and invading force), and he did so by writing his wife—not only the daughter of one of the half-dozen most important men in the Congress but also a lady residing in St. Louis and possessing splendid contacts with the press. Jessie Benton Frémont is to be applauded; she not only told

40 *Notes*, pp. 222–223.

Senator Thomas Hart Benton, she told the people of Missouri her husband's side of the remarkable story of his expedition to the far West.[41]

Another noteworthy letter is that headed "From the Plains. Letter from Solomon P. Sublette, bearer of dispatches to our Army in New Mexico," dated from Pawnee Fork, January 24, 1847. Here a notable mountain man and brother to one of the most famous of all mountain men—William Sublette—writes of the hardships of his journey southward from Independence to Santa Fe. The person to whom Sol Sublette is writing makes the letter even more fascinating, for he is none other than Sublette's old companion on the trail, Colonel Robert Campbell, a redoubtable mountain man himself as well as one of the great merchants of St. Louis. Campbell had of course given Sol Sublette's letter to Keemle and Field to print; it vividly exemplifies a not unusual means by which letters from the far West reached the *Reveille* office:

> I arrived at the *Fork* last evening, and to-day moved up the river about a mile, selected a situation, and will rest for twenty-four hours. While I am writing, the snow flakes are driving about my shelter on the wings of a very cold wind. It don't look promising for even an old *voyageur,* but I have no fears as to my ultimate success in getting through—not, however, without some difficulty. I met twelve teamsters yesterday, who are engaged with Harvey, of Boonville. They lost six mules at the *Point of Rocks*—stolen, they suppose—and in a snow storm at the crossing of the Arkansas their remaining mules perished with cold. Two of the men's feet are badly frozen.
>
> This is the third storm I have encountered since starting—what I mean by *storm* you will well understand—one of those old-fashioned, searching visitors, peculiar to this region. Thus far I have succeeded in keeping my mules in good order, by selecting good camping ground and carefully covering them from the weather; but from this forward the snow is so deep and camping grounds so unpromising, that I will leave my mules behind and take it afoot. I have, *sometimes,* on my journey, thought of your comfortable rocking chair and the warm fire which a few weeks since I enjoyed at your hospitable mansion—

41 *WR,* III (June 1, 1846), 878. Jessie Frémont's version of her husband's appropriation of the howitzer is termed "an absolute fiction" by Donald Jackson, "The Myth of the Frémont Howitzer," *Missouri Historical Society Bulletin,* XXIII (April, 1967), 205–214.

the recollection, even, amid this hurly burly of old winter's snow on the plains, is refreshing.

I took the new trail from Council Grove, and have found it better travelling for pack animals than the old road—more timber and better camping grounds.

From the best information I can gather, Capt. Murphy passed the crossing of the Arkansas about the 26th of December, and is no doubt by this time safe in Santa Fe.

Tell "*Bad Hand*" [Major Thomas Fitzpatrick, who figures also in the correspondence of "John Brown" at this time] that he need have no apprehension for my success, for if I have to abandon my mules in consequence of the snow, I will progress with less labor and more speed on foot.[42]

One gains from Sol Sublette's account a poignant understanding of just how the various letters from the far West reached the editorial offices in St. Louis and those comfortable St. Louis mansions with their hospitality, rocking chairs, and warm fires.

The men whose correspondence and dealings with the *Reveille* I have thus far mentioned are well known to history, and if not in every case makers and shakers, they were at any rate observers above-stairs as it were. But the *Reveille* also printed news from the faceless mass of men, such as the letters from an acting lance corporal who signed his four or five letters from Santa Fe only as G. W. S. This correspondent must have been both young and hardy as well as gifted with a naturally sunny humor. One of his letters metamorphosed into comedy the hardships of the volunteers' lives in Santa Fe. "The flour we use," he told the *Reveille,*

(which is called "Taos," on account of its being made principally there) is undoubtedly the cause of the dysentery which is so prevalent here. You would like perhaps to have some account of our quarters: Imagine to yourself a room of fourteen feet in length by eight in width, floor, "the mother earth"—on which we spread our blankets and robes (such as have any of the last). This is our sleeping chamber for seven men. For a kitchen we have a little room about six by fourteen, in one corner of which we have built an enormous fireplace

42 *WR*, III (March 8, 1847), 1197. For Fitzpatrick see B., "Major Thomas Fitzpatrick," *WR*, V (May 7, 1849), 2100 (dated Westport, May 1, 1849), giving details of the major's return from Bent's Fort, forty-six days out from Westport.

> which monopolizes about one-fourth of the whole room. This fireplace is as splendid a piece as I ever saw built of "dough-boys," (a large sunburnt brick about eighteen inches long and nine wide) rough, and with a perpendicular in accuracy of outlines, [like] a darky's leg. One consolation, it don't smoke! There is much sickness here at present; about twenty out of our company being daily on the sick report. The measles are prevalent, and the hospital is full.[43]

Most of the Missouri Volunteers who died in the campaign in New Mexico died not in the heat of combat but rather from disease or accident. The hardships they so courageously endured were directly the fault of a federal government as careless of human life at it was foolhardy in its international relations.

For all its vital importance to the future of the United States, the Mexican War was, even while it was waged, just another incident (if an important one) in the American saga of westward expansion, and the wagons rolled across the Plains, the Great Basin of Utah, and the Rockies to Oregon and California as relentlessly as a progression of hungry ants. That aspect of the movement west was constantly presented to readers of the *Reveille* and remains perhaps the most vivid impression one is left with after reading the seven volumes of the paper.

The latter years of the *Reveille* give ample evidence of its continuing interest in western expansion. One of its more noteworthy editorials was headed "The Prairies," in the issue of April 26, 1847. This unsigned piece shows Keemle and Field attempting to mold opinion not only among the St. Louis merchants but also among the officials of the federal government in St. Louis and Washington itself. "The increase of emigration and trade," assert the editors, "not only on the routes leading to Oregon and Santa Fe, but with the Indian tribes located on the head waters of the Missouri, has at length enlisted the attention of Government, and we perceive that some provision is about to be made for the protection of the emigrant and trader on our western plains." In sum, one observes here an acceptance of the dying away of the old nomadic fur trade of the mountain man, the entrepreneur in his pirogue, the Indian bringing in his

43 Signed E. W. S., I believe that this is a printer's error for G. W. S.; it is headed as one of the "Letters from New Mexico," *WR*, III (January 11, 1847), 1137.

beaver pelts to the great trading forts; in its stead is the emerging vision of a more settled bourgeois nation extending to the Pacific. The editorial continues: "The idea has suggested itself, while thinking on this subject, that trading posts, such as have been recently established at Council Grove by our friends *Boone & Hamilton,* might, under the charge of experienced men, effect the same purpose as these military posts, at a far less expense to the Government, and form, in fertile spots upon these great routes, the neuclei of future towns, where the emigrant might obtain supplies on his way, without having to undergo the delay and risk incident to carrying them over a long land journey."[44] Whether these remarks would tend to support or to qualify the classic Turner frontier thesis, I am not sure; but they do help to fill in the general design of the expansion westward in the latter 1840's. And it is true that a number of towns and cities arose by just such a historical process as the *Reveille* here suggests.

The evidence of Curry's abortive correspondence in the paper shows that Keemle and Field steadily maintained an interest in Oregon and upper California, even in the confused months of 1846. As Dale Morgan has shown, the *Reveille* was one of the first papers to print Patrick Breen's diary of his sufferings as a member of the Donner party, and the *Reveille*'s list of the survivors and of those who perished—reprinted from the San Francisco *California Star* of May 22, 1847—was widely copied.[45] By 1848 the tide of emigration to Oregon and California was rapidly swelling. For example, in its issue for March 20, 1848, the *Reveille* published a brief article, "Tourists to the Pacific," on its front page:

> We have received a letter from Alexandria, La., with regard to the Oregon route, &c. We reply, through our columns, as others may be thus answered:
>
> In the first place, unless the tourist should travel alone, or with an "express," it would be impossible to make the trip to and fro in one season. Caravans of emigrants, or traders' wagons, very seldom leave Independence before the 1st or middle of May, and then they travel so slowly that it requires three or four months to make the journey. Even if the tourist should arrive in Oregon in time to return

44 *WR*, III (April 26, 1847), 1254.

45 Morgan, II, 796, n. 209. See "Thrilling Journal," *WR*, IV (August 30, 1847), 1401; much of the page was devoted to this account of the Donner party.

to the States before winter, the chances of finding parties returning would be against him. The amount of money required, would, of course, depend altogether upon the party. The actually necessary expenditures would not be very great; but there are many incidental ones, such as "giving out" of horses, mules, &c., &c., to which parties on the plains are liable. The traveller should, by all means take mules in preference to horses. American mules are larger and better than Spanish mules. Never buy a Spanish mule that has white spots on its back—such have, at one time or other, been used as pack mules, and their backs will soon get sore. If the object be to hunt buffalo, the traveller should take with him several horses, but should not ride them steadily. Corn fed horses become weak after being a little while on grass, and are not fit to chase buffalo.

The traveller should also have a small covered wagon. It is very troublesome to drive pack mules; besides, there is the risk of losing them; wagons don't stray off or "stampede."

For arms it would be necessary to have a rifle, carrying from sixty to forty [balls] to the pound; a revolver, and a hunting or bowie knife. If the person is afflicted with ill health, and the system is not too much debilitated, the trip would doubtless do much good; but if, on the contrary, he is weak, and in a decline—it would either "kill or cure," perhaps the former.

In regard to provisions, we would advise tourists not to burden themselves with anything extra. A good stock of coffee, sugar, salt pork, or bacon, and flour; some tea, a sack or two of hard bread, with a small quantity of beans, would comprise all that would be necessary. A little saleratus would add much to the quality of bread. There will probably be a great deal of travel on the route this season, and from present appearances, parties will make an earlier start than usual.[46]

One recalls that just three years earlier, in its issue for March 24, 1845, the *Reveille* had published "John Brown's" letter advising emigrants to Oregon about the precise route that would be most advantageous for them to follow, as apparently at that time no single route had yet been altogether proven. And here, three years later, the *Reveille* is advising "tourists." Less than a year later alongside news of the cholera, that "dreadful scourge now prevailing in our valley," appeared two significant items, one of them a brief notice reprinted from the Cincinnati *Atlas*, and headed "The Rush for California."

46 *WR*, IV (March 20, 1848), 1625.

It seemed that a gentleman just returned to New York from Panama reported having gone to Chagres, crossed the Isthmus, and on seeing the immense crowd, "whose turns, according to barber's shop law, must come before his own . . . returned in despair. He found upwards of two thousand persons waiting for a passage. It is computed that there are 6,000 there now, all eager for a chance to reach San Francisco." California obviously had replaced Oregon as the goal for emigrants.

The next item was headed "Going to California" and was a practical piece of advice, with supporting statistics and details, as to how the prospective emigrant should outfit himself with "a species of property, such as wagons, harness, &c., very useful in the gold region." "To go in companies of ten persons, associating with other companies, so as to make a caravan sufficiently strong, the expenses" would run somewhat as follows: $900 for a wagon, harness, and eight good mules; $30 for ninety days, or nine hundred rations, of flour weighing 1,200 pounds; ninety rations of pork, weighing 675 pounds and costing $47; $30 for coffee, sugar, pepper, salt, and the like (about $3 per person); and $30 for "Cooking utensils, tin plates, coffee pots, camp kettles, &c." Added to this expense of $1,037—averaging $103.37 per person—one should "add expense of provisions, tents, mess apparatus, and ammunition" and an item called "contingencies," and the total would be "about $110.00 to each member of the Party." The aggregate weight of this load would not exceed 2,400 pounds; as the load of the wagon would be 4,000 pounds, "this would leave sixteen hundred pounds, or one hundred and sixty pounds for each man as private baggage." "If the party be poor," advised the *Reveille,* "they need go to no further expense, because a man can easily walk as far as the teams will travel in a day. But $90 will mount each man on a good mule, with trappings complete, making the entire cost of the outfit of transportation, for each, $200. Or, the party can purchase four mules and a light wagon for about $450, to ride in, making the cost of the whole only $155 to each person." And the *Reveille* concluded that as these calculations were made on "the supposition that no fresh meat would be killed on the route," consequently "all the game taken would be so much clear gain."[47]

[47] *WR,* V (January 8, 1849), 1963.

Not only good Americans but also the inhabitants of the Sandwich Islands had caught the fever; the islands had "become almost depopulated, the inhabitants having taken up the gold fever and . . . emigrating to California." And in another column under the heading "More Gold" was printed the news that "Col. Emory, of the topographical engineers, in his report of the expedition westward, from the mountains of New Mexico, along the course of the river Gila, speaks of having met with gold at several points on his route." A few adventurers (related the colonel) who ascended the Prieto River, which empties into the Gila, "hunting the beaver, washed the sands at night, when they halted, and were richly rewarded for their trouble. Tempted by their success, they made a second trip, and were attacked, and most of them killed by the Indians. My authority for this statement," Emory cautiously added, "is Landreau; though an illiterate man, he is truthful."

The myriad departures for the West were pessimistically viewed by some people, but not by the *Reveille*. Reprinting and commenting on "a most gloomy article with regard to the California drain upon our population," in the Hannibal *Courier*, the St. Louis paper refused to give up its habitual optimism. The *Courier* had cried: "The Curse of California—to the western States at least—has just begun." It argued, apparently, that the greater part of the emigration from Missouri was from "the producing classes," and it calculated "the reduction in produce, in consequence, at *one-fifth*!" Farmers, perennially an easily disgruntled group, were complaining that they were not going to produce anything that year beyond their home consumption, because farmhands were not only exceedingly scarce but outrageously expensive. To all of which the *Reveille* replied that "Immigration is not so rapid into our State as into others, but we have no fears of the prostration so gloomily looked forward to, while reporting weekly the arrival of two thousand sturdy Germans, English, and Irish."[48]

Besides the correspondence of George Law Curry, the *Reveille* published the letters of many another young emigrant bound for the Pacific Coast in the late 1840's.[49] John Francis McDermott has already

48 " 'The Curse of California,' " *WR*, VI (June 10, 1850), 4241.

49 I am currently compiling a checklist of items concerning the California Gold Rush that the *WR* published in 1848–50.

edited, for example, the travel letters that "Solitaire" wrote back to the *Reveille* when he went west in 1849.[50] As the editors happily recognized in that season of lemming-like migration, Robb was one of many such correspondents. An item entitled "Letters from the Pacific" in the *Reveille* for May 14, 1849, shows how Keemle and Field exploited their friends among the California emigrants. Alluding to one of their pseudonymous contributors known as "Hunt," author of a piece entitled "The Negro's Leap," which the paper had published just a year previously, the editors announced:

> We give on our first page a letter from a gentleman now on his way to the Pacific,—one among many whom we have made particular arrangements with for a regular and useful correspondence. "Solitaire's" letters will soon be reaching us; we shall in the meantime receive constant communications from the direct overland emigration [Robb was then proceeding to San Diego and thence to San Francisco by way of Corpus Christi, the Rio Grande, and the Gila River valley], and, in each case, from an unexceptionable source. "Hunt," whose first letter we give to-day, is Mr. E. W. Roberts, late of the *Prairie State Argus*, Jacksonville, Ill., and for five years past connected with the press of our neighbor State. Mr. R. was educated for the medical profession, he goes to California to observe persons and things, rather than to become an actual "digger," and we have every confidence that his letters will prove interesting in every sense.[51]

[50] John S. Robb ("Solitaire"), "Gold-Fever: The Letters of 'Solitaire,' Goldrush Correspondent of '49," John Francis McDermott, ed., *Missouri Historical Society Bulletin*, V (January, 1949), 115–126 (McDermott, Introduction, pp. 115–121); Pt. II, V (April, 1959), 211–223; Pt. III, V (July, 1949), 316–332; Conclusion, VI (October, 1949), 34–43. Robb's Gold Rush letters in *WR* are published in the *Missouri Historical Society Bulletin* as follows:

Part I: V (February 12, 1849), 2000 (dated Napoleon, Ark., January 24, 1849); V (February 19, 1849), 2008 (dated New Orleans, February 4, 1849).

Part II: V (March 12, 1849), 2033 (dated Corpus Christi, February 10, 1849); V (March 19, 1849), 2041 (dated Camp Missouri, Corpus Christi, February 12, 1849); VI (October 8, 1849), 3056 (dated San Diego, Cal., July 11, 1849); VII (July 22, 1850), 4292 (McDermott included this descriptive piece among the travel letters).

Part III: VI (October 8, 1849), 3056 (dated San Diego, Cal., July 9, 1849); *ibid.*, p. 3057 (dated San Francisco, Cal., July 18, 1849); *ibid.*, p. 3062 (dated San Francisco, Cal., July 20, 1849); VI (October 22, 1849), 3072 (dated Wood's Diggings, San Joaquin District, Cal., August 10, 1849).

Part IV: VI (October 29, 1849), 3080 (dated Sonoranian Camp, San Joaquin District, Cal., August 12, 1849); *ibid.* (dated Sullivan's Diggings, San Joaquin, Cal., August 15, 1849); *ibid.*, p. 3084 (dated Wood's Diggings, San Joaquin, Cal., August 17, 1849).

[51] "Letters from the Pacific," *WR*, V (May 14, 1849), 2106. "The Negro's Leap"

For all the high hopes the *Reveille* expressed for letters from Hunt, he disappointed them. Three of his letters—two dated from Independence and one from St. Joseph—were printed in the *Reveille* for May 14, 1849; another, dated from Camp Morgan, near Independence, appeared in the issue for May 28. Then silence, until the *Reveille* published Hunt's "Letter from California" in its issue for February 18, 1850.[52] Such an experience is representative; most of the Gold Rush letters the *Reveille* printed were dated either from a convenient embarkation point on a trail west—Corpus Christi, Chihuahua, Westport, St. Joseph—or from a settlement or town out in California. Relatively few reached the paper from the desert wilderness of the Plains or the Rockies, not only because of the overwhelming hardships of the overland journey but also because of the vagaries of such couriers as were available to take letters back to St. Louis.

When its correspondents reached El Dorado, usually they sent the *Reveille* a report of their first impressions—in the case of "Solitaire," several reports. Then, as one should expect, the youthful correspondents went their ways, became absorbed into the new way of life, lost touch with Missouri, and thus were unavailable to Keemle and Field in 1850 for the reporting of events in California. To take up space became a problem: where was California news to be had? On one occasion, the paper was reduced to reprinting a letter originally ad-

---

appeared in *WR*, IV (May 22, 1848), 1697; *ibid.*, p. 1699, carries a brief filler advising readers to "read this most spirited sketch, from one of our most valued correspondents. It is not only a fine descriptive effort, but it conveys a proper rebuke to the managers of the Illinois 'Underground Rail Road.' "

52 By "Hunt" in the *WR*: "Gold Fever—Progress—Ducks," V (February 12, 1849), 2003 (an indication of Roberts' gold fever); "Frontier Sketches," V (May 14, 1849), 2108 ([1] dated Independence, Mo., May 4, 1849, [2] dated St. Joseph, Mo., May 8, 1849); "The Emigration," *ibid.*, p. 2110 (dated Independence, Mo., May 2, 1849); "The Pacific March," V (May 28, 1849), 2118 (dated Camp Morgan, near Independence, Mo., May 11, 1849); "Letter from California," VI (February 18, 1850), 3109. A more prolific correspondent was "Mifflin," George Mifflin Harker, a newspaper reporter formerly connected with the St. Louis *Daily Union*. For Harker's emigrant correspondence to the *WR* in 1849–50, see Stella Drumm, ed., "Morgan Street to Old Dry Diggings, 1849," *Glimpses of the Past*, VI (April-June, 1939), 35–76. The last letters in Miss Drumm's collection were dated from "Mifflin's" encampment at Dry Diggings (var.: Old Dry Diggings), California, on February 2, 1850, and January 18, 1850, and were, respectively, printed in *WR*, VI (March 25, 1850), 4149 and 4151. Not gathered by Miss Drumm are two later "Mifflin" letters: "Times and Scenes in El Dorado," *WR*, VI (June 10, 1850), 4237 (dated Placerville, California, April 12, 1850), in which Harker complains that "I but seldom receive my 'Reveille,' and only three letters have reached me"; and "Letter from a Gentleman Digger," *WR*, VI (August 19, 1850), 4317 (dated Placerville, California, June 20, 1850).

dressed to the editors of the Washington *Union*, in preference, wrote Keemle or Field, "to boring our readers with anything of our own this morning." The truth was, of course, that the *Reveille* did not have a trusty set of California correspondents such as it had had from New and old Mexico in 1846–47. This letter, by R[obert] Semple, paints a relatively complete and succinct panorama of the Californian scene in the latter months of 1849 (it appeared in the *Reveille* for January 7, 1850) and attempts to say something concrete of the country and its resources. To assuage what he terms "the California fever," Semple gave "a *connected* view of the mineral and agricultural, as well as the commercial resources of California." The great Bay of San Francisco, he said, "may be considered our general harbor." "Sausalita," Sonoma, Napa, Benicia, Martinez ("a new town recently laid out by Mr. Wm. M. Smith"), Pueblo de San José, San Francisco were briefly described; some attention was paid to the vine-growing districts, even then well developed; and Semple declared that "a vast amount of gold in the 'Sierra Nevada' " and "very rich and extensive mines have been recently discovered in the coast range, which proves beyond a doubt that California is truly 'El Dorado.' "[53]

Semple's optimism was not shared by at least one knowledgeable correspondent of the *Reveille*; already California was a problem for Americans, for some of them an image as meretricious as it was grandiose. In the last extant issue of the *Reveille* came a letter headed "Mines of Col. Fremont" in refutation of the claims made by Semple and decrying the dazzling picture he limned.

The anonymous correspondent addressed "Messrs. Editors of The Reveille" and began by saying that as the "following extracts of a letter recently received from California" were "from a source . . . altogether reliable, you will perhaps serve the public by giving them publicity in your paper." The extracts were given anonymously, but the writer may well have been a person known to dozens of people in St. Louis; he specifically made an attack on the frenzy of speculation in gold-mining. "I and two others," he began, "are now engaged in the celebrated quartz vein, commonly known as 'Fremont's.' We have commenced operations here, and have got out some rich specimens of gold in its matrix, the quartz. As soon as practicable we shall get our machinery, and then our operations may more properly be said to have

[53] R. Semple, "California," *WR*, VI (January 7, 1850), 3165.

begun. So far as has yet been ascertained, this is the only quartz vein, bearing gold, on the west side of the Sierra Nevada." While the letter-writer went on to report the success of explorations of the new field by "Col. H. Jacobs, late U.S. geological Surveyor, and Prof. Shepherd, of Amherst College," he also reported the risks entailed in exploring for and in mining gold. "There are now at this place two companies from Washington City, one from Kentucky, one from Tennessee, one from Massachusetts, one from St. Louis, (Barton and Tyler,) one from Virginia, and one from Nashville. All these companies have costly machinery, and not a foot of a vein containing gold-bearing quartz to work. Rich times these, but ruin is coming, and quartz vein speculations will terminate the already bursting bubble of this El Dorado, for such it is in truth and in fact."[54]

Of all the correspondence the *Reveille* printed, this letter opens as fascinating avenues of speculation as any. First of all, the mention of Frémont in connection with California brings to mind the earlier letter from Frémont that the *Reveille* printed after being given it, in all probability, by his wife Jessie. Both the newly elected senator from the not-yet-admitted state of California and Mrs. Frémont were sailing back, via the Isthmus of Panama, to New York and Washington when the *Reveille* printed the anonymous letter about his landholdings and mining operation, and a major factor in Frémont's return east was his need to settle the question of his huge land grant, the Mariposa tract in the Sierra Nevada, and the problem of squatters on its seventy square miles, over forty-three thousand acres. Could Frémont have written the letter to a friend or a relative of Jessie's back in St. Louis, with directions to turn it over to the *Reveille* if doing so seemed wise? Or perhaps the anonymous prospector was really a young St. Louisan who was working for Frémont? Whatever the identity of the correspondent, one fancies that his first purpose was to deter speculators, prospectors for gold, and squatters from invading the Mariposa tract. The unknown correspondent freely admitted the success of Frémont's mining operation if only because the situation was too widely known in California and elsewhere to admit of denial. But his assertion that of the eight companies of easterners prospecting for gold in and near the Mariposa tract not a one had found "a foot of vein containing

54 *WR*, VII (September 23, 1850), 4363. This is the final issue in the Missouri Historical Society files of the *Reveille*.

gold-bearing quartz to work" is interesting, all the more so when immediately followed (as it is) by the unwarranted pessimism that warned: "Rich times these, but ruin is coming, and quartz vein speculations will terminate the already bursting bubble of this El Dorado, for such it is in truth and in fact." While these words were being read, Frémont was well on his way to wealth through "quartz vein speculations" on the Mariposa tract. Horace Greeley, who visited the Frémont estate in the summer of 1859, estimated that the two mills at Mariposa produced at least $250,000 worth of gold a year, at a cost of not more than $150,000; and of course Frémont engaged in other enterprises on a comparable scale, such as the raising and marketing of cattle.[55]

It was not the bubble of the Californian El Dorado that soon burst, but rather the much smaller, much frailer bubble of the *Reveille*. To change the metaphor, the *Reveille* sounded its final cheerful call to the West with its issue of September 23, 1850, and St. Louisans would no longer read "John Brown's" reminiscences of the Mexican War or "Solitaire's" Indian tales and accounts of river trips northward or the anonymous news of Californian gold fever. A century and two decades have passed since the end of the Mexican War and the discovery of gold at Sutter's Mill in California and the extension of our national boundaries to the Pacific. We are a middle-aged nation now, and a middle-aged nation, like a middle-aged man or woman, has a past. But in few places can that past have been reported more vividly, more energetically, more entertainingly that in the columns of the St. Louis *Weekly Reveille*, in the letters and comment of its correspondents and editors. These documents aid all those who would re-create a truthful, and therefore viable, image of America during the most crucial period of her westward expansion.

55 Horace Greeley, *An Overland Journey from New York to San Francisco in the Summer of 1859*, Charles T. Duncan, ed. (New York: Alfred A. Knopf, 1964), p. 270.

Letters from the West: A Survey of Reports by Travelers in the New Orleans *Picayune*, 1837–60

Nicholas Canaday, Jr.

IN THE YEARS prior to the Civil War, the New Orleans *Picayune* was one of those influential newspapers that focused eyes and ears on the West. In the case of the *Picayune,* partly no doubt because of the location of New Orleans but also because of the interests of its editors, the paper took the Southwest as its special province. The precise extent to which the *Picayune* reflects its readers' preoccupation with the various aspects of western travel, or on the other hand shapes this interest, cannot of course be determined, but the process no doubt was mutually reinforcing. The space given in the columns of the *Picayune* to travel accounts reprinted from various sources, casual letters from friends and acquaintances reporting home, news and articles reported from other newspapers, and especially letters, narratives, and sketches written in series by the *Picayune*'s own correspondents—all these attest to the interest in the rapidly expanding western horizon.

The New Orleans *Picayune* published its first issue on January 25, 1837. This first edition was the result of three years of planning by its founders, George Wilkins Kendall and Francis Asbury Lumsden, who were working as foremen in the printshop of rival New Orleans newspapers immediately prior to their joint venture.[1] The

[1] For the background information on Kendall, Lumsden, and the *Picayune* I am

two had met in 1833 when they had worked together in the shop of the *National Intelligencer* in Washington. When the *Picayune* was begun there were ten newspapers already serving the seventy thousand people of the busy city of New Orleans, and their newest competitor, named after the smallest Spanish coin then in circulation, was the smallest of the papers and also the cheapest. The first edition of four pages was printed in one thousand copies and all were sold. Within a week the circulation had almost doubled, and thus was launched a successful newspaper venture and an editorial partnership that lasted until Francis Lumsden's accidental death by drowning in 1860. A weekly edition of the paper, which had a large circulation in Texas as well as Louisiana, was begun on February 24, 1838.

George Wilkins Kendall of the *Picayune* became one of those legendary newspaper editors of the nation in an era of flamboyant, colorful journalism. Originally from New England, Kendall had worked twelve years for a dozen different newspapers in almost as many cities by the time he and Lumsden founded the *Picayune*. Kendall was then twenty-seven years old. In 1837 he had been in New Orleans only two years, and just as soon as the success of the newspaper was assured he began to travel again. His columns written throughout the nation and abroad, usually labeled "Editorial Correspondence," appeared frequently in the *Picayune* until his death in 1867. Lumsden and others managed the paper in New Orleans while Kendall was traveling, although when he was needed Kendall returned to that city sometimes for long periods of time.

I

The longest series of letters written by Kendall as a western traveler appeared in the *Picayune* beginning on June 17, 1841. By 1841 Kendall had become thoroughly caught up in the affairs of the Republic of Texas. Both houses of the Texas legislature had by February of that year passed separate bills favoring an expedition to Santa Fe as part of the general western expansion program and specifically to capture the rich western trade, of which Santa Fe was the focal point,

---

indebted to Fayette Copeland, *Kendall of the Picayune* (Norman: University of Oklahoma Press, 1943).

and channel it toward Texas ports on the Gulf. The expedition was organized, and Kendall left New Orleans in May bound for Austin to join it. The Mexicans viewed the Santa Fe expedition as more military than commercial, and after many vicissitudes the entire group was captured in September before reaching Santa Fe. The expedition had failed. Kendall spent seven months as a captive, most of the time as a prisoner in Mexico City. His release was finally accomplished, and he returned to New Orleans in May of 1842. In the meantime many of his adventures on the Santa Fe expedition had been chronicled in twenty-three letters to the *Picayune* published between June 17, 1841, and April 30, 1842.

Immediately upon his return to New Orleans Kendall began to prepare a book about the Santa Fe expedition. The narrative was published serially in the *Picayune* beginning June 1, 1842. There are twenty-one articles in June, twenty-two in July, and fifteen in August. Then in November another series of articles written by Kendall, this time sketches, began to appear. The series is introduced by an editorial on November 26, and sixty-two "Mexican Sketches" or "Santa Fe Sketches," as they were usually called, were published during November and December of 1842 and January, February, March, and April of 1843. Other newspapers reprinted many of the articles from each of the three series—the letters, the narrative, and the sketches—and together they are the raw material for the book that resulted when the expedition's press agent finally turned historian: George Wilkins Kendall, *Narrative of the Texan Santa Fe Expedition* (New York: Harper and Brothers, 1844).

Another series of articles about the ill-fated Santa Fe expedition—this series quite short—appeared in the *Picayune* during six consecutive days in May of 1842. Its importance is underscored by the fact that Kendall had not yet returned with his more complete account, and the New Orleans public was hungry for news. This series was written by Thomas Falconer, one of Kendall's companions on the expedition. It was introduced to the readers of the *Picayune* by an editorial on May 1 and began on May 3. Falconer, a young Englishman, had been captured with the main party of the expedition, but his immediate release was secured by the British minister in Mexico. Falconer had visited the imprisoned Kendall, and he brought news of him to his friends in New Orleans when Falconer returned there in March. Later the

Picayune published Falconer's articles as a pamphlet: *Thomas Falconer's Journal of the Santa Fe Expedition.* The publication of this pamphlet was announced in the *Picayune* on May 12, 1842.

Because of George Kendall's continuing interest in the Southwest, the commerce between New Orleans and Texas ports, and also the continuing migration westward that cleared through towns in northern Louisiana, the *Picayune* over the years following 1842 allotted many columns to news of Texas and the Southwest. By April of 1846 dispatches written by Kendall from the Mexican War began to appear. The *Picayune* chronicled his adventures as a reporter under fire in the months that followed. He returned to New Orleans in November of 1847, and four years later his book on the Mexican War was published.[2]

A brief and final series of western travel articles by Kendall appeared in the *Picayune* between August and November of 1851, the first letter on August 21. He had joined an expedition in St. Louis, commanded by an Indian agent, Colonel D. D. Mitchell, bound for an Indian council at Fort Laramie. Because of unexpected rainstorms and the theft of some of their mules by Indians, Kendall's party missed a scheduled rendezvous with another group at Fort Kearney in the Nebraska Territory. So Kendall's party went instead to a smaller council in Pawnee country, and when he returned to St. Louis he closed this series of a dozen letters. Thus in 1851 Kendall completed his last venture into the Plains for the *Picayune*.

II

Unlike the Kendall letters, the letters of Matthew C. Field to the New Orleans *Picayune* have recently been collected and edited. Matt Field—sometime actor, theater manager, newspaper reporter, and editor—first appeared in the columns of the *Picayune* in December of 1839. He had been hired as an assistant editor early that winter after spending the summer on the Santa Fe Trail and in New Mexico. His "Sketches of the Mountains and the Prairies," based upon his journal of that trip, which appeared in the *Picayune* between 1839 and 1841,

[2] George Wilkins Kendall and Carl Nebel, *War between the United States and Mexico, Illustrated* (New Orleans and New York: D. Appleton and Co., 1851).

have recently been published as a book, together with the journal itself: *Matt Field on the Santa Fe Trail*, edited by John E. Sunder (Norman: University of Oklahoma Press, 1960). Again in 1843 Matt Field ventured into the Plains for the *Picayune*, becoming the historian for the famous sporting expedition of Sir William Drummond Stewart. Letters from this expedition, together with sketches written for the *Picayune*, and supplementary material from his diary, have been published in Matthew C. Field, *Prairie and Mountain Sketches*, edited by Kate L. Gregg and John Francis McDermott (Norman: University of Oklahoma Press, 1957).

III

Two other important series of letters from the West that appeared in the *Picayune* prior to the Civil War have not yet been collected and edited. Because of the intense interest in the rush to California in 1849, the *Picayune* dispatched two veteran correspondents to report on the journey and the gold fields. Perhaps more accurately, James L. Freaner and John E. Durivage, both New Orleans newspapermen of some reputation, were determined to seek a new life in California, and the *Picayune* was fortunate in being able to make a contract with them for the reports of their adventure. There is no record in the *Picayune* that either ever returned to Louisiana. Twenty-four letters from Freaner and twenty-six from Durivage were published in the *Picayune* during 1849 and 1850.

James L. Freaner gained fame as a Mexican War correspondent for the New Orleans *Delta*.[3] The *Picayune* was much pleased to secure his services in this new assignment, as evidenced by its editorial column on February 20, 1849, announcing his departure:

> Among the passengers who left the city yesterday on the steamer Isthmus for Chagres, was Mr. James L. Freaner, on his way to California. We are happy to announce that we have secured the services of Mr. Freaner as a correspondent for this paper. California is to be the scene of extraordinary events, if we are not mistaken, ere the close

[3] Freaner as a competitor in the reporting of the war is dealt with at length by Copeland in *Kendall of the Picayune*.

> of this present year. . . . Our last telegraphic account from Washington represented that murders were "occurring hourly" in California. This is but the prelude to wilder scenes if some efficient Government be not provided. In any event, California for a year to come is to be the theatre to which the eyes of the world will be directed, and we are happy to have been able to engage as a correspondent there the services of a gentleman so well known for his perseverance and energy as Mr. Freaner. He acquired a reputation during the Mexican War for spirit, intelligence, and discretion which point him out as one of the best men in the country for a correspondent. His facilities for obtaining information will be second to no other man in the Territory, and we anticipate a series of letters from him which will make us thoroughly acquainted with the resources of the country and the events of which it is to be the theatre. We trust Freaner is to play an active and a profitable part in the golden drama, and that he will come back to us richer than Croesus and full of honors.

John E. Durivage, on the other hand, had been associated with the *Picayune* for a number of years. He too had been a reporter during the Mexican War: six signed letters from Monterrey published in the *Picayune* during July and August of 1847 had apparently attracted some attention. Further, during 1848 he made a tour of New York and New England, and nine signed letters in the *Picayune* between August and October of that year described his impressions of that part of the North. On March 4, 1849, less than a month after Freaner had left, the *Picayune* announced in its editorial column the departure of the second half of its reporting team:

> A large number of gentlemen leave this day on steamers for Lavaca and the Brazos, destined for California. Among them is Mr. J. E. Durivage, who has for several years been connected with this office. The seductions of California have been too much for him, and he has at last yielded. He proceeds immediately to the Rio Grande, thence taking his course . . . entirely by land . . . a fine field for his adventurous spirit, which will find more congenial sport in prairie travel, and in skirmishes with Comanches, than in gold digging. Our readers will recollect the letters from Mr. D. written from General Wool's headquarters, to which he was attached as a volunteer aide. He will continue his correspondence with the Picayune, recording therein his whole "travel history" till he reaches El Dorado. We

> promise great pleasure to ourselves and our readers from this source, and wish our friend as great a variety of adventures as his bold and ardent nature craves. He has our heartiest and warmest good wishes in his future career.

The *Picayune* now had correspondents on two of the principal routes to California. Freaner traveled via ship to Panama and then, after a much longer wait in the Isthmus than he had anticipated, via another ship to San Francisco. Durivage went on a ship to Brownsville, thence generally northwest along the Rio Grande to the vicinity of the Gila River, and then west to San Diego. Freaner arrived in California in June and Durivage in July.[4]

Freaner's letters to the *Picayune* began from Panama. His first letter was dated March 10 and published on April 1. In it he dealt with the difficulties that many travelers encountered in the route across the Isthmus, about seventy miles from Chagres to Panama by boat and overland, although his own trip was relatively easy. Five additional Freaner letters from Panama were published by the *Picayune* during April and May. All emphasized the expensive, unhealthful, crowded, and boring life experienced while awaiting passage to California. Black-market tickets originally bought in New York—and he takes the occasion to blame the "Yankees" for the speculators as well as for the intolerable delay—were selling for $600 to $1,000. Freaner's letters and other news from Panama prompted the *Picayune* to comment editorially on April 15: "It is estimated that there were at Panama at the end of March 1500 people *en route* to California; at Gorgona and Cruces 700 more. Much distress and some sickness is said to prevail upon the Isthmus. The large number of emigrants have, of course, nothing to do, and they busy themselves in all sorts of amusement. Gambling and frolicking are represented to us as being quite in the ascendant. Some companies which set out for California pledged neither to gamble nor drink have been forced to consider the transit across the Isthmus as a contingency not within their contemplation, and act accordingly."

There are no letters from Freaner published during June or July, but on August 4 there appeared his first letter from San Francisco. In

4 Freaner arrived in San Francisco aboard the steamship *Panama* on June 3 (*Picayune*, August 4, 1849). Durivage arrived in San Diego on July 1 (*Picayune*, August 7, 1849). The Panama route was supposed to be much quicker, but in this case the time saved was only about two weeks.

it he complained about his trip from the Isthmus: "Never, since the time old Columbus made his voyage of discovery . . . have the passengers of a vessel been more poorly provided for." He was amazed at the extravagant life in California, especially since "the value of real estate is almost beyond calculation, and the reality of prices surpasses everything that you can imagine." Details in the letter exemplified both themes, and life in California—including towns, mining camps, and ranches—was thoroughly described in the letters that followed, which were published in the *Picayune* between August and December. Freaner mentioned his team-mate Durivage only once, in a letter published on September 22. Then after the letter that appeared on December 9, 1849, there was an abrupt interruption in the series.

It was not until June 4, 1850, that the next two letters from Freaner appeared in the *Picayune*. These letters were dated April 20 and 30, and because of the delay in the news only excerpts were printed. An editorial comment introduced the letters and explained Freaner's silence of six months: "After an interruption caused, we regret to say, by a long and severe illness, we have received a couple of letters from Mr. Freaner, our correspondent at San Francisco. His first letter, dated the 20th of April, announced his complete restoration to health; but the second, dated on the 30th of April, speaks of a relapse, and the necessity of a trip into the interior for a change of air. He will visit the head of the Sacramento, and promises, if health permits, to communicate whatever may be interesting in those regions." On August 9 a letter was printed with the heading "Reading's Rancho, Head of the Sacramento Valley" and dated June 10, 1850. This letter included an interesting sketch of the new area, and Freaner promised to write more, but he failed to write until three months later, again from San Francisco. Two letters from that city and two letters from Sacramento City, the last one appearing in the *Picayune* on December 8, 1850, completed the series. A part of the letter dated October 19 from Sacramento City and published in the *Picayune* on December 7 described an occasion which Freaner may have felt was an appropriate close to his travel letters: "*Eds. Pic*—This morning the steamer from San Francisco brought us the glad tidings of the admission of California into the Union. The news was announced about two hours before daylight, by the firing of one hundred guns from the steamer. The signal was at once recognized by the community, and was followed by the discharge of firearms of all sizes and classes, from the old rusty flint lock to the polished revolver. Today is a day of general rejoicing."

The Durivage letters, published in the *Picayune* beginning in March of 1849, reflect from the outset Durivage's interest in the "congenial sport" of "prairie travel," as promised by the editors. The letters published through July described the trail—Roma, Mier, Monterrey, Saltillo, Chihuahua, Barranca, San Diego, and points in between. Durivage kept a detailed journal with daily entries. Three long portions of this journal were sent back for publication in the *Picayune*. On July 13 the *Picayune* published, in addition to a letter from Barranca, Mexico, a portion of his diary describing his travels on each day between April 9 and May 1. Then again on August 7 the *Picayune* published Durivage's first letter from San Diego and his diary of May 12 to June 20. Finally, on September 23 his travel diary of June 22 to July 1 appeared in the *Picayune*, together with another letter from San Diego.[5]

In the remaining months of 1849 Durivage's letters were sent from San Francisco and from Monterey, California, where he visited between August and October and reported to the readers of the *Picayune* in some detail the proceedings of the California Constitutional Convention. He mentioned his team-mate Freaner only once, in a letter published on September 18. Like Freaner, Durivage described mining camps, towns, and countryside. The following excerpt from a Durivage letter describing San Francisco, dated October 31 and published in the *Picayune* on December 9, 1849, may serve to exemplify his skill as a reporter:

> Mr. J. A. Rowe commenced operations last night with a circus company of very fair materials, and took in the very snug little sum of $3000—a pretty good beginning. There are two or three sets of Ethiopian serenaders in the city, who nightly lament the absence of Miss Neal, mourn over the fate of Rosa Lee, inform the public that they have just arrived from Alabama, or request, in the most earnest manner, to be carried back to Old Virginny. There are more new

[5] The travel diaries and all but one of the Durivage letters from the trail have been collected under the title "Through Mexico to California, Letters and Journal of John E. Durivage," in Ralph P. Bieber, ed., *Southern Trails to California in 1849* (Glendale, Calif.: Arthur H. Clark, 1937). One letter from Chihuahua, Mexico, dated April 31 and published in the *Picayune* on June 17, 1849, seems to have been inadvertently omitted from this collection.

gambling establishments than there are catfish in the Mississippi, and all have their peculiar attractions or "baits." In one is a very handsome Chilano girl, bejewelled like a dowager, who claps down her ounces as if they were so many brass buttons. At another . . . three comely-looking American girls tend bar, and are deep in the mystery of making rum punches, brandy smashers, and gin cocktails. In one is a band playing Hail Columbia; in another the Scotch bagpipes are wheezing away Roy's Wife; in another is a man blowing his brains out through a key bugle; in another an Italian, who beats the bass drum, plays the cymbals, plays the Pandean pipes, rings a set of musical bells on his head, and plays on several other instruments, all at the same time; then there is the banjo and the violin, the harps, the hurdy gurdies, and the grinding organs and monkeys. Add to all this sweet compound of sounds the rattling and jingling of money and dice on the tables, the clinking of glasses, the roaring of some inebriate, the rumbling of carts, the knocking and banging of carpenters, and you have a very faint idea of life in California.

In 1850 only four Durivage letters appeared in the *Picayune*. All were from San Francisco, and the last one of the series, dated December 21, 1849, was published in New Orleans on February 10, 1850. Then on April 29, 1850, a notice that appeared in the "California Edition" of the *Picayune*,[6] one of the periodic news-summary editions printed for shipment to California, indicated that Durivage had by then found employment with a newspaper in his adopted state: "NOTICE.—Mr. J. E. Durivage, of the 'Alta Californian,' San Francisco, is the duly authorized agent of the *Picayune*."[7]

The letters of James Freaner and John Durivage to the *Picayune* comprised the last series of letters from the West in that newspaper prior to the Civil War. News from the West during the 1850's continued to be of interest, as evidenced by the news stories, letters, sketches,

[6] The first "California *Picayune*," according to the editors, was "compiled expressly to suit the tastes and to supply the wants of our fellow-citizens in that distant but most interesting region," and was published on November 13, 1849.

[7] J. E. Durivage is mentioned as an editor of the *Alta California* and prominent citizen of San Francisco in the *California Historical Society Quarterly*, XXVI (December, 1947), 337; XXVIII (March, 1949), 34. Mahlon D. Fairchild, "Reminiscences of a 'Forty-Niner,'" *California Historical Society Quarterly*, XIII (March, 1934), 3–33, mentions seeing a former war correspondent of the New Orleans *Picayune* named "Freanor" in Panama in April of 1849. He adds that "Mr. Freanor, after coming to California and going to the northern part of the State, was killed by Indians in Trinity County in 1852" (p. 6).

and reprints from other newspapers dealing with the West that were scattered throughout the issues over the years. But long continued travel accounts in series seemed to have been put aside for a time by the editors of the *Picayune*. Even during the early years of the decade of the 1850's the columns of the *Picayune* began to reflect an increasing attention to the posture of the South in relation to the Union, and the tenor of the news and comment became increasingly excited, then strident, and finally desperate, as the nation moved along what seemed to be an inevitable path toward tragedy.

The Western Boatman: Half Horse, Half Myth

Richard E. Oglesby

> Whoo-oop! bow your neck and spread, for the kingdom of sorrow's a-coming! Hold me down to earth, for I feel my powers a-working! Whoo-oop! I'm a child of sin, *don't* let me get a start! Smoked glass, here, for all! Don't attempt to look at me with the naked eye, gentlemen! When I'm playful I use the meridians of longitude and the parallels of latitude for a seine, and drag the Atlantic Ocean for whales! I scratch my head with the lightening and purr myself to sleep with the thunder! When I'm cold, I bile the Gulf of Mexico and bathe in it; when I'm hot, I fan myself with an equinoctial storm; when I'm thirsty I reach up and suck a cloud dry like a sponge; when I range the earth hungry, famine follows in my tracks! Whoo-oop! Bow your neck and spread! I put my hand on the sun's face and make it night in the earth; I bite a piece out of the moon and hurry the seasons; I shake myself and crumble the mountains! Contemplate me through leather—*don't* use the naked eye! I'm the man with the petrified heart and biler-iron bowels! The massacre of isolated communities is the pastime of my idle moments, the destruction of nationalities the serious business of my life! The boundless vastness of the great American desert is my enclosed property, and I bury my dead on my own premises! Whoo-oop! bow your neck and spread, for the Pet Child of Calamity's a-coming![1]

And come they have, all those Pet Children of Calamity, those half-men, half-horse, half-alligator keepers of the keelboats, gasconading down the halls of time, led by the biggest, brashest member of the entire fraternity, Mike Fink. Larger than life they loomed on the

[1] Samuel L. Clemens, *Life on the Mississippi, The Works of Mark Twain*, IX (New York: Harper and Brothers, 1903), 22.

early nineteenth-century American horizon, and distance has only enhanced their magnitude to the point where reality has long since been lost. They had something, that handful of swaggering extroverts who, for a brief moment in history, were spotlighted for providing the energy which moved the crude boats carrying American commerce on western waters, something that, though they really contributed next to nothing to the growth of the nation's mid-section, caused them to become legendary in their own time, and fit subjects for the myth-makers of Disneyland West. What that something was has been a matter for conjecture ever since, at least among students of literature, folklore, and the American character, but heroes they were to their contemporaries, and heroes they remain.

Hero seems a strange title to be applied to the likes of Mike Fink, James Girty, Big Bill Sedley, and the rest, for the noble qualities usually associated with heroic stature were noticeably lacking among boatmen. Yet theirs was not the heroism obtained after time had deposited a patina on their reputations, effectively covering their faults and gilding their characters. Indeed, it was the very faults and lack of character attributed to the boatmen which made them demigods in the eyes of the plodding pioneer farmers populating the West. The boatmen were definitely not respectable, which gave them a certain charm, especially in the view of youth. They ignored the law, in fact went far out of their way to flout it on occasion, which endeared them to the ordinary, law-abiding citizens who hated legality, as it always appeared to work against them and in favor of eastern speculators, but who could not quite bring themselves to break its bonds. In short, the boatmen seemed to be the expression of the alter ego of the pioneer farmers, the effusive side of their nature which rarely showed, or got the chance to show. Since most farmers never saw a boatman in the flesh, it was easy to assign to him all the repressed desires and urges the pioneer had, whether or not they were deserved.

But those who manned the sweeps, strained at the cordelles, and pushed the poles on western waters were more than mere toughs who defied authority. In a real sense, the boatmen were among American society's first dropouts, and, as such, commanded a certain respect and admiration, to say nothing of publicity. Not only did the rivermen reject the Puritan Ethic and the normal social restraints of the times, they went against the whole grain of western and American society.

The business of the American West during the heyday of the boatmen, which began after the close of the Indian wars of the Northwest and ended with the coming of the steamboat, was the conquest of the wilderness, a work both difficult and unremitting. There were endless forests to be felled, cabins to be raised, ground to be plowed, crops to be planted, harvested, and marketed, roads to be cut, cities to be erected, civilization to be created. In this process there was little rest, no leisure time, and, while this strenuous life had its satisfactions, for most of the individuals involved, pecuniary rewards were practically nonexistent. Subsistence was attainable, but there was little to be made beyond that.

Not for the boatmen the enormous task of building a nation, not even when the labor and sacrifice were glorified by such phrases as "Manifest Destiny." Not for him either the prevailing wage of from fifty cents to a dollar a day[2] for doing the same hard work without benefit of land. Life was too short to be spent in drudgery, particularly when the rivers offered escape. Boatmen were always in demand, for certain commodities—salt, flour, whiskey—had to be moved from place to place regardless of the costs of transport. Wages on the rivers were good, generally exceeding, sometimes by twice,[3] the prevailing rate for labor, and the work was far lighter, the responsibilities negligible. To be sure, the boatmen were periodically called upon to perform prodigious feats of strength, and, occasionally, as on a trip from New Orleans to the Ohio valley, they would have to sustain labor for months on end. But much of their time was spent lolling indolently on deck while the current pushed the boat, blackguarding with riverbank residents or passing crews,[4] waiting only for nightfall and the opportunity to spend their coins and swallow a few drams of whiskey.

In addition, the boatmen traveled. They got out of the highly circumscribed world of the woods to see new places, do new things,

[2] The prevailing wage scale varied from time to time and place to place, and several travelers noted it between these figures. John Palmer, *Journal of Travels . . .* (London: Sherwood, Neeley, and Jones, 1818), p. 66; and James Flint, *Letters from America*, in Reuben Gold Thwaites, ed., *Early Western Travels, 1748–1846* (32 vols., Cleveland: Arthur H. Clark, 1904–06), IX, 114, 126, are good examples.

[3] This wage, too, varied, and depended on what the boatmen could get from their employers. Normally they received more from wealthy travelers than for ordinary voyages. A good summary can be found in Leland D. Baldwin, *The Keelboat Age on Western Waters* (Pittsburgh: University of Pittsburgh Press, 1941), p. 88.

[4] Palmer, *Journal*, p. 63.

enjoy new climates. They went where whiskey was plentiful, women were complaisant, and opportunities to demonstrate their manhood were available in profusion. The riverfronts at Pittsburgh, Shippingsport, and St. Louis were boisterous enough, but "The Swamp" in New Orleans and Natchez-under-the-Hill were meccas of the free and easy life of the boatmen. Small wonder that an aura of romance quickly enveloped them, obscuring the often grim facts of their actual condition, and making their profession "irresistible to the young people who live near the banks of the river,"[5] and to all Americans who wished, perhaps only vicariously, to shed the commonplace and partake of adventure. The boatman became a folk hero to incurably romantic Americans, who apparently had need of one after the business of fighting a revolution and developing a workable government was completed.

Not only did myths and legends quickly proliferate regarding the boatmen and their multifarious activities, but sentimental poems were penned rhapsodizing the carefree and happy life on the rivers, with William O. Butler's "The Boatman's Horn," which appeared in the Lexington *Western Review* in 1821,[6] a good indication of how maudlin they could be, and how early they developed. Thus, almost contemporaneously with his appearance on the rivers of the Midwest, the boatman made his entrance into the halls of American mythology. But the legendary glories of his existence could be imagined by anyone, whether or not he was familiar with the boatmen; in fact, as was the case with most early writing about the West, it was better if the authors were totally ignorant of anything beyond the Appalachians.

As the era of the keelboat and flatboat passed into history, westerners began to collect and print the stories and legends of the boatmen, usually centering them, as did Morgan Neville in his "Last of the Boatmen," published in Cincinnati in 1828,[7] around Mike Fink. Neville's was first, but the tales rapidly multiplied, and were avidly devoured by westerners and easterners alike. The pages of the *Western General Advertizer* were a particularly rich source, and some of the

5 Timothy Flint, *Recollections of the Last Ten Years . . .* (Boston: Cummings, Hilliard, and Co., 1826), p. 15.

6 William O. Butler, "The Boatman's Horn," reprinted in *Western Pennsylvania Magazine of History*, I (1918), 26.

7 Morgan Neville, "The Last of the Boatmen," *The Western Souvenir* (Cincinnati: James Hall, 1828).

best stories in it were collected by the editor, Charles Cist, in *Cincinnati Miscellany,* which he printed in 1845.[8] The Crockett Almanacs spread fictional accounts far and wide, and such authors as Emerson Bennett and Joseph Field gave them some sort of respectability. Many other authors grasped at the boatmen as a theme, and new stories were continually invented down to the end of the nineteenth century, with still others added in the middle of the twentieth.[9]

All of this literary activity concerning the life and times of Mike Fink and his cohorts not only completely obscured the boatman as a real, live human being, but had a great deal of significance in the development of American literature. It fitted into the growing awareness on the part of early nineteenth-century writers that American themes were not only popular, but could be important as well. The grandly exaggerated tales of Mike Fink stealing sheep with the aid of chewing tobacco, or going to court in his keelboat, or shooting the scalplock off an Indian helped lay the basis for an American strain of humor without which Mark Twain might not have been able to exist.[10] Perhaps more noteworthy, some critics have seen in the terrible eye-gouging fights, the revolting descriptions of Natchez-under-the-Hill, the bloody assaults of the river pirates so graphically described by these early writers the beginnings of realism in American fiction.[11]

Not all critics have taken so kindly to the contributions of keelboat literature to the American tradition. Henry Nash Smith saw the "boasting, swearing, drinking, gouging" boatmen as the antithesis of the true hero in early America, Daniel Boone,[12] as did Vernon Louis Parrington, who said:

> The world that provided a stage for the courage of Daniel Boone and the fighting qualities of George Rogers Clark bred also the Davy Crocketts and Mike Finks and Col. William Suggses, who discovered

[8] Charles Cist, *Cincinnati Miscellany* (2 vols., Cincinnati: Caleb Clark, 1845–46).

[9] Walter Blair and Franklin J. Meine, eds., *Half Horse Half Alligator: The Growth of the Mike Fink Legend* (Chicago: University of Chicago Press, 1956), pp. 19–20.

[10] Bernard De Voto, *Mark Twain's America* (Boston: Houghton Mifflin Co., 1932), pp. 240 ff., has a good discussion of the development of American humor, as does Constance Rourke, *American Humor* (New York: Harcourt, Brace and Co., 1931).

[11] Walter Blair and Franklin J. Meine, *Mike Fink; King of the Mississippi Keelboatmen* (New York: Henry Holt and Co., 1933), p. 268.

[12] Henry Nash Smith, *Virgin Land: The American West as Symbol and Myth* (New York: Vintage Books, 1957), p. 61.

> there opportunities for the development of less admirable qualities; and it engulfed in its depths a host of nameless adventurers who drifted into the wilderness settlements, drank and quarreled and begot children, suffered from chills and ague, spread a drab poverty along the frontier, and were put away under ground and forgotten by the more fortunate who salvaged prosperity from the abundant wreckage.[13]

Parrington did admit, however, that the tales of the boatmen contributed to the development of American humor, though he apparently got no fun out of it. Arthur K. Moore, in his most provocative book, *The Frontier Mind*, even went so far as to say, "All things considered, it is reasonable to regard the 'half horse, half alligator' of Kentucky as an approximation of reality and as a projection of the metropolitan imagination into the forest." I am not sure he was really convinced of the first part of that statement, but Moore described the boatmen as "an embodiment of the brutal, amoral content of primitivism,"[14] and went on to deplore the boatmen, and the publicity they received, as doing severe damage to the development of the American character.

All of these speculations are based on the romance of the boatmen, and the fiction that grew thereupon, but have little relation to the actual men who worked the rivers. What were they really like? Unfortunately, historians throw little light upon the subject. Although their researches have discovered that the boatmen, at least some of the more notorious of the breed, were not particularly savory characters, historians, too, have been unable to escape the glow of romance tinting everything the boatmen touched. Sometimes they spoke soberly and carefully, as did R. Carlyle Buley: ". . . the western boatmen did their part as nation builders, and deserve a place in history as well as trappers and teamsters, farmers and missionaries, prospectors and railroaders";[15] or more exuberantly, like Thomas D. Clark: ". . . underneath their uncouth habits and their eternal drinking and fighting they carried with them the will power of western civi-

13 Vernon Louis Parrington, *Main Currents in American Thought* (3 vols., New York: Harcourt, Brace and Co., 1927–30), II, 138.

14 Arthur K. Moore, *The Frontier Mind* (Lexington: University of Kentucky Press, 1950), pp. 134–135.

15 R. C. Buley, *The Old Northwest; Pioneer Period, 1815–1840* (2 vols., Bloomington: Indiana University Press, 1950), I, 440.

lization. They were endowed with a spirit of defiance which made them noble pioneers";[16] or capitulating entirely, as did Bernard De Voto: "They were the lees of America but their labor was enormous and their gusto greater still. They warred inimitably upon one another and then allied for the spoilation of the tender when the boats tied up beside the little towns. They swaggered down the streets while the citizenry trembled. They drank what pleased them: they levied on shops and poultry runs; they marched upon brothels where white whores worn out in the cities competed for their favors with black wenches and mullatoes . . . the boatmen immortally violent, heroic, unconquerable."[17] But like their literary confreres, historians skirted the reality because the myth was more appealing, and well may be more significant.

About the only legitimate sources of direct information about the boatmen as they really were are the writings of the hundreds of travelers who passed through the Midwest during the pre-steamboat era. Europeans and Americans alike, these travelers carried in their baggage strong prejudices which colored their accounts and make them difficult to use. Some were violently anti-American and anti-democratic and sought examples to prove the generally degraded and uncivilized state in which they felt the frontiersmen lived. Others were just as strongly pro-American, and, in their excitement about the democratic experiment, chose very carefully their illustrations of life in the West, and tended to portray the backwoodsman in the most favorable light. There were even a few of these spectators who were as hopelessly romantic as the later myth-makers, and some of their narratives are fair competition for the Crockett Almanacs. Yet they were on the scene, and the testimony they offer is all we have.

The vast majority of travelers, whether hostile or sympathetic, who bothered to comment on the boatmen, agreed on five major characteristics which they saw exhibited: the propensities to fight, drink, swear, steal, and frequent houses of ill repute. All of these were scandalous activities in the morality of the times, particularly so to Englishmen, who presumed that the lower classes, into which they lumped the boatmen simply because that was the bottom of the scale,

16 Thomas D. Clark, *The Rampaging Frontier* (Indianapolis: Bobbs-Merrill Co., 1934), p. 95.

17 De Voto, *Mark Twain's America*, pp. 59–60.

should act with proper decorum and respect for their betters. With the exception of thievery, these are the same characteristics repeatedly emphasized by the myth-makers as examples of the exuberant love of freedom possessed by the boatmen, and indicate that folklore and fiction had some basis, however tenuous, in fact. The mythology, however, demonstrated that the boatmen were fearless fighters and backed down to no one, had an infinite capacity for alcohol and women, and possessed a vulgar vocabulary without peer. In other words, the boatmen could do all those things a teenager dreams of doing without any apparent ill effect on his health, well-being, or moral stature. When stealing was mentioned in folklore, and no less a personage than Mike Fink was so accused, it was always in the form of play, or a huge practical joke, and therefore not accountable to any ordinary standards. Even when Mike and his men were mentioned as broaching the wine casks entrusted to their care aboard a keelboat, it was only a case of high-spirited men taking a bit early their deserved reward for a difficult and dangerous journey. The facts do not always evoke the same interpretation.

The boatmen of the western waters had a strong reputation for lawlessness, but they had come by it honestly. In the days before the Louisiana Purchase, the boatmen, on their arrival at Natchez, regularly took an oath of allegiance to the king of Spain in order to be admitted to Spanish territory.[18] From that bit of deception it was easy to graduate to the practice of skinning merchants out of entire cargoes by telling them that their boats had been sunk by snags. William Faux told of a man who had engaged in trade on western rivers, but who had quickly retired from the business because, as he said, "Produce is surrendered to enterprizing men, as they are called, on the rivers, but who frequently prove to be thieves; for if the boat is *stove in*, or markets are bad or dull, there are no returns; you hear no more of either produce or boat-men."[19] This experience was not, apparently, uncommon. Henry M. Brackenridge had to take the captain of a boat on which he had taken passage to court in order to recover his goods, which had been impounded by the captain "for the purpose of specu-

18 Charles Wilkinson to Judge Harry Innes, in Mary Verhoff, *The Kentucky River Navigation*, Filson Club Publications, No. 28 (Louisville: John P. Morton Co., 1917), p. 224.

19 W. Faux, *Memorable Days in America*, in Thwaites, ed., *Early Western Travels*, XI, 151.

lating upon them."[20] Thomas Nuttall was fleeced by some malevolent boatmen,[21] as was Christian Schultz, who warned, after spending $35 to become educated, "You must never, on any account, advance money to your boatmen."[22]

Even traveling alone in a skiff a wayfarer had to be wary of theft, one remarking, "It would be imprudent to sleep ashore and leave goods in a boat on the river, boatmen being much blamed for stealing."[23] As a paying passenger aboard a keelboat, a careful individual kept his hands in his pockets at all times. James Flint, who saw very little he liked in the West, reported that one of his traveling companions missed a knife. He accused the boatmen of theft, whereupon "a degraded wretch offered to buy the fork."[24] The smart tourist going downstream from Pittsburgh, as practically all of them did, utilized the same means found practicable by Gorham Worth and his companion. They calculated that "safety was of more importance than speed . . . and . . . determined to take an ark rather than a barge, as by doing so we should avoid the necessity of employing boatmen—at that day a class of men rather reckless rowdies, that were not to be trusted."[25] So the boatmen, as least some of them, were unprincipled sharpers, and their brand of lawlessness does not seem to fit into the categories of practical jokes, exuberant spirits, or an excess of democratic zeal. It was just common criminality.

As fighters the boatmen were known far and wide, as was their particular brand of combat, known as "rough and tumble," wherein no holds were barred, and gouging, biting, and kicking were the approved techniques. From reading the keelboat literature one comes away with the feeling that every boatman wore a black eye-patch as a symbol of his participation in, and survival of, one of these gory matches. Many travelers remarked on these encounters. Said James

20 Henry M. Brackenridge, *Recollections of Persons and Places in the West* (2nd ed., Philadelphia: J. B. Lippincott, 1868), pp. 186–188.

21 Thomas Nuttall, *Journal of Travels into the Arkansas Territory*, in Thwaites, ed., *Early Western Travels*, XIII, 75.

22 Christian Schultz, Jr., *Travels on an Inland Voyage* (2 vols., New York: Isaac Riley, 1810), I, 193.

23 Flint, *Letters from America*, p. 92.

24 *Ibid.*, p. 113.

25 Gorham A. Worth, *Recollections of Cincinnati from a Residence of Five Years* (Albany: Charles Van Benthuysen, 1851), reprinted in *Historical and Philosophical Society of Ohio Quarterly*, XI (1916), 19.

Flint, "Fights are characterized by the most savage ferocity. Gouging, or putting out the antagonist's eyes, by thrusting the thumbs into the sockets, is part of the *modus operandi*. Kicking and biting are also ordinary means used in combat; I have seen several fingers that had been deformed, also several noses and ears, which have been mutilated, by this canine mode of fighting."[26] John Woods described the boatmen as "much given to drinking whiskey, fighting, and gouging, that is, they fight up and down, trying to put out each others eyes with their fingers and thumbs, and sometimes biting off each others noses and ears. A man, who resides near me, had the top of his nose bitten off, in one of these brutal frays, some years since. This is their common manner of fighting. . . ."[27] But neither of these gentlemen saw an actual "rough and tumble."

That such battles took place there can be no doubt, as Fortescue Cuming remarks on a pair of boat crews getting drunk and starting a "battle royal, in which some of the combatants attempted to gouge each other, but my boat's company interfering, separated them, and quelled the disturbance,"[28] but, in the final analysis, everyone's impression of one of these fights comes from the description of what must have been the grandest, if that is the word for it, of them all.

> Bulk and bone were in favor of the Kentuckyan; science and craft in that of the Virginian. The former promised himself victory from his power, the latter from his *science*. Very few rounds had taken place, or fatal blows given, before the Virginian contracted his whole form, drew up his arms to his face, with his hands nearly closed in a concave, by the fingers being bent to the full extension of the flexors, and summoning up all his energy for one act of desperation, pitched himself into the bosom of his opponent. Before the effects of this could be ascertained, the sky was rent by the shouts of the multitude; and I could learn that the Virginian had expressed as much *beauty* and *skill* in his retraction and bound, as if he had been bred in a menagerie, and practised action and attitude among panthers and wolves. The shock received by the Kentuckyan, and the want of breath, brought him instantly to the ground. The Virginian never lost his

26 Flint, *Letters from America*, p. 138.

27 John Woods, *Two Years' Residence . . .*, in Thwaites, ed., *Early Western Travels*, X, 255.

28 Fortescue Cuming, *Sketches of a Tour to the Western Country*, in Thwaites, ed., *Early Western Travels*, IV, 303.

> hold, like those bats of the South who never quit the subject on which they fasten till they taste blood, he kept his knees in his enemies body; fixing his claws in his hair, and his thumbs on his eyes, gave them an instantaneous start from their sockets. The sufferer roared aloud, but uttered no complaint. The citizens again shouted with joy. Doubts were no longer entertained; and bets of three to one were offered on the Virginian. The Kentuckyan not being able to disentangle his adversary from his face, adopted a new mode of warfare; and, in an imitation of the serpent which crushes such creatures to death as it proposes for its food, he extended his arms around the Virginian and hugged him into closer contact with his huge body. The latter disliking this, cast loose the hair and convex eyes of his adversary, when both, folded together like bears in an embrace, rolled several turns over each other. The acclamation increased, and bets ran that the Kentuckyan "*would give out,*" that is, after being mutilated and deprived of his eyes, ears, and nose, he would cry out for mercy and aid. The public were not precisely right. Some daemon interposed for the biggest monster; he got his enemy under him, and in an instant snapt off his nose so close to his face that no manner of projection remained. The little Virginian made one further effort, and fastening on the underlip of the mutilator tore it over the chin. The Kentuckyan at length *gave out,* on which the people carried off the victor, and he preferring a triumph to a doctor, suffered himself to be chaired around the ground as the champion of the times, and the first *rougher and tumbler.*[29]

In sickening, if detached, detail, this account, purportedly by an eyewitness, appeared in Thomas Ashe's *Travels in America,* published in London in 1808. Shortly after the book's appearance in America, Ashe, the first to discover that a book attacking America could be a moneymaker, was branded as, if not a liar, at least a plagiarizer. It was quickly discovered that most of his description of the West was taken verbatim from an edition of Zadok Cramer's *The Navigator,* probably the one published in Pittsburgh in 1806, a fact which Cramer himself indignantly noted in later editions,[30] and *Travels in America* has since

29 Thomas Ashe, *Travels in America . . .* (London: William Sawyer and Co., 1808), pp. 97–98.

30 Zadok Cramer, *The Navigator* (8th ed., Pittsburgh: Cramer, Spear, and Eichbaum, 1814).

generally been discounted as a valid source. Nonetheless, novelists and historians alike quote directly from this rather questionable foundation when looking for verification of the bloody battles of the keelboatmen. They have to, for it seems to be about the only source.

Other travelers were not so impressed with the fighting qualities of the boatmen. On one occasion a boatman was singing lustily on a Sunday in violation of a local law and one of the local rustics told him to be quiet or else. "The boatmen, perceiving that he was assailed by a stronger man than himself, gave up the contest."[31] Christian Schultz, who witnessed a confrontation at Natchez, complete with screaming challenge and reply, noted, "they went at it like two bulls, and continued for half an hour, when the alligator was fairly vanquished by the horse,"[32] with no mention of kicking, biting, or gouging. The frontiersman's outlet for his highly charged emotions was physical combat, and the boatman was no exception to this rule. However, his peculiar methods, particularly the crowing challenge, largely put on for the benefit of wide-eyed tourists, put him all out of proportion. Estwick Evans came closest to the truth, remarking, "I have often heard of the low conversation said to prevail among the boatmen of the west; and also of their quarrelsome and fighting habits. All these practices are much less than they are represented to be."[33]

With regard to drinking, swearing, and whoring, western sojourners found much to condemn in the boatmen. Drinking, particularly, horrified most travelers, though perhaps they should have been aware that alcoholism was almost endemic on the frontier. A pair of Moravians were particularly shocked when their boatmen "began drinking to such excess that they did not know what they were doing. They poured this horrid drink, by the pint, down their throats."[34] As seafarers, fresh-water variety, the boatmen were given a daily ration of alcohol, with extra "fillees" granted upon need of excessive exertion

31 Flint, *Letters from America*, p. 109.

32 Schultz, *Travels*, II, 145.

33 Estwick Evans, *A Pedestrious Tour*, in Thwaites, ed., *Early Western Travels*, VIII, 261.

34 "Diary of the Journey of Br. and Sr. Kluge and Br. Luchenback from Goshen on the Muskingum to White River, March 24 to May 25, 1801," in Lawrence H. Gipson, ed., *The Moravian Indian Mission on White River* (Indianapolis: Indiana Historical Bureau, 1938), p. 94.

to round a point or get off a sandbar, but the boatmen went beyond that to adopt what one traveler called "Dr. Aldrich's five reasons for drinking

> *Whiskey*, a friend, or being dry,
> Or least we should be by and by,
> Or, any other reason why."[35]

Occasionally the boatman's propensity for drink could work to the advantage of the shrewd traveler, as William Richardson told his men, "in case either of them fell asleep in their watch such should go without whiskey for a week."[36] He had no trouble.

Swearing was offensive to cultured ears, and some travelers, like Estwick Evans, preached to the men against it,[37] but Evans admitted he had little long-term success. Said James Flint, "their swearing is excessive and perfectly disgusting,"[38] and most others agreed, although the language of the boatmen seems no more vulgar than that of the teamsters, who moved other voyagers by land. The swearing and drinking seemed to go together with the brothels of the river towns, particularly Natchez, where the redoubtable Christian Schultz was embarrassed one early morning by coming aboard his boat and disturbing "the morning slumbers of exactly one quarter of a dozen of the copper-colored votaries of the Cyprian Queen, who it seems had undertaken to enliven the idle hours of our Canadian crew."[39] Such things tended to make "Low Natchez . . . a true Gommorrah,"[40] and "without exception, the most licentious spot that I ever saw."[41] But there was a Low Natchez on every frontier, and in not a few civilized places as well, a fact which, though they did not like to admit it, most travelers recognized.

On the other hand, there were travelers who viewed such things not as vices, but as an outgrowth of the hardships and privations forced

35 Palmer, *Journal*, p. 66.

36 William Richardson, *Journal from Boston to the Western Country and down the Ohio and Mississippi Rivers to New Orleans, 1815–1816* (New York: Valve Pilot Corp., 1940), p. 21.

37 Evans, *Pedestrious Tour*, p. 260.

38 Flint, *Letters from America*, p. 113.

39 Schultz, *Travels*, II, 136.

40 Charles Sealsfield, *The Americans as They Are; Described on a Tour through the Valley of the Mississippi* (London: Hurst, Chance, and Co., 1828), p. 108.

41 Richardson, *Journal*, p. 34.

on humanity by the frontier, and made due allowance for them. Andrew Ellicott found boatmen hard workers and said, "Our success [at navigating low water] was owing to the large number of people we had with us, and whose quiet submission to unusual hardships does them great credit."[42] The ubiquitous Christian Schultz exclaimed, "I was confirmed in the good opinion I had formed, that the Kentucky sailors in general, although a rough, yet are a more amiable class of citizens, than they have been represented to be."[43] In recommending keelboat use to his readers, Zadok Cramer called boatmen "Experienced and careful" of the goods assigned to them,[44] and John James Audubon used such terms when describing his crew as "Generously Inclined," "good Natured," and "happy."[45] Perhaps the most revealing commentary came from the hundreds of travelers who said absolutely nothing about boatmen, even when they journeyed by keelboat.

From the testimony of travelers, then, it appears that the boatmen as a class were a more or less normal frontier group. They exhibited certain distinguishing peculiarities, and though they contained in their midst far more than the normal allotment of the profligate and lawless, they were generally just normal, rough human beings going through a difficult and dangerous business. Their numbers were not great—Morris Birkbeck noted in 1818 that there were about two thousand men engaged in boating on the Ohio,[46] and that figure seems reasonable. Add another thousand for the New Orleans-to-Natchez trade and the total is probably pretty close to the number of boatmen active at any given time. Their contribution to the commerce of the West, in terms of bringing badly needed goods up the Mississippi and Ohio rivers from the Gulf, was slight. In 1808 not more than thirty boats reached Louisville from New Orleans,[47] and though that number increased somewhat in later years, the goods carried scarcely dented the demand, and certainly the efforts of the

42 Andrew Ellicott, *The Journal of Andrew Ellicott . . .* (Philadelphia: Budd and Bartram, 1803), p. 17.

43 Schultz, *Travels*, II, 115.

44 Cramer, *Navigator*, p. 38.

45 Donald C. Peattie, ed., *Audubon's America* (Boston: Houghton Mifflin Co., 1940), p. 138.

46 Morris Birkbeck, *Notes on a Journey in America* (London: Severn and Redington, 1818), p. 77.

47 Frank H. Dixon, *A Traffic History of the Mississippi River System* (Washington: G.P.O., 1909), p. 10.

boatmen had little impact on the westward movement. Their fame, therefore, came from the fictional rather than the actual side of their business.

The mythological keelboatman as folk hero filled, and probably still fills, an American need. He fits in well toward the head of the galaxy of American paladins, the ranger, the long hunter, the mountain man, the cowboy. His very human side was too prosaic to merit much attention at the time, and thus it has been ever since. So the real boatman, dirty, drunken, and disgusting, or brave, generous, and amiable, depending on which travelers you consult, will ever remain in well-deserved obscurity, covered completely by the myth he only partly helped to create. The epitaph of the actual half horse, half alligator was written by a historian over a generation ago. "Some of them actually bore the marks of the draft horse in large callouses on their arms and shoulders, products of the setting pole and the sockets of the keelboat. Their resemblance to alligators was less evident but not wholly lacking, certainly not when they ate."[48]

Thus Americans, desirous of creating a larger-than-life figure to express to themselves as well as to the rest of the world some of their inner feelings about what they were accomplishing in the way of conquering the wilderness, and unable to fabricate one strictly from imagination, turned to the boatmen. Ignoring the evidence offered by travelers, magnifying some of the boatman's attributes, ignoring others, and inventing still others, Americans found in their men of the western waters the expression of their exuberant optimism, boisterous sense of freedom, the glory they took in physically defeating the frontier, and their unquenchable sense of humor. To such a creature, the real boatman was almost irrelevant. May he rest in peace.

[48] Charles H. Ambler, *A History of Transportation in the Ohio Valley* (Glendale, Calif.: Arthur H. Clark, 1932), 50.

Western Travelers in Quest of the Indian

Donald D. Miner

> . . . The Indians that I have had an opportunity of seeing in real life are quite different from those described in poetry. They are by no means the stoics that they are represented; taciturn, unbending, without a tear or a smile. Taciturn they are it is true, when in company of white men, whose good-will they distrust, and whose language they do not understand. . . . When the Indians are among themselves, however, there cannot be greater gossips. . . . They are great mimics and buffoons, also, and entertain themselves excessively at the expense of the whites with whom they have associated, and who have supposed them impressed with profound respect for their grandeur and dignity.[1]

Such were the observations of Washington Irving in comparing the real and the romantic Indian while touring on the prairies in 1832.

We get a much more impassioned revelation of this same truth from Charles Augustus Murray's *Travels in North America*,[2] which presents his account of six weeks' residence among the Pawnees in the summer of 1835. He suggests that

> the Indian, among whites, or at a garrison, trading-post, or town, is as different a man from the same Indian at home as a Turkish "Mollah" is from a French barber. Among whites, he is all dignity and repose; he is acting a part the whole time, and acts it most admirably.

1 Washington Irving, *A Tour on the Prairies*, John Fràncis McDermott, ed. (Norman: University of Oklahoma Press, 1956), p. 44.

2 *Travels in North America during the Years 1834, 1835, & 1836; Including a Summer Residence with the Pawnee Tribe of Indians in the Remote Prairies of the Missouri* . . . (2 vols., London: R. Bentley, 1839).

> He manifests no surprise at the most wonderful effects of machinery—is not startled if a twenty-four pounder is fired close to him, and does not evince the slightest curiosity regarding the thousand things that are strange and new to him; whereas at home, the same Indian chatters, jokes and laughs among his companions—frequently indulges in the most licentious conversation; and his curiosity is as unbounded and irresistible as that of any man, woman, or monkey on earth.

It was as a much disgruntled and disillusioned traveler that Murray returned to Fort Leavenworth where but six weeks previously he had been so impressed with the "tact" and "self-possession" of the Pawnees and their "haughty, impenetrable reserve."

From boyhood Murray had been an ardent admirer of James Fenimore Cooper, from whose Indian romances he had garnered many of the concepts of Indian customs and character which he jettisoned on the plains of Kansas. In the summer of 1834, Murray, while traveling by steamer up the Hudson River, discovered Cooper to be a fellow passenger; they had met previously at the famed breakfast table of Samuel Rogers, the Scottish poet. He does not record the gist of their conversation, but that they discussed to some extent a common interest—the Indian—is likely indeed. In St. Louis in June, 1835, Murray met George Catlin, who encouraged him in his plans for making an excursion on the prairies.

Both Cooper and Catlin might very well be included among the writers Murray censures in this stricture: "Every hour I spent with the Indians, impressed upon me the conviction that I had taken the only method of becoming acquainted with their domestic habits and their undisguised character. Had I judged from what I had been able to observe at Fort Leavenworth, or other frontier places . . . I should have known as much of them as the generality of scribblers and their readers, and might, like them, have deceived myself and others into a belief in their 'high sense of honour'—their hospitality—their openness and love of truth. . . ."

In spite of Murray's ultimate disappointment with the real Indian, he has left us some of the best sketches of Indian life and character in frontier literature. And in addition to his valuable account of the Indians, Murray himself provides an excellent study for students of western travel. For with his eager anticipation of a storybook West peopled with Cooperian savages, he is the personification of the romantic traveler whose real journeys can never compare with his imaginary ones. Fortunately for us, Murray had accumulated a good body of exceptional material before deciding that the Indian—at least the Pawnee—was a subject unworthy of a traveler's attention.

On July 7, 1835, Murray, accompanied by a small party, set out from Fort Leavenworth with 150 Pawnee warriors on their way to join their tribe, which had begun its trek to the summer hunting grounds. Murray was to accompany them in their summer hunt. During the first night on the trail Murray's horses strayed, and while his attendants searched for them the next morning the Pawnees moved on. It took Murray's party two days of hard riding to catch up. Though impressed with the Indians' ability to thrive on a Spartan diet—the *pomme blanche* being their sole nourishment for days at a time—he was equally disturbed by the difficulty of preparing meals for his own party while the Indians continually begged food or ransacked his provisions. On different occasions as Murray lay ostensibly asleep he noticed the attempts of the Indians to lure his dog from his side. One day the dog failed to come when he called: he could but conclude that the dog had furnished a meal for hungry Indians, though he could hardly make a scene over it. The Indians' legendary hospitality was by this time much suspect.

Before arriving at the main Pawnee camp it became necessary for Murray to trade his jaded mount for a fresh one. He made a deal with the younger Patalacharo, a chief of the Grand Pawnees. The chief got Murray's horse for the loan of a fresh one. But much to Murray's disgust, Patalacharo continued to use the weary animal as a pack horse. When the animal could go no farther, the chief demanded that his own horse be returned to him. This was indeed a dilemma, for should Murray return the animal, the Indians would consider him weak and subject him to further extortions; on the other hand, Patalacharo was, in addition to being a chief, a man of "gargantuan proportions" and was reputed to have already killed two or three men. But as a physical specimen, Murray himself was not inadequate: with a strained boldness he challenged the brave to come and take the horse at his own peril. Murray continued to ride, but this was an inauspicious beginning to a summer with the Pawnees.

In the first two weeks of his adventure Murray had discovered conspicuous blotches in the veneer of the noble-savage legend. The

Indian's publicized sense of hospitality and his supposed great love for the steed that bore him across the plains were but fiction; and in contrast to his reputation as the proud stoic, he too frequently proved to be a beggar and a haggler—annoying in his unbridled curiosity and boorish in his person and manner.

But Murray's initial disappointment in the Indian was soon forgotten in his enthusiasm for the color and excitement of Indian life. How vividly he describes the panorama of the Indian village as he first saw it!

> Upon an extensive prairie gently sloping down to a creek, the winding course of which was marked by a broken line of wood here and there interspersed with a fine clump of trees, were about five thousand savages inclusive of women and children; some were sitting under their buffalo-skin lodges lazily smoking their pipes; while the women were stooping over their fires busily employed in preparing meal and maize for these indolent lords of the creation. Far as the eye could reach, were scattered herds of horses, watched . . . by urchins, whose whole dress and equipment was the slight bow and arrow, with which they exercised their infant archery upon the heads of the taller flowers, or upon any luckless blackbird perched near them. Here and there might be seen some gay young warrior ambling along the heights, his painted form partially exposed to view as his bright scarlet blanket waved in the breeze; while his small fretful horse was scarcely to be recognized under the variety of trappings with which the vanity of his rider had tricked him out. . . .

Murray's love for hunting and his skill as a marksman made the buffalo hunt a great challenge for him. In his journal he vividly recreates the tension of the moment at which buffalo were first sighted: "On the 22nd [July] my long cherished curiosity was destined to be gratified; loud and deafening cries of 'Tahara! tahara!' (buffalo) ran from one end of the line to the other, and all became bustle and confusion. Some young men went in their gayest attire, others vaulted naked on their unsaddled horses; in all about a thousand sallied forth in search of the enemy." Most of Murray's days were spent in the hunt, and in that time he killed many buffalo with his short-barreled German rifle.

Other moments of danger and excitement included a raid on the Pawnee horses by an Arikara war party, an attack by the Cheyennes, and a stampede. Each occurred at night and set the entire village in chaos: "I never heard such a continual confusion of sounds," Murray writes. "The council of Pandaemonium, or the tower of Babel, could scarcely equal it. Women chattering, children crying, men singing, or rather yelling their war songs, dogs howling, horses neighing, and asses braying!" In this manner he describes the Arikara raid. All in all there was adventure and activity enough to make him forget for a time the more unseemly aspects of savage life.

But it was not the portrayal of the adventure or turbulence of the Indian's life that makes Murray's account exceptional; it was rather his penchant for noting the bizarre and the comic elements of the Indian's personality. This enabled him to portray much of a little-observed aspect of the Indian, and allows the Indian to become in the pages of his journal what he has had so little opportunity in literature to be—a human being.

Murray notes the humor of the gustatory feats of the Pawnee and re-creates his own sad plight in numerous eating contests with his insatiable hosts or in his bold attempts to indicate gratitude for such hospitality by gorging himself at each of six successive feasts given in his honor. He laments the impossibility of sleeping in an Indian lodge where a half-dozen squaws—after what should have been an exhausting day's work—gossip and giggle through the night, while outside the lodge "upwards of four thousand" dogs continue their horrible serenade. He reveals that the Indian—like all parents—dotes on his children, spoiling them beyond anything seen by the average white man. The Plains warrior, though impassive in regard to inflicted pain, may "moan and whine under the toothache or colic in a manner that among us would shame 'a sick child.' " And in all his bestowing of presents the Indian is only investing in greater returns. Nowhere is the Indian's ego, his joy in personal adornment, better illustrated than in Murray's travel account: "I have seen some dandies in my life," writes Murray—"English, Scotch, French, German, ay and American dandies too; but none of them can compare with the vanity or coxcombry of the Pawnee dandy." He includes a couple of excellent sketches of such Indian fops, but they are unfortunately too long to be included here.

Thus the first few weeks of Murray's residence with the Pawnees were filled with the color and action typically associated with Indians, tempered by the everyday peculiarities and idiosyncrasies of Indian character. But soon enthusiasm for the hunt waned and his aesthetic sensibilities became dulled by exposure. The sun became hotter and the rain wetter, the mosquitoes and the vermin of the lodge more persistent, and the pervading stench of the Pawnee village more noisome. And his journal dwells on vermin and filth, indolence, avarice, and treachery. For some time the other members of his party had wished to return to civilization, and after an attempt was made on his life when he strayed too far from the protection of the camp, he too decided that his visit should be terminated. He writes: "On the night of the 7th I scarcely slept at all, so excited was I at the prospect of our prairie journey, and I may add, so delighted at exchanging, even for greater hardships, the confinement, the vermin and the dirt of the Pawnee lodges."

In the summer of the following year Murray visited Cooper at Otsego Hall. Though Murray records nothing of their conversation, that they dwelt at some length on the differences between real and romantic Indians is indicated by a letter from Cooper to Murray written many years after the visit: "All your dégout for the Indians could not overcome that which is truly heroical in their character, and . . . you have been obliged to paint a little *en beau* will ye, nil ye. I was confoundedly afraid you were about to throw dirt on some of my pictures, when I heard you were in the field, for you were in a somewhat savage state of mind, yourself, when we conversed on this subject."[3] By the time this letter was written, Murray had, as Cooper indicates, published an Indian romance, whose Delaware and Osage characters bore little resemblance to any of his Pawnee hosts. Murray remained firmly convinced that the Pawnees were the most treacherous of all the North American Indians.

How different a picture of Pawnee Indian life is drawn by John Treat Irving, who visited those tribes in 1833, just two years before Murray's tour! Like Murray, Irving had an eye for the droll and the bizarre, but unlike Murray, he includes no hint of villainy in the character of the Pawnee. Nor does he include the more noxious aspects

[3] Cooper to Murray, Philadelphia, November 19, 1844, in James Franklin Beard, ed., *The Letters and Journals of James Fenimore Cooper* (4 vols., Cambridge: Harvard University Press, 1960–64), IV, 490–491.

of Indian life so graphically presented by Murray. He did not, however, live in intimate contact with them as Murray did.

It was in early August of 1833 that twenty-year-old John Treat Irving, nephew of Washington Irving, arrived at Fort Leavenworth as a member of an expedition headed by Henry Leavitt Ellsworth, Indian Treaty Commissioner. Ellsworth had led a similar expedition the previous year to the Osages; on that occasion Washington Irving had served as unpaid secretary pro tem. Perhaps it was from his uncle that young Treat Irving had contracted the contagion of frontier wanderlust; it was certainly somewhat due to his uncle's influence that he became a member of the 1833 expedition.

And again it was perhaps Washington Irving himself who was the literary prototype of many of the qualities which he found in Treat's account of his tour among the Pawnees—*Indian Sketches* (1835).[4] These sketches, he suggests, "present some of the most spirited, lively and familiar views of Indian life that I have met with. . . . We have not had much as yet of the comic of Indian character; writers have all represented the Indian according to a conventional and artificial model; this unhackneyed youngster presents them as they are."[5]

Treat Irving also had great ability for creating western landscape, for revealing either the splendor or the loneliness of the prairies. "It was late upon a fine glowing afternoon in July," he writes, "that we first crossed the Indian frontier, and issued from the forest, upon a beautiful prairie, spreading out as far as the eye could reach, an undulating carpet of green, enammeled with a thousand flowers, and lighted up by the golden rays of the setting sun." And in contrast to the pied beauty of the prairie, he describes its solitude: "There is a deep silence in a western wilderness. No sound is heard, not even the note of a bird to break the deathly stillness."

Though he was impressed with the western landscape, the aspect of the frontier most eagerly anticipated by Irving was, of course, the redskin warrior of the Plains. Naturally his party had seen Indians in the frontier towns, but they had not been of the "wild" variety, standing on their own soil. The expedition had traveled but a short distance

4 John Treat Irving, Jr., *Indian Sketches, Taken during an Expedition to the Pawnee Tribes, 1833*, John Francis McDermott, ed. (Norman: University of Oklahoma Press, 1955).

5 Irving to Aspinwall, New York, May 31, 1835, in *ibid.*, p. xlii.

beyond Independence, Missouri, when an Indian was sighted—a Shawnee, whose romantic charisma quickly faded as they drew near him:

> A feeling of disappointment, mingled with sorrow, came over us as we rode up to this solitary being. At a distance our fancies had painted him possessed of all that was noble in the Indian character; but a newer view dispelled the illusion. He could not have been older than thirty, but intemperance had left its mark upon his features. His hair was thick and matted, and hung nearly to his eyes. His legs were covered with leggings of deerskin, ornamented with a yellow binding. Over a dirty calico shirt he wore a long surtout coat, with immense brass buttons; and upon his shoulder he bore a long and heavy rifle. . . . So,—these are the Indians! This is a specimen of the princely race which once peopled the wilds of America. . . . We were disappointed. . . .

At Fort Leavenworth but a few days later, however, Irving's disappointment in the civilized Shawnee Indian was fully eclipsed by the awe with which he observed a Sac warrior who personified all the nobility of the legendary romantic savage:

> . . . never had I beheld such a princely fellow. He stood unmoved as we came up, viewing us with a calm, cold, but unwavering gaze. His eyelids never drooped; nor was the eye averted for an instant as it met our look. A large blanket, here and there streaked with vermilion, and ornamented with hawk bells, was so disposed around his folded arms, that it left bare his finely formed shoulder and half his high and sinewey chest. . . .
>
> As we approached he drew himself up, and threw his head slightly backward with an air of haughtiness which well became his high stern features. He seemed to feel like a proud but desolate being. Upon his head was bound an eagle's plume, but it was crushed and broken. Could it be emblematic of the broken spirit of his own tribe? Their power was gone; their strength was withered; they were scattered to the four winds of heaven; the bones of their bravest warriors were whitening the prairies and their chief [Blackhawk] was in bondage in an unknown land.

But it is not such romantic portraits—standard in so many travel accounts—which make *Indian Sketches* unique; instead, it is, as Washington Irving suggested, the genre sketches presenting the Indian as a human being that make his account so. Treat Irving is little concerned with religious rites, languages, Indian history, or ethnology, nor even with the details of the expedition which took him there. He prefers to amuse himself—and his reader—by limning the follies of man as exemplified in the Indian. Thus we have an unprecedented and unimitated drama of the irony, farce, and slapstick in the Indian's pomp, vanity, and personal peculiarities, with an occasional glimpse of conjugal infelicity and domestic tragedy. Irving's levity is weighted now and then by a confirmation of Thoreau's observation that "the mass of men lead lives of quiet desperation" (even the Indian).

For nearly a month the expedition was delayed at Fort Leavenworth while preparations for the tour in the Platte River area continued. Councils were to be held with different tribes in that area—principally the Pawnees—presents were to be distributed, and treaties signed; also arrangements were to be made for a general peace council at Fort Leavenworth in October.

The days dragged by for Irving as the preparations continued, so he decided to visit the village of the many Kickapoos he saw about the fort. "They received us in their usual calm manner, and we were satisfied," he writes; "for the welcome of an Indian is shown more by actions than words. There is no superfluous expression of feelings which he never had—he never makes use of hypocrisy—he receives you with a good will or not at all." He describes a pair of Indian lovers he observed as they wandered about the prairie, "full of affection and slovenliness; unwashed but devoted"; and a "fat blowzy squaw" fleeing the wrath of her stick-wielding husband, a "diminutive, spider-legged Indian, who looked as if he had withered away under the gall of his own disposition."

About September 1 (Irving provides few dates) the tour commenced. On the evening before departure, Irving was, of course, excited. "There was a mystery and shadowy danger," he writes, "which threw a high excitement around the whole expedition. Nothing was positive about the wild tribes we were to visit. It was known, that their numbers were large; it was reported, that they were cruel and unsparing in their nature; that they looked upon the whites as their bitterest enemies, and carried on a war of extermination against the whole race." That bit of apprehension which would have been natural to any twenty-year-old at such a time was surely much augmented by the terrible Indian-atrocity stories which were devised to amuse them on the night before their departure.

They set out at midday traveling in a northerly direction toward the village of the Oto and the Missouri Indians on the Platte River, some twenty miles from its junction with the Missouri. From there they would move along the Platte until reaching the Pawnee villages. "There is but little variety on the prairie," he writes. "The life of one day is the life of a month; yet there is an excitement about it. The killing of a deer is an era in the day. The appearance of a hunter upon a distant hill would give birth to a thousand speculations. . . . The sight of footprints in the grass would be the foundation of a hundred wild fancies."

Upon approaching the Oto village two days later, they were given the customary Indian welcome to important guests: a throng of Indian braves galloped toward them, "pealing out scream upon scream, brandishing their spears, and whirling their tomahawks around their heads." At the very moment when it seemed as though they were to be trampled, the Indians separated, whirling to each side of them, leaving all "enveloped in a cloud of dust."

While entering the village, the braves continued to careen and cavort about them in a wild display of horsemanship. The horse of an old Indian who had been particularly daring fell while crossing a gully, throwing his rider into the mud and bringing a loud shout of laughter at his expense. "For a moment he stood glaring about him like an angry tiger," Irving writes; "then raising his withered arm, he shook it at the crowd. 'Laugh on! laugh on!' exclaimed he, 'I am old and feeble now; but there was a time when you would not have dared to have done this.' "

After one week in the village they had become the audience for the sly jokes of all the old warriors, for which they pretended great satisfaction, though the wit lay hidden in the language. "The old squaws," he writes, "would hold us by the button, and whine into our ears some lugubrious tale of misery, equally unintelligible." The children, over their shyness, played about their tents, "teasing the black cook, or frightening the oxen." Clusters of children sat nearby, gambling away arrows given them by their parents.

The Iotan chief, Irving suggests, may have been "lord paramount of the village," but within the confines of his own lodge he was but the harassed husband of five squaws. "While we were eating with him, the old man took the opportunity to disburthen his heart. He let us into a knowledge of the miseries to which he was subjected from their caprices; and the difficulties which he found in maintaining a proper discipline where there were so many mistresses and but one master."

When invited to the lodge of a secondary chief, the big Kaw, their unexpected company for dinner brought on a domestic crisis: "Occasionally he cast toward his helpmate a deprecating glance, like that of a whipped dog—his eye seemed to say, 'I know I was wrong in bringing them; but I beseech you to keep quiet now, and you may scold as much as you please when the visitors have gone.' " When the hastily boiled dried buffalo meat proved to be tough, their embarrassed host apologized, thus drawing upon himself a barrage of invective from an already disgruntled squaw, who took this remark as a direct affront. The chief finally lost "all restraint and sent back a fire as hot as was given." But at last the chief realized that he could not match the acidity of his wife's tongue, and silently he began to look about the lodge until his eye came to rest on a large stick. The wrangling ended.

> To dress and ornament himself with trinkets and geegaws [writes Irving] is the delight of a savage. . . . Scarcely a day elapsed but a little group would collect before our tents for the purpose of ornamenting themselves. . . . When the toilette was completed, a surprising change came over the young warriors. They would fling their blankets ostentatiously around them, and with a lordly air lounge through the town; looking first at one of the young squaws, then at another; and occasionally condescending to speak to some dirty-looking brother. . . . When they had finished their perambulations, they would mount upon the top of one of the highest lodges, and stand for hours to be gazed at by the different idlers. . . .

On September 21 Ellsworth and the Otos met in council and signed a treaty. On the following day presents were distributed to all the Indians, and the Indians in return performed a buffalo dance for their guests. In early October the expedition departed for the Pawnee villages. Again they were upon the prairie.

As the expedition came into sight of the Grand Pawnee village they could see "that the hills surrounding it were black with masses of mounted warriors." A single horseman came forward to greet them, and at a signal from him, "the masses moved forward to circle about them in one dark dense flood," performing an even more frightening demonstration of horsemanship than that given by the Otos. "There is something in the fierce, shrill scream of a band of Indian warriors, which rings through the brain, and sends the blood curdling back to the heart," Irving writes. Ellsworth was then approached and greeted by the head chief of each of the Pawnee villages, then by the lesser chiefs. Many Indian braves among the crowd stepped forward to extend the stem of their pipe to the lips of Ellsworth, a signification of their pledging to make a gift of a horse to him.

The council was held on October 9 and the treaty signed the next day. On the following morning the expedition was ready to depart for the Republican village, but not before the Indians had presented the horses they had promised. Although a few of the horses were splendid animals, it soon became evident that many of the pledges had been made in a moment of excitement and regretted at leisure. For the horses brought forth shortly degenerated into a "collection of the maimed, the halt, and the blind. One after another they came lingering up," writes Irving, "until one Indian alone lagged behind. The chief inquired for him, and was told that he had gone out to search for his animal. Ten minutes elapsed. At last there was a movement in the crowd, and a sly-looking, old white-headed Indian made his way through it. In his hand he held the end of a long buffalo tug: the other was secured to his horse. Such a horse! he was blind of both eyes; his tail had been cut off short to his rump; his ribs stood out in bold relief; and his very joints creaked, as he walked stiffly after his leader." The old Indian chuckled as he disappeared into the crowd.

The Republican village was located on the Loup Fork of the Platte about twenty miles from that of the Grand Pawnees. In this village they were given the same tumultuous welcome, and, as customary, treated to many successive feasts of boiled corn and buffalo meat. After a number of such treats, the interpreter brought word "that three of us had been invited to attend at the lodge of one of the older warriors, who had prepared something which he thought would be more acceptable than buffalo flesh and corn." After a cordial welcome and much small talk, their host told his squaw to bring forth the delicacy. The three curious guests sat staring at a large kettle, containing something of an orange color, hanging over the fire. For some time the squaw stood patiently spearing into the kettle with a sharp-pointed stick without success in retrieving its orange contents. At last she brought forth a boiled *pumpkin,* which she divided among her dismayed guests. "We fell to, desperately therefore, under the vigilant eye of our fat host," Irving writes, "who was continually plying us with fresh pieces, according to the laws of Indian hospitality, and to refuse which would be regarded as a slight. How we managed to get through that vegetable feast, I can hardly say; it was one of the severest trials of the whole of our campaign. . . ."

They stayed but a few days in the Republican and Tappage villages and then began their return trip to the garrison. Somewhere in the vicinity of the Big Nemaha River, Irving became separated from the expedition while hunting and spent a few days traveling alone over the prairies before making his way back to the garrison. Treaties had been signed by most of the tribes of the area by the middle of November. By November 17 Irving had left the frontier.

The attraction which the frontier held for those who wished to escape from the "stultifying" influences of civilization is well indicated in the following passage from the journal[6] of the Swiss artist Rudolph Friederich Kurz:

> From my earliest youth primeval forest and Indians had an indescribable charm for me. In spare hours I read only those books that included descriptions and adventures of the new world. . . . Now primeval forests exist only in inaccessible mountain fastnesses; cultivation extends even to the snow-capped peaks. Man's habitations spread over the whole earth; there are churches and schoolhouses without number; yet where are men found dwelling together in unity? Where does sober living prevail? Or contentment? I longed for unknown lands, where no demands of citizenship would involve me in the vortex of political agitations. I longed for the quietude of immemorial woods where no paupers mar one's delight in beauty, where

[6] J. N. B. Hewitt, ed., Myrtis Jarrell, trans., *Journal of Rudolph Friederich Kurz, an Account of His Experiences among Fur Traders and American Indians on the Mississippi and Upper Missouri Rivers during the Years 1846 to 1852*, Bureau of American Ethnology *Bulletin 115* (Washington, D.C.: Smithsonian Institution, 1937).

> neither climate, false modesty, nor fashion compels concealment of the noblest form in God's creation; where there is neither overlordship of the bourgeois nor the selfishness of the rich who treasure their wealth in splendid idleness, while the fine arts languish.

In this manner Kurz begins the journal which presents his experiences on the western frontier of America during the years 1846–52. During that time he traveled to St. Louis, St. Joseph, Council Bluffs, and Fort Berthold and Fort Union (located in what is now North Dakota).

Since his boyhood Kurz had entertained one great passion: the creation of a gallery of paintings depicting the Indian in his native habitat. Later when he had become interested in art, he felt that by observing savage man he would be able to realize the romantic ideal of antique man, completely unspoiled by civilization and its social institutions.

In 1846 Kurz traveled from Le Havre, France, to New Orleans, intending to go on to Mexico from there. But because of the Mexican War he decided to perform his observations of primitive man on the Missouri River prairies instead. He arrived in St. Louis on January 17, 1847. The next year he spent chiefly in that area, making extensive sketches of the forests on the Cahokia River, just across the Mississippi from St. Louis. "I forgot everything else in my wonder at the loveliness of that display," he writes. There he found the primeval forests which had been so much a part of his dreams. During the summer he traveled up and down the Mississippi, sketching the Mormon temple in Nauvoo, the Piasa bird on the bluffs above Alton, scenes at Galena, the Fox Indians at Rock Island, and the Choctaws in New Orleans. But by April of 1849 he had become restless "to travel and to contemplate the deep woods, to study the buffalo and the red man. . . . I had already accomplished something in the pursuit of my aims," he writes: "primeval woods, prairies, and river I had observed at every season of the year. . . . Now I longed to study Indians and wild animals." On April 5 he left for St. Joseph.

There he found a wide variety of Indian tribes—Kickapoo, Iowa, Oto, Potawatomi, and Fox. "They conduct themselves in a very dignified manner," he writes. "Indians who came to see me in the autumn served as models for sketches and portraits. First came six of the most notable Fox Indians. . . . I took the greatest pleasure in those grandees;

they bore themselves with a dignity so natural, so distinguished, that I was filled with admiration. . . . I found in them delicate tact in manners, nobility of feature, and dignity in bearing."

But Kurz was most impressed with the Iowas, whom he characterizes as clean, brightly dressed, and "stately in bearing. On the whole they wear very little clothing," he writes; "in midsummer with the exception of the breechcloth and blanket, they wear no clothes at all. So I had at last my long-desired opportunity to study the antique from living models."

So impressive were the Iowas that Kurz began to spend his evenings in the lodge of Kirutsche, an Iowa chief, whose pretty seventeen-year-old daughter Witthae was not the least of the attractions of that lodge. For months Kurz pursued his studies in the language, customs, and habits of the Iowas while visiting the village almost daily. In January, 1850, he married Witthae and bought her a new outfit of the Indian type, "though Witthae herself would rather have adopted the European mode. . . ." The marriage lasted but a few weeks, for the girl soon became bored living in town away from her people. She ran away and Kurz resolved not to ask her to return. "That was the end of my romantic dream of love and marriage with an Indian," Kurz writes. "Brief joy!"

With Witthae gone Kurz soon became restless and moved north to Savannah. There he began to speculate in horses, hoping to obtain means for further travel, but his enterprise failed. Hoping to find employment at the fur-trading posts in the North, be boarded a steamer in mid-June, 1850, bound for the Upper Missouri, where he knew he would be able to observe Indians and wildlife in an even more primitive setting. His luck changing for the better, he managed to find employment as clerk under James Kipp at Fort Berthold in the land of the Mandans.

"How fortunately I am placed!" he writes on July 23. "What favorable opportunities for studying the Indians! . . . The Herantsa Wirussu are a magnificent people—the women possess little beauty of face but are splendidly formed. These Indians have a noble mien that is classic—all about me are living models of the antique."

But Kurz had scarcely begun to sketch the Indians at Fort Berthold when his affinity for misfortune was reconfirmed: cholera raged among the tribes, and his drawing was considered the source of this plague. (Epidemics had broken out previously following the visits of Catlin and Bodmer.) So Kurz restricted his activities to covert sketches. Eventually he alone remained free of cholera: this, of course, was proof enough for the Indians that he was "bad medicine."

On September 1, 1850, in order to pacify the Indians and remove him from danger, Kurz was transferred to Fort Union. There Indian subjects were everywhere: "In this Babylonian confusion of languages among the representatives of various nations it is hard to master one single dialect," he writes; "Assinboin, Crow, Herantsa, Cree, Mandan, and even Blackfeet all mingled together, and then mixed up with English, French, Spanish, and German." He spent eight months there sketching Indians and wildlife.

But by February, 1852, Kurz notes in his journal: "life at this fort has become more and more a dull routine, as less that is new or novel has presented itself for my study." On April 19 he left Fort Union to begin his long return journey home. Though his aspirations to become a renowned artist never succeeded, both his drawings and his journal are an invaluable addition to frontier literature.

Yet Kurz was pleased with the Indian as he found him: "I was so happy not to have been disappointed in the woodlands and forests," he writes; "they were, I found, far more rich, included more that was original, and the Indians were of a more noble type than I had ever dreamed." But there is that in Kurz's experience which mocks the romantic vision of primeval forest and savage life which he brought to America to test on the frontier.

The "sober living" he hoped to find was not a part of frontier life as he found it. For he discovered the fur trade to be a cutthroat enterprise, offering a rather precarious existence for most, certainly for himself. The Indians he presents are a rather wretched people, much of whose lives is characterized by frustration and futility. The "quietude of immemorial woods" he left behind him at Cahokia, for one of his chief complaints while living in a fort was lack of privacy; it seems that the Indians came and went so freely about his room that he could do little work. And he had but exchanged the paupers of Europe for the redskin paupers of the frontier, for he discovered the Indians to be constant beggars and often thieves, sometimes out of actual necessity. Because of the Mexican War he had to forgo an equable climate for the frigid winter of a Dakota prairie. Though he managed to leave behind him the "demands of citizenship," he soon became involved in the intrigues of fur-trading and preoccupied with America's political problems. The frontier did provide the means for developing his aesthetic theories, yet he failed to obtain the recognition he had sought: the Swiss public had little interest in Indian life—and critics even suggested that his paintings were not realistic.

Thus much of his journal presents anything but a romantic picture of the frontier and the Indian, for he was there during a particularly harsh period of time. But he does leave an authentic record of real Indians and a graphic picture of what life was like for those living on the frontier at that time. In his account one also finds beauty and adventure, along with the youthful enthusiasm and excitement which might be expected of the young traveler on the western frontier.

Another account of life at a fur-trading post on the Upper Missouri is left us by Henry Boller, whose *Among the Indians, Eight Years in the Far West, 1858–1866*[7] re-creates the experience of his four-year residence at Fort Atkinson among the Gros Ventres, Arikaras, and Mandans. It is perhaps due to a disposition somewhat less saturnine and introspective than that of Kurz that Boller creates a much more pleasant and appealing picture of the frontier. Then, too, Boller was in the area when disease was not widespread as it had been while Kurz was there.

In spite of this basic contrast, there is a great similarity in the experience of the two men. Like Kurz, Boller, throughout his youth, cherished a romantic vision of life on the frontier. In boyhood he kept scrapbooks of clippings pertaining to wild animals, and in imitation of a copy of one of George Catlin's books he began a gallery of pictures on the walls of his room. Throughout his boyhood and into his college years he continued to dream of going to live on the frontier. He left college as a senior without graduating and refused a clerkship in his father's business, preferring instead to pursue his dream. In March, 1857, he and his father traveled from their home in Philadelphia to St. Louis, probably to explore the possibilities of his entering the fur

7 Milo M. Quaife, ed. (Chicago: Lakeside Press, 1959).

trade. In May, 1858, Boller was again at St. Louis, and on this occasion obtained a position as clerk of the "Opposition" firm of Clark, Primeau, and Company. On May 23 he embarked for the frontier.

The annual departure of the fur company's steamboat from St. Louis for the Upper Missouri was, as Boller describes it, a colorful and exciting scene: "Crowds thronged the levee watching the bustle to and fro and the last hurried preparations for starting. Black volumes of smoke pour from the tall chimneys, the waste steam escapes with a hoarse roar, and a few preliminary turns of the wheels add to the fast increasing excitement. Curiosity-seekers crowd the cabin, peering into every nook and corner. . . ."

A few days later they had left civilization behind and crossed the borders of the frontier into Sioux country. More than twelve hundred miles above St. Louis they met the first large body of Indians—a band of Yankton Sioux awaiting their annuities, now on board the steamboat in charge of the Indian agent. "Their white skin lodges scattered over the broad green prairie, the horses feeding in all directions, and the gay dresses of the Indians on the river's bank formed a wild and picturesque scene," he writes.

The next event of note came when a party of Sioux ordered that the steamboat be landed. When the boat continued its course, the party opened fire. "Our Dakota friends, finding their efforts to stop us unavailing, rode furiously off, with gleaming weapons and fluttering pennons, forming a striking picture as their outlines became sharply defined against the clear, blue sky while cresting the hills in their wild gallop."

"It was at the close of a beautiful day in June," Boller writes, "when we laid up in sight of Fort Pierre, the first trading-post on the river. All that night our ears were greeted with the unaccustomed sound of the wolves howling in every direction."

In late June they arrived at Fort Clark, which, along with Fort Primeau, was "completely infested with rats," imported by the company steamboat. The Indians had at first been highly gratified in having been distinguished by this unique acquisition, but shortly afterward had come to regret the distinction.

The Ricarees (Arikaras) Boller saw at Fort Clark "were savage-looking Indians and more sullen and insolent than any we had yet met. The men had villainous countenances, which in many cases were disfigured by the loss of an eye, either from accident or disease . . . owing to their filthy habits and smoky lodges." Beyond the village he observed circles of human skulls, with medicine poles in the center bearing "propitiatory offerings to the Great Spirit. The dead, dressed in their best garments, are laid on scaffolds in the open air."

Near the Mandan village, at the mouth of the Little Knife River, the steamboat stopped at sundown to cut wood, as usual. Boller describes his amusement at watching an Indian setting out on a hunt load his fusee: "After a double handful of powder, he put in nine half-ounce balls one upon another, with a large wad of red flannel between each. The gun was literally loaded halfway up to the muzzle, and it seemed to me as if the safest place when fired off would have been directly in front."

In answer to those who have presented the Indian as an unrelenting stoic, Boller includes numerous scenes indicating otherwise. One such scene is his description of the amours of a young brave and his "little squaw," while traveling on the steamboat: ". . . never was lover more devoted to his prairie bird. Their favorite haunt was in the shade of the pilothouse. Here they enjoyed themselves to their heart's content, and derived inexhaustible amusement from painting their swarthy countenances with vermilion in all the variations their vivid imaginations could devise. After one coat of paint had been laid on, they would mutually admire each other, then upon due deliberation, would rub it off and try another fashion."

One cannot but envy this young man as he exults in all he sees, who discovers in reality all the romance which has for so long loomed on the horizon of his imagination. "The scenery from this point grows bolder and more imposing," he writes. "Ranges of towering clay bluffs of the most fantastic shapes, often resembling gigantic ruins, meet the eye. All colors are here depicted, from the darkest blue to a bright vermilion, and when the rays of the sun light up their walls and towers the effect is picturesque in the extreme, reminding one of castles in the Old World."

In late June or early July (Boller gives no date) he reached Fort Atkinson. "At length I had arrived at my destination in the Indian country," he writes. "For years it had been a cherished project to penetrate the heart of the wilderness and see the Indians as they really were, those too far beyond the pale of civilization to have felt the corrupting influences of its overflow. As the steamboat that had brought me here rapidly pursued her course down stream I realized my complete separation from all former associations. . . ."

That night he lay on a bunk of cottonwood plank softened with a half-dozen buffalo robes, after a meal of dried buffalo meat and *pommes blanches*.

Boller soon gained the opportunity to observe Indians at length, for he was surrounded by Indian idlers most of the day. "The idlers," he writes, "the *gentlemen* of the village, having taken their morning bath in the river and made their toilets, which at this season seemed to consist simply in readjusting the breechcloth, wend their way to the fort, loitering around and peering into the different houses in hopes of being asked to eat, an invitation which they never consider amiss, and always cheerfully accept."

> All the wild Indian tribes look upon the whites as an inferior race [writes Boller], pretty much in the same light that we formerly regarded plantation Negroes: They have the idea that the earth is one vast plain resting upon four huge turtles, and that the whites occupy a very small corner of it, while the rest is the . . . domain of the Indians. . . . The poorest vagabond of a redskin that roams over the prairies, with little else than a breechcloth to hide his nakedness, thinks himself infinitely richer and better in every respect than his Great Father, the President of the United States. . . . The Indians look upon all Americans . . . as a nation of traders, who get their goods from a cunning people beyond the big water. . . .

Among Boller's sketches revealing the human qualities of the Indian is a particularly memorable one of an old Sioux living among the Gros Ventres and Arikaras, a "highly accomplished sinner," and a "boundless liar," whose stories were told with such a "serio-comic air" that one had to be amused. "All day the old Doctor, as we styled him, would sit, surrounded by a coterie of his friends, regaling them with numberless lies, but all so plausible that his delighted audience listened with gaping attention. The kettle was constantly on the fire, for the Doctor's hospitality as a host was proverbial, and as long as there was anything in the cabin to eat he entertained plenty of company." One day the old Indian, observing Boller read a book, had a flash of intuition. Inquiring how he might obtain such a book, he was overwhelmed when Boller graciously presented him the one which he was reading. Then at the Indian's urgent request Boller wrote in the book a few sentences in Sioux, dictated by the Indian himself. Later that same morning Boller noted a large crowd gathered about the residence of the old Sioux. There before the crowd sat his friend the Doctor, "with the book open before him, his eye intently fixed upon the page, moving his lips as if reading, and occasionally turning over a leaf. He had on a pair of heavy silver-rimmed spectacles, and as might be expected, looked profoundly wise." When one of his audience expressed doubt of the Doctor's literacy, the Sioux read through the lines written by Boller, and then, pushing his silver spectacles back upon his forehead, handed the book to Boller and asked that he read the same lines. As Boller finished, the Doctor cast an amused glance at him as if to confirm this new bond between them.

Boller saw much in the Indian's life which was colorful and amusing. His account is a series of remarkable landscapes and sketches of Indians busily engaged in proving themselves human, both in folly and valor. The color and romance he emphasizes; the hardship, suffering, and horror he subordinates. Yet there is much which indicates that life on the frontier at that time was continuously heightened by a pervading sense of the threat of imminent catastrophe or death. Boller describes an Indian woman dropping behind on a journey to kill the smallest of her three children because it was too young to travel; a tragedy in which the three splendid sons of a half-blood hunter are found after having been butchered by a Sioux raiding party on one of a never-ending series of raids and counter-raids; and the perennial bouts of starvation and suffering which were so much an accepted part of the Indian's life.

But the ultimate effect of Boller's narrative is the re-creation of a frontier exhibiting all the qualities promised in so many glowing encomiums by western travelers. In the Preface to his book Boller writes: "I shall ever look back upon the years spent in the Indian country as among the pleasantest of my life, and if in all my dealings with white men I had found the same sense of honor that characterized my savage friends, my appreciation of human nature would be much higher."

Such is the romance and excitement of the western frontier and the Indian as seen through the eyes of these four travelers who ventured beyond the fringes of civilization between 1833 and 1860. Because of their articulate expression of their perspectives and impressions, they offer an excellent sampling from the spectrum of traveler types who journeyed west to observe the Indian.

Charles Augustus Murray, with his romantic preconceptions of the Indian, is a striking illustration of the many travelers who were doomed to disappointment and disenchantment. For the Indian—though he was definitely aware that he had an image to maintain and could and did stage many impressive performances for white visitors—also had an everyday life, one far removed from that of the fictitious noble savage. Murray's stint among the Pawnees was a harsh but convincing testimony to this fact. On the other hand, John Treat Irving creates such a pleasant and amusing mural of Pawnee life that Murray might well have questioned whether Irving had actually met the Pawnees. Certainly there can be but little doubt that Irving's hosts were presenting their best profile to the view of this important delegation from Washington; but at the same time, Irving was seeking a different quality in his observation of the Indian: his particular interest was in noting the human characteristics of his subject. It might have been predicted with some assurance that he would not be disappointed in his quest.

Rudolph Friederich Kurz was, of course, an artist, and as such his quest had to do with line, form, and color. Like Murray, he brought with him many illusions about the Indian, but when these were ground away through the attrition of reality, he found adequate compensation in that the Indian proved compatible to his aesthetic and commercial needs. Henry Boller is representative of still another class of travelers. He came to the frontier with a romantic picture of the Indian and frontier life, but such was his nature that he returned from the frontier some years later with his romantic view still intact. How then is one to know where reality lies?

Indeed, one can but agree with Murray when he denigrates savage existence; or with Irving when he suggests that the Indian is quite normally human in his behavior and is perhaps even more interesting than the romantic depiction of him; or with Kurz when he expounds upon the beauty of a Dakota landscape and the symmetry of form in his Indian models in one breath, and then with the next laments the bleakness and monotony of frontier life; nor can we even quarrel with Boller when he proposes that he found the Indians—the same Indians whose morality Kurz deprecates to a great extent—more honorable than the great majority of whites he had known. The upshot of all this might appear to be that the early West was all things to all people—the sole determinant being one's perspective. We should certainly infer such from the many conflicting impressions of that host of travelers roaming about the West during this era. At least we can definitely be sure that there would have been general acclaim of the thesis that all in all it was a tour well worth taking.

Jean Louis Berlandier: A French Scientist among the Wild Comanches of Texas in 1828

John C. Ewers

WHEN I WAS A BOY in western Pennsylvania, concerned adults used to call a lad whose zest for life far outran his respect for the proprieties "wild as a Comanche." Just why the Comanches were selected as the epitome of "wildness" I did not know. But I now believe that had I been a white settler on the Texas frontier a century ago I probably would have shared that opinion of the Comanches. As a matter of fact the Comanches posed a serious threat to the lives and property of enemy tribesmen as well as to whites for fully 170 years—from 1705 until 1875.

Anthropologists consider the Comanches, a Shoshonean-speaking tribe, to be an offshoot of the Shoshoni Indians of Wyoming. They were unknown to history prior to 1705. In that year they were seen on the frontier of New Mexico, raiding for horses. Within a half-century thereafter the well-mounted Comanches acquired firearms through trade with the Wichitas farther east, and, driving the Apaches before them, pushed southeastward to the vicinity of San Antonio, the capital of the Spanish province of Texas. By the early years of the nineteenth century the Comanches had extended their raiding operations southward beyond the Rio Grande, plundering Spanish ranches and settlements, stealing horses and mules, and carrying off women and children into captivity. Spanish authorities in both New Mexico and Texas knew the Comanches as the largest and most aggressive

Indian tribe south of the Arkansas and between Santa Fe and San Antonio. Estimates of their widely scattered population reflected the fear in which they were regarded more accurately than their true numbers. The Spanish commonly estimated them at thirty thousand. And in 1818 a reputable officer of the U.S. Army, Colonel W. A. Trimble, quoted that same figure in a report to the Secretary of War, even though he estimated the Comanches had lost four thousand of their number in a severe smallpox epidemic only two years earlier.[1]

When Mexico gained her independence from Spain in 1821, that new republic inherited New Spain's perennial problem of what to do about the dread Comanches on her northern frontier. Mexico continued New Spain's policy of defending that frontier through a chain of widely spaced military posts, known as presidios, lightly and inadequately manned by small troops of cavalry. In 1827 Anastacio Bustamante, Military Commander of the Internal Provinces (an able officer, who was later to become president of Mexico), managed to negotiate a tenuous peace with some of the easternmost of the Comanches at the presidio in San Antonio. And it was during the next year—1828—when these Indians rode into San Antonio to renew the peace and to trade buffalo meat and bear grease for weapons and ammunition, that Jean Louis Berlandier first met them.

Berlandier was then a young man, about twenty-three years of age, far from home. His date of birth is uncertain, but he was born about 1805, of a very poor family, near Fort de l'Ecluse, a French boundary fortress a short distance from Geneva, Switzerland. As a youth he became an apprentice in a pharmaceutical house in Geneva. An ambitious lad, he taught himself Latin and Greek in his spare time. Auguste-Pyrame De Candolle, the famous Swiss botanist, was favorably impressed with the boy, and admitted him to his classes. As

1 Colonel Trimble's report of August 7, 1818, to the Secretary of War is reprinted in Rev. Jedediah Morse, *A Report to the Secretary of War of the United States on Indian Affairs* (New Haven, Conn.: Converse, 1822), pp. 256–260; his estimate of the Comanche population appears on p. 374 of that volume. The best sources on the eighteenth-century Comanche are two books of Spanish documents edited by Alfred Barnaby Thomas, *Forgotten Frontiers* (Norman: University of Oklahoma Press, 1932), and *The Plains Indians and New Mexico, 1751–1778* (Albuquerque: University of New Mexico Press, 1940); and Herbert E. Bolton's *Athanase de Mezières and the Louisiana-Texas Frontier, 1768–1780* (2 vols., Cleveland: Arthur H. Clark, 1914). The best modern study of the Comanche is Ernest Wallace and E. Adamson Hoebel, *The Comanches, Lords of the South Plains* (Norman: University of Oklahoma Press, 1952). The authors of this book make no mention of Berlandier, and apparently had no knowledge of his studies of the tribe.

Berlandier progressed in his studies, De Candolle opened the herbarium of the Academy to him, and took him on his own field trips. In 1824, probably before his twentieth birthday, precocious Berlandier published a monograph on gooseberries in the *Memoires* of the Society of Natural History of Geneva which demonstrated his promise as a botanist.

Soon thereafter, Lucas Alamán, Minister of Foreign Affairs of the Republic of Mexico and a former student of De Candolle, informed that Swiss scientist that he was seeking a biologist to accompany a Mexican scientific expedition into Texas. De Candolle recommended Berlandier. So it was that when the Mexican Comisión de Limites left Mexico City on November 10, 1827, elaborately equipped with a wagonload of scientific books and instruments, French-born and Swiss-trained Berlandier was a member of the party.[2]

Even though its responsibility for determining the boundary between Mexico and the United States gave this Comisión de Limites its name, its mission was a much broader one, and included the scientific exploration of Texas. And make no mistake about it, this was a well-organized expedition of able men, and one which compared favorably with any exploring expedition the United States had sent into the trans-Mississippi West prior to that time. It was led by General Don Manuel de Mier y Terán, a highly qualified and experienced engineer. The pioneer American colonist in Texas, Stephen F. Austin, who came to know General Terán well, and who relied upon his observations for the location of the principal towns in Texas on his own map of 1829, considered Terán to be the most scientific officer in the Mexican Army. Terán's professional staff included Lieutenant José Mariá Sánchez, as artist and cartographer, Raphael Chovell, from the School of Mines, as mineralogist, and the Frenchman, Berlandier, as biologist.

Among the specified responsibilities of the Comisión were those of obtaining information on the customs, dispositions, and habits of the native tribes, as well as estimates of their numbers. And we know

2 The little that is known of the background on Berlandier is well summarized in the chapter titled "In Defense of Jean Louis Berlandier" in Samuel Wood Geiser, *Naturalists of the Frontier* (Dallas, Tex.: Southern Methodist University Press, 1948), pp. 30–54. No portrait of Jean Louis Berlandier is known.

that Terán himself, as well as Lieutenant Sánchez and Berlandier, all took these particular responsibilities seriously.[3]

Moving northward at a rather leisurely pace, the Comisión crossed the Rio Grande into present-day Texas at Laredo on February 2, 1828. Leaving Laredo eighteen days later, they continued northward through the uninhabited desert, subsisting on toasted and ground corn cakes with brown sugar (known as *pinole*). After eleven days' march they reached San Antonio (then known as San Fernando de Béxar), a small frontier town of less than fifteen hundred inhabitants, on March 1, 1828.

Although Berlandier traveled extensively during the next sixteen months (even making a short round trip by sea to New Orleans), he spent a goodly share of that time in the neighborhood of San Antonio, collecting, drying, and preserving numerous plant specimens. I have seen some of these specimens, still well preserved, and labeled in Berlandier's own hand, in the Gray Herbarium at Harvard.

In late summer of 1828 Berlandier first met bands of Comanche Indians—warriors, wives, and children—who rode into San Antonio and encamped in the open plaza. That fall Berlandier accepted an invitation from Colonel José Francisco Ruiz, an officer at the presidio, to accompany him and a party of sixty to eighty Comanche Indians, under Chiefs Reyuna and El Ronco, on a bear and buffalo hunt in the region northwest of San Antonio—an area that had not been adequately and correctly mapped.

Accompanied by thirty dragoons and some citizens of San Antonio who had licenses to hunt for meat, the party left San Antonio on November 19. Berlandier noted that the Comanches had more than three hundred horses. He was fascinated by the ease with which these Indians moved their camp, and set up and dismantled their lodges;

3 The organization, staffing, and the complex mission of the Comisión de Limites are explained in Ohland Morton's *Terán and Texas* (Austin: Texas State Historical Association, 1948), pp. 42–56. This volume also provides extensive biographical information on General Don Manuel de Mier y Terán (1789–1832). On June 9, 1828, General Terán submitted a report on the Indian tribes of Texas which was published under the title "Noticia de las tribus de salvages conocidos que habitan en el Departamento de Tejas, y del numero de familias de que consta cada tribu, puntos en que habitan y terrenos en que acampan," in *Sociedad de Geografía y Estadística de la República Mexicana, Boletín*, segunda epoca, II (1870), 264–269. Lieutenant Sánchez' lively diary of his travels with the Comisión de Limites in Texas, translated by Carlos E. Castaneda, and published under the title "A Trip to Texas in 1828," *Southwestern Historical Quarterly*, XXIX (1926), 249–288, contains numerous observations on the Indians he saw in Texas.

but he was appalled by the laxness of their security at night. They experienced several false alarms when anticipated attacks by Apache enemies failed to materialize. Nevertheless, Berlandier was impressed by the speed with which the Indian warriors moved to meet the anticipated attack, and he noted that the women also prepared to defend themselves with bows and arrows.

Game was scarce during the early days of this journey. The Comanches appeased their hunger by killing skunks, removing the anal glands, cutting off the heads and legs, burning off the hair, and after taking out the entrails, broiling them in the fire. And Berlandier could not refuse their offer of some of this meat. He found it was not disagreeable, but resembled young pig.

When the Comanches killed a white wolf, Berlandier observed that the Indians highly valued its hide, attributing supernatural powers to it. They made quivers of it, and also believed that arrows exposed to the smoke of burning white wolf's hair would always wound an animal.

Berlandier observed that the Indians were smoking the dried leaves of a plant they called *temiacha* (the smooth sumac), mixed with tobacco. He found and identified a flowering plant they called *puip*, the chewed roots of which they used for healing wounds, squeezing the juice into an open wound. He noted that the Comanches made a yellow dye from the root of a kind of barberry, and that they used an artemisia in their ceremonial steam baths.

On the sixth day the Comanches parted company with the whites near the Guadalupe River, intent upon returning to their distant villages. The whites turned northward toward the Pedernales and did find and kill buffalo. After the hunt they traveled southward through the Frio Canyon, and returned to San Antonio on December 18.[4]

Berlandier probably met the Comanches on several occasions after that—in San Antonio. But there is no indication that he ever traveled with them again. Yet he seems to have regarded that excursion as the highlight of his extensive explorations in Texas.

The French scientist did not return to Europe. After he concluded his service with the Comisión de Limites in Matamoros, across the Rio Grande from Texas, he continued to reside in Matamoros,

[4] Berlandier's account of this expedition appears in an article, "Caza del Oso y Cibolo, en el Nor-oeste de Tejas," *El Museo Mexicano*, III (1844), 177–187.

married a Mexican woman, and earned a comfortable living through the practice of medicine. Although he maintained his interest in science until his death in 1851, Berlandier published but little. I have found only three publications based upon his explorations in Texas. The first is an exceedingly rare sixteen-page leaflet, probably published by a local press in 1832, entitled *Memorias de la Comisión de Limites. Historia Natural. Botánica,* comprising a technical description of eleven newly proposed species and four new genera.[5]

The second is a lively description of that hunting excursion with the Comanches and Colonel Ruiz, published in a short-lived popular journal *El Museo Mexicano* of Mexico City in 1844, under the title *Caza del Oso y Cibolo, en el Nor-oeste de Tejas.*

The third, jointly authored with Rafael Chovell, *Diario de Viage de la Comisión de Limites,* published in Mexico City in 1850, includes a verbatim reprinting of his 1844 article on the bear and buffalo hunt. This also is at least relatively rare. It was priced at $150 the last time I saw it listed in a book-dealer's catalog.

Berlandier was drowned while attempting to cross the San Fernando River, south of Matamoros, in 1851. He was only about forty-six years of age at the time of his death. In December, 1852, Secretary Joseph Henry of the Smithsonian Institution helped Lieutenant (later General) Darius Nash Couch to obtain a leave of absence from the U.S. Army in order to "make a scientific exploration of the country south of the Rio Grande." In February, 1853, Lieutenant Couch purchased Berlandier's papers and scientific specimens from his widow in Matamoros. These papers and objects are now widely scattered, but safely preserved. His zoological materials, including a significant manuscript on the mammals of Mexico (including Texas), are in the Smithsonian Institution. The Gray Herbarium has a number of his botanical manuscripts, a handsome series of water colors of plants, and many plant specimens collected both north and south of the Rio Grande. A very extensive collection of his papers relating to the Comisión de Limites is in the Western Americana Collection at Yale. With them are a number of interesting maps, field sketches, and landscape views executed during the exploration. The Library of Congress

[5] I. M. Johnston provides a modern botanist's critical evaluation of this rare contribution in "A Neglected Paper by Jean Louis Berlandier," *Contributions from the Gray Herbarium of Harvard University,* n.s., LXX (1924), 87–90.

has one of several versions of his journals of his travels in Mexico, written in his own hand and in his native French. Certainly Berlandier was one of the most prolific writers among the explorers of the American West during the first half of the nineteenth century, even though only a small percentage of his writings have been set in type.

As an ethnologist I have been most interested in Berlandier's materials on the Indians. His ethnological specimens, though few in number, are of excellent quality. They are preserved in the U.S. National Museum. A majority of the tribally identified artifacts are from the Comanches, and they are uniquely important because they comprise the earliest documented specimens from that tribe.

Berlandier's most important ethnological manuscript is a lengthy and detailed description of the Indians of Texas in the Thomas Gilcrease Institute of American History and Art, Tulsa, Oklahoma. Although the date of 1830 appears on the title page, internal evidence proves that it was not completed before 1834.[6] It is accompanied by a unique series of water colors of sixteen Texas tribes (some of them extinct since 1860 or earlier) executed by Lino Sánchez y Tapia, a Mexican artist who was Berlandier's scientific illustrator, and who died in 1838. A number of these illustrations are after original sketches by Berlandier himself.[7]

In preparing Berlandier's materials on the Indians of Texas for publication I have been impressed by the fact that, even though he considers more than forty tribes, he devotes a high proportion of his description and of his discussion to the Comanches. In fact, I believe Berlandier's account is the nearest approach to a well-rounded ethnography of the Comanche Indians written by any observer of that tribe during the days before the buffalo were exterminated on the southern Plains and the wild Comanches were pacified.

The coverage is both broad and remarkably detailed. Berlandier (on the authority of Colonel Ruiz) estimated the Comanche population around 1830 at 12,500, which appears to me to be a realistic

6 This manuscript, in Berlandier's native French, bears the title *Indigenes nomades des Etats Internes d'Orient et d'Occident des territoires du Nouveau Mexique et les deux Californies. 1830.*

7 Others of the illustrations of Indians are after originals by Lieutenant José Mariá Sánchez, the artist-cartographer of the Comisión de Limites. That both Lieutenant Sánchez and Berlandier had considerable artistic talent is proven by examples of their original works in the Western Americana Collection at Yale.

estimate. He described the summer and winter range of the tribe, and identified the tribal allies and enemies. Berlandier's biological interests may be reflected in his descriptions of Comanche physical appearance, his efforts to determine their life span, his discussion of their diseases and illnesses, and his explanation of the periodicity of smallpox plagues among them. His botanical interest is revealed in his attempts to identify the plants used by those Indians for medicinal purposes such as the treatment of syphilis, the hastening of delayed menses, the soothing of toothache—and even as an insect repellant.

As a firsthand observer of the Comanches, Berlandier's data on clothing, weapons and war equipment, skill as horsemen, and trade with the whites are probably based upon what he saw with his own eyes in San Antonio and on his six-day march with a party of Comanches. But he went far beyond these observations to describe the Comanche life cycle—the birth of a baby, postnatal care, cradling, the education of youth, sex life (both normal and abnormal practices), marriage, adultery, the role of women in camp life and on the warpath, treatment of the aged, and death, burial, and mourning customs. Not only did he describe Comanche methods of hunting buffalo, but he also told how they lanced bears and hunted other mammals, including wild horses and wild cattle. He explained the tribal government, the causes of intertribal warfare, and the making of war and peace. His manuscript is especially rich in its description of Comanche warfare—how war parties (both large and small) were organized, how they moved against the enemy, how they employed wily strategems to catch their enemies by surprise, and just how they took scalps. The Comanche no-flight warrior society—its organization, equipment, activities, and special privileges—is described in detail. The torture of prisoners, the vilification of dead enemies, and the occasional practice of cannibalism are gruesomely defined.

Nor does Berlandier neglect to describe Comanche recreations and to explain their religious beliefs—their veneration of the sun, their individually owned medicines, and their conceptions of life after death.

Where did Berlandier acquire this wealth of information on Comanche life and customs? Surely he did not observe all this during six days of travel with a Comanche hunting party, and occasional visits with the Comanches in San Antonio. Nor did this French scientist fabricate these details from his own imagination. He did obtain a very large part of his Comanche data from another white man, a man who had known the Comanches over a period of years, and much more intimately than did Berlandier. That man was Colonel José Francisco Ruiz, the man who invited Berlandier to accompany him on that hunting excursion northwest of San Antonio with the Comanches in 1828.

No other white man in Texas at that time had a more intimate knowledge of the Comanches than did Colonel Ruiz, or was more respected by them than he was. Born in San Antonio in 1780, Ruiz was sent to Spain to be educated. After his return to Texas he managed his father's ranches on the Nueces. In 1803 he became San Antonio's first schoolmaster, conducting his classes in his own home. A patriotic Texan, Ruiz joined the revolutionists in their attempt to overthrow Spanish rule in Texas in 1811. After the revolutionary forces were decisively defeated by the Royalists in the Battle of the Medina River on August 18, 1813, Ruiz had to flee for his life. He found refuge among the Comanche Indians, and lived with them for eight years. He was living in Natchitoches, Louisiana, in the fall of 1821, after Mexico gained its independence from Spain. Then Gaspar Lopez, Commandant General of the Eastern Interior Provinces, offered him a full pardon if he would use his influence with the Comanches and Lipan-Apaches as a commissioner to those tribes on behalf of Mexico. He accepted and later was commended for his services. Ruiz still later became an officer in the Mexican Army serving at several of the presidios in Texas. He was one of the signers of Texas' Declaration of Independence in 1836, and served the Republic of Texas both in its Senate and as a negotiator with the Indian tribes, who knew him to be a friend. Ruiz died in 1840, some eleven years before Berlandier's death.[8]

Berlandier did not fail to give credit to Colonel Ruiz in his writings on the Comanches. In them I have found no fewer than eighteen references to Ruiz as Berlandier's authority on a particular custom, or as the person who provided a specific example to illustrate a custom. Undoubtedly Berlandier had seen enough of the Comanches to ac-

8 A biographical sketch and portrait of Ruiz appear in the pamphlet *José Francisco Ruiz, Texas Patriot,* by Walter G. Stuck (San Antonio, Tex.: Witte Memorial Museum, 1943).

quire a feeling for their culture, but he relied upon Colonel Ruiz to supplement his own observations and thus to enable him to enrich and to to round out his description of Comanche culture.

As a scientist who asked nothing of the Indians except the truth about their own way of life, Berlandier shared none of the prejudices of many of his predecessors or followers who wrote about the Comanches and their Indian neighbors. He did not see them through the eyes of a missionary, a soldier, a trader, a government official, or a settler on the Indians' land. He was a trained observer with an insatiable curiosity and a keen eye for significant details. And he had an orderly mind, capable of organizing and relating ideas. In addition this Frenchman wrote simply and clearly and with a considerable charm—attributes not commonly found in the writings of men of science. He recognized the Comanches and their Indian neighbors not as wild, untameable creatures of nature, but as human beings, men of considerable intelligence, capable of learning to live in an organized society and of adapting to changed conditions of life on the frontier of white settlement. I believe that in the future Berlandier will be remembered as one of the most enlightened and one of the best amateur ethnographers of the American West during the frontier period.

Perhaps this still little-known Berlandier might be compared to that much better-known, mature German natural scientist, Maximilian, Prince of Wied-Neuwied, who traveled up the Missouri River in 1833, spent some eleven months among the Indians, and wrote a classic account of the tribes of the Upper Missouri. But I should prefer to compare him to another natural scientist of a slightly earlier period—Thomas Say, the zoologist of Philadelphia. During the period 1819–20 Say served as field naturalist for the Long expedition west of the Mississippi, and like both Berlandier and Prince Maximilian, he became intensely interested in the Indian tribes he encountered. During the winter of 1819–20, while he lived at the field station of Engineer Cantonment, on the Missouri River above present-day Omaha, Say not only collected mammals, birds, fishes, and insects and described them, but he also wrote one of the best descriptions of the Omaha Indians to be found in the literature, and one which Prince Maximilian recommended to his own readers. Like Berlandier, Say did not rely entirely upon his own observations. He derived a great deal of his information on Omaha customs from John Dougherty, Indian subagent and interpreter, who had lived for eight years on the Missouri and spoke several Indian languages.[9]

During the following summer (1820) Say accompanied the Long expedition up the Platte River to the foot of the Rocky Mountains, south to the headwaters of the Arkansas, and back eastward by way of the Arkansas valley. While descending the Arkansas he met some of the tribes of the southern Plains—the Arapahos, Kiowas, Kiowa-Apaches, and a few Comanches. These contacts were brief, and Say had no companion who knew these tribes as well as did Colonel Ruiz. But he did make written observations on these Indians. Unfortunately, only a few days before the party reached the frontier post of Fort Smith, three of the enlisted men deserted, taking with them Say's precious notebooks.[10]

This was a serious loss of knowledge of the Indians of the southern Plains of the 1820 period. But it is a consolation to know that much of that information must have been regained by a fellow biologist, Jean Louis Berlandier, who, with the assistance of the knowledgeable Colonel Ruiz, began his studies of the Comanches and their neighbors on the frontiers of Texas only eight years after the Long expedition returned to civilization.

[9] Say's account of the Omaha Indians appears in Edwin James, *Account of an Expedition from Pittsburgh to the Rocky Mountains, Performed in the Years 1819, 1820*, in Reuben Gold Thwaites, ed., *Early Western Travels, 1748–1846* (32 vols., Cleveland: Arthur H. Clark, 1904–06), XIV, 288–321, XV, 11–136. In his letter to the Secretary of War requesting John Dougherty's appointment as Indian subagent and interpreter on the Missouri, September 25, 1819, Benjamin O'Fallon stated that Dougherty "is a Kentuckian—but has lived, between this and the yellow stone, for the last 8 years and speaks several Indian languages tolerably well" (*Territorial Papers of the United States*, XIV (1949), 564.

[10] Stolen and never recovered were Say's journal, his notes on Indian manners and customs, and two vocabularies of Indian languages. The theft occurred on August 31, 1820, and was reported in *The Journal of Captain John R. Bell, Official Journalist for the Stephen H. Long Expedition to the Rocky Mountains, 1820*, Harlin M. Fuller and LeRoy R. Hafen, eds. (Glendale, Calif.: Arthur H. Clark, 1957), pp. 256–257.

Roads West from St. Louis

William B. Baker

ON MAY 12, 1823, Paul Wilhelm of Wuerttemberg left St. Louis with the intention of talking with Auguste Chouteau, at his farm on the bluffs of the Missouri beyond Florissant, before joining at St. Charles the fur company keelboat on which he was to travel up the river. Not able to find a satisfactory saddle horse, he started out in a one-horse, open, two-wheeled cart. The road to St. Charles, he found,

> after one has passed the last houses of St. Louis, leads, for two English miles over hills which are overgrown with bushes of hazelnut, oak, walnut, and sumac. After that one travels thru prairie for six or seven miles. The prairie, however, is not merely a grass-covered piece of land but also supports a mass of tall weeds and low wooded plants. . . . The road so far proved to be tolerable, but the thunderstorms which came one after the other had not left a dry thread on me. My clothes, however, soon dried in the intense heat which beat upon us between showers. . . . Beyond the prairie there came again a hilly region whose underbrush consisted of hazelbushes. . . . [At Florissant] the road becomes extremely bad. In the lowlands, especially in the hollows the horses sank above their knees in the black mud. My driver seemed to be a past-master in upsetting the cart. Often, at the worst places, I had to jump from the cart to avoid breaking my neck in the upsetting.[1]

A month later at Franklin, having found travel by water extremely slow, Prince Paul decided to go by land to the mouth of the Kansas

[1] Paul Wilhelm, Duke of Wuerttemberg, *First Journey to North America in the Years 1822 to 1824*, William G. Bek, trans., *South Dakota Historical Collections*, XIX (1938), 231–232.

River. "From Franklin a tolerable road leads to the mouth of this great river," he had learned.

What Prince Paul considered a "tolerable road" raises the question of what a bad road might be. The route of his journey, except for the first day, is probably approximated by the road shown leading from Franklin through Liberty in Figure 1. Following are some of his observations pertaining to the roads and the means of transportation.

June 12, 1823. From Franklin to Pierre à la fleche (Arrow Rock).

> Saddle horses could not be provided here [Franklin] any better than in St. Louis. Only weak and worn out animals were offered. I had to be content to take an extremely wretched, frail, one-horse cart, which on the morning of my departure was yet hastily repaired with common nails. In this rig I was to make a journey of many miles over a poorly opened road. It really meant that I should walk this distance, for in the cart was just room enough for the driver and my very scant baggage. A boy of fourteen undertook the job of driving this conveyance thru an unknown, wild country, where human habitations were often miles apart. . . . The rough trail, which was dignified with the name of road was so poor that the traveler often lost it from sight altogether. It contained also so many trees that were broken down by the wind and so many swampy places, that I often spent hours in overcoming these hindrances. Before one reaches the Kansas river the Missouri must be crossed two times. The first time at Pierre de la fleche and the second time this happened in the neighborhood of Tabeau creek. The road to Pierre de la fleche, a distance of twelve English miles from Franklin by way of the river, led through a sparsely inhabited region. The first two miles of the way were passable. . . . In a deep hole our cart broke for the first time, but after a stay of two hours it was temporarily repaired by Caillou who had fortunately provided himself with an ax. . . . Thru swampy forest we made seven more miles, during which time I had ample occasion to make unpleasant observations concerning the lack of skill of our young American driver. About four o'clock in the afternoon we reached an isolated house opposite Pierre de la fleche. Here lived the owner of the ferry boat which took one across the river. . . . Nothing remarkable occurred while crossing the river in the flat-bottomed square-ended boat. It required almost an entire hour to get across, as the vessel had to be pulled half a mile up the stream.

June 13, 1823. From Pierre à la fleche to a house in the prairie.

To the first and nearest dwelling in the prairie was a distance of twenty-eight English miles, a stretch which one could make in one day during the dry season in the summer. We followed the track of a wagon which must have preceded us some time, but whose tracks were still recognizable to the trained eye of my companion. In this manner we traveled till noon in an intense heat, thru a grassy plain that extended apparently unendingly to the west and south, being interrupted only occasionally by scattered wooded spots. . . . My little driver was afraid to spend the night on the prairie. He allowed the exhausted horse scarcely the necessary noon-day rest and after half an hour drove on. . . . With the setting of the sun the oppressive heat became somewhat less, and at eleven o'clock in the night we reached a lonely cabin. . . .

June 14, 1823. From the house in the prairie to the house of a German immigrant. The account of this day's travel omits any comment dealing with the road or the lack of a road.

June 15, 1823. From the German immigrant's house to Blufftown.

As we had to travel on the ridge of a chain of hills that slope to the Missouri we had the greatest difficulty in making headway with our conveyance over the poor and stony road. Finally we reached the river where we purposed crossing, near a little, now abandoned town of Brington. . . . From Brington to Pierre a la fleche they reckon sixty English miles which distance we made in two and a half days. On account of the wretched condition of our wagon and the bad roads, I had made almost the entire distance on foot, which was especially difficult on the fifteenth because of the hilly and stony ground. . . . On the left bank the road was extremely bad and uneven. I had to travel either thru bottomless morass and great stretches of standing water, or over hard, bumpy, sun-baked clay roads. Much of the region was overgrown with impenetrable vegetation and thorny bushes, in part also with nettles as tall as a man. Here our conveyance broke down completely.

June 17, 1823. From Blufftown to Liberty.

Finally, on the next morning, after much effort, there was found an old horse, almost blind, on which my belongings, and in case of extreme fatigue, myself were to be transported to the little town of

> Liberty. . . . The way led either thru woods and thru a number of creeks, whose crude bridges had been washed away, or along steep, uneven hillsides, on which my pack horse often stumbled and fell, so that I even feared I should not get to Liberty alive. After traveling twelve miles I saw the bank of the winding Fish creek, Riviere aux Poissons, which is navigable in canoes, is rather deep and muddy, and whose water is gray and bad tasting. We crossed on a flat-bottomed boat and stopped at the house of a farmer for an hour. It was the first house which we had seen since morning. . . . Not until it had become dark, about at nine o'clock, did we reach Liberty, after a day's journey of almost twenty-six English miles.[2]

It is really no surprise that the St. Charles road or its extension to the Kansas River even at such a late date as Prince Paul's travels should still be no more than a rough trace through the wilderness where the traveler had to carry axe and spade to reclear the way of fallen trees and new growth. Roads beyond the Mississippi were slow in being developed for the good reason that the principal business on the frontier was trade with the Indian tribes along the Missouri. The river was the great road to the Northwest. Pedro Vial, it is true, made his way across the Plains from Santa Fe to St. Louis in 1794, Zebulon M. Pike led an exploring expedition to New Mexico in 1806, traders from Missouri in 1822 took caravans to Santa Fe, but it was not until 1825 that the road to Santa Fe was surveyed.[3] The Overland Trail to the Rocky Mountains, Oregon, and California by 1840 was well known but the fearful state of the "road" in 1849 is vividly reported in many a Gold Rush diary. Wherever navigable rivers existed, they were preferred. Land roads were auxiliary to waterways.

A road system out of St. Louis would have begun, of course, as soon as there was some place to go to. When Delor's village (later known as Carondelet) was begun in 1767 five or six miles to the south, a road would have linked the two settlements. For a number of years, however, St. Louis and Ste. Genevieve, seventy miles apart, communicated by river or by the road from Cahokia to Kaskaskia through the

2 *Ibid.*, pp. 289–301.

3 Noel M. Loomis and A. P. Nasatir, *Pedro Vial and the Roads to Santa Fe* (Norman: University of Oklahoma Press, 1967); Donald Jackson, ed., *Journals, with Letters and Related Documents. Zebulon Montgomery Pike* (2 vols., Norman: University of Oklahoma Press, 1966); Kate L. Gregg, *The Road to Santa Fe* (Albuquerque: University of New Mexico Press, 1952).

American Bottom on the eastern bank of the Mississippi. It was only in 1779 that Fernando de Leyba, Lieutenant Governor of the Western Illinois, as a defense measure ordered a road opened along the right bank so that the two principal towns would have a land route usable when the river might be closed by ice.[4] The *voitures* of the French before and after this date traveled on the waters of the Mississippi, not over what some have romantically pictured as *el Camino Real.* Westward a road to Blanchette's village at Les Petits Cotes (St. Charles, Missouri) would have been cut over the prairies and through the woods soon after 1769, since for some purposes it would be more convenient to use riding horse or cart to travel twenty miles overland than to boat forty miles up the two rivers. Nicolas de Finiels' map (Figure 2) of the region around St. Louis (1797–98) pictures for us the local network of roads but these remained the roughest of cart tracks uncertainly marked and for strangers often difficult to follow.[5]

It was only in 1815 that official attention in Missouri Territory was directed to the matter of roads. Let me turn to the beginnings of these roads immediately westward from St. Louis, ancestors of today's great highways.

Roads west from St. Louis have been important despite the presence of the rivers and the relative ease of river travel, even after the steamboat eased the labors of going upstream. There were, then as now, times when the river was in an angry or icy mood. As the day came to occupy the lands of Missouri as well as to cross them for goals farther west, the role of the road was great either in providing access routes for the traveler engaged in local movement or in the very purposeful travel of the migrant with a wagon who for some reason chose to go by land.

It is probably safe to assume that the traveler headed west from St. Louis during the first half of the nineteenth century knew little of the roads he would encounter. For specific information pertaining to these same roads the present-day student of western travel often finds

[4] Lawrence Kinnaird, *Spain in the Mississippi Valley* (3 vols.), *Annual Report of the American Historical Association for 1945* (Washington, D.C.: G.P.O., 1945), I, 348.

[5] Published for the first time in A. P. Nasatir, *Before Lewis and Clark: Documents Illustrating the History of the Missouri, 1785–1804* (2 vols., St. Louis Historical Documents Foundation, 1952), I, 94. Roads east of the Mississippi were equally bad. For a description of the road from Louisville by way of Vincennes to St. Louis in 1796 see John Francis McDermott, ed., "The Western Journals of Dr. George Hunter, 1796–1805," *Transactions of the American Philosophical Society*, n.s., LIII, Pt. 4 (1963), 27–29.

himself in much the same plight as the early traveler. Looking into a printed work such as *A Description of the Roads of the United States* by John Melish (Philadelphia, 1815), one finds the road to St. Charles laid down as the only one leading from St. Louis. H. S. Tanner's *American Atlas* (1823) shows three routes, however, headed west from St. Charles. But the fact that other roads existed is well established from more regional sources. The earlier map by Nicolas de Finiels, for instance, indicates four routes, including the St. Charles road, extending from St. Louis. Part of the discrepancy, then, may be attributed to difference in scale.

Some idea of the roads encountered by travelers of the period can be obtained through examination of county and state documents, especially the cartographic record. There are certain admitted weaknesses to such an approach. Most immediately notable is the fact that the surveyor's view was often made, though not always, before significant traffic had developed. This disadvantage is perhaps partially offset by the insight that may be gained from documents expressing the concerns of the inhabitants for the establishment of roads where none existed. Again, some of their problems with existing roads can be found in their petitions for improvements and changes in road location as they knowingly or unknowingly participated in the establishment of road patterns that would endure far longer than the transportation devices they used.

Three groups of documents supply the foundation for a view of certain early roads westward from St. Louis. First is a set of 523 file folders dating from February 22, 1815, to February 5, 1874, containing petitions and other records related to the establishment of roads in St. Louis County and in some instances beyond. Second, a series of plat books of road surveys makes up a loosely related set of maps. Although these were originally records of the City of St. Louis, they are now a part of the records of the St. Louis County Highway Department and are housed in the vault of the St. Louis County Recorder of Deeds. The set of files has suffered from the attrition of time. The letter of transmittal from the St. Louis County Highway Engineer to the Recorder of Deeds contains a list of 147 files missing at the time of transfer in 1963.[6] The original "Road Index" of the files remains

6 "Missing Files Folder," in Old County Road File, St. Louis County Highway Department Records, Recorder of Deeds Office, Clayton, Mo.

in the Sewers and Paving Office, St. Louis City Hall.[7] Third, a brief look at some of the roads across Missouri will be approached through the use of materials, especially road plats and field notes, in the Missouri State Archives.

An act passed by the legislature of the Territory of Louisiana on July 9, 1806, called for "a surveyor, and three disinterested householders" to view a proposed road, and "to survey and mark out the same of a sufficient width, by the nearest and most practicable course, and make and return a plot thereof. . . ."[8] There is a very real probability, however, that the roads existing in 1803 were little altered until 1815. The first action recorded in the Old County Road File (Folder 1), dated February 22, 1815, is an order "to survey lay out and mark a Public Road from James Ferry on the Missouri to town of St. Louis" filed with "a plot of said road of Fifty feet wide as by the plot hereunto answered more fully appears."

A look at the "Road Index" will show the from-to relationship in road establishment. Admittedly, travel ultimately develops as a two-way phenomenon; however, there is good reason to suspect that a preponderance of the impetus may initially be unidirectional. Interpretation of directional tendencies for road establishment by road name is at best risky. It can, of course, be the result of the manner of expression of the time. Nevertheless, it is suggested that at the outset the interest in road establishment tends to be, in large part, unidirectional, and that those having substantial financial interests will most often be instrumental in the initial establishment of roads. Insofar as this is true there is meaning in the full road name as it appears in a document such as the "Road Index." Additional understanding may also be gained from the names of the petitioners for the roads.

Three of the first four roads identified in the "Road Index" are entered as leading from St. Louis. The first four roads listed with the date of earliest dated document in the file are:

1. From St. Louis to Hall's, James' or Spring ferry (February 22, 1815)
2. From Point Labbadie (on the Missouri) to St. Louis (January 25, 1818)

7 "Road Index," Cabinet 13, Sewers and Paving Office, St. Louis City Hall. Only the original handwritten copy contains full road titles and later annotations.

8 *Laws of the Territory of Louisiana* (1806), Chap. 28, sec. 1.

3. From St. Louis to St. Charles (October 15, 1818)

4. From St. Louis by St. Ferdinand to St. Charles and from St. Ferdinand to St. Charles (April, 1820, first two documents not dated)[9]

These roads or routes followed nearly the same courses as shown on Finiels' map (Figure 2). The next four roads established were links connecting the lines radiating from St. Louis, thereby providing a means of peripheral travel. Of the next twenty-two roads, six were peripheral, that is, not identified as terminating at St. Louis; thirteen were from an outlying location to St. Louis, and only three were identified as from St. Louis to an outlying point. Two of the roads were additional routes to St. Charles. Of the next seventy entries in the "Road Index," fifty-four were peripheral roads, two were from outlying locations to St. Louis, and thirteen were from St. Louis to outlying points. The suggestion is advanced that there was an initial period of consolidation for the first four roads, lasting until 1820. During the second period, which lasted a little more than a decade, there was substantial concern in outlying settlements for the establishment of roads by which products could be transported to market. Concern during the third period, which continued to the end of the record in 1874, was chiefly with completion of the network by outlying communities and various points on the trunk routes.

Considering the first one hundred roads, those established between 1815 and 1845, the terminals were as follows: to ferries, twenty-one; to mills, seven; to taverns, seven; to mines or salt licks, three; to bridges, two; to fords, two. Terminals such as towns and other roads are not included. The unusual predominance of ferries as terminals and focal points is explained by the unique location of St. Louis in which travel westward called for crossing the Missouri or Meramec rivers or proceeding by a narrow strip of land between the two. Both streams are much too large for the bridge-building capabilities of the early part of the period.

The following petition reflects the role of certain economic activities in the demand for new roads.

> To the Honorable the Judge of the Circuit Court now holding said court within and for the County of St. Louis.
>
> The petition of the subscribers inhabitants of the township of

[9] Old County Road File, Folders 1–4.

St. Louis in said County humbly showeth—That your petitioners labour under great inconvenience for want of a road or highway to lead from the Horse Mill of Reuzin Sappington to the mill belonging to Wilson Hunt on the River De Peres and from thence to the town of St. Louis. Your petitioners therefore pray your honor to appoint persons to view and lay out the same according to law and they will ever pray, etc May 23, 1818.

Respectfully your
obedient servant.
[48 signatures][10]

Although the need for roads is easy to visualize, the conditions pertaining to the roads themselves are more difficult to reconstruct. Chapter 28 of the *Laws of the Territory of Louisiana* (1806) makes no mention of minimum requirements for road surfaces. "An Act concerning Public Roads and Highways" of the Laws of the Territory of Missouri dated January, 1814 (Chap. 115, sec. 4), however, establishes limits, although they would be intolerably lenient at present. "All public roads laid out as now in use, or which shall be hereafter laid out, shall be cleared of all trees and brush at least twenty feet wide, and such limbs of trees as may incommode horsemen or carriages, shall be cut away and no stump shall exceed twelve inches in height."

Let us turn to an examination of two roads from St. Louis, both of which were not only of great importance to local travelers, but also were routes followed by many migrants moving westward. An unusual opportunity to view some of the conditions along roads of the past is provided by the field notes and maps of the road surveyors. Unfortunately such a view is provided, if at all, only at widely spaced intervals of time. It is happy for us that this was a period of cartographic eloquence. Through the 1830's, the practice of making detailed sketches of land features adjoining the right of way was subject to the individual talents of the surveyor; however, by 1845 an act pertaining to state roads in *The Revised Statutes of the State of Missouri* (Chap. 115, Art. II, sec. 9) directed that the surveyor

shall note in a suitable field-book, the courses and distances of the route surveyed, the direction, breadth and average depth of water courses, and such other prominent features of the country, and prom-

[10] *Ibid.*, Folder 10.

> inent objects and places near, or over which such road shall pass, as may be conveniently obtained, together with such other topographical information as the commissioners may deem expedient. . . .
>
> The commissioners shall cause to be made, for the use of the state, a complete and accurate connected map of the whole route of such road, embodying thereon the several plats directed to be made out by the surveyor for the use of the several county courts, with such topographical information as may have been obtained during the survey.

That the practice of making somewhat detailed traverse maps of both state and county roads was established at least as early as 1826 is indicated by an unsigned and undated map in the Old County Road File drawn in 1826 by René Paul.[11] The eastern half of this map shows Mulhall's Grocery across from the adjoining Methodist, Catholic, and Presbyterian graveyards just outside St. Louis (Figure 3). Not only points of common interest such as burial grounds and the grocery are shown, but the residences and cultivated fields of individuals as well.

For the St. Louis area the drawing of road traverses reached its high point during the tenure of William H. Cozens, County Surveyor, and his deputy Clement W. Coote in 1845 and 1846, apparently in response to the law of 1845. Their work makes up County Road Plat Book C.[12] The maps, however, are based on surveys made at different dates through the 1830's.

Since a road to St. Charles pre-dated the period under consideration, let us look at the departure from St. Louis, in September, 1845, as described in the field notes of William H. Cozens and the drafting of Cozens and Coote in a map entitled "Map of the Southern St. Charles Road. From the City of St. Louis, to the Missouri River opposite the town of St. Charles" (Figures 4, 5, 6, and 7).

The accompanying field notes disclose that rock surfacing of the route was progressing in an irregular or broken fashion. Both the map and field notes show that there were two hotels near the pond in the Grand Prairie. Bonhomme Road branches south a short distance east of the Old French Tavern.

11 *Ibid.*, Folder 3.

12 Plat Book C, St. Louis County Highway Department Records, Recorder of Deeds Office, Clayton, Mo.

As we approach the terminal opposite St. Charles, the field notes point to "Chauvins house on left, old road on right . . . an Ash 18" dia . . . travelled road on right, field on left . . . to a stake at the foot of a hill near a large Elm tree—Thence— . . . a large Walnut tree . . . entre old field . . . a stake on the right bank of the Missouri River opposite the upper End of the town of Saint Charles" (Figure 7).

The traveler upon reaching the river had a view of St. Charles similar to that represented by J. C. Wild in 1841 (Figure 8). St. Charles was the major dispersal point for routes on the north side of the Missouri River.

In a somewhat similar fashion, though less prominent as a dispersal point, the town of Manchester was also a place of first destination for the long-distance traveler as well as a focal point for some local travelers. This road, an extension of which paralleled the Missouri River on the south to Jefferson City, offered the advantage of being the only road westward not requiring the use of a ferry within a short distance of St. Louis. That portion of the road in St. Louis County is presented on two plats, the first of which is entitled "The State and County Roads from the City of St. Louis to the Town of Manchester" (Figure 9), drawn by Cozens and Coote in 1845, from survey notes for the state and county roads in 1838 and 1830, respectively.[13] The portion from St. Louis to the east fork of the River des Peres, however, was surveyed as late as December, 1844 ("Field notes of the Manchester Road. Beginning in the centre of Market Street opposite the SW corner of the St. Louis Court House Square, Thence with Market Str. . . .").[14] Beginning at station no. 28 of the survey, the field notes trace the road "to the E End of the bridge over the East fork of the River des Peres . . . intersects the *State Road* . . . enter Widow Berry's field with consent . . . leave field enter woods . . . old road on left . . . opposite D. C. Sutton's house where set 8 Mile post (cedar) on right with old road . . . through the woods the old road on the right . . . a ford over the River des Peres."

The bridge mentioned above is presumed to be the same bridge as the one for which plans are found in Plat Book C (Figure 10)[15] identified as "Plan and Elevation of Bridge, to be Constructed Over

13 *Ibid.*, Plate 10.
14 *Ibid.*
15 *Ibid.*, Plate 14.

the River Desperes," drawn in September, 1839. It will be noted that it was a covered bridge with broken stone abutments and cut stone pillars. It seems reasonable to assume that this bridge is representative of some of the better bridges built over small streams during the period.

The field notes of the road from St. Louis to Manchester end in an appropriate fashion: ". . . with Main Street in the town of Manchester to a cross street at Tripletts. Distance 19 Miles . . . from St. Louis" (Figure 11).[16]

A companion map, entitled "State and County Roads from the Town of Manchester to the Franklin County Line," has two independent sets of field notes for surveys made in 1831 and 1838, and the composite map was made in 1845, by Cozens and Coote (Figure 12).[17] As may be seen from the map, just a small portion of the land west of Manchester was cleared at this time. Only seven houses are shown on both routes, and three of these were within the first three miles west of Manchester. In the remaining distance of approximately twelve miles the traveler would pass three more houses if he went by the new state road or only two if he followed the old county road. Fittingly, the field notes of the state road end at "the county line 32 Miles and 71 chains from St. Louis marked on a BOK (black oak) 24" dia left of the road at a creek which runs North."[18]

The roads previously described were part of a system of eight roads that were the subject of "An Act to Provide for Laying Out and Opening Certain Roads in the County of St. Louis . . ." which was approved February 11, 1839.[19] This act made official the basic routes that had been growing for over a half-century. As has been noted on the detailed survey maps, many nearly parallel branches of roads developed as an easier route or grade was sought or in the attempt to avoid the deep ruts made by the repeated passing of loaded wagons.

With the basic roads established attention turned increasingly to road quality and the condition of the surface, and the law became more specific, stating: "the commissioners shall locate the routes over such ground, as may be conveniently, and finally, and with as little

16 *Ibid.*, Plate 10.

17 *Ibid.*, Plate 11.

18 *Ibid.*

19 Horatio M. Jones and Alexander Marlin, *Laws of the State of Missouri Specially Applicable to St. Louis County* (St. Louis: Missouri Democrat Office, 1861), pp. 354–359.

expense as possible, graduated so as not to exceed 5° elevation. . . ." The act also provides that "The county court . . . shall cause the roads established under this act to be cleared of trees, and other obstacles and opened 60 feet wide; and all stumps, rocks, and other obstructions, shall be taken up to a depth of not less than one foot. . . ."[20]

Mud was a major concern in the middle 1880's. Olley Williams, writing for the *Western Journal* in 1848, said, "If some of us have waded through mud almost to our knees for the last quarter century, there is no reason for entailing this state of things upon our children." Williams apparently held little hope for state action, stating that "it is out of the question ever to expect the State of Missouri or a majority of her inhabitants, to go for internal improvements of any magnitude."[21] J. B. Moulton, St. Louis County Engineer in 1852, showed the situation by a map somewhat unusual for the time, which survives thanks to the Missouri Historical Society of St. Louis (Figure 13). The map shows the type of surface for the eight major routes with their paralleling and intertwining antecedents. The statement in the upper left is addressed "To the Members of the Senate & House of Representatives from St. Louis City & County in the Missouri General Assembly" and calls for expedition of road improvements. A table is provided which indicates the mileage and other information for each road. For example, the cost varied from $4,500 per mile for Bellefontaine Road to $8,600 per mile for Carondelet Road (Figure 14).[22]

In its attempts to get out of the mud, St. Louis County did not escape the plank-road craze of the 1850's. This subject has been treated elsewhere[23] but is introduced here through the "Map of the Central Plank Road From St. Louis to Log Church" (Figures 15 and 16), drawn in 1851 by B. A. Alderson and J. B. Moulton. It, too, shows the splitting and intertwining of old and new roads.

Thus far attention has been focused upon the roads that would be encountered in the first day's travel from St. Louis. A brief ex-

20 *Ibid.*, p. 358.

21 Olley Williams, "M'Adamized Roads in St. Louis County," *The Western Journal*, I (1848), 679.

22 J. B. Moulton, "A Map of St. Louis County Missouri, Showing the conditions of Roads improved . . ." (1852), MS.

23 North Todd Gentry, "Plank Roads in Missouri," *Missouri Historical Review*, XXXI (April, 1937), 272–287.

amination of state roads may give some idea of conditions beyond St. Charles or the Franklin County line. It will not be necessary to establish the relationship of antecedent trails and traces to the present road pattern of this area because this has been well demonstrated.[24]

Viewed broadly, the first roads into the interior of Missouri paralleled the Missouri River, or went only as far as Potosi in the Missouri lead district. With this exception, the road pattern resembled the major river pattern, as is to be expected in a pioneer land. The pattern is shown as it had developed by 1836, on Tanner's "New Map of Missouri with its Roads and Distances" (Figure 1). With increasing boldness roads were placed through open country to shorten the distance required by those that closely followed the wandering of the river. One such road parallels the Gasconade River, a tributary of the Missouri, and another strikes south from Independence, with no apparent relationship to the drainage pattern. The route to Santa Fe, to be sure, leads southwestward from Independence into the Great Plains. This was the first decade of a three-decade period of state road establishment.

Again, the law figures prominently in the records of roads. The law relating to the availability and placement of the records upon which a detailed examination rests reads: "Such map, with a copy of the field notes of the survey, and all grants of the right of way, taken as hereinafter provided, shall be forwarded by such commissioners, together with a full report of their proceedings, to the governor, to be by him deposited in the office of the secretary of state."[25] Compliance with the law produced more than 180 packets or containers of documents dealing directly with roads which are on file in the Missouri State Archives. Nearly all of the records are from the four decades between 1830 and 1870, although relatively few roads were established in the last of these decades. The law requiring plats to be continuous produced some probably unanticipated results. Many are several feet in length, which necessitated rolling. The rolled maps constitute a collection occupying forty-six boxes which usually contain one map and accompanying field notes. The surveyor of one road evidently experienced difficulty in obtaining paper of appropriate dimensions,

24 Martha M. Wood, "Traces in Early Missouri, 1700–1804," *Missouri Historical Review*, XXXVIII (October, 1943), 12–24.

25 *The Revised Statutes of the State of Missouri* (1845), Chap. 151, Art. II, sec. 12.

but solved the problem by using the back of green-flowered wall-paper.[26]

An examination of the records discloses that most roads and most state road mileage did not develop as through routes linking the extremities of the state, but rather developed as loosely related segments of less than one hundred miles in length. Such an examination also indicates the concerns of the inhabitants and those officials responsible for road placement. These are pointedly illustrated by a letter to Governor John Edwards.

> To his excellency the Governor of Missouri We the undersigned commissioners who were appointed by our last legislature to view and locate and mark out a state road from Weston in Platte County by the way of Bloomington to St. Joseph in Buchanan County would report to his excellency the following: we met in the town of Weston on or about the 10th of May 1845 we employed the necessary assistants and after each of us were duly qualified to our respective duties we proceeded: we found the routes exceedingly difficult on account of uneven and marshy grounds and contentions of individuals by the way over whose lands the road is compelled to pass to have a practicable route, we adjourned and continued from time to time (on account of much rainy weather) till we completed the location, we then proceeded to take relinquishments most persons to whom we applied relinquished, some few were absent consequently not heard from, we have made our reports to the respective courts of Platte & Buchanan Counties our work is by them received, and charges allowed, we finally, agree in this report though our route is far from being a rectalineal line, yet it is capable of being made a good Stage route perhaps the best ground over which a road can pass from point to point and will be of utility to the travelling community our distance and further particulars are shown by our plats and field notes from under the hands of your obedient Servants this the 9th day of August A.D. 1845.
>
> Lenard C. Prunty
> William Flannery Commissioners[27]
> James Carter

[26] "State Road leading from the town of Bucklin in Linn County to Green Castle in Sullivan Co. filed Jan. 25, 1860," MS map. Maps and Plats of State and County Roads, Missouri State Archives, Jefferson City.

[27] Maps and Plats of State and County Roads, Box 6, Missouri State Archives.

To view a westward continuation from St. Charles, the map of the road from St. Charles to the town of Mexico is presented (Figure 17). The map is of austere form, showing little more than the essentials of the survey. The accompanying field notes, however, are quite complete, treating the distance of eighty-six miles in 273 entries. The subject matter is similar to those presented earlier, except that increased emphasis is placed on slope and alternate passage from woods to prairie. The field notes indicated that this road "ran with" the Boonslick Road[28] for a short distance, but unlike the better-known Boonslick Road never developed into a major route. Such was the case of many roads to land-office towns. There remains, nevertheless, an unusually detailed and objective description of the country traversed on the way to the land office.

The map of the northern portion of the "State Road From Independence to Batesville" (Figure 18) is presented not as an example of cartographic excellence but as a map portraying a route west from Independence in 1841. The spacing of fields along the road gives an idea of the emptiness of the land. The accompanying field notes contain 162 remarks for a distance of seventy-one miles chiefly dealing with topographic characteristics.

By the 1850's a very high proportion of the papers deal with requests for changes in existing roads. A substantial majority of the cases called for making the road coincide with fields now defined by the rectangular land survey. The petitions pointed out the disadvantages to the landholder whose property was divided by the diagonal passage of a road through his field. There followed a long period of increasingly rectalinear roads. After all, the addition of a few yards here and a few more there mattered little to local wagon traffic. The roads in many instances were losing to the railroads their role as cross-country routes.

As the first period of state road establishment and surveying passed with the dislocations of the Civil War and with the coming of railroads, the maps produced in conjunction with the road surveys became increasingly precise and confined to the details of road construction. And so the period of eloquence in road survey maps ended.

[28] Kate L. Gregg, "The Boonslick Road in St. Charles County," *Missouri Historical Review*, XXVII (July, 1933), 307–314; XXVIII (October, 1933), 9–16.

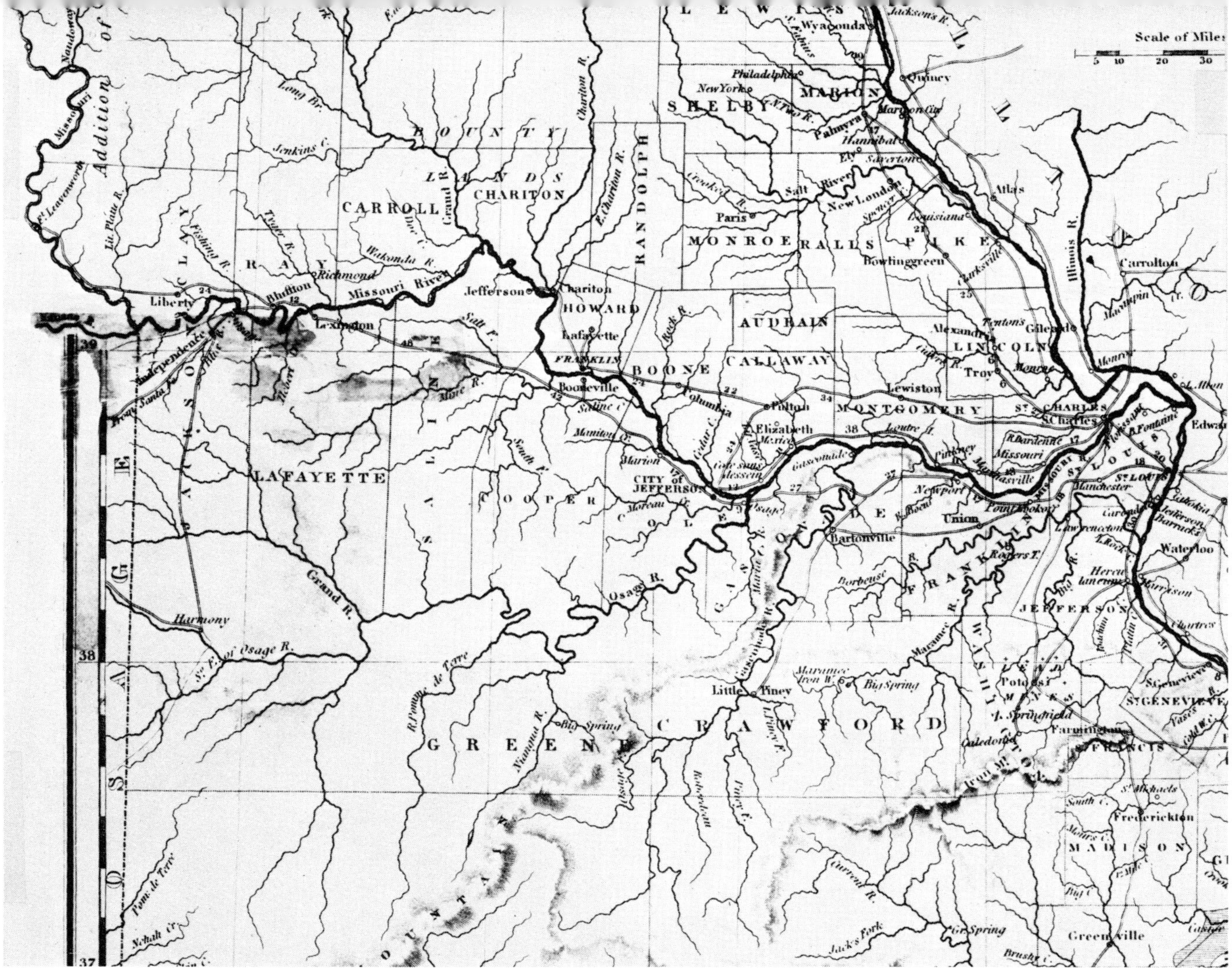

FIGURE 1. *Section of "New Map of Missouri with its Roads and Distances." By H. S. Tanner, from* Tanners Universal Atlas *(Philadelphia: H. S. Tanner, 1836), Plate 28. Courtesy of the Missouri Historical Society, St. Louis.*

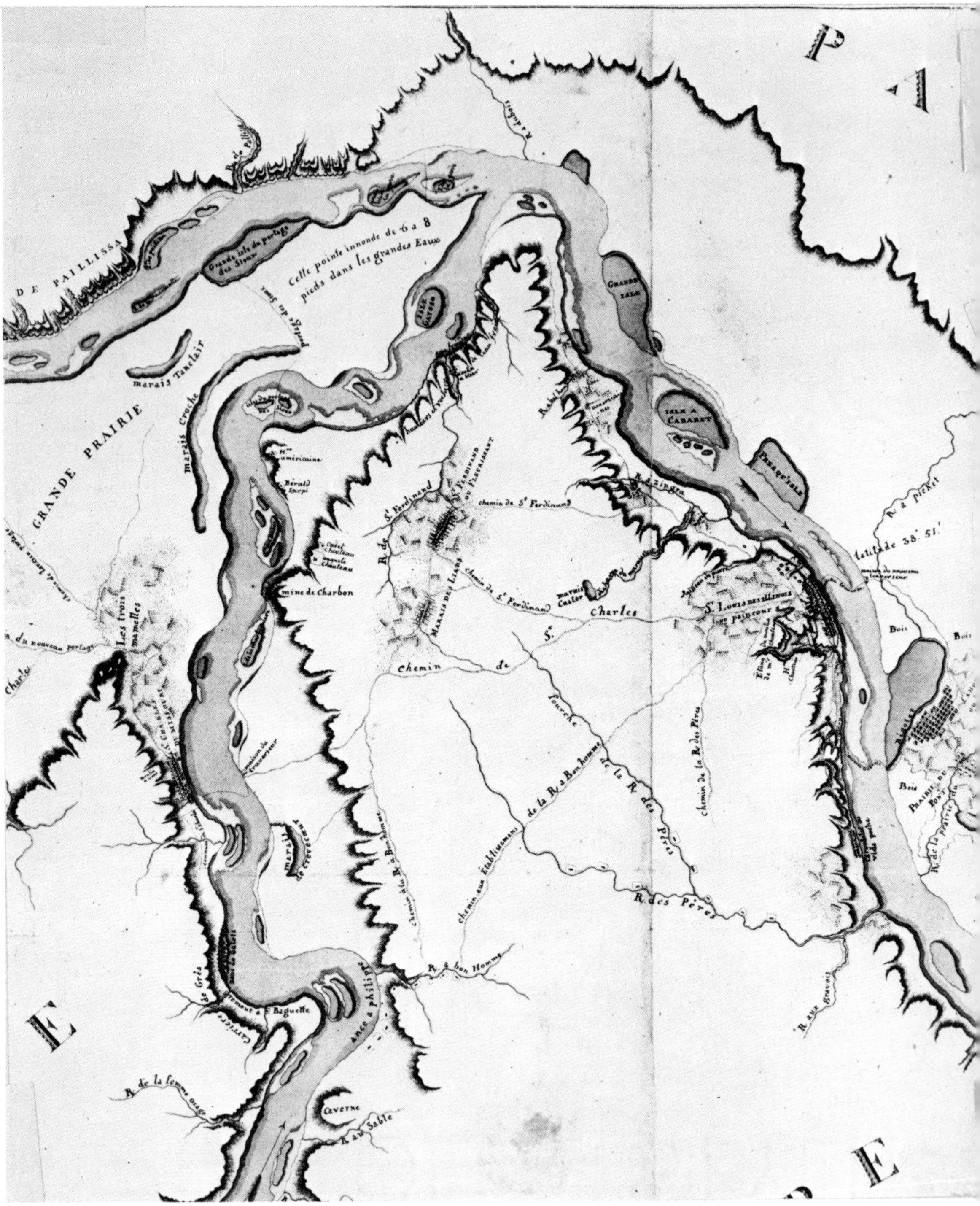

FIGURE 2. *Section of N. de Finiels' map of Upper Louisiana, 1797–1798, "Carte d'une Partie du Cours du Mississippi," showing network of roads from St. Louis to St. Charles, Missouri. Original in Bibliothèque Nationale, Plans et Cartes.*

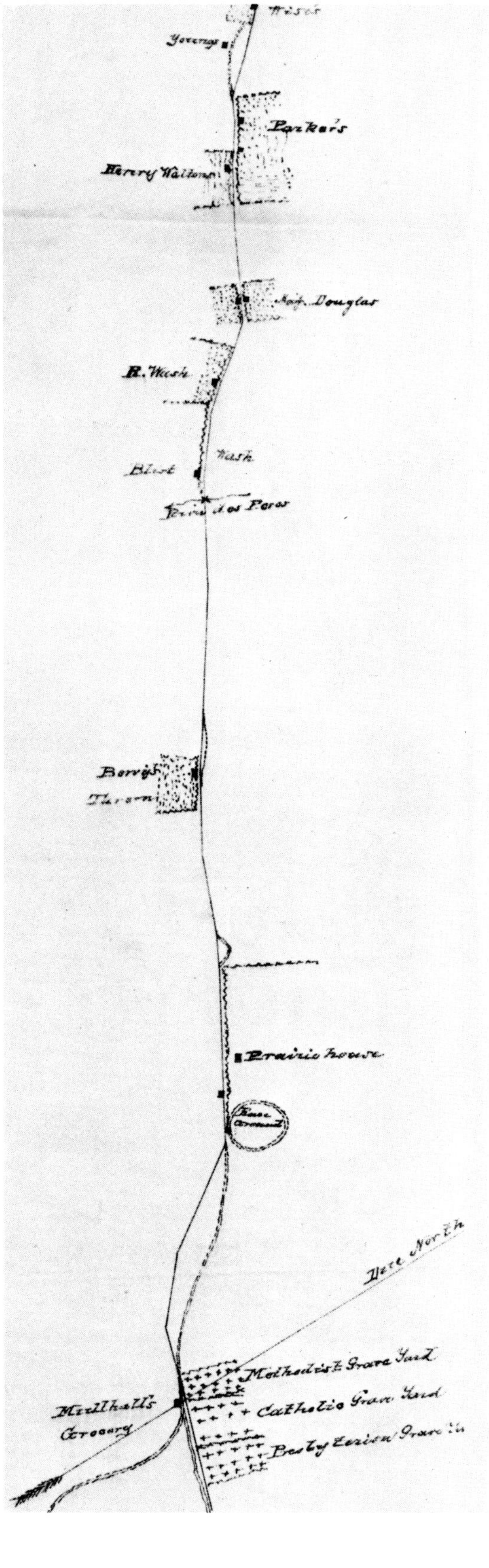

IGURE 3. *Eastern portion of an untitled map of the oad from St. Louis to St. Charles. Presumably by René Paul in 1826. Old County Road File, St. Louis County Highway Department Records, Recorder of Deeds Office, Clayton, Mo.*

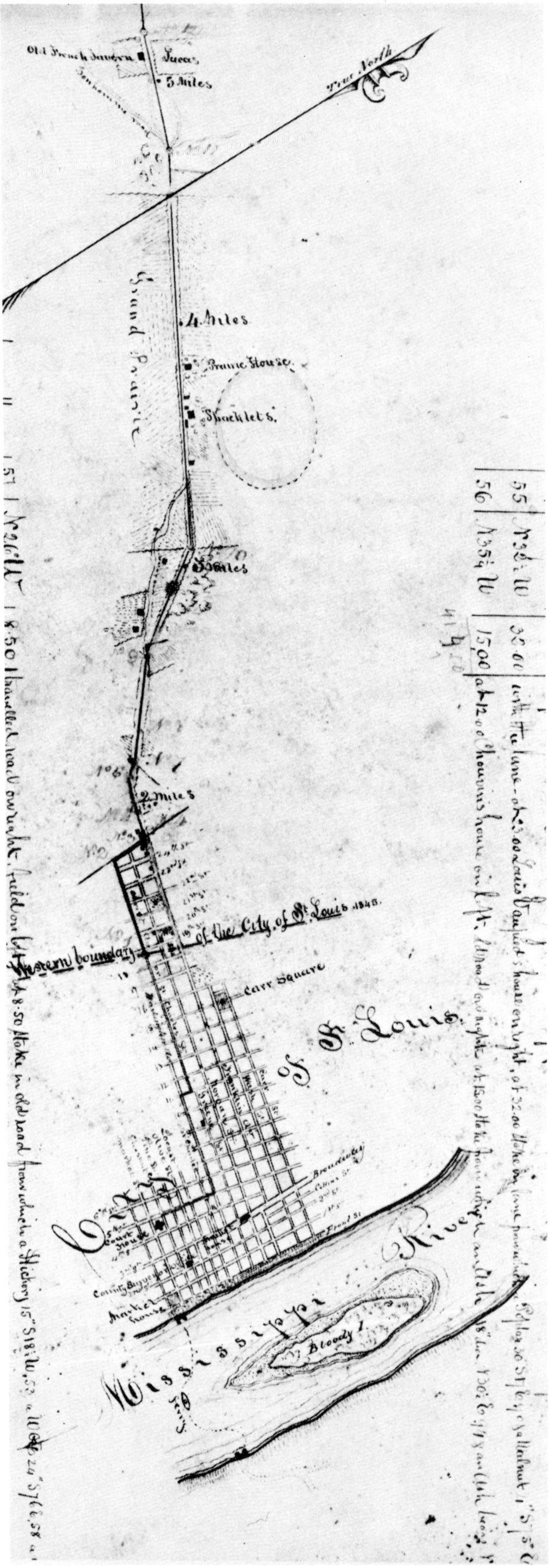

FIGURE 4. *Section 1 of "Map of the Southern St. Charles Road. From the City of St Louis, to the Missouri River opposite the town of St. Charles." By William H. Cozens and Clement W. Coote, 1845. Plat Book C, Plate 1, St. Louis County Highway Department Records, Recorder of Deeds Office, Clayton, Mo.*

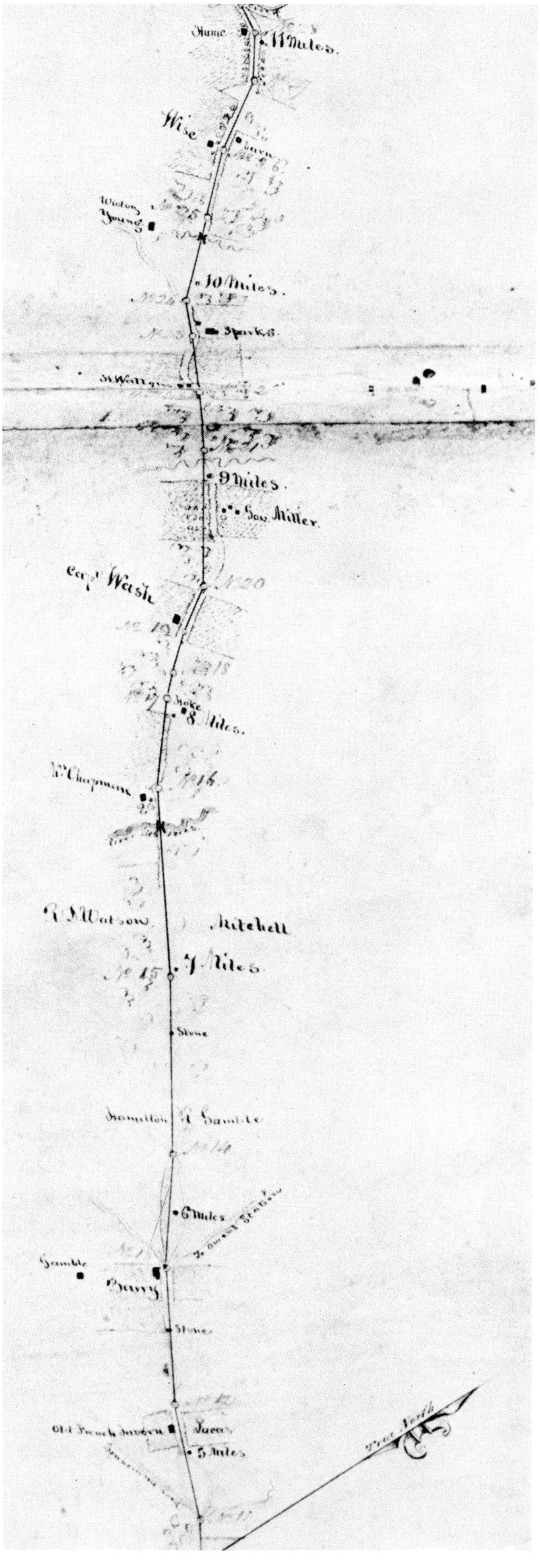

IGURE 5. *Section 2 of "Map of the South-rn St. Charles Road. . . ."*

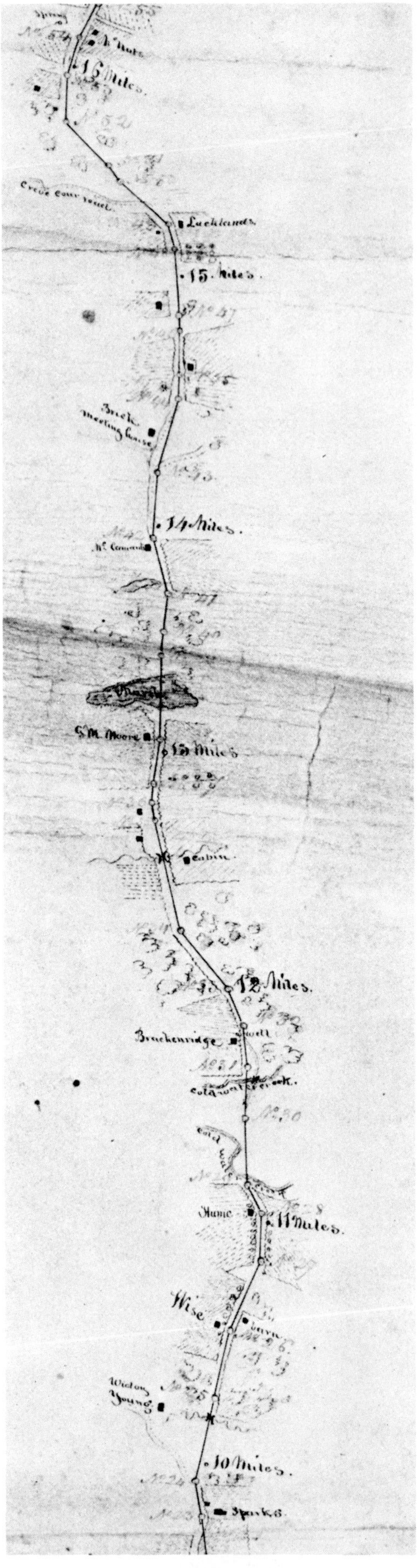

FIGURE 6. *Section 3 of "Map of the Southern St. Charle Road. . . ."*

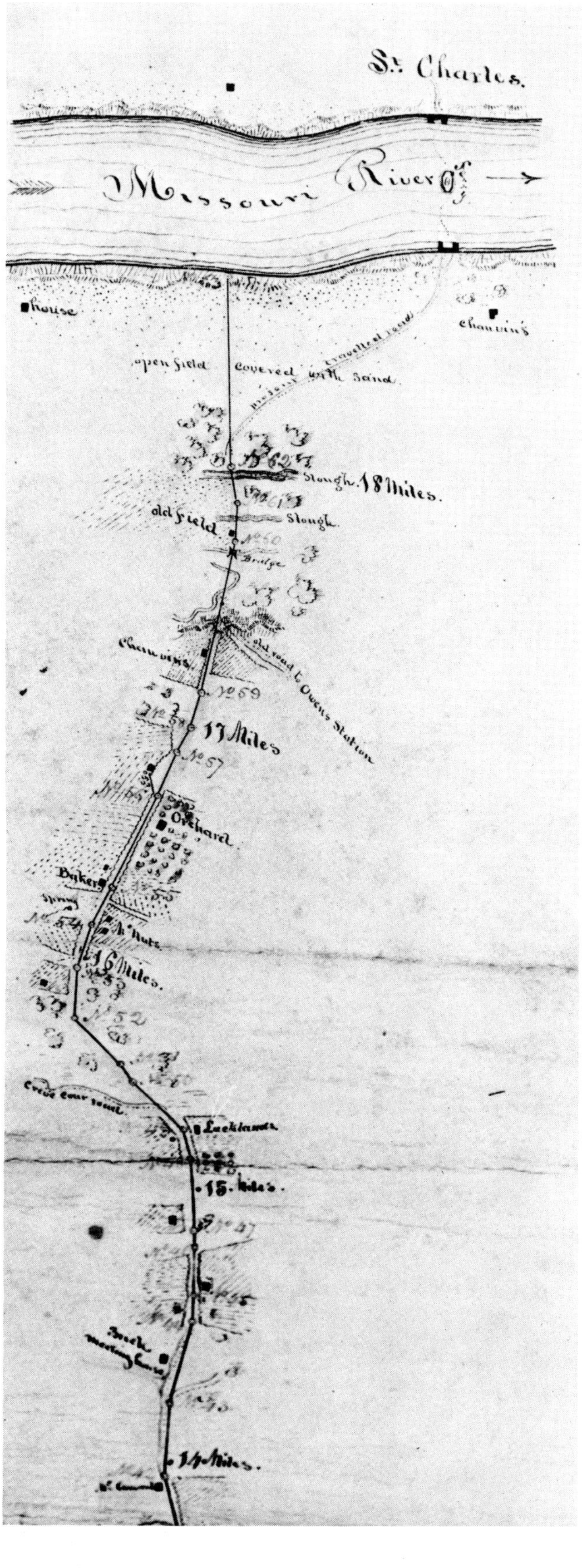

IGURE 7. *Section 4 of "Map of the South-*
rn St. Charles Road. . . ."

FIGURE 8. *"View of St. Charles." Lithograph by John Caspar Wild, from Lewis F. Thomas, ed.,* The Valley of the Mississippi Illustrated in a Series of Views *(St. Louis: Republican Printing Office, 1842), Plate VII. Courtesy of the State Historical Society of Missouri, Columbia.*

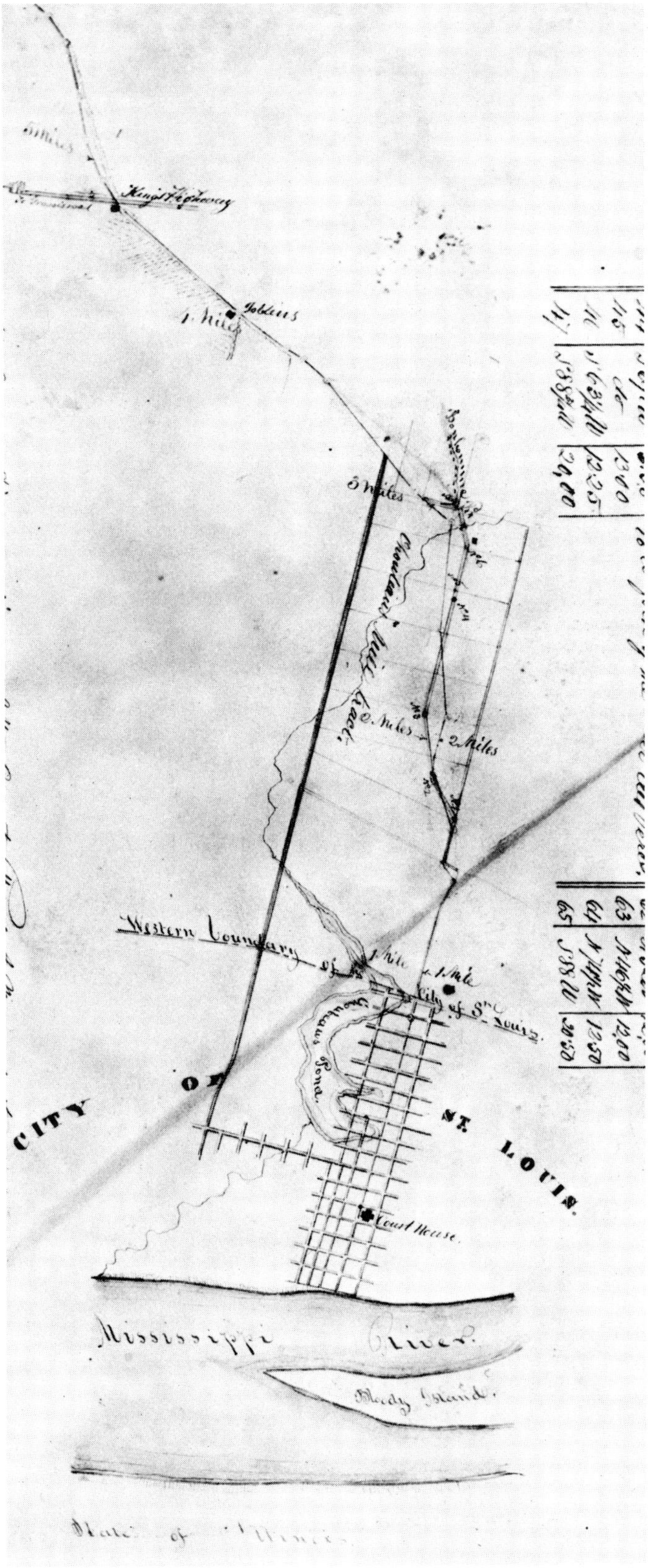

FIGURE 9. *Eastern terminal of "The State and County Roads from the City of St. Louis to the Town of Manchester." By William H. Cozens and Clement W. Coote, 1845. Plat Book C, Plate 10, St. Louis County Highway Department Records.*

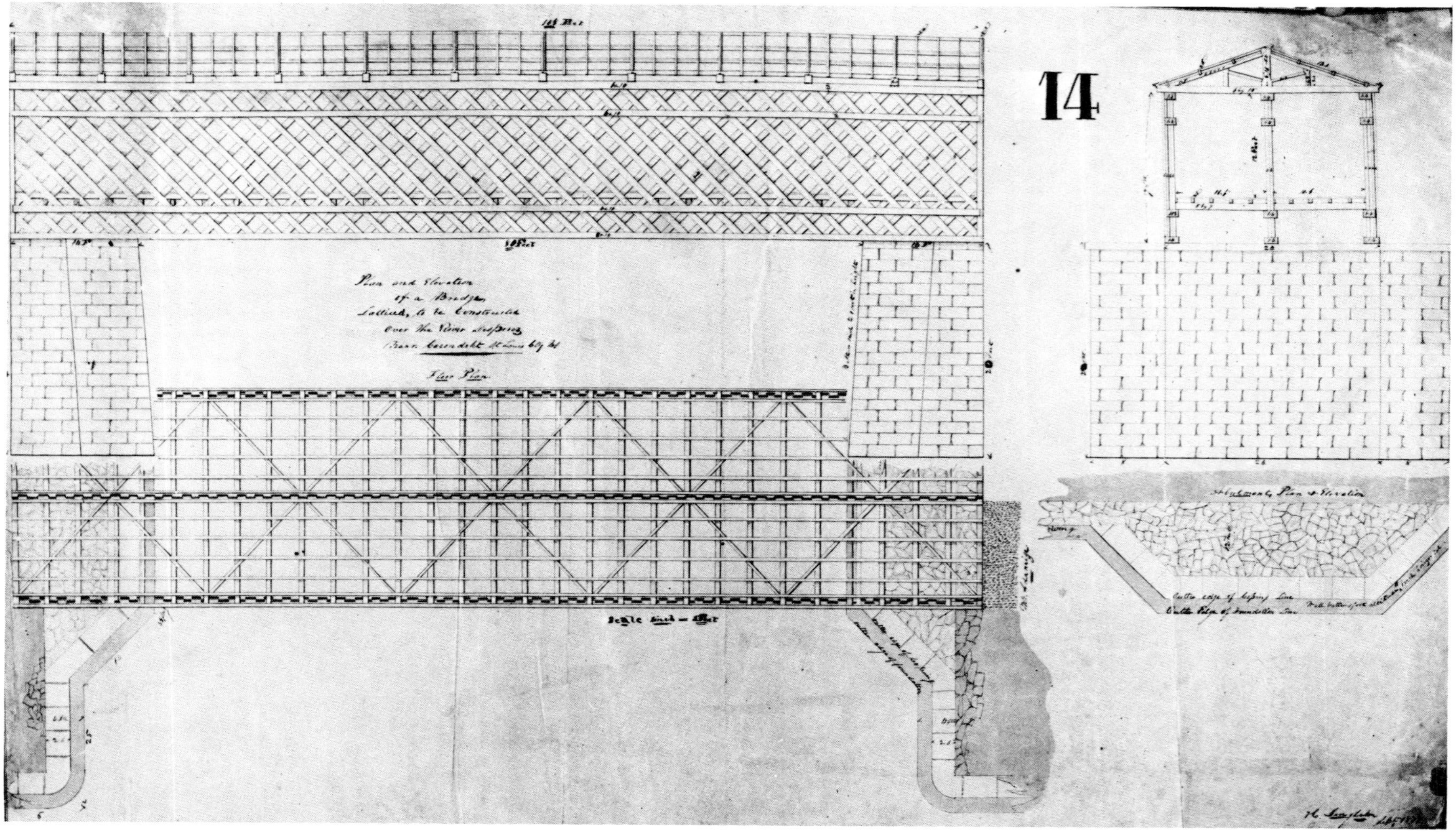

FIGURE 10. *"Plan and Elevation of Bridge, to be Constructed Over the River Desperes." By H. Singleton, 1839. Plat Book C, Plate 14, St. Louis County Highway Department Records.*

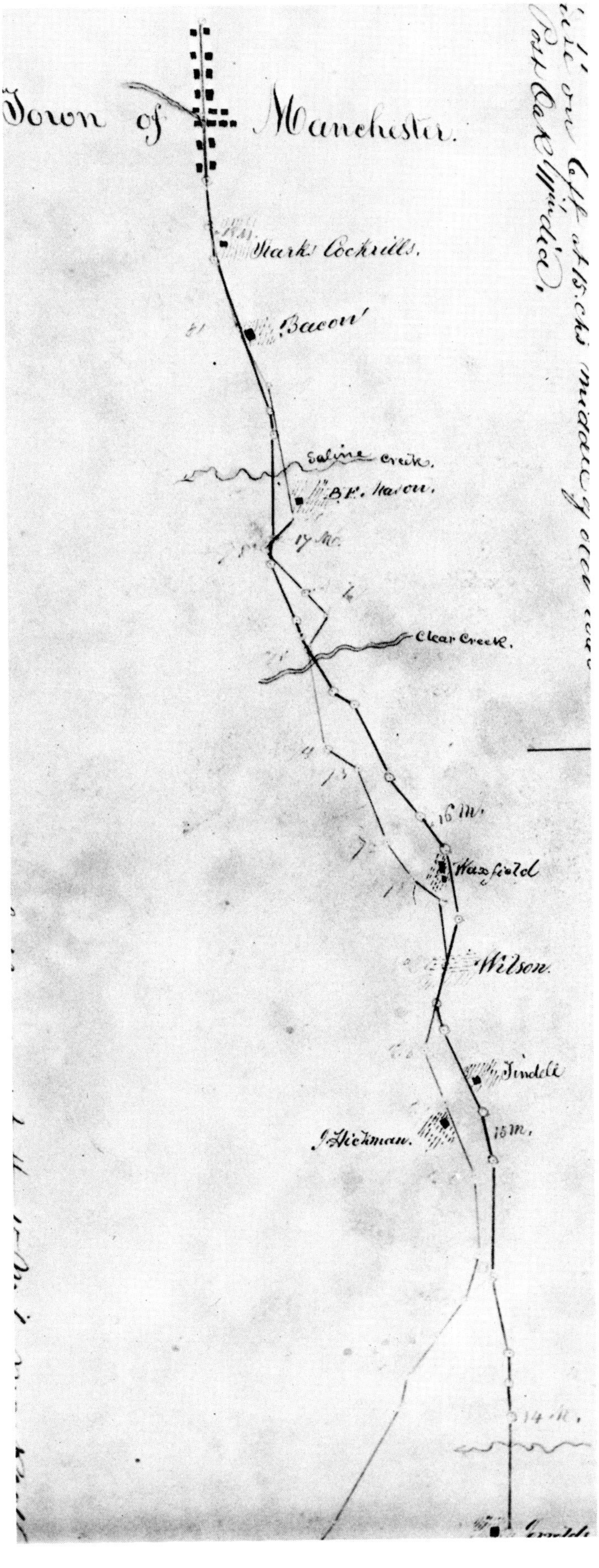

FIGURE 11. *Western terminal of "The State and County Roads from the City of St. Louis to the Town of Manchester." By William H. Cozens and Clement W. Coote, 1845. Plat Book C, Plate 10, St. Louis County Highway Department Records.*

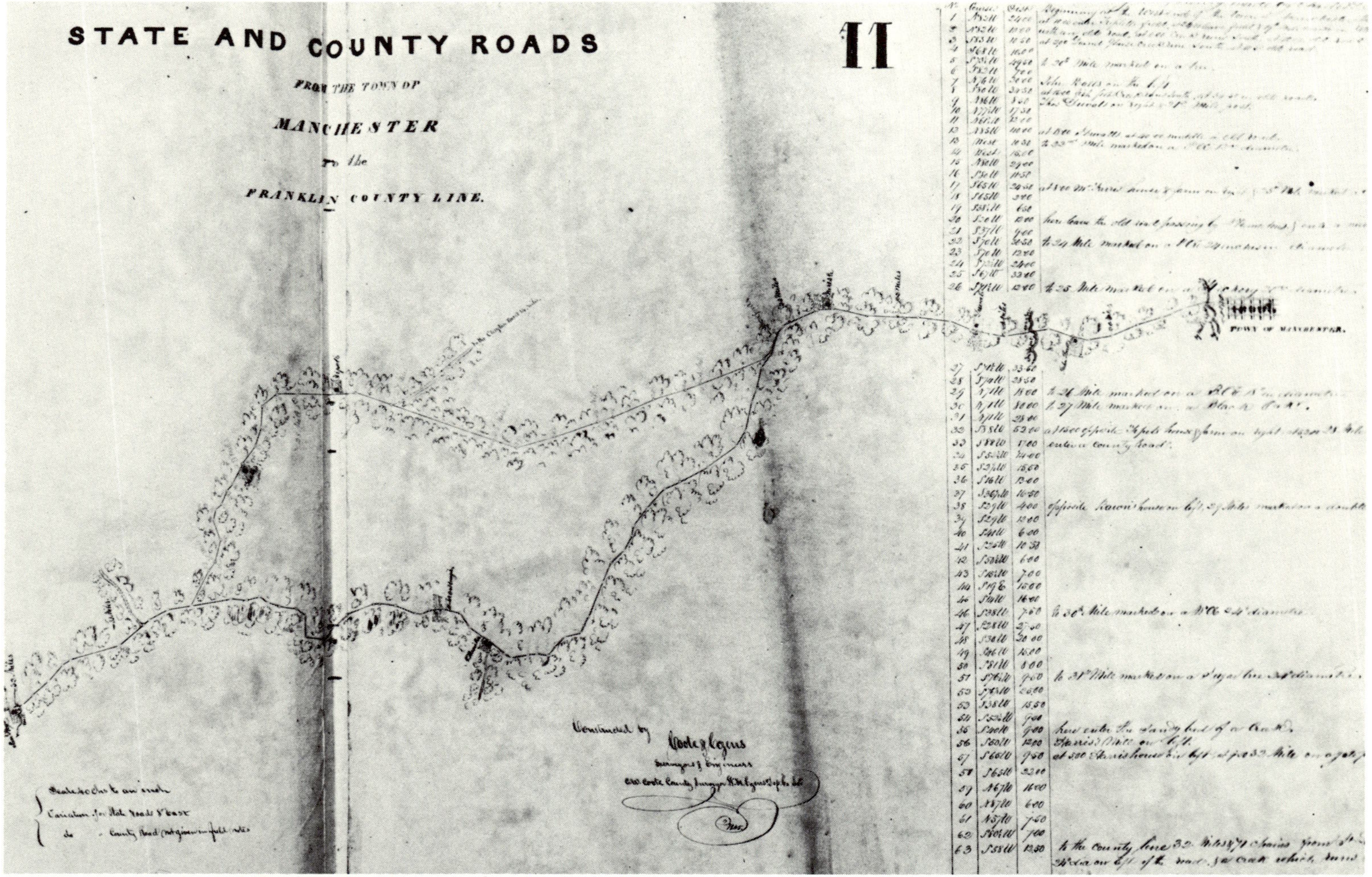

FIGURE 12. *"State and County Roads from the Town of Manchester to the Franklin County Line." By William H. Cozens and Clement W. Coote, 1845. Plat Book C, Plate 11, St. Louis County Highway Department Records.*

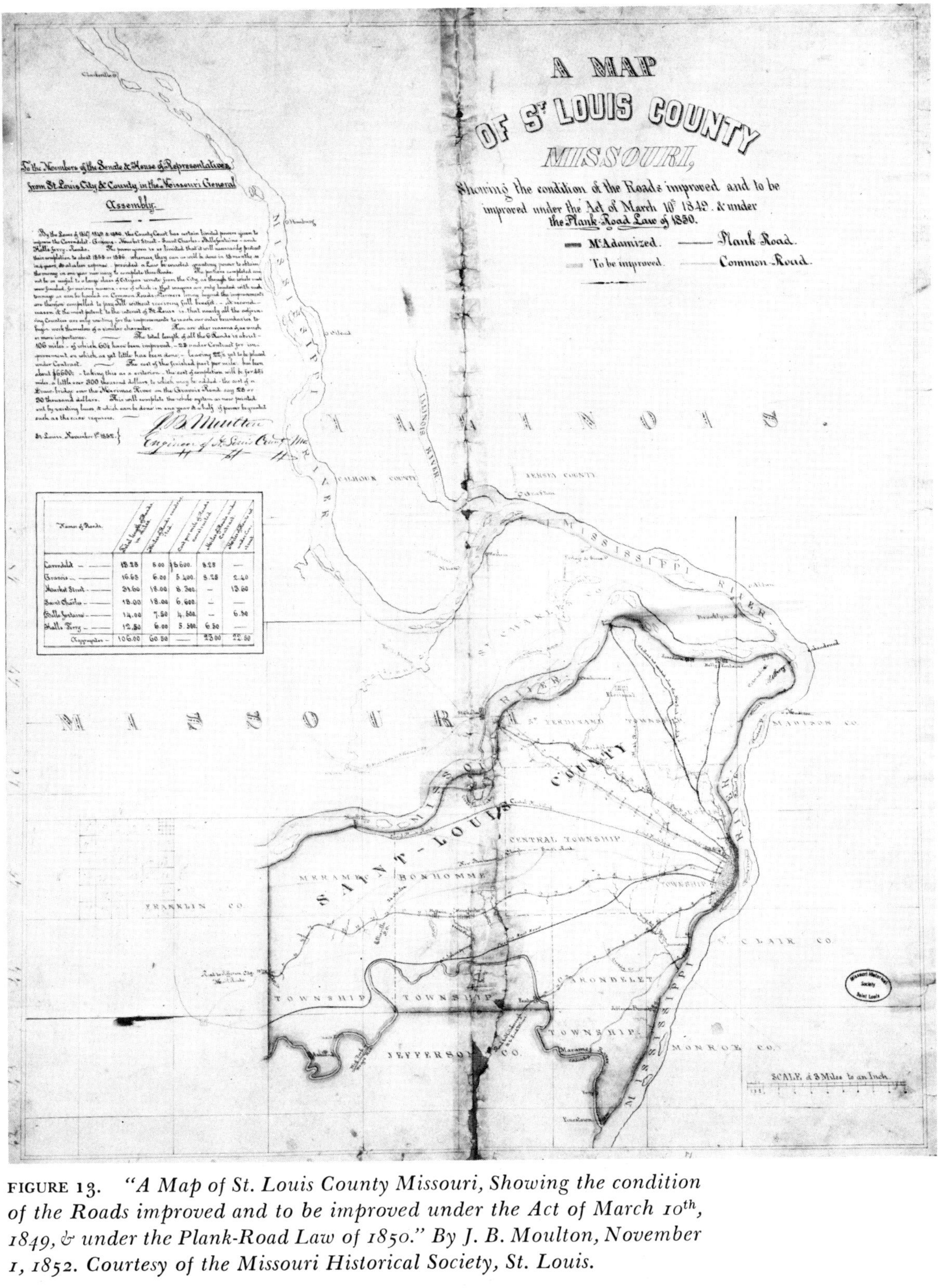

FIGURE 13. *"A Map of St. Louis County Missouri, Showing the condition of the Roads improved and to be improved under the Act of March 10th, 1849, & under the Plank-Road Law of 1850." By J. B. Moulton, November 1, 1852. Courtesy of the Missouri Historical Society, St. Louis.*

FIGURE 14. *"Carondolet* [sic] *(Vuide Poche)." Lithograph by John Caspar Wild, from Thomas, ed.,* Valley of the Mississippi, *Plate VIII. Courtesy of the State Historical Society of Missouri, Columbia. Wild's original gouache painting hangs in the St. Louis Mercantile Library.*

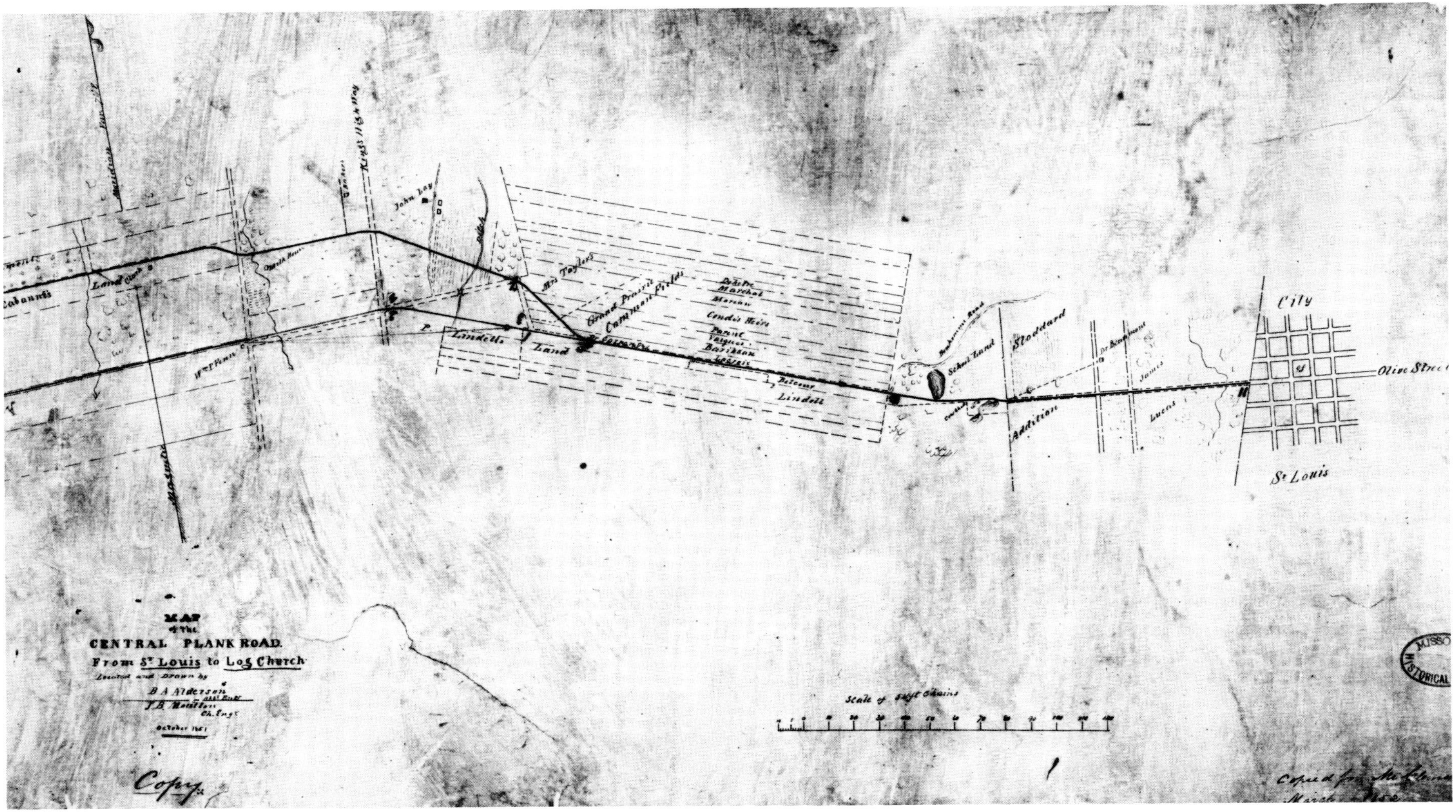

FIGURE 15. *Eastern section of "Map of the Central Plank Road From St. Louis to Log Church." By B. A. Alderson and J. B. Moulton, October, 1851, copy, March, 1852. Courtesy of the Missouri Historical Society, St. Louis.*

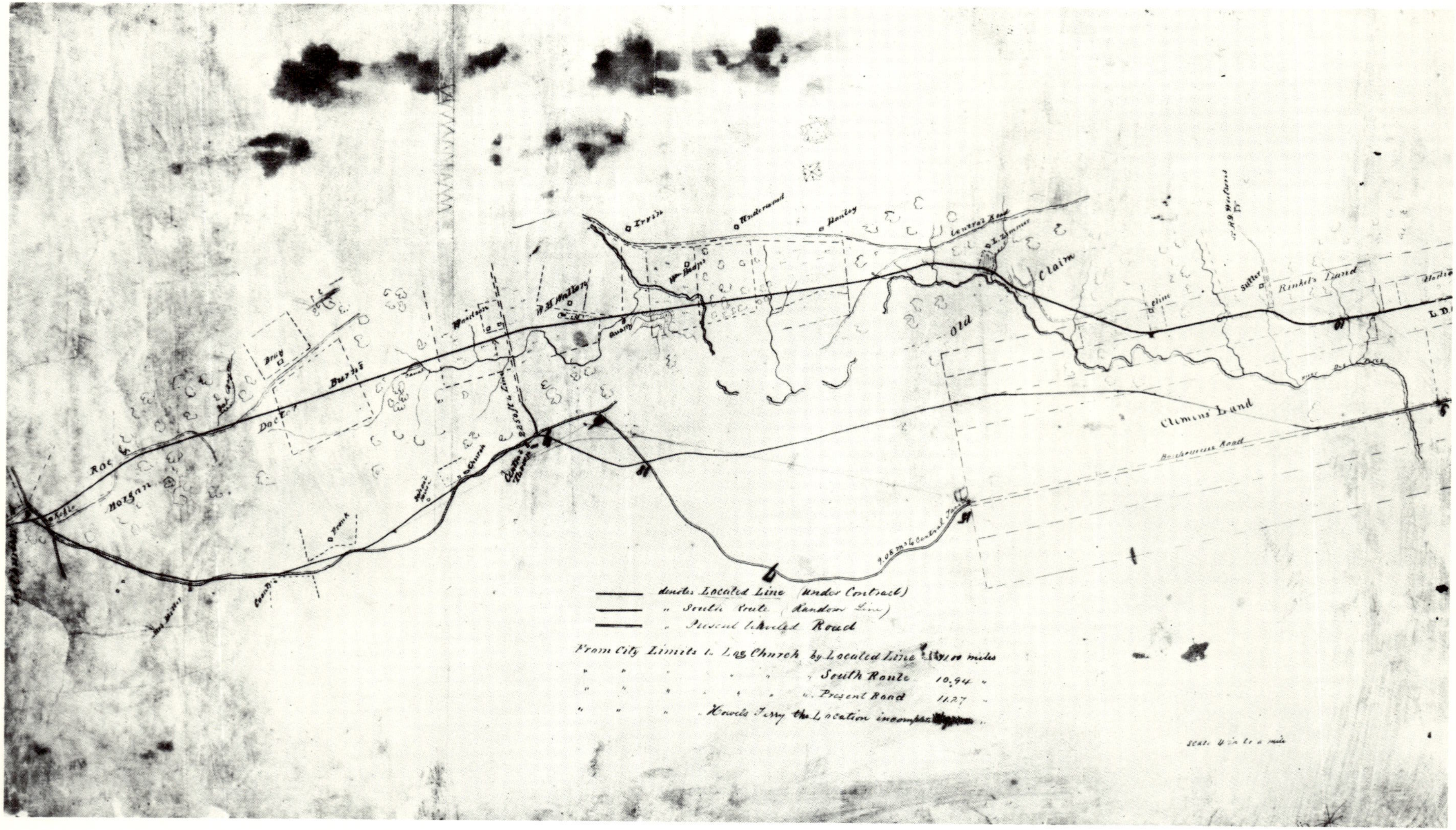

FIGURE 16. *Western section of "Map of the Central Plank Road From St. Louis to Log Church."*

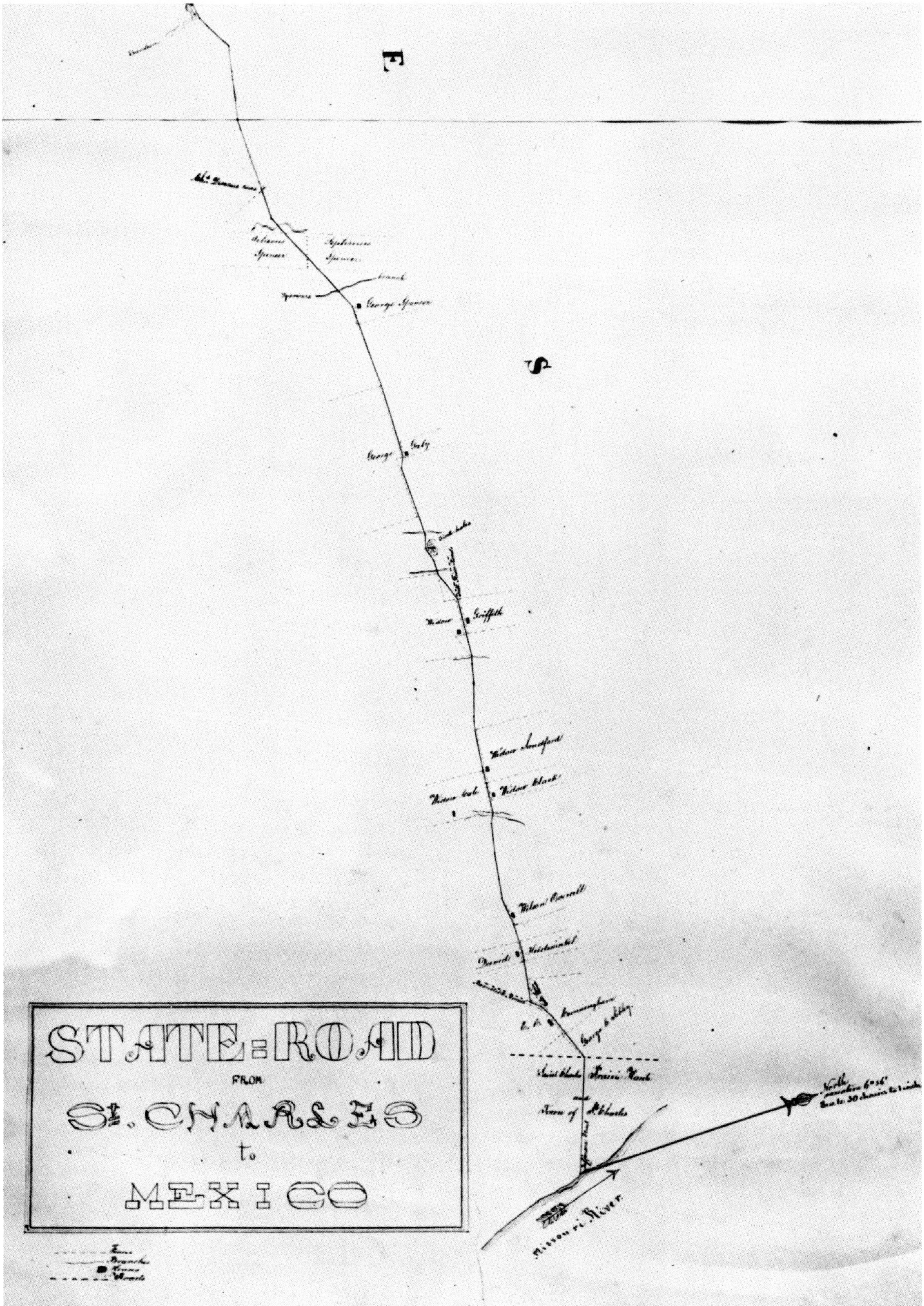

FIGURE 17. *Eastern portion of "State Road from St. Charles to Mexico." From "Plat and field notes of a State road from the town of Saint Charles in the County of Saint Charles to the town of Mexico in the County of Audrain. Filed July 28th, 1847." State and County Road File, Box 2. Courtesy of the Missouri State Archives.*

FIGURE 18. *Northern portion of "State Road From Independence to Batesville." July 10, 1841. State and County Road File, Box 25. Courtesy of the Missouri State Archives.*

Index

Contributors

WILLIAM B. BAKER, Associate Professor of Earth Sciences at Southern Illinois University, Edwardsville, was born in Springfield, Missouri, and, after a lengthy interruption by World War II and a short career as an airline pilot, was graduated from Southwest Missouri State College. He received his Ph.D. in geography from the University of Nebraska and taught for a time at the University of Tulsa. His field of research is the geographic form of settlements and he is preparing a bibliography of early maps of the middle Mississippi Valley.

JOHN PORTER BLOOM, born and reared in Albuquerque, received his B.A. degree in inter-American affairs at the University of New Mexico in 1947 and a Ph.D. in American history at Emory University in 1956. He spent seven years in college teaching, including four years at Texas Western College (now the University of Texas at El Paso), and four years as historian and historical editor in the National Park Service. Since 1964 he has been with the U.S. National Archives, Washington, D.C., as editor of *The Territorial Papers of the United States* and senior staff specialist in Western history. He was one of the organizers of the Western History Association and for five years Secretary-Treasurer of that organization. He has published articles on the Mexican War period in New Mexico and northern Mexico and is working on a book about American soldier life in the war with Mexico.

NICHOLAS CANADAY, Jr., Associate Professor of English at Louisiana State University, received his Ph.D. at the University of Florida in 1957. Although his scholarly publications have hitherto been related to American fiction, he has long maintained an interest in American studies. He was graduated from Princeton University in the American Civilization

Program, and his doctoral work in Florida was directed by Professor Harry R. Warfel. He was Fulbright Lecturer in 1963–64 at Kanazawa University, Japan, where in addition to his teaching he assisted in the planning of an American Studies Program. Critical articles by him have appeared in *Studies in American Literature* (1960), *The South Central Bulletin*, University of Houston *Forum, Studies in Short Fiction*, and *Papers on Language and Literature.*

JOHN C. EWERS joined the Park Service in 1935, was Curator of the Museum of the Plains Indians at Browning, Montana, from 1941 to 1944, became Curator of Anthropology in the U.S. National Museum (Smithsonian Institution) in 1946, was named Planning Director of the new Museum of History and Technology in 1956, Assistant Director in 1959, and Director in 1964. Since 1965 he has been Senior Ethnologist, Smithsonian Office of Anthropology. He has been much interested in Indian culture and his books on this subject include *Plains Indians Painting* (1939), *Artists of the Old West* (1965), and *Indian Life on the Upper Missouri* (1968). He edited Catlin's *Okepa* (1967), has written on Lewis and Clark, the mountain man, Zenas Leonard, and has published numerous articles in the *Smithsonian Institution Annual Reports* and in various historical journals.

JOHN T. FLANAGAN, Professor of English at the University of Illinois since 1949, has taught at the University of Minnesota and Southern Methodist University. He was a Fulbright Lecturer at Bordeaux, France, in 1952 and in Belgium in 1960. He lectured in Kyoto, Japan, in 1962 and at the Universities of Moscow and Leningrad in the spring of 1963. His special interest is in the literature, culture, and folklore of the Middle West. He was editor of *America Is West* (1945) and author of a biography of James Hall (1941). He has collaborated in several anthologies, notably *Folklore in American Literature* (1958) and *Research Opportunities in American Cultural History* (1961). He has contributed to various *festschriften* and has published about a hundred articles in academic and historical journals.

HERMAN R. FRIIS left teaching at Southern Illinois University to become Geographer-Archivist in the National Archives. In 1952 he became Chief of the Cartographic Records Division, in 1959 Chief of the Technical Records Division, and in 1962 was named Senior Specialist in Cartographic Archives, which is equivalent to a research professorship. He is a fellow of the American Geographical Society and Society of American Archivists. Since 1946 he has been a member and a chairman of committees in the National Academy of Sciences—National Research Council, in the federal government, and in professional organizations. He received the Outstanding Achievement Award of the Association of American Geographers. His most recent (March, 1967) publication is *The Pacific Basin: A History of Its Geographical Exploration*, which he edited. He is now Director of the Center for Polar Archives but also remains one of our leading cartographic specialists for the western frontier.

ARCHIBALD HANNA, Jr., Curator of the Western Americana Collection of the Yale University Library, is a native of Worcester, Massachusetts. He received an M.S. in library science from Columbia University in 1949 and in 1951 his Ph.D. from Yale. During World War II he served in the U.S. Marine Corps, acting as a Japanese language translator in the central Pacific. He joined the staff of the Yale Library in 1949 and was appointed William Robertson Coe Librarian in 1952 as well as Librarian of the Franklin Collection. He became Curator of these collections in 1955 and was also appointed a Research Associate in Yale's History Department in 1960. He has watched Yale's great holdings in Western Americana more than double since 1952. His biography of John Buchan (Lord Tweedsmuir) was published in 1954.

NICHOLAS JOOST, Professor of English at Southern Illinois University, Edwardsville, is a graduate of the University of Florida and received his Ph.D. from the University of North Carolina in 1947. He has taught at Northwestern and Loyola universities and served on the editorial staff of *Poetry* magazine from 1951 to 1954. He was Research Consultant in 1957–58 at the Worcester Art Museum under a grant from the Bollingen Foundation. In 1963–64 he was a Fulbright Lecturer in the Netherlands. He was President of the St. Louis Westerners for the year 1967–68 and is editor of *Papers on Language and Literature*, the critical periodical of Southern Illinois University. His numerous articles have appeared in various historical and literary journals, and he is the author of several books, among which are *Scofield Thayer and the Dial* (1964), *Years of Transition, The Dial, 1912–1920* (1967), and *Ernest Hemingway and the Little Magazines: The Paris Years* (1968).

JOHN FRANCIS McDERMOTT, Research Professor of Humanities at Southern Illinois University, Edwardsville, has edited, among other books of western travel, three Missouri River narratives: *Up the Missouri with Audubon: The Journal of Edward Harris* (1951), Thaddeus Culbertson's *Journal of an Expedition to the Mauvaises Terres and the Upper Missouri in 1850* (1952), and *Audubon in the West* (1965). In 1965 he was chairman of a Southern Illinois University (Edwardsville) conference on the trans-Mississippi West, the papers of which were published in 1967 under the title *The Frontier Re-examined.* His latest books are *An Artist on the Overland Trail: The 1849 Diary and Sketches of James F. Wilkins* (1968) and *Before Mark Twain: A Sampler of Old, Old Times on the Mississippi* (1968). The latter is the initial volume in a series entitled "Travels on the Western Waters" which he is directing for Southern Illinois University Press.

DONALD D. MINER completed his undergraduate studies at Washington University in St. Louis and in 1967 received an M.A. degree in English from Southern Illinois University, Edwardsville. Now teaching in the Technological College of the State University of New York at Cobleskill, he plans to continue his graduate studies in American literature. He has under way several research projects on frontier subjects, including an anthology of verbal sketches of the "human" Indian extracted from narrative accounts by western travelers.

DALE L. MORGAN, B.A., University of Utah, 1937, began his prolific scholarly career as editor of the WPA Historical Records Survey in Utah in 1938. Since 1954 he has been a member of the Bancroft Library staff at the University of California at Berkeley. Not to mention a great quantity of articles and edited documents published in historical quarterlies, he is the author or editor of at least thirty volumes of western Americana, including *The Humboldt: Highroad of the West* (1943), *Jedediah Smith and the Opening of the West* (1953), and *The West of William H. Ashley* (1964). His latest book (edited in association with Eleanor T. Harris) is *The Rocky Mountains Journals of William Marshall Anderson,* published by the Huntington Library in 1967. Numerous awards testifying to his contribution to our knowledge of the American West have included a Guggenheim fellowship. At the present time he is primarily engaged in a guide to California manuscripts in the Bancroft Library, following up the guide to Pacific and western manuscripts published in 1963.

RICHARD E. OGLESBY, Ph.D., Northwestern University, 1962, has taught at Eastern Illinois University and is now Assistant Professor of History at the University of California at Santa Barbara. A contributor to the *Missouri Historical Society Bulletin* and other historical quarterlies, he is the author of *Manuel Lisa and the Opening of the Missouri Fur Trade* (1963). He is now engaged in editing Christian Schultz's account of his private explorations on the Ohio and Mississippi rivers in 1807–08, *Travels on an Inland Voyage,* for a new series of reprints of "Travels on the Western Waters" being inaugurated by Southern Illinois University Press. He is also at work on a biography of the early nineteenth-century fur trader, Pierre Menard. He was a contributor to *The Frontier Re-examined* (1967).

DWIGHT L. SMITH, a frontier and western historian, has taught at Indiana Central College and Ohio State University and is now Research Professor of History at Miami University. He has also been a visiting professor at several other universities in the United States and Canada and has served as consultant to the American Bibliographical Center, Santa Barbara, California. Author or editor of articles in numerous historical journals and of several books, he has specialized in travel accounts. His works include *The Western Journals of John May* (1961), *Down the Colorado* (1965), *Western Life in the Stirrups* (1965), and *The Photographer and the River* (1967). The two-volume *Exploring and Surveying the Colorado River* is in press. He is currently preparing for publication a Pike's Peak journal and a trans-Canada overland diary from manuscript holdings of the Newberry Library.